64.95

D1034158

The Motet in England
in the Fourteenth Century

Studies in Musicology, No. 94

George J. Buelow, Series Editor

Professor of Music
Indiana University

Other Titles in This Series

The Motet in England
in the Fourteenth Century

by
Peter M. Lefferts

UMI RESEARCH PRESS
Ann Arbor, Michigan

Produced and distributed by
UMI Research Press
an imprint of
University Microfilms, Inc.
Ann Arbor, Michigan 48106

Library of Congress Cataloging in Publication Data

Lefferts, Peter.
The motet in England in the fourteenth century.

(Studies in musicology ; no. 94)
Revision of thesis (Ph.D.)—Columbia University,
1983.
Bibliography: p.
Includes index.
1. Motet—500-1400—History and criticism.   2. Music—
England—500-1400—History and criticism.   I. Title.
II. Series.
ML2931.2.L44   1986   783.4'0942   86-6900
ISBN 0-8357-1722-4 (alk. paper)

This book is dedicated to my parents.

Contents

List of Figures

List of Tables

Preface

The polyphonic music of fourteenth-century England, created during the century and more between the Worcester fragments and the Old Hall manuscript, is one of the last major repertoires of medieval music to be unearthed. What has been uncovered is a vigorous musical tradition relatively independent of contemporaneous developments in France and Italy in the genres cultivated, in the techniques of rhythmic and harmonic language and large-scale form, and in notation. These remains, still largely unfamiliar even to specialists in medieval music, are comparable to the French and Italian fourteenth-century repertoires in size and number of sources, though we lack even a single integral codex. The present volume examines in detail one important insular genre of this period, the motet, in light of all surviving music.

This study was inaugurated in a graduate seminar under the direction of Ernest Sanders at Columbia University in the spring term of 1976. The seminar was devoted to editing the surviving complete motets of fourteenth-century English provenance. Its transcriptions provided the original impetus for the present work. Revised and augmented by this author, they were shared with Professor Frank Ll. Harrison during the final stages of his preparation of *Motets of English Provenance, Polyphonic Music of the Fourteenth Century,* XV (Paris and Monaco, 1980). Professor Harrison invited me to be responsible for editing and translating the texts of the 36 motets in his volume. That was accomplished over the spring and summer months of 1978, assisted in part by a travel grant from Columbia University that allowed me to spend June through August of that year in England. Research undertaken then convinced me that though a major project based solely on the complete motets was not viable, incorporation of the fragments would provide sufficient scope and perspective for a substantial study.

In this book it has not been possible to present more than a small fraction of the hundreds of pages of transcriptions of the texts and music of fragmentary, unperformable motets prepared in the course of research. Upon request, this material is available from the author on microfilm. Facsimiles of nearly all the relevant sources are happily now available in Harrison and Wibberley's volume in the series *Early English Church Music* (see the bibliography).

I would like to acknowledge a number of individuals and institutions who have helped me during my research and writing. Primary among them are Ernest Sanders, Leeman Perkins, and Joel Newman of the Department of Music, Columbia University, who read and criticized drafts of the manuscript. Frank Ll. Harrison, Margaret Bent, Roger Wibberley, Roger Bowers, Anthony Pryer, Susan Rankin, Andrew Wathey, Adrian Bassett, and Bruce Barker-Benfield have been generous with help, encouragement, and information on many topics, not in the least about new sources. The Martha Baird Rockefeller Foundation for Music and the Whiting Foundation provided financial aid that made possible a year off from teaching to read and write over the 1979–80 school year, and supported research trips to England in the summers of both 1979 and 1980. The Graduate School of Arts and Sciences of Columbia University has supported this work through fellowships, teaching assistantships, and the travel grant mentioned above; the University of Chicago has provided further assistance in the form of research funds and computer time for the preparation of the manuscript.

Last, I would like to thank my wife Laura for her patience and encouragement, suggestions and criticisms, and cheerful help in getting the work done.

A Note to the Reader

Bibliographic references in the footnotes and critical reports are made throughout by short titles; for fuller information please consult the bibliography. Manuscripts are mainly cited by shorthand *sigla* that follow the form of citation in RISM B/IV/3-4 and *The New Grove Dictionary*; a complete list of manuscripts cited may be found in appendix 1.

The normal thirteenth- and fourteenth-century custom is to identify a motet by the incipit of its duplum, but this practice will not be followed. Rather, the incipit of the triplum will be used for identification. If it is missing, the duplum incipit will be cited. In the absence of any incipit the first legible words of the uppermost surviving part will be used. Manuscript *sigla* are cited in the text, tables, and figures only if pertinent to the specific point being made. A finding list of motets, arranged alphabetically by incipit, is given at the beginning of appendix 2.

Commonly Used Abbreviations

AH	*Analecta Hymnica.*
AS	Frere, *Antiphonale Sarisburiense.*
CEKM I	Apel, *Corpus of Early Keyboard Music,* I.
CMM 39	Günther, *The Motets of the Manuscripts Chantilly.*
CS	Coussemaker, *Scriptorum de Musica.*
CSM	American Institute of Musicology, *Corpus Scriptorum Musicae.*
EBM	Stainer, Stainer, and Stainer, *Early Bodleian Music.*
EECM 26	Harrison and Wibberley, *Manuscripts.*
GS	Frere, *Graduale Sarisburiense.*
MSD 2	Dittmer, *The Worcester Fragments.*
NOHM	*New Oxford History of Music.*
PMFC I	Schrade, *The Works of Philippe de Vitry.*
PMFC V	Harrison, *Motets of French Provenance.*
PMFC XIV	Sanders, *English Music of the Thirteenth and Early Fourteenth Centuries.*
PMFC XV	Harrison, *Motets of English Provenance.*
PMFC XVI–XVII	Harrison, Sanders, and Lefferts, *English Music for Mass and Offices,* I–II.
TECM I	Stevens, *Treasury of English Church Music,* I.
WMH	Dom A. Hughes, *Worcester Medieval Harmony.*

I, II, III, IV in context usually refer to the voice-parts of a motet, counting from the top down.

s, m refer to syllabic or melismatic semibreves.

l, b, s, m refer to long, breve, semibreve, and minim in the critical commentary (L, B, S, M are occasionally used, especially in number schemes).

c.o.p. refers to ligatures *cum opposita proprietate.*

1

Basic Issues

Introduction

The motet was the most actively cultivated genre of polyphonic music in France and England from the first decades of the thirteenth century to the middle years of the fourteenth, when it gave over that role in France to the polyphonic chanson and in England to Mass Ordinary settings. On the Continent Paris was the first major center of compositional activity, though motets were composed in outlying regions as well. Motets in the French tradition are found in collections assembled in locations all across western Europe, from Spain to the British Isles and Poland. Integral motet codices, plus numerous fragments, have held the attention of scholars on this repertoire since the late nineteenth century. It has been surveyed, catalogued, edited, and analyzed extensively. As is the case with French and Italian polyphonic secular song of the fourteenth century, the contents of most Continental motet sources have been transcribed in at least two modern editions.

The contributions of musicians working in areas peripheral to the Parisian cultural orbit are only imperfectly recognized. This has led in particular to a serious underestimation of the independence and importance of compositional activity in England.[1] The fact that English music has languished in relative obscurity is in part due to the vagaries of musicological scholarship but also (and not coincidentally) due to the lack of sizeable integral manuscripts, the anonymity of English composers, and the apparent diversity and obscurity of their working environments. Since the Second World War a handful of scholars have made important contributions to the study of the late medieval English motet, most prominently Jacques Handschin, Luther Dittmer, Ernst Apfel, Ernest Sanders, and Frank Ll. Harrison.[2] The most extended treatment has been that by Sanders in his 1963 dissertation, "Medieval English Polyphony," and subsequent 1973 survey, "The Medieval Motet."

This study takes Sanders's work as a point of departure and concerns itself with the motets in circulation in England in the fourteenth century. These compositions are diverse in form, style, and origin, yet form a reasonable corpus for study on account of important features they hold in common. Most were composed in England and are distinct in many ways from contemporaneous Continental pieces. Those insular motets that date from ca. 1300 to ca. 1340 or 1350 form a relatively closed and homogeneous body that is as a whole from a slightly more recent generation of composers than the motets of the seventh and eighth fascicles of *F-MO*. They are contemporary with the more advanced motets of *F-Pn 146* (the *Roman de Fauvel*), the bulk of the motets attributable to Philippe de Vitry, and the early motets of Guillaume de Machaut. The line of development they continue, however, is insular in its antecedents, richer in its variety of formal approaches than Continental practice, more reflective on the whole of the versification of the texts set to music, and innovative in notation and in numerical control of phrase lengths. At the same time it is conservative both in its cultivation of an idiomatic harmonic language and in its surface rhythmic activity. The later part of the repertoire, dating from midcentury to ca. 1400, is represented by many fewer sources and pieces, and contains many more imported Continental motets, some given new texts to suit English preferences in that regard. It also includes insular pieces with varied approaches to the reconciliation of Continental notation and style with local practice.

The English and the French knew each other's music. Politics and intellectual life made this inevitable, and it is testified to by the theoretical tradition as well as the musical sources (though there are virtually no insular sources of the polyphonic French chanson). The timing and degree of influence exerted by each culture on the other are, however, issues on which scholars have come to very different general conclusions. Bent has written that "the indigenous English repertory between the Worcester Fragments and Old Hall has no demonstrable continental links, and seems to have remained quite separate in style, techniques, and notation until the very late fourteenth century."[3] Sanders, on the other hand, has written: "it would appear that no indigenous English motet techniques were maintained beyond the middle of the century." He goes on to say, "Yet our knowledge is unfortunately far too fragmentary to permit any definite conclusions."[4] The present study, especially the information brought forward in chapter 2, fills in some of the gaps in our knowledge, sketching out a middle ground between these two disparate summary positions.

The dimensions of the repertoire under consideration can be stated only approximately. Adopting for the moment a rather broad definition of what constitutes a motet, there are about 35 sources to be dealt with, containing about 130 motets. Sixty-odd of these are complete or completable, and there is a similar number of fragments. About 110 of the total are English, and the rest are of probable foreign authorship.[5] Because of the nature and condition of the present manuscript remains (pastedowns, flyleaves, covers for documents, and the like) many of the so-called complete motets actually require extensive restoration of music and texts if they are to be studied and performed. At the same time, many of the fragments are integral folios with one or more whole voice parts (due to the *cantus collateralis* layout in the original manuscript) and hence may be profitably investigated for information about the motet's length, form, style, and subject matter. Incorporation of information on the fragments makes possible a much clearer view of the genre than is available from the complete motets alone. In many of the categories established in the course of this study, there are instances where only one or two (or even no) complete examples survive.

The preliminary tasks of this research were bibliographical and philological—controlling all the available source materials and establishing accurate readings of the notes and texts of all the musical remains.[6] The major endproducts of this research are embodied in chapters 2 through 4: a comprehensive typology of the motets' formal structures and compositional techniques; an assessment of the notations used in the motets in light of English and Continental notational systems of the thirteenth and fourteenth centuries; and discussion of text content and versification. The remainder of chapter 1 will review certain issues involving boundaries and definition of the motet genre, problems of chronology and style, and some observations on motet sources (this will not, in general, be a source-oriented study).

Boundaries and Definition of the Motet

Defining the repertoire for this study involves problems in the setting of both generic and temporal limits. Genre definition involves fundamental questions about both compositional approach and function, and for that reason it will be dealt with first. To begin with, it will be useful to recall features of the motet as it was cultivated on the Continent in the later thirteenth and early fourteenth centuries. It was then, as a rule, a composition a3 with two upper voices, each having its own text, over a tenor cantus firmus that was the lowest of the three by range and was fashioned by the rhythmic patterning and repetition of a melisma drawn from responsorial psalmody (or from elsewhere in the corpus of plainchant). In England there were, in addition to such motets built on a cantus firmus, motets built over a *pes*, a voice of tenor function that is either freely composed or perhaps drawn from the popular sphere, often featuring strict or varied ostinati.[7]

In addition to the *pes* motet a3, the English also wrote freely composed motets a4 with two lower voices sharing tenor function. These free motets may be monotextual and have conductus-like melismatic preludes, interludes, and postludes. What is essential to the character of these motets—what seems to have made them motets in English eyes—is the stratification of function, range, melodic material, and to a lesser degree, rhythmic activity, between those voices that are texted, hence in the foreground of the composition, and that voice (or those voices) never texted and serving as a structural skeleton or foundation.[8]

The motet on a cantus firmus has a kinship to another English genre, the troped chant setting, that was cultivated extensively in the thirteenth and early fourteenth centuries. These chant settings are polytextual and notated in the musical sources in parts. The tenor, whether laid out in patterned rhythms, in irregular rhythms, or simply as a series of even longs, is a single statement of a plainsong or some well-defined subsection of a chant such as the soloist's portion of a responsorial chant. The two parts composed above it bear texts troping the words of the chant. These new words are often artfully written and aligned so that the syllables of the tenor text are articulated simultaneously in all three voices. Table 1 lists thirteenth- and fourteenth-century English troped chant settings.[9]

Though troped chant settings are very similar to motets in technique and source layout, they are distinguishable by a number of features: there is no repetition of tenor *color*; liturgical specificity is clear and contextuality assumed for the performance of the setting; the melody and syntax of the chant determine most features of overall form; and the text is closely allied to that of the tenor.[10]

However, by the early fourteenth century the line between the two genres often becomes hard to draw. Just as in the conductus and rondellus genres, there is an apparent hybridization (or perhaps better, a convergence) of features of chant settings with those of the motet. This is particularly true in regard to text, where it is impossible to draw a neat line of demarcation between simple assonance and a tropic relationship, loose or close, between upper voices and the tenor, and texts may abandon a close aural relationship with chant text to incorporate instead a regular verse structure. (For more on the aural relationships between texts, see chapter 4.) Troped chant settings often show isoperiodicity of phrase structure, either established for an entire piece, as in *Salve mater* (*WF*, 64), or interrupted at sectional boundaries, as in the *Cjc 23* fragments; the tenor may be irregularly rhythmicized while supporting such a regular phrase structure, as in *Ianuam quam clauserat* (*Onc 362*, 1).

Further blurring the distinction between genres are those compositions in which a whole chant is repeated either in part or in its entirety. For instance, the hymn used as the tenor of *Jhesu redemptor* is stated four times, the antiphon used as the tenor of *Parata paradisi porta* is stated one and four-

Table 1. English Troped Chant Settings

Introit

Salve sancta parents-T.Salve sancta parens	WF, 9; Ob 60, 1
Salve mater-T.Sancta parens	WF, 64
Hac die nobili-T.Gaudeamus omnes	Ob 60, 2

Kyrie

Christe lux mundi-T.Kyrie (Orbis factor)	WF, 1
Lux et gloria-T.Kyrie (Lux et origo)	WF, 2; Ccl, 2
Kyrie fons pietatis-T.Kyrie (Fons bonitatis)	WF, 29; Ob 60, 9
O paraclite regens-T.Kyrie (Rex virginum)	Ccl, 1
Virgo mater salvatoris-T.Kyrie	Cfm, 1

Gloria

Rex omnium lucifluum-T.Regnum tuum	Ob 60, 11; LoHa, 1.2
Decus virginitatis-T.Salve virgo(Regnum tuum)	WF, 33
Spiritus et alme-T.	US-Cu, 5
Spiritus procedens	WF, 43

Gradual

Benedicta.Virgo Dei	WF, 80a
Benedicta Domina	WF, 3
Beata supernorum-T.Benedicta.Virgo Dei	WF, 26
Virgo que fructifero-T.Virgo Dei genitrix	CAc 128/6, 1
Virgo paris-T.Virgo Dei genitrix	WF, 14
Virgo decora-T.Virgo Dei genitrix	Osa 1/2; Ob 14, 8

Tract

Gaude Maria virgo-T.Gaude Maria	WF, 35

Alleluia

Ave maris stella V.Hodie Maria virgo	Cjec 1, 8/8a
A laudanda legione V.Ave Maria	Cjec 1, 9
Alleluya Christo iubilemus V.Dies sanct.	Ob 400, 1
Alleluya clare decet V.P(ost partum?)	Ob 400, 2
Adoremus ergo natum V.Vidimus stellam	Ob 400, 3
Ave sanctitatis speculum	Ob 400, 4
Ave Maria gratia plena V.Assumpta est(?)	Ob 400, 5
V.Post partum virgo	Ob 400, 6
Ave magnifica V.Post partum virgo	Ob 400, H; WF, 19
Ave Maria ave mater V.Nativitas gloriose	Ob 400, I
V.In conspectu angelorum	Ob 400, K
Alleluya dulci cum V.Fit leo fit Leonardus	Ob 400, L
Alleluya musica canamus V.Hic Franciscus	Ob 400, M
V.Fulget dies	Ob 400, N
Alleluya canite V.Pascha nostrum	WF, 27
Alme iam ad gaudia V.Per te Dei genitrix	WF, 28

Table 1. (continued)

V.Gaude virgo gaude	WF, 45
Alleluya psallat V.Virga iesse floruit	WF, 46
V.Letabitur iustus	WF, 49
Gaude plaude V.Judicabunt sancti	WF, 50
V.Fulgebunt iusti	WF, 51
Alme veneremur diei V.Justi epulemur	WF, 52
V.O laus sanctorum	WF, 54
Alleluya moduletur Syon V.Veni mater gracie	WF, 55
Ave magnifica Maria V.Dulcis Maria(?)	WF, 56
V.Regis celorum mater	WF, 57
V.Nativitas gloriose	WF, 81

Offertory

Felix namque Maria   WF, 4

Versicle

Sursum corda   WF, 63

Sanctus

Sanctus Tro. Unus tamen est divinus	WF, 58
Sanctus Tro. Adonay genitor	WF, 59
Sanctus Tro. Deus ens ingenitus	WF, 60
Sanctus Tro. Et eternus Deus	WF, 61
Sanctus Tro. Ex quo omnia pater	WF, 62
Sanctus Tro. Et eternus Deus	WF, 77

Prose

Inviolata integra-T.Inviolata integra   WF, 42

Responsory

O Judea et Jerusalem	Ob 60, 3/4
Descendit de celis	Ob 400, 7
Descendit de celis	Ob 400, 8

Antiphon verse

Crucifixum Dominum-T.Crucifixum in carne   WF, 96

14th-Century Whole-Chant Settings Written in Parts

Introit

Salve sancta virgula-T.Salve sancta parens   Ob 652, 4

Gloria

Regnum sine termino-T.Regnum tuum	WF, 80
Regi regum enarrare-T.Regnum tuum	Onc 362, 12
Rex visibilium-T.Regnum tuum	Ob 7, 3

Gradual

Trinitatem veneremur-T.Benedicite   Lbl 24198, 5

Alleluia

Alta canunt-T.?Alleluia pascha nostrum	Onc 362, 8
Alleluya rex piaculum	TAcro 3182, 2
Ave prolem parienti	Llc 52, 1
Astra transcendit-T.Alleluya V.Assumpta est	Llc 52, 2
Assunt Augustini	Llc 52, 3
Solis vel syderis	D-W 499, 1
Alleluya concrepando	D-W 499, 2
Quartus.Tenor pro iiii	D-W 499, 3
Alleluya confessoris	D-W 499, 5

Responsory

Ianuam quam clauserat-T.Iacet granum	Onc 362, 1

Antiphon

Rosa delectabilis-T.Regali ex progenie	Onc 362, 18
Doleo super te-T.Rex autem David	Cgc 512, 7
Ave miles-T.Ave rex gentis	Ob 7, 7
Parata paradisi porta-T.Paradisi porta	Lpro 261, 1

Hymn

Veni creator spiritus-T.Veni creator	Ccc 65, 1
Jhesu redemptor-T.Jhesu redemptor (4x)	Cfm, 2

Prose

Salve cleri-T.Sospitati dedit egros	Ob 81, 4

Sequence

Balaam de quo-T.Epiphaniam (2 verses)	Onc 362, 4
Jhesu fili-T.Jhesu fili virginis	DRc 20, 3

Psalm tone

Quare fremuerunt-T. (2x)	Lbl 1210, 9

Benedicamus Domino

Beatus vir-T. (2x)	Lwa 12185, 3
Humane lingue-T. (2x)	Lbl 40011B, 17

Related settings

Nunc dimittis	Cjc 23, 1
Speciosa facta	Cjc 23, 2
Quis queso	Cjc 23, 3
Crucifixus surrexit. Dicant nunc Iudei	Cjc 23, 4

Settings of Non-Liturgical, Integral Tunes

French-Texted Tenors

Ade finit-T.A definement (3x)	Onc 362, 7
Caligo terre-T.Mariounette	Onc 362, 9

Table 1.   (continued)

Solaris ardor-T.Mariounette	Onc 362, 10
Triumphat hodie-T.Trop est fol	Lbl 24198, 7
Herodis in atrio-T.He hure lure (3x)	DRc 20, 1
Deus creator-T.Doucement (3x)	Ob 7, 14
Alma mater-Tenor de Alma mater	BERc 55, 1
Exulta Syon filia-T.En ai ie bien (6x)	F-TO 925, 1
Ma insuper-T.Or sus alouete	F-TO 925, 2
Valde mane-T.Va dorenlot (7x)	F-TO 925, 3
Syderea-T.Se i'avoie a plaingant (3x color)	F-TO 925, 7

English-Texted Tenor

Vide miser-T.Wynter (3x)	F-TO 925, 9

Latin Devotional Lyrics

Civitas nusquam-T.Cibus esurientum	Onc 362, 5
Frondentibus-T.Floret (3x)	Ob 7, 6
Barrabas dimittitur-T.Babilonis flumina (3x)	BERc 55, 4
Laus honor vendito-T.Laus honor Christo (3x)	Cpc 228, 3
Corona-T.Cui proclamant (6x)	F-TO 925, 4

Some Unidentified Tenors (whole chants or integral tunes)

Inter choros-T.	WF, 79
Patrie pacis-T.	Cgc 512, 12
O dira mens-T.	F-Pn 23190, 4
Soli fines-T.	US-SM 19914, 3
Augustine par angelis-T.Summe presul (3x)	Ob D.6, 2
Triumphus patet-T. (3x)	Lbl 1210, 2
Mulier magni meriti-T. (peslike, 3x)	Cgc 512, 1
Orto sole serene-T. (peslike, 4x)	Cgc 512, 9

fifths times, and the *Benedicamus* melody of *Beatus vir* is stated twice. (These and other instances are noted in table 1.) Moreover, one finds single statements of French-texted tunes as tenors, multiple statements of integral tunes with Latin texts, and single or multiple statements of unidentified tenors that appear to be whole chants or integral tunes. To draw a generic distinction between chant settings and motets on the basis of the number of repetitions of a melodic *color* is purely arbitrary. So is the guideline that if a melody set once in its entirety is Gregorian the piece is a chant setting, while if it is not plainsong the piece is a motet. In this light, and given the fact that fourteenth-century motet sources do not appear to discriminate between whole-chant settings and motets, the fourteenth-century whole-chant settings listed in table 1, along with the settings of integral tunes, will be considered as motets for the purposes of this study.[11]

The Function of the Motet

The problem of genre definition also involves the issue of the function of the motet. Here we must confront the most unsettling gap in the present account of the motet in England, namely our knowledge about its compositional milieu and performance contexts. Little hard evidence of any sort connects the repertoire to the personnel and routines of the musical establishments that must have sung it. Except within very broad limits we do not know where the motets were written or for whom, how widely they were disseminated and through what means, where and when they were performed or by whom, how long they remained in circulation, or when or for what reasons they eventually were discarded.

On the Continent, at least in Parisian circles, the motet became in the early thirteenth century a sort of aristocratic chamber music for an educated elite at court, among the clergy, friars, and monks, and at the university. This is clear from the subject matter of vernacular and Latin texts, the independent circulation of some texts, the general contents of manuscripts containing motets, and references to motets in specialized writing on music and other literature.[12]

What sorts of institution served in England as centers of composition and performance of the motet? On the basis of the provenance of the manuscripts in which the fragmentary English remains have been preserved as covers, flyleaves, pastedowns, and the like, "an almost exclusively monastic picture arises."[13] However, due to the parlous state of the sources, one can only speculate about the degree to which the present remains preserve a representative sampling of the kinds of sources in which the motet repertoire was likely to be found. By an ironic twist of fate, the materials at our disposal today are almost without exception the refuse from books already discarded in the fourteenth and fifteenth centuries that only survive as a byproduct of bookbinding at active scriptoria such as the one at Worcester. If a book of polyphonic music escaped the consequences of the stylistic or generic obsolescence of its contents, then it was probably lost during the destruction or dispersal of monastic libraries at the Dissolution, or in later Protestant purges. Furthermore, the fourteenth-century materials we have tend to reflect patterns of medieval library preservation in general (e.g., as from the Benedictine houses at Bury St. Edmunds, Durham, and Worcester), as can be seen by comparing data in Neil Ker's study of surviving books from medieval English libraries with Margaret Bent's listing by determinable provenance of English music sources from the late thirteenth century to about 1400.[14] Only when much more archival work has been done on all late medieval English musical establishments capable of singing polyphony will we know whether the important musical centers are well represented in the extant sources, but those sources point strongly to the largest abbeys and monastic cathedrals.

In a stimulating, resourceful, and iconoclastic contribution to the inaugural issue of the *Journal of the Plainsong and Medieval Music Society*, Christopher Hohler has countered the evidence of the sources, arguing instead that London and the court were the centers of production and reception for the polyphonic repertoire, which might then have been disseminated to rural monasteries and country towns via the schools at Oxford. The distinction between the producers and consumers of motets is an important one to remember, and indeed there is no direct and independent testimony that motets were mainly written at, and circulated from, the large rural monasteries—or put another way, that the English music culture was polycentric rather than monocentric. However, the kinds of evidence provided by the texts suggest that at least through the late fourteenth century the motet was cultivated for England's larger abbeys and monastic cathedrals, and that on balance these institutions were the likely points of origin as well.

Archival material thrusts the issue of provenance in yet a different direction. Harrison's pioneering work in *Music in Medieval Britain* stresses the likelihood of a new and predominating role for secular foundations in the cultivation of polyphony by the later fourteenth century. This observation has been followed up by Roger Bowers in an exhaustive survey of nonmonastic choral institutions in the English church from 1340 to 1540.[15] Bowers summarizes the picture presented by archival research as follows:

> The performance of fourteenth-century church polyphony was undertaken by the most musically literate members of the choirs of the major churches and of the various royal and aristocratic household chapels, of which, at any given moment, there were probably never more than thirty-five or forty where written polyphony was performed. These choirs included those of the major secular churches (the nine secular cathedrals and a handful of collegiate churches), a declining number of monasteries (principally Benedictine and Augustinian), the sovereign's Chapel Royal, and an increasing number of private chapels maintained within their households by the most senior churchmen and aristocracy.[16]

It is possible that the stylistic shift toward Continental models and the importation of Continental repertoire around and after midcentury, as well as the relatively smaller number of motets surviving from this later period, can be explained by the decline of the monasteries and the modeling of the repertoire of the new foundations, especially aristocratic chapels, along French lines, with the abandonment of motets in favor of the three-voice score repertoire as a frequent constituent of services.[17] Perhaps, too, if this shift took place, there was a concomitant shift in the functional role of the motet, affecting above all the number of motets kept in an active repertoire and the frequency with which any motet might be sung.

Motet texts will be discussed at greater length in chapter 4, but the following points need to be anticipated here. First, the texts suggest an ecclesiastical milieu and a liturgical or devotional function for the motet; most are sacred and can readily be associated with a specific feast day of the church year. Second, some concern saints who are particularly associated with monasticism, such as Saint Benedict, Saint Augustine, or Saint Martin of Tours, and a few additional scattered textual references also point to the cloister. We know little more about when in the daily round of services a motet may have been sung (at mass, in the offices, during processions, after compline, at votive services or Memorials) or where (from the pulpitum, in choir, in the chapter house, cloister, or refectory), and to what degree the performance context was fixed at all comparable institutions or may have varied with locale and order.

One approach to the question of liturgical placement is straightforwardly contextual. A motet (presumably like a troped chant setting) might have been performed in exactly that location in the liturgy from which its cantus firmus (or text) is derived, serving as a substitute for a ritual genre of plainsong.[18] This is an initially attractive thesis, but not without its problems. For instance, it fails to account for any of the free pieces and motets with non-Gregorian tenors. Further, because of the diversity of Gregorian sources of tenors, the motet cannot be associated categorically with one or even a small number of liturgical contexts.[19] Also, very few liturgical texts are set literally in motet style; other genres, discant and cantilena, exist for the setting of purely liturgical texts.

Approaching the problem in another way, one can gain insight into possible places for motets to be performed in the liturgy by canvassing service books for references to places where (and occasions when) polyphony was permitted. Harrison has done pioneering work in this area in an important chapter of *Music in Medieval Britain* ("The Polyphony of the Liturgy: 1100–1400"). He finds specifications for polyphony used both as a direct substitute for ritual items and as a nonritual interpolation, "which is nevertheless liturgical when used in a service."[20] An exhaustive search of all the relevant materials (a well-defined but daunting task) would certainly seem called for. The survey ought to be broadened to include the identification of all the kinds of supplementary material, monophonic as well as polyphonic, that appear in English sources as accretions to (or substitutes for) the standard chants and texts of the liturgy. Along the same lines, it would also be useful to know what monophonic genres were still being newly composed in England in the thirteenth and fourteenth centuries. These data would help to clarify for the music historian the degree of flexibility and accommodation of the liturgy to all new forms, presumably including the motet. It is unfortunate that there is nothing comparable to the services for the Feast of the Circumcision at

Beauvais that would provide for any English institution so much concrete evidence about the inclusion of new material into the mass and offices.[21]

Harrison has proposed a neat, plausible distinction between free and cantus firmus items, specifying a narrow range of performance contexts that can account for both as nonritual, but liturgical polyphony. He hypothesizes that as a rule the polytextual cantus firmus motet with tenor based on a mass chant was sung at mass by soloists in the pulpitum, perhaps even with the accompaniment of the organ, "to break the silence of the priest's silently spoken Canon of the Mass, after the Sanctus but before the Elevation."[22] Motets might also be *Deo gratias* substitutes at mass (but not in the office) in response to the deacon's "Ite." Free pieces, including conductus, rondellus, and voice-exchange motets on a *pes* were sung in the office in choir as unaccompanied *Benedicamus* substitutes ("cantus in loco Benedicamus") at the end of lauds or vespers. Less commonly, motets on a tenor might be *Benedicamus* substitutes in the office, in the event they are based on office chants or have the words "Benedicamus Domino" incorporated at the end of their text(s).

Harrison's theory, though perhaps more satisfactory than the contextual approach, lacks a convincing mass of direct evidence to back it up and so remains in a kind of scholarly limbo, as yet unproven but unable to be dismissed. Two pillars underlying the historical basis of the theory, his conjectures on clausula and conductus function, have been attacked recently by specialists.[23] The theory is also vulnerable to an objection already raised for the contextual theory. That is, there is no sign that there ever was any systematic recourse to a particular category of chant for motet tenors, nor any sign that any repertoire indicated a consistent performance context by concentration on motets with either mass tenors or office tenors to the exclusion of the other.[24]

The appearance of *Deo gratias* motets in the Machaut mass, the Missa Tournai, the Fountains fragments, Old Hall, and Bent's reconstructed choirbook (*H6*), and the location of motets in general at the end of Old Hall, suggest that the motet both on the Continent and in later fourteenth-century England was primarily associated with the Mass. On account of where they have been added, Bent calls the second layer of motets in Old Hall "sanctus sequels."[25] A number of the earlier fourteenth-century English motets (*Ave miles*, *Beatus vir*, and *Zorobabel abigo*) incorporate some form of "Benedicamus Domino" into their texts, and two have a *Benedicamus* chant as tenor (*Beatus vir* and *Humane lingue*). This evidence does give some support to a part of Harrison's thesis. Yet in terms of the whole, the number of motets which can be so singled out on the basis of text content is small, thus indicating their exceptional nature rather than that theirs was an exclusive, primary, or even typical function of all motets.[26] This problem cannot be pursued to any firm conclusion in the present study.[27] However, it should be observed that Harrison's distinction between free and cantus firmus pieces, which was followed in the division of material between PMFC XV and XVI, will not be followed here. The motet repertoire will be considered separately from the conductus and rondellus repertoires, but no generic distinction on the basis of function will be made between free and cantus firmus motets, or between monotextual and polytextual motets, in the English corpus.

Temporal Limits

In regard to the temporal limits placed on this study, reasonable and natural boundaries exist approximately at either end of the fourteenth century.[28] There are many characteristic features and continuous lines of development that link the thirteenth- and fourteenth-century English motets, but there is at the same time a marked shift in the notation, musical style, technical forms and procedures, subject matter, and relation of word to music in English polyphony around 1290 to 1300. This shift, triggered in all probability by exposure to Franconian and Petronian notational and stylistic developments on the Continent, provides a distinct terminus. As defined by the musical sources, the thirteenth-century repertoire extends mainly up through the Worcester fragments and slightly later related sources, which are excluded here save for a few fourteenth-century palimpsests entered into the earlier material. Some motets of probable thirteenth-century origin survive in later sources, and are considered along with more advanced pieces in this study.[29] On stylistic grounds, a few sources in Franconian notation are better classed as of the very late thirteenth century than of the early fourteenth, in particular *Lwa 33327*. On the other hand, *F-TO 925*, because of its concordance to *Onc 362* and the notation and rhythmic language of its fragment … *ma insuper*, is taken for present purposes to be of the very early fourteenth century.

The later boundary is set toward 1400 by the nine motets in Old Hall (five from the first layer and four later additions) and those in roughly contemporary or slightly later sources, such as the eight or more motets in Bent's reconstructed manuscript (*H6*),[30] Sandon's Canterbury fragment *Cant 3*,[31] and motets by Dunstable and his generation, all of which are excluded. Motets from English sources with nonmotet concordances in the first layer of Old Hall (*Lbl 40011B* and *Omc 266/268*) are included. This later terminus is a stylistic juncture at the point when isorhythmic technique in the motet turns consistently to tripartite and quadripartite structures marked by sectional changes of mensuration and complex diminution schemes. There is also the adoption of minor prolation and of iambic minim-semibreve motion under major prolation, as well as the introduction of complex syncopations and displaced rhythms on several levels of mensural organization, including the simultaneous juxtaposition of voices in different mensurations with minim equivalency.

Chronology and Style

Within the termini established at both ends of the century, a loose chronology of sources and pieces can be established that is anchored by few firm dates. This relative chronology is rather elastic and can be stretched or bunched to fill the era in question continuously, if not totally uniformly, with the repertoire that we have at hand. In regard to the earlier end of the era, Hohler has observed accurately, if a little acerbically, "I have not noticed in the literature any indication of the kind of evidence which entitles a musicological connoisseur to distinguish the notation of 1295 from that of 1301."[32] At the other end of the century, Andrew Hughes has discussed possible dates for an Old Hall motet that vary by over 30 years.[33] The discrepancy in suggested dates for the composition of the motet *Sub arturo plebs* reaches 50 years.[34] In light of the general lack of external evidence on which to base absolute dates for individual motets and sources, no piece-by-piece chronology of the motet corpus can be attempted. It will be useful, however, to outline the basic premises for the relative chronology of sources, motet types, and occasionally, individual pieces that underlies this study.

The manuscript sources offer evidence whose value has not yet been fully realized. A detailed paleographical and codicological survey of the motet manuscript fragments, involving review by experts in various archival sciences, remains to be undertaken.[35] We need careful assessments of the age and provenance of the contents and manufacture of the present parent (or "host") manuscripts and their bindings. The musical leaves themselves must be assessed for the implicit size of the uncutdown musical manuscripts from which they came, for their ruling and layout, for the characteristics of their music and text hands, and for what all this can possibly tell us about their ages. The paleography of text and music hands is well understood by musicologists in a broad historical framework, but of course precision is notoriously difficult to attain by this kind of analysis. The paleographer is inclined to defer to the musicologist's familiarity with musical style in any joint effort to come up with a fairly refined date for a source. As one consequence, it must be recognized that we usually lack the tools to distinguish a later copy from a version whose copying may be close to the date of composition.[36] Hence we must be vague not only about the origins of a repertoire but also about the span of time it may have been in circulation.

A second source of evidence on chronology is the evolution of notational forms and mensural organization, along with their intimately correlated style features, namely the range of rhythmic units employed and the rhythmic units used for declamation. Again, this is an evolution whose broad outlines are well understood but whose timing is not securely enough established to provide guideposts for a detailed chronology. (For a survey of these features in the motet repertoire, see chapter 3, table 13.) A logical resource for chronology would be a comparison between Continental and English practice. The "conservative attitude towards the rhythmic surface of the music"[37] in early fourteenth-century England, along with native innovations in notation and a concentration on formal rather than notational inventiveness, make direct comparison with the Continent only that much more difficult in this regard.

Comparative style analysis gives us a number of other yardsticks for musical differentiation along stylistic gradients that may be taken as roughly equivalent to chronological or evolutionary gradients. It will be useful to take up a number of these features for review with regard to the English motet repertoire.

Range

Range is one of the critical parameters for control of counterpoint in vocal polyphony; it is governed both by purely compositional considerations and by the makeup of the performing forces for which the piece is intended. Aspects of range as an element of style include: (1) the total range spanned by all parts; (2) the range of the polyphonic framework, i.e., the average width of counterpoint between the outermost parts; (3) the ambitus of individual parts and the degree of stratification or overlap between parts; and (4) the location of the overall range both within the Odonian gamut and with respect to the final of the motet.

For late medieval polyphony, one can say in general that total range, the width of counterpoint, the ambitus of individual voices, and the tendency toward stratification (terracing) of ranges all increase over time. In the early thirteenth century the overall range is usually no more than an octave to a tenth, with a fifth to an octave for the average width of counterpoint. By the end of the century the total range increases to a twelfth or a thirteenth, with an octave as the usual width of counterpoint. In the Continental repertoire this remains the norm throughout the fourteenth century, though in exceptional cases, such as a few of the Petronian motets of the first decades, and in later examples, in particular some isorhythmic motets a4, a fifteenth or sixteenth is reached in overall range. Roger Bowers has shown, through painstaking analyses of English sacred music over the periods ca. 1320 to 1390 and ca. 1350 to 1450, that "two octaves emerges as the normal practical working limit of overall compass."[38] He goes on to argue that a fifteenth or sixteenth must be a natural upper limit on the performing potential of the ensemble for which this repertoire was intended.[39]

English motets of the first half of the century already frequently exploit a tonal range of around two octaves. They constitute perhaps the first polyphonic repertoire to do so consistently. In those of widest range, the average width of counterpoint often exceeds an octave, frequently touching a tenth or twelfth. (For a list of the motets ordered by ascertainable total range, see table 2.) As with all such stylistic features, one cannot make very fine chronological distinctions on this basis. Nonetheless, there is a striking contrast between motets that date from perhaps the 1260s and 1270s (such as those in *US-PRu 119B, Cjc 138, Cjec 5,* or *D-Gu 220*) and those of 60 or 70 years later, such as the duet motets of *Lbl 1210* or *DRc 20.* On the earlier side are motets with overall ranges of a ninth to an eleventh, with an average width of counterpoint of only a fifth, and voices almost completely sharing the whole range, with much voice-crossing.[40] By contrast, the duet motets have an overall range of a fifteenth or sixteenth, with individual part ranges of as much as a tenth, eleventh, or thirteenth, without voice-crossing in partwriting. The average width of counterpoint is an octave, but there is a great diversity of interval content in the outer-voice framework (from sixths to twelfths), rather than the consistency seen in the earlier motets.[41]

Four-Part Writing

Three-voice partwriting is a universal norm from the late twelfth century through the midfifteenth century. In Notre Dame polyphony there is a small number of organa, conductus, and clausulae a4; and the motet a4 is cultivated for a short time in the early thirteenth century, as represented by the collection of such pieces in the second fascicle of *F-MO.* Resurgence of four-voice writing on the Continent comes over a hundred years later, in the 1330s, with the later motets of de Vitry and Machaut. The English, on the other hand, cultivate four-voice writing, particularly in troped chant settings and the motet a4, throughout the later thirteenth and early fourteenth centuries with a distinct upturn in output in the later period.[42] As a percentage of the surviving repertoire, motets a4 make up a more significant part of the fourteenth-century corpus than of the thirteenth-century corpus, although they never come to predominate, going from about 20 percent of the thirteenth-century number to about 40 percent of the fourteenth-century number.

If the motet a3 in its normal scoring (tenor plus texted duplum and triplum) is represented texturally as 2+1, then one possible scoring for the motet a4 is 3+1, representing the inclusion of an additional texted upper part. (The term for the fourth part is, straightforwardly, quadruplum.)[43] This is the scoring of early French motets a4 and also of a small number of English examples, mostly of the thirteenth century.

Another possible scoring for the motet a4 is 2+2, which indicates that there are two texted and two untexted parts.[44] The fourth voice in such pieces is low in range like the tenor and has a clearly subordinate, tenorlike function.

Table 2. Comparative Data on Overall Range

a. *Statistical Comparison with Other Repertoires*

Source	Range (number/percent)									Sample
	9th	10th	11th	12th	13th	14th	15th	16th	17th	
PMFC XIV	6/19	3/9	7/22	8/25	4/12	4/12				32
F-MO 7&8 fasc.	1/1	22/24	22/24	36/40	8/9	2/2				91
F-Pn 146 & de Vitry			2/7	6/22	10/37	6/22	3/11			27
Machaut			1/4	4/16	13/54	4/16	2/8			24
PMFC V				7/21	18/55	3/9	3/9	2/6		33
CMM 39				1/7	8/53	3/20	1/7	1/7	1/7	15
14th-C. Continental in England				2/8	14/58	3/13	5/21			24
14th C. insular	1/1			7/9	16/22	22/30	19/26	8/11	1/1	74
Bowers's data	--------------30/8---------------				113/28	120/30	103/26	27/7	5/1	398

b. *14th-Century Insular Motets by Determinable Range*

10th   Trinitatem veneremur

11th   ----

12th   Ade finit   ?Regina iam
          Civitas nusquam
          Corona virginum
          Herodis in pretorio
          Iam nubes
          Suffragiose

13th   Alma mater   ?Detentos a demonibus
          Candens crescit   ?Venit sponsa
          Excelsus in numine
          Fusa cum silentio

Table 2.   (continued)

Ianuam quam
Inter usitata
O homo
O pater
Petrum cephas
Salve cleri
Triumphat hodie
Triumphus patet
Tu civium
Vide miser

14th	A solis-Ovet	?Alta canunt
	Balaam de quo	?Augustine par angelis
	Caligo terre	?Beatus vir
	De flore	?Inter choros
	Solaris ardor	?Laus honor
	Suspiria merentis	?O crux vale
	Thomas gemma	?Parata paradisi
	Virgo Maria	?Quid rimari
	Cuius de manibus	?Regi regum
		?Regnum sine termino
		?Soli fines
		?Veni creator
		?Viri Galilei
15th	A solis ortus	?Assunt Augustini
	Ave miles	?Radix Iesse
	Barrabas dimittitur	?Zorobabel abigo
	Doleo super te	
	Exulta Syon	
	Frondentibus	
	Hostis Herodes	
	Mulier magni meriti	
	Orto sole	
	Patrie pacis	
	Quare fremuerunt	
	Regne de pité	
	Rosa delectabilis	
	Rota versatilis	
	Valde mane	
	Virgo sancta Katerina	
16th	Jesu fili	?Baptizas parentes
	Rex visibilium	?Hac a valle
	Te domina	?Lux refulget
	Zelo tui	?Salve sancta
17th	Jhesu redemptor	

Table 2. (continued)

c. *14th-Century Continental-Style Motets in Insular Sources*

12th	Firmissime fidem	
	Degentis vita	
13th	Amer amours	?Alme pater
	Apta caro	?Parce piscatoribus
	Domine quis	?Virginalis concio
	L'amoreuse flour	?Nec Herodis
	Mon chant	
	Musicorum collegio	
	Omnis terra	
	Pura placens	
	Sub arturo	
	Tribum quem	
14th	Ad lacrimas	?O vos omnes
	Rex Karole	
15th	Deus creator (English?)	
	Humane lingue (English?)	
	Inter amenitatis	
	Vos quid	
	O canenda	

There are two ways in which this voice may behave. In some motets it accompanies the tenor cantus firmus, filling in counterpoint above or below the tenor as necessary and serving as the lowest sounding voice whenever the tenor rests. Its role is an essential one so the part cannot simply be omitted to lighten the texture, but it is usually not patterned rhythmically the way the tenor is, and may be more active. This is the kind of fourth voice found, for example, in isoperiodic motets such as *Petrum cephas* and *Ianuam quam clauserat.*[45]

In other English motets a4, especially in the large-scale free compositions with voice exchange, the role of the fourth voice in a 2+2 texture is slightly different. Here the two lower parts are almost entirely equivalent. They may have identical ranges and rhythmic activity and share melodic material through exchange. Often this form of two-voice substructure (with or without exchange) is effectively only a single voice, with fragmentation of the lower part into two through hocket. (For examples, see figures 1 and 19 in chapter 2.) In other motets, such as *Rota versatilis,* the two lower voices may have slightly differentiated ranges and fixed harmonic functions. The effective

Table 3.   English Motets a4

13th Century:

3+1

O nobilis nativitas
O quam glorifica
Pro beati Pauli (I)
Pro beati Pauli (II)
Spirans odor
(Sancta parens)

2+2

Ave miles de cuius
Campanis cum cymbalis
Dona celi factor
In odore
Loquelis archangeli
O mors moreris
Opem nobis on Thoma
Super te Ierusalem
Virtutum spolia
(Sumer canon)

14th Century:

3+1

Exulta Syon
Inter choros
Orto sole
Solaris ardor
Trinitatem veneremur

2+2

A solis-Ovet	Orto sole
Absorbet oris	Peregrina moror
Alta canunt	Petrum cephas
Apello cesarem	Quid rimari
Assunt Augustini	Regi regum
Augustine par angelis	Regina iam discubuit
Ave miles	Regne de pite
Candens crescit	Regnum sine termino
Cuius de manibus	Rota versatili
Detentos a demonibus	Salve cleri
Flos regalis	Salve sancta
Hac a valle	Soli fines
Hostis Herodes	Syderea celi
Humane lingue	Thomas gemma
Ianuam quam	Triumphat hodie
Inter choros	Tu civium
Laus honor	Ut recreentur
Lingua peregrina	Veni creator
Lux refulget	Venit sponsa
Maria mole pressa	Virgo Maria

O crux vale	Viri Galilei
O homo	Zorobabel abigo
O pater	

Insular Terminology for Lower Voices in Motets a4

Quartus cantus

Ave miles de cuius
Dona celi factor
Loquelis archangeli
O mors moreris
Opem nobis O thoma

Candens crescit
Hostis Herodes
Ianuam quam
O homo
Petrum cephas

Quadruplum

Alta canunt

Quadruplex

Ovet mundus

Quadri(.)ivium

Cuius de manibus

Contratenerem

Humane lingue

Primus Tenor & Secundus Tenor

Motet	*Surviving part names*
Candens crescit	Tenor primus
Quid rimari	Tenor primus
Flos regalis	Kyrie. Tenor primus
	Kyrie Seconde
Textless	Tenor secundus
(*Lwa 12185*, 5a)	

Table 3.   (continued)

Super te ierusalem	Primus tenor
Nec Herodis	Primus tenor
Thomas gemma	P(rimus tenor)
	Secundus tenor
Ut recreentur	Secundus tenor
Detentos	Secundo tenore
Textless	Primus
(*Ccc 8,* 3a)	
Ave miles	Tenor ii
Salve cleri	ii

texture in these motets a4 is, in any event, mostly in three real parts, with only occasional bars of true four-part writing. Extensive use of imperfect consonances facilitates four-part writing by making more consonant pitches available, especially in an increased contrapuntal field, but fully independent four-part counterpoint cannot be sustained for any substantial length of time because of the homogeneity of rhythmic motion in all voices, coupled as it often is to parallel voice leading.[46]

It is tempting to see an effort to distinguish between the various possibilities for scoring in a 2+2 texture in the terminology used to label the lower parts in English motets a4. The evidence has been assembled in table 3. There is too little of it to draw firm conclusions. One attractive interpretation is that the terms "Tenor" and "Quartus cantus" are used when these voices are stratified by range and/or function, and that the terms "Primus tenor" and "Secundus tenor" are used when the two parts are a perfectly equivalent pair. On the other hand, it may be that Quartus cantus is the earlier designation and Secundus tenor the later. However, the use of both kinds of terminology in concordances of *Candens crescit* suggests that the different modes of nomenclature were equivalent, simply reflecting what are perhaps regional preferences.[47]

The form of the final cadence provides one interesting measure of style change among the motets a4. The earliest either cadence awkwardly to an 8–5 sonority with doubling, or else cadence to an 8–5–3 sonority. Table 4 lists pieces with the triadic final. These appear exclusively in thirteenth-century sources with the exception of *O homo*, which argues for an early date of composition for this piece.[48] Later motets a4 cadence either to 8–5 or to the more progressive 12–8–5.[49] Scarcely any English motets a3 cadence to 12–8, a final sonority which is significantly more common among fourteenth-century Continental motets a3. It is, at any rate, safely to be regarded as more progressive than a close on 8–5.[50]

In addition to an observation on how pieces end, it can be useful to

Table 4. Motets a4 with Triadic Final

Sumer canon	Lbl 978, 5	F-final
Pro beati Pauli	WF, 70	C-final
Super te Ierusalem	WF, 95	F-final
Loquelis archangeli	WF, 18=66	F-final
Campanis cum cymbalis	Ob 60, 13	F-final
O homo de pulvere	Onc 362, 17	D-final

observe how pieces begin. Most motets a3 begin on an 8–5 sonority, and most motets a4 do likewise, either by doubling or by resting in one voice (usually the duplum or the second-lowest part). This convention is abandoned in a small number of fourteenth-century English examples: *Zelo tui* and *Doleo super te* both begin with the triplum briefly unaccompanied; *Jhesu redemptor* begins the opposite way, with tenor and duplum only; and *Petrum cephas* begins with triplum and quartus cantus only, in what may be a gesture towards a Continental-style *introitus*.

Imperfect Consonances and Harmonic Style

Finally, an important guide to relative chronology is offered by the handling of imperfect consonances in contrapuntal interval combinations. The English preference for a full, rich sonority of thirds, sixths, and tenths in their polyphonic writing is a marked feature of insular style from the early thirteenth century on. One can observe in both motet and cantilena repertoires an evolution from the use of 5–3 sonorities to more progressive 6–3 and 10–5 sonorities, along with an increasing use of a more diverse vocabulary of interval combinations such as 8–6, 10–6, 10–8, 12–8, and 12–10. This can be correlated with a contrapuntal grammar in which they appear with increasing frequency in chains of parallel imperfect intervals, moving in quickening note values. In particular, with regard to the motet Harrison has observed the phenomenon he calls "pre-cadential protofaburden." This is found in some relatively early fourteenth-century motets where three voices move in semibreve values while the tenor rests. In later motets there emerges the texture Harrison calls "protofaburden-parlando," with longer chains of 6–3s.[51] This parallelism finds a direct counterpart in the writing of cantilenas, and as with the cantilena, becomes less of a feature later in the century, when the full English sonorities are used in a more varied contrapuntal environment.[52]

Table 5.   The Sources: Provenance and Estimated Age

14th-Century Insular Motet Sources, by Sigla

BERc 55	Yorkshire (household accounts)
Ccc 65	Worcester?(RISM); Benedictine
Cfm	Coxford; Augustinian
Cgc 512	Norwich; Benedictine
Cpc 228	
CAc 128/2	
DRc 20	Durham; Benedictine
D-W 499 (W3)	St.Thomas, Arbroath
F-Pn 23190	
F-TO 925	
Llc 52	
Lbl 1210	Cistercian?(Harrison)
Lbl 24198	St.Thomas, Dublin; Augustinian
Lbl 28550	Robertsbridge; Cistercian
Lbl 40011B	Fountains; Cistercian
Lbl 40011B*	Fountains; Cistercian
Lli 146	
Lpro 2/261	Thurgarton; Augustinian
Lwa 12185	Surrey (household accounts)
Ob D.6	Daventry; Cluniac/Benedictine
Ob 7	Bury St. Edmunds; Benedictine
Ob 81	
Ob 143	
Ob 594	
Ob 652	
Omc 266/268	
Onc 57	Christ Church, Canterbury; Benedictine
Onc 362	London?(Hohler); Canterbury?(Lefferts)
TAcro 3182	
US-NYpm 978	a royal chapel?(Harrison)
US-PRu 119A	Revesby; Cistercian
US-SM 19914	St. Osyth; Augustinian
US-Wc 14	
WF	Worcester; Benedictine
Yc	Shouldham?; Gilbertine
GB-YOX	

Rough Chronology of the Sources

	Harrison PMFC XV and "Ars Nova"	Sanders
Circa 1300-1330		
F-TO 925		
Lbl 40011B*		

Ob 652			
Onc 362	1	ca.1320	1
Lbl 24198	4		3
Ob D.6			
US-PRu 119A			
WF			
CAc 128/2			
Ob 81	2	ca.1330	2
Onc 57			

Circa 1330-1360

Lpro 2/261			
Cfm			
Ob 7 (front)	5	ca.1340	4
Ob 594			
Cpc 228			6
Yc			
Lbl 1210	3		
Cgc 512	6	ca.1336-55	7
DRc 20 (front)	7	ca.1350-60	8
Lwa 12185			5
BERc 55			
Lbl 28550			
Llc 52			
Ccc 65			9
TAcro 3182			
Lli 146			

Circa 1360-1380

Ob 7 (rear)
DRc 20 (rear)
F-Pn 23190

US-SM 19914
Ob 143
US-NYpm 978
Omc 266/268

Circa 1380-1400

GB-YOX	
Lbl 40011B	8
US-Wc 14	

A Provisional Chronology of Sources

Table 5 presents the sources for the motet in England in the fourteenth
century, listed first alphabetically by *sigla,* with an indication of provenance,
and then in roughly chronological order.[53] Similar though less inclusive lists
are published by Harrison (in "Ars Nova" and again, implicitly, by the
ordering of material in PMFC XV) and Sanders ("English Polyphony," p.
438). This table is provided as a reference point for the remarks on the ages of
pieces and sources that will be made from time to time in the following pages.
The dates represent informed guesses, for the most part.[54] They are not to be
understood as being as firm and objective as they might seem to be on account
of the specificity suggested by this listing.

2

Typology of Motet Structures

Large-scale features of design are of particular interest in the study of the English motet. Since a motet is as much constructed as composed, it will normally have both audible form and inaudible order,[1] an architectural plan based on elementary principles that dictates for each motet an overall shape and internal details of phrasing and counterpoint (some immediately perceptible and others only revealing themselves to the patient student). The most striking feature of insular motets in terms of compositional procedure is that their musical structures are limited to variations on a small number of recognizable models or formal archetypes. Surviving motets and fragments are particular realizations of these types, each individualized through specific ways of handling cantus firmus, text, and the numerical proportions of phrase lengths and sections. These consistent methods of approach, though few, are in fact more diverse than those found in Continental motets from contemporaneous sources.[2]

In an examination of the structure of any motet, the tenor must be taken as the point of departure. One reads the motet "from the bottom up," observing the tenor's patterns of rhythmic and melodic repetition and then looking to the other voices for correspondences in musical phrase structures and counterpoint. The most basic subdivision among motet types followed here distinguishes between two structural or compositional categories: (1) isomelism, where musical repetitions in the tenor are accompanied by repetition of musical material in the upper voices; and (2) periodicity (in particular, isoperiodicity) of phrase structures in two or more voices.[3]

Among the motets categorized as isomelic are those exhibiting strict and varied voice exchange, strophic repeat with variation, and refrains. In many of these motets it is apparent that composition actually proceeded "from the top down," with a loosely patterned (or nonpatterned) tenor that was freely composed or else disposed ad hoc so as to support a tuneful texted voice with symmetrical melodic periods. As a result most isomelic motets are markedly sectional or have prominent strophic features. They are built out of a series of well-defined musical units with clearly articulated boundaries corresponding to textual strophes, and melodic variation is an important stylistic feature, especially in the freely composed pieces. One of the most vigorous and distinctive of these indigenous motet types is the motet a4 with five sections of voice exchange followed by a coda.

The motets with periodic phrase structures are designed to express simple numerical schemes through interlocking musical phrases of rationally controlled length. Periods of these phrases may be uniform throughout a motet, or may be mixed in various ways. Especially in isoperiodic motets, a rhythmic module defined by the phrase beginnings and endings may replicate itself several times in the course of the motet, thus defining a sectional structure that is audible. Conceptually, however, the periodic motets must be regarded as through-composed. Theirs is a musical fabric in which textual strophes overlap without sharp internal divisions articulated by cadences observed in all parts. A particularly clear-cut type of periodic motet is the isoperiodic duet motet with *medius cantus*. The isomelic and periodic categories are not mutually exclusive, as will be seen in a number of examples, but the distinction between them is generally useful.[4]

The typology reveals that a rather chaotic collection of whole compositions and fragments from many sources can be assembled into rational categories accommodating practically all the extant material. That this is possible suggests that although the great bulk of the repertoire is lost (and with it, undoubtedly, many fascinating and original motets), we can get a sense of its range, its variety, and the consistency of its compositional techniques from those motets we do have. In the following pages the various motet types will be described with some examination of the shared or unique features of the motets falling under each heading, and with some mention of those motets that depart to some extent in their stylistic and formal relationships from the more clearly defined types.

Isomelic Motets

Motets with Strict Voice Exchange

The thirteenth century. The most important group of isomelic motets is that in which exact voice exchange occurs over a repeating tenor. A significant number of these pieces survives in late thirteenth- and early fourteenth-century sources, and they show a continuity of approach to motet design over the entire period (perhaps ca. 1270 to 1330). Independent compositions built on a succession of periods of voice exchange may be free or possess a cantus firmus, and may be either monotextual or polytextual. Those that are both free and monotextual lack both of the essential criteria of the motet as it developed on the Continent, namely polytextuality and a rhythmically patterned *cantus prius factus* as tenor. For this reason Harrison regards them instead as rondellus-conductus and sees in such a cantus firmus–based voice-exchange piece as *Ave miles* a hybridization or fusion of the techniques of rondellus-conductus and motet; therefore he labels it a rondellus-motet.[5] However, there is evidence that in the usage of English musicians, voice-exchange compositions on a *pes* (freely composed tenor) were regarded as motets rather than as a species of conductus.[6] Terminology such as "rondellus-motet," in its suggestion that norms have been contravened or boundaries crossed in the fashioning of a piece, conveys the common background of both rondellus and voice-exchange techniques in England but blurs the important technical difference between rondellus and motet, or between conductus and motet. This distinction needs to be made with clarity precisely because of "the close stylistic relationship that unites conductus, rondellus, and freely composed motet in the English repertoire of the thirteenth century."[7]

Voice exchange (*Stimmtausch*) occurs when two voices alternately present the same music over a double-versicle tenor. In a rondellus, all voices begin together and proceed through periods of exchange. The rota, a related musical phenomenon, is a round canon at the unison in which all voices participate.[8] One could conceivably describe voice exchange as a rondellus in two parts imposed on a repeating tenor. However, a true rondellus is a self-contained entity whose counterpoint is complete in and of itself, so the application of the term in cases where "voice exchange" would be more apt seems a misnomer (see figure 1).[9]

Rondellus and voice-exchange techniques in thirteenth-century English compositions occur in conductus, troped chant settings of Alleluias, independent voice-exchange motets, and independent rondelli.[10] These are listed in table 6. In each category the pieces are tabulated in an order representing a chronology based on style features. The style criteria include range (increasing overall span, width of counterpoint, and width during rondellus section), units of declamation (from longs to longs and paired breves and finally to longs and breves in alternation), manuscript layout (in score or parts), and notation (from premensural notation to English mensural notation and finally to Franconian notation).

Parallels in the evolution of rondellus and voice-exchange techniques are clear. It is probable that both have their origin in the constructivist techniques of contrapuntal invention found in conductus *caudae*. Most voice-exchange and rondellus passages, when not melismatic, bear a single text, in one voice at a time. Rare instances of simultaneous texting of all voices in typical conductus fashion are seen in *Salve mater* (two-thirds of a rondellus section), and in *Salve rosa florum* and *Equitas in curia* (voice-exchange passages). Like conductus, the independent rondelli and voice-exchange motets often have

Figure 1.   Voice Exchange, Rondellus, and Rota

Voice-Exchange		Rondellus		Rota			
ab	*a2*	*a3*	*a4*	a	b	c	d ...
ba	ab	abc	abcd		a	b	c	d ...
XX	ba	cab	dabc			a	b	c	d ...
		bca	cdab				
			bcda				

melismatic preludes, interludes, and postludes. Like motets in general, the independent rondelli and the later conductus and conductus-rondellus are written in parts, and *Fulget celestis curie* even has the simultaneous declamation of two different texts.[11] No later examples of rondellus a3 survive; the abandonment of this technique is undoubtedly due to the progressive expansion of range that had taken individual voice parts to a twelfth (in *Fulget celestis*) or a fourteenth (in *Regis aula*), representing an extreme upper limit on the practical range demanded of singers in thirteenth- and fourteenth-century polyphony. It seems reasonable to postulate that the progressive tendency toward four-voice writing in English polyphony found the functionally stratified voice-exchange motet better suited for development than the equal-voiced rondellus.[12] Further, another innovation, the adoption of cantus-firmus technique in voice-exchange motets, was simultaneous with the widespread extension of free composition to motets a4 through the replacement of the *pes* by a two-voice supporting substructure. Voice-exchange motets a4 may be successors to the rondellus but they are linear descendants of the exchange motet a3.

Before any discussion of fourteenth-century motets with voice exchange, it will be useful to demonstrate the facture of such compositions in the thirteenth century so as to clarify points of continuity and contrast. Two later thirteenth-century voice-exchange motets strikingly similar to each other in design, *Quam admirabilis* (*WF*, 16) and *Dulciflua* (*WF*, 41), illustrate the earlier motet's features.[13] In both motets, conductus-like melismatic preludes and postludes frame four sections of texted exchange. Each has a freely composed tenor whose repetition scheme may be diagrammed as xxy AA BB CC DDz, where exchange occurs over each double versicle and capital letters represent texted sections. In numerical terms, the two motets are proportioned as follows:

Quam admirabilis
131L = 2(16L)+4L + 2(10L) + 2(10L) + 2(12L) + 2(12L)+7L

Dulciflua
122L = 2(14L)+5L + 2(8L) + 2(12L) + 2(8L) + 2(12L)+7L

Table 6. Rondellus and Voice Exchange in 13th-Century English Music

Rondellus

1) in conductus ("conductus-rondellus"), written in score or parts

Integra inviolata	Ob 489, 3	score
Salve mater gracie-Salve		score
mater misericordie	Ob 489, 1b/2	
	=Ob 591,3	
Flos regalis	Ob 489, 1	score
O laudanda virginitas	Ob 591, 1	score
Amor patris	WF, 20	parts
De superne sedibus	WF, 5	parts
Quem trina polluit	WF, 69	score
	=Du, 1	
In excelsis gloria	WF, 93	parts
	=US-Cu, 4	
Karisma conserat	Onc 362, 14	parts
Regis aula	US-PRu 119A, 1	parts
	=Lbl 24198, 32	

2) in organal settings of Alleluias, where ascertainable

Gaude plaude	WF, 50
Alleluia Christo	Ob 400, 1
Alleluia clare decet	Ob 400, 2
Adoremus ergo natum	Ob 400, 3
Ave sanctitati	Ob 400, 4
Ave Maria plena	Ob 400, 5
Alleluia ave Maria	Ob 400, I
.....	Ob 400, K
Alleluia dulci cum	Ob 400, L
Alleluia musica canamus	Ob 400, M

3) in independent rondellus and "rondellus-motets" in parts

Kyrie rex Marie	Ob 497, 2 (in score)
Ave virgo mater	WF, 25
Munda Maria mater	WF, 21 (rota)
O venie vena	WF, 13 (motet + rond.)
Orbis pium	US-Cu, 8 (motet + rond.)
...ha mundi gloria	Ob 60, 7
...sine macula	Ob 60, 8
Ave mater Domini	Ccc 410 (in score)
Stella maris	US-Cu, 6
Christi cara mater	US-Cu, 10
Gaudeat ecclesia	WF, 94
Fulget celestis curia	WF, 31
	=Onc 362, 16

Table 6. (continued)

Voice Exchange

1) in conductus, written in score or parts

Salve virgo tonantis	Ob 3, 3	score
...angelorum agmina	WF, 90	score
Ave credens baiulo	Ob 257, 4	score
Salve rosa florum	WF, 92	score
.....	WF, 107	score
Regina regnans	WF, 89	score
Equitas in curia	Cgc 820, 1	parts
Sanctorum gloria laus	Onc 362, 21	parts

2) in organal settings of Alleluias, where ascertainable

Ave magnifica	WF, 19
(=Alle psallite)	=WF, 56
	=Ob 400, H
	=F-MO, 322 (Rok8.339)
Alleluya psallat	WF, 46
Alme veneremur	WF, 52
Alleluya moduletur	WF, 55
Re(gis)	WF, 57
Alleluya Christo	Ob 400, 1

3) in independent motets written in parts

Virgo regalis	WF, 12
Sumer canon (rota on pes)	Lbl 978, 5
Salve Symon (rota on pes)	Cjec 5, 7
Sanctorum omnium	WF, 23
Sol in nube tegitur	WF, 17
Puellare gremium	WF, 76
Alleluia celica rite	US-PRu 119A, 3
Loquelis archangeli	WF, 18
	=WF, 66
O quam glorifica	WF, 10
Patris superni	US-Cu, 7
Tota pulchra es	US-PRu 119A, 2
Quam admirabilis	WF, 16
Dulciflua	WF, 41

Notes

1) The conductus do not include pieces from continental sources that Falck suggests might be English.
2) Some of the conductus-rondellus have voice-exchange *caudae.*

Quam admirabilis has a single text, each of whose four stanzas is sung and then repeated, while *Dulciflua* has a single text of eight brief stanzas arranged in four pairs so each section sets one pair without any textual repetition from one voice to the other. The subject matter in both cases is the BVM. Finally, each of these two motets is notated in a rhomboid-breve variety of English mensural notation. *Dulciflua* has the paired breves of alternate third mode while *Quam admirabilis* has binary longs and breves with an unusual proliferation of semibreves. (See chapter 3, figure 22.)

The fourteenth century. The manuscript *Onc 362* contains a pivotal repertoire in the apparent evolution of the voice-exchange motet, namely two surviving intermediaries between the corpus of voice-exchange motets a3 in English mensural notation and the later motets a4 in Franconian notation. They are *Balaam de quo* and *Excelsus in numine*. Both are a3 but in Franconian notation; indeed, in *Balaam* there is declamation and hocketing in semibreves.[14] *Excelsus* is constructed on a freely composed *pes* that is identified in the manuscript as "Tenor de Excelsus." *Balaam*, on the other hand, is built on a cantus firmus.[15] It is the first exchange motet surviving in England to have this feature and, as in later examples, its text tropes the chant verses. In regard to the handling of text, *Balaam* is single texted, repeats each verse on exchange, and has a coda to the first texted section where both upper voices declaim together (on "exhibit stella"); *Excelsus* has two different texts identical in versification that are heard alternately, except at the end of each half of the motet where, in brief codas, they are heard simultaneously.

Formally, these motets are the last of an old bipartite design also seen in *Sol in nube*, *Alleluia celica rite*, and *Tota pulchra*.[16] They are divided by a central cadence and double bar into two slightly unbalanced halves, and begin with a melismatic prelude. Each half of *Balaam* ends with an elaborate textless *cauda*, while each half of *Excelsus* ends with a texted coda, as has just been mentioned. The numerical proportions and tenor design of these motets may be represented as shown in figure 2.[17] Both motets are of high musical interest, *Excelsus* for its lyrical melodies and *Balaam* for the way in which both the internal repetitions and restatement of the *Epiphaniam* chant are exploited to construct a form of substantial complexity using a technique that Dalglish calls "hocket variation."[18]

From the similarities in design shown by the pairs of voice-exchange motets just discussed, it is clear that their composers were working to create uniquely individualized interpretations of a conventional design or common archetype for voice-exchange motets a3. The fourteenth-century exchange motets a4 (for which see table 7) generally follow one of two such models with much the same kind of fidelity. In idealized form these are (i) a motet with five sections of exchange in which exchange occurs between every successive pair

Figure 2. *Excelsus* and *Balaam:* Numerical Proportions and Tenor Design

Excelsus   90L = 14L+2(8L)+2(8L)+5L + 2(8L)+2(8L)+7L
            $\times$ AA   BB   C   DD   EE   F

Balaam   108L = 4(5L+5L+4L) +   4(4L+4L+5L)
           aab AAB aab aab   CDE CDE cde cde

Table 7. 14th-Century Voice-Exchange Motets

Voice-Exchange Motets a3
Balaam de quo
Excelsus in numine

Five-Section Motets a4 with Coda (and Related Pieces)
Ave miles
Cuius de manibus
O pater excellentissime
Triumphat hodie
Salve cleri

Quid rimari cogitas
Viri Galilei
Rota versatilis

Large-Scale Sectional Voice-Exchange Motets a4
A solis ortus-Ovet mundus
Hostis Herodes impie
Rota versatilis
Absorbet oris faucibus

Varied Voice Exchange
Virgo Maria
Tu civium

Thomas gemma
Te domina

Other Voice Exchange
O homo de pulvere
Barrabas dimittitur

Regnum sine termino
Alta canunt
Rex piaculum

of musical phrases, over a two-voice supporting substructure that itself is undergoing a coincident exchange, followed by a coda; (ii) a motet with four sections of exchange, in which exchange does not occur after every musical phrase (corresponding to a few verses or a stanza of poetry), but rather after a longer, self-contained unit of four musical phrases (corresponding to a pair of four-line stanzas or to four three-line stanzas), over a two-voice substructure that repeats without exchange. These possibilities may be diagrammed as in figure 3 for a single period of exchange. Here a1, a2, a3, a4 bear text; A, B, X, Y do not. As figure 3 shows, text is not repeated in (i) but is repeated in (ii). A single five-section motet, *O pater excellentissime*, occupies an intermediate formal position between the alternatives just given. Each of its five sections may be represented as in figure 4.

To illustrate the degree to which motets of the first type adhere to a norm of five sections of exchange followed by a coda, some data on these motets are given in figure 5, which will serve as a point of departure for a number of observations. First, all the motets except *Quid rimari* and *Viri Galilei* have five sections of exchange, and all save for *Salve cleri* and *Rota versatilis* have a coda. In three (*Ave miles, Cuius de manibus,* and *Quid rimari*) this coda is melismatic, while in three others (*O pater, Viri Galilei,* and *Triumphat hodie*) it is texted.[19] Both upper parts of *Triumphat hodie* were apparently underlaid with text throughout.[20] In all the others a single text is sung without repetition, the upper parts alternating in the singing of consecutive stanzas. Saints, rather than the BVM, predominate as subject matter.

The presence of a cantus firmus in half the compositions affects tonality and the numerical proportions between sections. All the pieces on a chant tenor are tonally closed compositions with a D final, while those that are free have either a C or F final. The two motets on F, *O pater* and *Quid rimari*, are remarkably similar in melodic style and in the dovetailing of the two lower parts in a simple hocket (see figure 6). The cantus firmus for *Salve cleri* is the Saint Nicholas prose *Sospitati dedit egros*, whose double versicles underlie four sections of exchange and set eight stanzas of text that paraphrase and expand upon the corresponding verses of the prose. The first section is free, lacking any apparent cantus firmus or prior model for its text, and is constructed in two overlapping 14L phrases. The other sections are identical in length aside from the second, which lengthens the duration of the first syllable, thus adding a bar to the phrase. *Triumphat hodie* is built on a secular French tenor (*Trop est fol*) whose repetitive musical form, AA BB AA BB AA, is also conveniently designed for exchange, and dictates the alternation of 7L and 4L units. The texted coda of the motet is built on one further statement of the first part of the tenor, AA, with elaborate hocketing between the lower voices. The tenor of *Ave miles*, on the other hand, has no repetitive structure of its own and as a result is divided in fairly arbitrary fashion. The lengths of

Figure 3.   Models for Fourteenth-Century Voice-Exchange Motets

(i)			(ii)	
a1	B		a1 a2 a3 a4	B—————————
B	a2		B—————————	a1 a2 a3 a4
X	Y		X—————————	X—————————
Y	X		Y—————————	Y—————————

Figure 4.   Design of One Section of *O pater excellentissime*

a1 a2	B—————	or in more detail	a1	a'2	B	B'
B—————	a1 a2		B	B'	a1	a'2
X—————	X—————		X	Y'	X	Y'
Y—————	Y—————		Y	X'	Y	X"

with a coda that may have had the form:

a1	b2'
B	A'
X	Y'
Y	X.

the sections of this motet, like those of *Cuius de manibus*, *Quid rimari*, and also to some extent *Rota versatilis* (but not *O pater*), seem governed by a scheme in which the first section is the longest, the second is the shortest, and the following sections grow slowly in length. *O pater*, by contrast, is designed as an arch form with the longest section toward the middle.

One exceptional motet fragment, *Viri Galilei*, is best described in conjunction with the five-section voice-exchange motets. It has a unique approach to voice-exchange construction a4 in six sections followed by a texted coda. Only one of its two lower parts survives; it is designed as a series of double versicles that are themselves repeated, i.e., AA BB CC CC AA BB D. Tenor melodies A, B, and C are closely related and share their final two bars as a refrain. The surviving upper part makes good counterpoint with itself if exchange is assumed within each section (e.g., AA), hence counterpoint a3 is restorable and the reconstruction of a fourth (lower) part is straightforward. In texture and melody the style is very much like that of the two F-final motets exerpted in figure 6. *Viri Galilei* can be said to mix the techniques of voice exchange with varied strophic repetition, and the composition as a whole is a series of variations punctuated by a refrain. The text has a complementary design. It consists of five variations or paraphrases on a text that is finally heard in its original form only in the sixth (final) section; this text, familiar from the Ascension Day liturgy, is there set in full save for its final two Alleluias, which have been appropriated for the short coda.

Figure 5. Dimensions of Five-Section Voice-Exchange Motets

Motet	Subject	Final	cf?	Range	Total Length/Phrase Lengths
Ave miles	St. Edmund	D	cf	15th	96L = 2(15L)+2(5L)+2(8L)+2(9L)+2(9L)+5L
Cuius de manibus	BVM	C	free	14th	95L = 2(12L)+2(6L)+2(7L)+2(8L)+2(11L)+7L
O pater	St. Bartholomew	F	free	13th	152L = 2(12L)+2(14L)+2(14L)+2(16L)+2(14L)+10L(?2x5L)
Triumphat hodie	St. Lawrence	D	cf	13th	73L = 2(7L)+2(4L)+2(7L)+2(4L)+2(7L)+14L(2x7L)
Salve cleri	St. Nicholas	D	cf	13th	124L = 2(14L)+2(13L)+2(12L)+2(12L)+2(12L)
Quid rimari	BVM	F	free	14th	72L = 2(12L)+2(5L)+2(8L)+2(8L)+7L
Viri Galilei	Ascension	F	free	14th	100L = 2(8L)+2(8L)+2(8L)+2(8L)+2(8L)+4L
Rota versatilis	St. Katherine	C	free	14th	336L = 2(54L)+2(38L)+2(18L)+2(40L)+2(27L)

Note: Phrase lengths do not always add up to the total length when there is overlapping. Actual, not elided phrase lengths are given above. For instance, the first section of *Ave miles* is actually 29L = 14L + 15L (two elided 15L phrases); the first section of *Quid rimari* is 23L = 11L + 12L; and the first section of *Salve cleri* is 26L = 2(13L), i.e. two elided 14L phrases.

Figure 6. The Opening Phrases of *Quid rimari* and *O pater*

Quid rimari cogitas

O pater excellentissime

Large-scale sectional voice exchange. The large-scale sectional voice-exchange motets are another distinct type. There are four or five of them extant, a number that depends upon whether one regards *A solis ortus* (*Ob 81*, 1) and *Ovet mundus* (*Ob 81*, 2) as one motet or two (while accepting that the very fragmentary *Absorbet oris–T.Recita formosa* (*Lbl 40011B**, 1*/6*) should be classified with this group). These motets have lengths approximately double those of the pieces discussed so far. Each section sets four musical phrases in long, balanced melodies of great individuality and distinction that are interrelated either as pairs with *ouvert* and *clos* cadences, or by recurring patterns of declamation, cadential figures, and similar melodic contours. All sections close with a short melismatic "turn-around" or linking figure that effects a transition either into a repetition or on to the next period. The two lower voices have overlapping but stratified (rather than identical) ranges, with the designation "Tenor" reserved for the lowest voice, which usually sounds the root of all 8–5 harmonies. The "Quartus cantus" (or "Quadruplex" in *Ovet mundus*) lies, on average, a fifth above. Rather than write these two voices out twice in full, their repetition is indicated by the rubric "Recita" at the end of each section. The dimensions of these motets and the phrasing in the texted voice are given for comparison in figure 7.

That the archetypal form of these motets has four sections is not self-evident, given the few examples of this type and the fact that only one, *Hostis Herodes*, incontrovertibly has four sections. But something can be said in favor of the proposition. One must first of all account for the fact that there are five sections in *Rota versatilis*. By comparison with *Hostis Herodes* in regard to the length, mensuration, and declamation of each section, the first section of *Rota* stands out; it is unusual in notation and by far the longest. I propose that *Rota* has been composed with an extra section in accordance with the "fivefold" convention for voice-exchange motets discussed above, and thus can be said to reflect two archetypes.[21]

If taken as one motet, *A solis ortus* and *Ovet mundus* would have the same number of sections, with roughly the same features and dimensions, as *Hostis Herodes* or sections two through five of *Rota versatilis*. They survive on adjoining openings of *Ob 81* and are followed immediately by *Hostis Herodes*. It is tempting to propose that this source preserves two adjacent large-scale motets (in different layouts, as will be discussed), one on Christmas followed by one on Epiphany.[22] The evidence suggesting that *A solis* and *Ovet* are a single extended work is first of all stylistic: they are structural twins; their notation and part-ranges are the same and they have similar clefs; they share tenor contours, melodic motives, and second-mode rhythms. In regard to harmony, all the large-scale voice-exchange motets have similar "*pes* harmony," with a very limited tonal vocabulary based on tonic and supertonic chords. *Rota* is a closed tonal unit on C with a significant amount of motion to

Figure 7. Dimensions of Large-Scale Voice-Exchange Motets

```
A_solis_ortus-Ovet_mundus

Section length          Doubled              Phrases
                        (in perfect L)

1.  44L                 88L                  12 12 10 10 L
2.  72B (36 imp. L)     48L                  18 18 18 18 B
3.  36L                 72L                   9  9  9  9 L
4.  72B (36 imp. L)     48L                  18 18 18 18 +6 B
    + 6B "turnaround"    2L

            total:     258L


Hostis_Herodes

1.  44L                 88L                  12 12 10 10 L
2.  60B (30 imp. L)     40L                  12 12 18 18 B
3.  34L                 68L                   8  9  8  9 L
4.  72B (36 imp. L)     48L                  18 18 18 18 B
    - 4B "turnaround"

            total:     244L  (-4B)


Rota_versatilis

1.  54L (27 x 2L)      108L                  ?
2.  38L                 76L                  10 10  8 10 L
3.  54B (18L?/27L?)     36L                  12 14 13 15 B
4.  40L                 80L                  10 10 10 10 L
5.  54B (27 imp. L)     36L                  14 14 14 12 B

            total:     336L
```

Remarks: In *A solis–Ovet,* the 6B "turnaround" links the statements of the final section; it is sung once and stands outside of the regular 72B phrase structure. The linking "turnaround" in the last section of *Hostis Herodes* falls within the 72B phrasing; possibly the final long may be considered to hold through the number of B required at the end in order to complete the number structure. Note that for totals, all numbers have been converted to their equivalent in perfect longs.

B♭; *Hostis Herodes* opens on D and closes on C, with sectional cadences on C; *A solis* and *Ovet* both open on D, with the former closing on D and the latter on C. A final cadence to D for *A solis* is uncharacteristic of free compositions, which usually end on F, C, or G. Thus *A solis* taken alone is abnormal in this regard, while as one piece, *A solis–Ovet* would have nearly the same tonal characteristics as *Hostis Herodes.*

The use of hymn paraphrase in *A solis* and *Hostis Herodes* also bears on the present question. In each of these compositions the opening stanza of the hymn beginning with the same words is paraphrased in the opening two stanzas of the motet text. Further, both motets quote the opening melodic phrase of their respective hymn tunes in the initial bars of the top voice, as can be seen in figure 8. These well-known hymns for Christmas and Epiphany are closely related. Both texts were originally drawn from a single source, *A solis ortus*, the ancient acrostic hymn on Christ's life by Caelius Sedulius (d. ca. 450), and the tunes most commonly associated with them are identical except in their respective opening phrases. Melodic quotation in the motets therefore occurs precisely and exclusively where the two hymns differ. In light of these circumstances the lack of any hymn quotation in *Ovet mundus* can be taken to indicate that it is not an independent piece.

The conclusion that *Ovet mundus* is just a subsection of *A solis* also follows, perhaps most strongly, from an examination of texts. The verses for *Hostis Herodes* are a free expansion of the hymn stanza, telling the Epiphany story of Herod and the Wise Men based on the account in Matthew 2:1–12. There are shifts in the narrative viewpoint every two stanzas and a striking use of direct discourse as Herod raves in stanzas three and four. Together *A solis ortus* and *Ovet mundus* tell the Christmas story in similar fashion, freely expanding their hymn stanza following the account in Luke 2. Here, too, there are shifts in the narrative viewpoint corresponding to the four sections of the motet and a use of direct discourse in the second section. Parallels in versification also tend to associate *A solis* with *Ovet*. All these arguments taken together suggest that *Ovet* is not the second of three similar motets but rather the second half of *A solis ortus*, a motet that together with *Hostis Herodes* forms a Christmas-Epiphany pair with similar form and dimensions for each member.

The foregoing does not establish that *A solis* and *Ovet* are unsatisfactory if sung independently. (Were they sung at different times on Christmas Day?) Indeed, their manuscript layout, covering an entire opening per piece, speaks rather strongly for their separate identities, granted the extreme rarity in English sources of a motet being copied into more than a single opening.[23] Nothing in *Ob 81* suggests the necessity of a page turn from one opening to the next, either in layout, ornamentation of initials, or rubrics. The following does, however, need to be considered. *Hostis Herodes* fits on a single manuscript opening because it has been written out in a different format than is used for *A solis-Ovet*. In its layout no repetition or voice exchange is explicitly called for; rather, the music for each section is written out once, with voice I singing the texted part in the first and third sections and voice II singing the texted part in the second and fourth sections. Though there is no indication in the source, this format can be regarded as a method of condensing the full layout of the voice-exchange composition, either for an abbreviated performance or merely to save space. Such a hypothesis is given credence by the transmission of *Rota versatilis*. In two sources *Rota* was apparently written out in full (*Ob 652* and *Lbl 40011B**) while in a third (*Lbl*

Figure 8.   Comparison of Hymn and Motet Incipits

24198) it was presented in the same "condensed" format as we find for *Hostis*. Perhaps in view of the unusual length of *A solis-Ovet* the *Ob 81* scribe took some economies in the layout of a second example rather than dispose similar works in the same way.

Motets with Varied Voice Exchange

The Caius motets. Voice exchange is a crucial feature of a number of fascinating motets that apply the principle in a more varied and musically creative way than seen above. For instance, *Virgo Maria* and *Tu civium* are virtually twin compositions, the first on Mary and the second on Saint Peter, that appear as consecutive motets in the Caius college manuscript *Cgc 512*. *Virgo Maria* is laid out across a single opening in two lengthy voice-parts, each of which occupies one page. From these, two other voices are to be realized by singers beginning halfway through the parts at a point marked in each by an asterisk. In *Tu civium* four voice-parts are written out one after the other with only a double bar to separate each from the next. *Virgo Maria* has presumably been performed in its entirety when all singers have sung both halves of the part they began. A similar performance with exchange between pairs of voices can be presumed by analogy for *Tu civium*. Hence both are motets a4 (2+2) and can be diagrammed formally by a simple voice-exchange scheme (see figure 9). Performance of either as a true rondellus, presumably following the form diagrammed in figure 9 or something similar, is precluded by a number

Figure 9.   Motet a4 (2+2) Voice-Exchange Scheme and Rondellus

Voice Exchange	Rondellus
ab	abcd
ba	badc
cd	cdab
dc	dcba

of factors: the layout of *Virgo Maria*, the overall range that would be demanded of the singer, and the careful stratification of the voices into two pairs by range, texting, and features of counterpoint. In these respects they are much like the other voice-exchange motets examined above except that here all four voices bear text. These two motets are surely the least conventionally "motet-like" in the repertoire.[24]

The Caius motets share many features beyond their formal structure, including length (twice 70L for *Virgo Maria* and twice 72L for *Tu civium*), the same binary mensuration of long, breve, and semibreve, some melodic-rhythmic figures, and a G final. There are interesting differences, however, in their tonal language. *Virgo Maria* has a strong secondary emphasis on C and stresses that pitch's sub- and supertonic harmonies, including their colorful superposition in a sonority of three stacked thirds: B♭-D-F-A. *Tu civium* lies approximately a third higher in overall range than *Virgo Maria* and emphasizes harmonies secondary to G on subtonic F and confinal D, including a sustained pedal on D.[25]

The texts of these motets make little sense if taken out of musical context. Wibberley tries to explain their chaotic character by making the assumption that regular poetry has been randomly distributed across the polyphony. In the case of *Virgo Maria* he has been able to extract several Marian poems from the motet's four texts by tracing rhymes and verses linearly through all four voices. His attempt ultimately accounts for almost every word, but the poems so extracted are not particularly convincing on their own merits, and it is not comforting to have to suggest they were distributed across the lines of the motet without any rational method.[26] Rather, it seems more probable that what is provided as text for these motets was written to fit a finished composition and was designed to underline and emphasize musical interrelationships between the voices of the motet. The kaleidoscopic nature of the musical fabric, with its ever-changing texture of melodic duets in thirds and sixths, hocketing between pairs of voices, voice exchange on several rhythmic levels, larger structural repetitions, and recurring melodic tags, accommodates a similarly varied verbal play between the voices of the motet through the use of assonance, echo-rhymes, textual hocketing, homo-declamatory patter, and varied text exchange paralleling musical voice exchange. The lack of balanced phrases and regular periodicity in the music forestalls the use of conventional poetry. The result is a harmonious tapestry for the ear, the audible appearance of order and structural interrelationship from moment to moment without any clear controlling design.

The musical periods in *Virgo Maria* and *Tu civium* may be approximately represented as in figure 10. Almost all the periods are 4L units or multiples of 2L units, with some overlapping.[27] The high degree of repetition and variation in each motet is immediately apparent. In *Virgo Maria* the *a* section functions as an introduction of 8L. At the structural midpoint (46–49) there is a shift from a strong secondary harmonic emphasis on D, the supertonic of C, to B♭, the subtonic. Section *d* and its variations feature extensive patter duet.

In *Tu civium* the first 19L are an introduction somewhat independent of what follows. At *b* there is a duet similar to passages in *Virgo Maria*. The letters *r* and *r″* stand for a musical tag that recurs as a refrain. There are lengthy pedal points on D and then on G at *d* and *d′*, respectively; hocket sections occur at *e*. The use of repetitive two-bar cells is seen first at *c*, which is constructed in pairs of phrases, i.e., 9–10, 11–12; 13, 14; 15–16, 17–18. The last pair overlaps the repeat of *a*. At *f*, following the procedure seen at *c* and also in the counterpoint over the preceding pedal points, the figure picked up from 64–65 is spun out in similar 2L units.

In both Caius motets voice exchange is not merely a feature of performance practice but integral to the contrapuntal texture throughout. See, for example, sections *e* and *e′* in *Virgo Maria* (50–53, 53–57, 61–65) or the *e* sections of *Tu civium* (30–33, 40–48). Among the various melodic and rhythmic turns held in common by these motets, one is particularly prominent, the patter figure in *Virgo Maria* that is also the refrain tag in *Tu civium*. The Caius exchange motets show how freely varied voice exchange, in the medium of the limited English *pes* harmony, becomes the road to considerable structural complexity and display of formal artifice.

Other varied voice exchange. Two further motets have interesting additive structures based on varied voice exchange within a static *pes* harmony. These are *Thomas gemma* (a4) and *Te domina* (a3). The construction of *Thomas gemma* is at one time strict and quite free, well-determined and yet curiously irrational. The motet works even more rigorously than *Virgo Maria* or *Tu civium* in four-bar units.[28] These correspond to statements of three different versions of a four-bar *pes*,[29] which themselves undergo some variation during the course of the motet. There are 29 four-bar units in all, arranged roughly as five sections framed by hocketing refrains and bounded by an introduction and a coda. The musical materials are structured as in figure 11. There is clearly an intentional formal structure here and a varied reuse of distinct yet related materials, not merely the stringing together of recurring formulas.

Figure 10. Formal Design in the Twin Caius Motets

Virgo Maria

b. 1-8	8L	a		Intro.
9-13	5	b	⎤⎤	
14-21	8	c	⎟⎟	
22-24	3	b'' ⎦	⎟	X (16 + 12 = 28L)
25-28	4	d ⎤	⎟	
29-32	4	d'	⎟	
33-36	4	d'' ⎦	⎦	
37-41	5	b' ⎤⎤		
42-49	8	c' ⎦	⎟	
50-53	4	e ⎤	⎟	Y (13 + 16 = 29L)
54-57	4	e'	⎟	
58-61	4	e''	⎟	
62-65	4	e' ⎦⎦		
66-70	5	d'''		Coda

Repeat in full.

Tu civium

b. 1-4	4L	a ⎤	Intro.
5-8	4	b	
9-15	7	c	
16-19	4	a' ⎦	
20-25	6	d ⎤	X
26-29	4	rr' ⎦	
30-35	6	e ⎤	Y
36-39	4	a' ⎦	
40-45	6	e ⎤	Y'
46-49	4	a' ⎦	
50-55	6	d' ⎤	X'
55-58	3	r' ⎦	
59-64	6	d''	X''
65-70	6	f ⎤	Coda
71-72	2	r' ⎦	

Repeat in full.

Figure 11.   Musical Structure of *Thomas gemma*

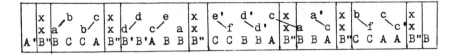

Or more schematically

```
Intro/R/i/R/ii/R/iii/R/iv/R/v/R/Coda
```

where R is a hocketing refrain over B''.

In figure 11 an x represents the hocket sections built on a variant of B. The other small letters represent text-bearing melody, and lines drawn between them indicate exchange of text. Particular melodic material and versions of the *pes* occur together (a, d, e with B; b, e, f with C; c with A), though there is not necessarily melodic voice exchange when the *pes* immediately repeats (for example, units 11–12) and textual exchange between voices does not always correspond to melodic voice exchange (for example, units 3–4 and 4–5). Two points of articulation in this structure (one would hesitate to call either a structural midpoint) are defined after the third hocket unit. One occurs at unit 14, where the role of first partner in textual and melodic exchange passes from voice II to voice I, making a division of the whole motet into 13+16 units. Two units later, at the textual midpoint, the predominant rhyme changes from "-ate" to "-atus," making a divison of the whole into 15+14 units.

As in the Caius motets, the problems of prosody and sense in the texts of *Thomas gemma* are inseparable from the nature of the musical texture. The exchange structure and hocketing must be taken into account, and further, it must be recognized that when a voice relinquishes the dominant melodic role, the text it proceeds to sing is likewise subordinate. Hohler reacts to the resulting language by saying, "The piece is frivolous; it can never have made much sense. The upper voice looks like a farsing of a poem in honour of S. Thomas of Canterbury (though if it is, I have never met the poem) but the second voice is really plain nonsense. It is verbiage designed to carry music."[30] He is perhaps a bit harsh on the second text, which seems no better or worse than the first. Layout of the texts in parallel vertical columns (see figure 12) clarifies their verse structure.[31] Subordinate words are indented to the right of each column, and the hocketing words are interlocked in the middle of the page.[32] Two primary texts emerge which are regular in rhyme, syllable count, and stress (*8p6p*); they form ten pairs of lines framed by introductory and concluding verses. The change in end rhyme can be seen to divide the text neatly in half.

The foregoing analysis of text and music describes features of *Thomas gemma* without suggesting the compositional strategy by which the composer originally arrived at its form. There seems no familiar procedure at work here. It is possible to see a loose five-section form with introduction and coda, but it is not clear why 29 has been used as the total number of units, and no simple number structure is apparent.

Figure 12. Text Structure in *Thomas gemma*

```
PRIMARY TEXT I            HOCKET        PRIMARY TEXT II
-----------------------------------------------------------------
Thomas gemma Cantuarie                  Thomas cesus in Doveria

                     primula
                          emulo
                     fide pro tuenda
                          lesus


                    cesus in           a divina repentina
                    ecclesia           mira caritate
        a divina repentina
        mira caritate                                 fulgens
                    fulgens            matutina vespertina
                                       lucis increate
        matutina vespertina
        lucis increate                               gratia


                          rivulo
                     gratia
                               patulo
                     late


                    tibi nova          sublimaris curia manens
                    reparate           in eternitate
        sublimaris curia regis
        pro fidelitate                                patris
                    tua                a ruina repentina
                                       per te liberate
        a ruina leti bina                             sunt sane
        per te liberate
                    sunt a fece        tu doctrina medicina
                    et ab amaro        serva sanitate


                     malo
                          tremulo
                     frivolo
                          sub dolo


a sentina serpentina                                 purga
gentes expiate
                     et a viciis       a sentina serpentina
                                       gentes expiate
```

Figure 12.   (continued)

```
singularis nuncuparis                              dirige
gratia ditatus
             super                       singularis nuncuparis
                                         gratia ditatus
hinc perfectos et electos                            super
tu es sublimatus                                 Remo atque

                          Romulo
                    rivulo
                               tremulo
                    madido


                pie sanans                tu per sanctos et electos
                egros                     pie sublimatus
preciosis (et) generosis                            merito
gemmis tumulatus
                aureis                    peris in ecclesia
                                          decora tumulatus
                    modulo
                           stimulo
                    tumulo
                           primulo


cum decore vel honore                                de sancto
pie laureatus
             in celis                    in honore et decore
                                         pie laureatus
inter cives celicos                                  gaudiis
digne veneratus
                Thoma                    inter cives celicos
                nunc pro                 summe veneratus

                    populo
                           querulo
                    stimulo
                           celo
tempestatis caritate                                 sine fine
fervida rogatus.                         manens tam beatus.
```

Te domina presents similar problems in determining the compositional procedure underlying an unusual motet and in making sense of the text's versification and language. Like *Thomas gemma*, *Te domina* is built in periods of varied voice exchange on a repeated tenor *color*. Here, however, the tenor lacks any strict rhythmic pattern, so it never repeats in symmetrical units over which exact exchange could take place. Above the tenor the upper voices take turns (six times apiece) in the role of the predominant melodic texted voice. As in *Thomas gemma*, the subordinate voice is lower in pitch and often rests, but carries text. However, no verse structure with regular rhymes and line lengths emerges when the text is laid out in accordance with the musical design; this is because phrases are not regular in length or declamatory rhythms. (See figure 13, where the primary and secondary texts are determined by according primary status to text sung to continuous melodic phrases, especially versions of the archetypal melodic arches to be discussed shortly.) The two texted voices share much melodic material, as explained below, but the exchange in which they participate is in the first place an alternation of roles without necessarily any immediate repetition of text or melody.

The tenor melody, a *pes*-like ostinato, has not been identified as a Gregorian cantus firmus. It is written in irregular groups of longs and long-rests, and none of the four and a half statements of the *color* is exactly like any other in rhythm. The *color* itself also differs slightly in each restatement, though the variation usually amounts only to a difference in the number of times a pitch might be repeated. In fact, pitch repetitions aside, it is closely related to the *pes* tenors of two thirteenth-century English motets, *Sol in nube* (*WF*, 17) and *Tota pulchra* (*US-PRu 119A*, 2), and to the tenor of *Thomas gemma* as well. (See figure 14.) This strongly suggests that its origin is non-Gregorian. A very high degree of isomelodic linkage coordinates the tenor and upper parts. That is, certain melodic figures consistently recur against the same tenor elements. These melodic figures may be seen as entirely derived from two archetypal melodic arches, the first (ab) rising from C to C1 and falling back to G, the second (cd) rising from D to D1 and falling back to F. If the tenor *color* is broken into two segments (i and ii), then ab is associated with the first half of each and cd is associated with the second half of each (the melodic cadences to F). From these essentials we can generate a map of the typical counterpoint over a single statement of the tenor *color* and compare it to the more complex and varied treatment of the components of the archetypal melodies in the finished motet. (See figure 14.)

Te domina is extraordinary in its degree of melodic recurrence and motivic play, and remarkable in its adaption of an apparent *cantus prius factus* to this approach. Certainly, composition of this motet was simultaneous in all parts rather than a process of successive addition of voices to a predetermined, patterned tenor. The text here is an afterthought—poetry for music whose assonances reflect rather than generate the larger form, though declamation may have played a role in determining local rhythmic features.

Other Voice Exchange

There are a few remaining cantus firmus motets with voice exchange that do not fall neatly into any of the preceding categories since they do not have large-scale, multiple double-versicle design in the tenor or the comprehensive reliance on voice exchange seen thus far. In the case of two motets, *O homo*

Figure 13. Text Structure in *Te domina*

```
PRIMARY TEXT I              HOCKET        PRIMARY TEXT II
-------------------------------------------------------------
Te domina regina                          Te domina Maria
pariendo protulit virgo                        Iesse virgula
sola paritura sine semine
             laus patrie                  tu germina protinus
             celestis                     odorifera
                                          profers redolencia
nitens sidus in ethere
in caligine
             mundi                        O florigera
             sine crimine                 delens et obprobria
                                          a malicia
                                          avaricia
                                          sola deputata
nos serva domina                                   subdolis
celi rosario
privilegium
             O flos odor                  decore superasti
                                          lilia purpurea
                                          modulancium
lucens nitore vario                                et carmina
mater honoris                                      et
             flos genus                   primula
                                          per tibi data
                                          nato nata
virgineum                                 privilegia
pia sublimia                                       coronata
                                                   O
                      consilia
                          viola
                      per imperia
                               convivia
                      visita
                          da solacia
                   ignaros            via previa
                   reos per           nostra post exterminia

                      secula
                          funeris
                      criminalia
peregregia                                       fata
rosa demere                                      O
               predilecta                 tripudiorum
               candidata                  dulcis materia
                                          laudis immemoria
                                          preconizata
                      piacula
                          miseris
                      poli luminis
loca nos in gloria.                       nobis succure Maria.
```

considera and *Barrabas dimittitur*, a threefold statement of the tenor underlies varied voice exchange. The second section of each is a freely varied version of the first, with exchange between upper parts; the third section is freer yet in counterpoint but is fundamentally a strophic variation upon the first. The exchange is more literal in *O homo considera*, and further, within its tenor there is one near-exact restatement of melody that is matched to voice exchange embedded within each of the three larger sections. *Barrabas* has a looser relationship betwen sections. In particular, the third introduces new material, including dramatic oscillations on the words "hely lamazabathani" and a rise in tessitura with canonic imitation at "hinc clamavit."

In *Regnum sine termino* exact voice exchange occurs twice, taking advantage of the two melodic double versicles embedded in its tenor, the Gloria prosula *Regnum tuum solidum* (shaped A BB CC D). In *Alta canunt*, a

Figure 14.   Musical Elements of *Te domina*

Figure 14. (continued)

Tenor of *Sol in nube* (WF, 17)

Tenor of *Tota pulchra* (US-PRu 119A, 2)

Tenor of *Thomas gemma*

Figure 14. (continued)

Actual pattern of use in *Te Domina*.

I:	IN a'b' cdd'	da'b	a'd' cd'	b'a'b'	bd'
				HH H	H
II:	IN ab'b	abb'b"b" cd	a'b a'b	b'b"c'd b"cd	a'b
T:	A	B	C	D	E

I, II: voices I and II
T: tenor
A-E: colores in the tenor
IN: introduction
H: hocket section

fragmentary motet whose tenor is lost, the counterpoint of the surviving texted voice with the extant quadruplum, and the amount of melodic repetition in each, suggest that the original motet was constructed in loose periods of strophic repetition and varied voice exchange. Since the text tropes the *Alleluia Pascha Nostrum*, the chant melody was probably the cantus firmus and the melodic repetition inherent in the *Alleluia* melody probably determined the motet's contrapuntal structure. Just how the chant may have been disposed is not clear. One final example, *Rex piaculum*, from the later fourteenth-century source *TAcro 3182*, shows that voice-exchange techniques were not wholly abandoned after the first few decades of the century, and in fact were apparently still associated with the genre of troped chant settings of the Alleluia in which they flourished in the later thirteenth century.

Strophic Repeat with Variation

In reference to the thirteenth-century English motet repertoire Sanders has noted that "almost all of the *pedes* of the freely composed motets without *Stimmtausch* also exhibit features of repetition, some with variation, some without."[33] Later examples among motets built on a cantus firmus show a predilection for isomelic exploitation of tenor repetition to have continued at least through the earlier part of the fourteenth century. Composers took advantage of whatever opportunities presented themselves in tenor behavior. *Civitas nusquam*, for example, shows repetition of counterpoint only where the music of the first 10L is repeated upon partial restatement of the tenor in the final 10L, and in *Alma mater*, the return of counterpoint follows the repetition scheme of the rondeau used as cantus firmus.

Strophic repeat with variation is a particularly prominent feature of the important group of motets distinguished by a tenor (usually an integral, non-Gregorian tune) that is stated two or three times in its entirety.[34] The sources of these tenors are quite varied, and include French chansons, Latin devotional songs, and *pes*-like free melodies. (See tables 1 and 8.) Where the tunes themselves incorporate reiterated phrases (the ABAA form of the hymn melody in *Laus honor* is but one example among many) the opportunities for repetition of material are further multiplied. The overt reuse of material does not indicate poverty of invention on the part of composers. As in *Barrabas dimittitur* and *O homo considera*, the motets with varied voice exchange on threefold tenors mentioned above, economy of means becomes an opportunity for the clever variation and permutation of musical ideas. Less overt is the particularly fine use of motivic repetition within and between strophes in *A de finit*. Phrase design in motets with strophic repetition usually overlaps sectional boundaries so that repetitions of counterpoint are embedded in the fabric of the piece rather than clearly articulated for emphasis as they would be in a strict voice-exchange motet. As a result,

Table 8.   Motets Exhibiting Strophic Repeat with Variation

Motet	*No. of Tenor Repetitions*
O homo considera	3x
Barrabas dimittitur	3+1/3x
Ade finit	3x
Rex omnipotencie	2x
Solaris ardor	ABBAA
Alma mater	ABAAABAB
De flore martirum	2x
Deus creator omnium	3x
Doleo super te	2x
Duodeno sydere	3x
Laus honor	2x
Mulier magni meriti	3x
Nos orphanos erige	3+1/3x
Princeps apostolice	2x
Civitas nusquam	1+1/4x
Parata paradisi porta	1+4/5x

Motets with similar layout and declamation in s but without marked strophic repeat:

Frondentibus	3x
Triumphus patet	3x
Herodis in atrio	3x
Caligo terre	ABBAA

periodic phrase structures are not precluded if the tenor is appropriately patterned, and motets of this type normally have some periodicity in phrase design. In others a shift in texture, like the introduction of canonic imitation in the third section of *Barrabas dimittitur* or the hockets introduced midway through a number of the *F-TO 925* motets, introduces contrast that perceptibly marks off strophes.

A number of the complete motets with strophic repetition and breve-semibreve declamation have attracted comment in the literature for their high amounts of reiterated material and internal detail. For instance, Dalglish describes *De flore* as a variation motet with isomelic features; Sanders analyzes *Mulier magni meriti* as a paired strophic variation with refrain; and Sanders (following Handschin) observes how the melodic repetition in the cantus firmus of *Doleo super te* allows the construction of a motet whose second half is a close variation upon the first half (Handschin's pithy comment: "Thus isorhythmicity is confounded with isomelodicity").[35] *Nos orphanos* provides a dramatic example of the high degree of literal repetition that can be found in this type of motet (see figure 15).

Figure 15. Strophic Repetition in *Nos orphanos*

Refrain Motets

The motets discussed so far in this chapter consist of a number of discrete sections whose lengths are related by simple musical relationships or numerical proportions. Only in some of the motets exhibiting strophic repeat with variation do periodic phrase structures interlock voices in patterns that tend to obliterate clearly defined sections (though here there is repetition in the unit length of the period). Otherwise, the motets may be viewed as built up linearly in blocks of counterpoint arranged in series. Given this sectional construction, it is not surprising to find instances where refrains are used to define or clarify structure. There are refrains or refrain-like effects in several motets already discussed, including a hocket refrain in *Thomas gemma*, the repetition of material at the end of the sections of *Mulier magni meriti*, and the little recurring tag in *Tu civium*.[36] Four further examples, two of them very fragmentary, clearly show the exploitation of a distinct textual and musical refrain in which both elements are stable and distinguished in melody and versification from the more varied periods they punctuate (see table 9).[37] One of these motets, *Candens crescit*, has first-mode rhythms with declamation on long and breve; the others, *Suspiria merentis, Rogativam potuit*, and *Surgere iam est hora*, are all in second mode with breve-semibreve declamation.

Though both upper voices of *Candens crescit* are texted, this motet must be considered a polyphonic setting of the tune in voice II, "Candens lilium columbina," that gives the whole piece its shape and drive. Overall, this musical shape is a rondo-like ABABA, with the second B slightly varying the first in its opening bars and the second and third A bearing the same text, hence functioning as an explicit refrain. The tune in voice II divides musically into two pairs of *ouvert* and *clos* phrases. In A, each phrase of the pair is 8L in length and subdivides in half, so that A can be represented as ax ax'. The B section is articulated as two 12L phrases, each of which consists of three 4L subphrases, so that B can be represented as bb'x bb'x'. The *ouvert* and *clos* motives (x and x') are the same in A and B. Voice I provides a counterpoint to voice II in the same register, with overlapping phrases. The irregularities of musical phrase in voice I, and chains of identical rhymes in its text, make clear that it was conceived after voice II as a complement to it. Beneath all this, voices III and IV together create the texture of a single supporting part through a constant alternation of short motives in hocket-like fashion.

Suspiria merentis is the only other refrain motet that survives complete. It is built over a cantus firmus that is a varied ostinato of six pitches. Each of its five sections is built on a pair (or in the case of the fourth section, two pairs) of phrases arranged melodically as *ouvert* and *clos*, followed by the refrain, which is likewise an *ouvert* and *clos* pair. Every section has parallel phrases in the upper parts and ends with the same cadential pattern and chiming "-are"

Table 9.   Refrain Motets

Candens crescit:	ABABA
	= axaxc′ bb′x bb′x etc. (voice II)
Suspiria merentis:	AR BR CR DR ER
	= aa′ rr′ bb′ rr′ cc′ rr′ dede rr′ fg rr′
Rogativam potuit:	. . . . R AA R
	=. . . . rr′ ab ab rr′
Surgere iam est:	AR BR CR
	= aa′ r bb′ r cc′ r (r=xx′y)

rhyme in voice I. The literal recurrence of the refrain has been taken advantage of by the scribe of *Cgc 512*, who wrote it out in full only once in the manuscript. Subsequent repetitions are indicated in each voice part by a textual cue that is set off by strokes, e.g., //Spiritus alme//Seculare// or //Sancte spiritus//tedia//, and further indicated by a sign (in the staff above) resembling a Greek letter *pi* or a doubled *t* in the cursive script of the text hand.

Two motet fragments have strong similarities in paired-phrase design and melodic facture to the pieces just reviewed. *Rogativam potuit* is preserved on a page from a musical rotulus now folded into *Ob 652*. Only a little more than half (the second half) of a single voice remains, including two statements of the refrain and the intervening section. As in *Suspiria* and *Candens*, the refrain is composed of a melodic double versicle with *ouvert* and *clos* phrase endings. The structure of the surviving section (from "Deus ecce") is similar in design to, though larger in scale than, the fourth section of *Suspiria* (from "Cur id a quo"). The text of this section of *Suspiria* has four-line stanzas that are set as four 3L musical phrases of 14 syllables each, paired in couplets AB AB. In *Rogativam*, however, there is twice the amount of text: four four-line stanzas are set to four 6L phrases of 32 syllables each, related as AB A′B′. Unfortunately no tenor for *Rogativam* survives, but it must have had a repeating structure like the tenor of *Suspiria*.

Just as there are both free and cantus firmus–based voice-exchange motets, so there exists, in addition to the refrain motets just discussed, a fragment of one remarkable specimen built on a Gregorian melisma. This fragment is *Surgere iam est hora*. Its tenor is *Surge et illuminare*, the opening melisma of the verse of the Epiphany gradual *Omnes de Saba*. The cantus firmus is an appropriate choice on account of its internal repetition: there is a melodic double versicle on "*Surge*" that is followed by a ten-note extension on "*illuminare*" (see figure 16). This *color* must be stated three times in all, though only the second and third statements are preserved. In each statement the double versicles are given a different internally repeating rhythm while the extension is repeated identically, thereby laying the groundwork for a refrain structure with overall form AA'R BB'R CC'R.

The tenor design is mirrored in the duplum, which is carefully crafted so that its musical and textual repetitions overlap the tenor's and its own musical phrase boundaries, while at the same time parallel verses of the poem are set to parallel musical lines. The rhythmic variations in the tenor have a correspondence in the varying versification and increasing length of stanzas in the duplum text, with a consequent acceleration in the rate of declamation from the first section through the third section. It is likely that the missing triplum had repetitions of text and music that directly coincided with its musical phrase structure, though doubtless these were not precisely coincident with those of either duplum or tenor. It is worth noting, too, that the refrain in the duplum is itself a mini-AA'B setting.

I suggested above that *Candens* is a polyphonic setting of the tune carried by voice II, but there is no external evidence indicating that this tune had a prior existence. Do the polyphonic refrains of *Suspiria, Rogativam,* and *Surgere* preserve preexistent tunes? Given the compositional constraints apparent in each motet, it seems unlikely, though impossible to rule out. The melodic style in the refrains is certainly close to what we commonly regard as a popular, even dance-like idiom, and it definitely colors the melodic style of the other parts in these motets (see figure 17). It is testimony to the vitality of the insular motet that it could produce forms of such transparent charm and ingenuity.

Motets with Periodic Phrase Structures

Periodicity refers to a regularly recurring element; when the term is used in regard to the motet that element is a musical phrase length. Many of the motets already discussed in this chapter, including those with strongly defined sectional or "strophic" form such as the motets with strict voice exchange or the refrain motets, have features of periodic phrase structure. Periodicity may be found in one or more voices of a motet, usually (but not always) including the tenor. In a part with periodicity, phrase lengths may vary in some predetermined way, but more usually they are equal. If the same period is repeated uniformly in two or more voices of a motet, then these voices (and the motet as a whole) are characterized as "isoperiodic." Where the periods of the motet voices differ, one may speak of "mixed periodicity." In such a situation

Figure 16. Refrain Motet Double-Versicle Melodies

Figure 17. The Melisma on "Surge et illuminare"

there may be occasion to speak of a double structure if a voice seems to have sufficient independence from the tenor in melody and phrase design to suggest that it is a *cantus prius factus*. It is useful to distinguish a third type of periodicity, "subdivided-module periodicity," in which the repeating module is not itself a single long phrase, but rather is made up of a number of shorter phrases of mixed periodicity; this more elaborate modular structure may be interrupted or reset so as to replicate exactly over restatements of the tenor pattern rather than continuing from the beginning of the motet to the end.

Isoperiodic motets are the most numerous and clearly defined class of periodic motets in the English repertoire (see table 10). In a typical case an adjustment is made to the lengths of the initial phrase in each voice so as to stagger or displace subsequent phrases to avoid strictly parallel phrases in two or more parts. This offset is made up at the very end of the motet by a compensating increase or reduction in the length of the last phrase in each part. For instance, if the length of the period is 5L, then the phrases of the voices in a motet a3 might be laid out as in figure 18. This creates a module of phrases and phrase rests of the unit length that replicates itself strophically throughout the composition. The module may be rigorously isorhythmic as well but in fact seldom is.[38] Usually, however, it is isodeclamatory. That is, the motet's phrases are all identical in declamatory patterning; we may speak of a "declamation profile" that is constant whatever the variety in melismatic subdivision of the regular units of declamation. As a consequence, isoperiodic motets normally have poetic texts with regular verse structures that are paired in length and versification. In fact, regular poetry is associated generally with periodicity and balanced phrase structures; isoperiodicity is merely an important example of this. Granting that the composition of an isoperiodic motet involves the coordination of regularly versified texts with a rigidly constructed numerical phrase scheme, a composer could conceivably begin to work with either the determination of a preferred modular number or the choice of a conventional versification scheme as a starting point. Given a modular number and uniform declamation in some pattern, versification is dictated. Given a poem (or any predetermined verse pattern) and a declamation pattern, the modular number is dictated.

Isoperiodic Motets with Long-Breve Declamation

A clear generic subdivision of isoperiodic motets in the English repertoire occurs between those that have declamation on long and breve and those that have declamation on breve and semibreve. Within each of these subdivisions there is a single predominant type: for the former, motets with broadly patterned tenor similar to *Petrum cephas*, and for the latter, duet motets with *medius cantus* similar to *Jesu fili*.

Table 10. Isoperiodic Motets and Other Periodicity

Motets (by increasing modular number)	Module (in L)	No. of Periods	Length (+coda)
I.a. *Isoperiodic with long-breve declamation*			
Vas exstas	7	10	70
Regi regum (wc)	7	12	84
Ianuam quam (wc)	8	14	112
Solaris ardor (wc)	9	6	54
Templum eya	9	8	72
Virgo sancta	9	10	90
Petrum cephas	9	12	108
Lux refulget	9,6,4	10,2,3	90,12,12
Jhesu redemptor	10	8	80
Ut recreentur	10,12	8,7	80+4,84+10
Salve sancta (wc)	12	3	36+20
Inter choros (wc)	12	5	60+4
Rex sanctorum	12	6	72
Veni creator (wc)	12(2x6)	9.5(19)	114
Dei preco	14(2x7)	4(8)	56
Maria mole pressa	15	6	90
I.b. *Isoperiodic with breve-semibreve declamation*			
Duet motets with medius cantus			
A solis ortus (*Lwa*)	4	12.5	50
Rosa delectabilis	4	15	60
Jesu fili	4	16	64
Fusa cum silentio	8(2x4)	7.25	58
Quare fremuerunt	8	12	96
Zelo tui langueo	8	16.25	130
Others isoperiodic with breve-semibreve declamation			
Rex visibilium (wc)	4	9	36
Suffragiose	2	21	42
Iam nubes	4	11	44
II. *Mixed periodicity* (Upper voices; tenor)			
Exulta Syon	11, 10, 8; 9		
Syderea celi	7; 2		
Valde mane	9, 8; 8		
Corona virginum	10; 12		
Ade finit	13, 11, 9; 4		
Vide miser	15, 14, 13, 12, 11; 24(4x6)		

Table 10.   (continued)

Iam nubes	4; 9
Detentos a demonibus	17; 7
Regina iam discubuit	17; 5
Venit sponsa	17; 11
Parata paradisi porta	13, 12, 9, 8, 6; 14
De flore martirum	9, 8, 6, 4, 2; 7

III. *Subdivided-Module Periodicity* (see Figure 25)

Mulier magni meriti
Princeps apostolice
Orto sole
Beatus vir

Figure 18.   Hypothetical Isoperiodic Motet a3

$$7+5+5+\ldots\ldots+5+3L$$
$$6+5+5+\ldots\ldots+5+4L$$
$$5+5+5+\ldots\ldots+5+5L$$

In the *Petrum cephas* type, the phrase rests in the texted voices, and often even more strikingly, the pattern of notes and rests in the tenor, make a distinctive visual configuration in the manuscript source (see figure 19). This orthography is especially characteristic of the motets with large modular numbers. Variations in texture and in the rhythmicization and patterning of the tenor in these pieces are in large part due to the fact that a high proportion of whole chants are set this way, with all the problems inherent in trying to accommodate the chant to the modular scheme. Motet-like troped chant settings in *Cjc 23*, *D-W 499 (W3)*, and *LIc 52* do not sustain isoperiodicity for very long before it is halted at sectional boundaries of the chant with a cadence in all voices, whereas motets on whole chants strive to sustain continuity of phrase patterning from beginning to end. The evidence suggests a possible line of development for the *Petrum cephas* type: first, motets with three isoperiodic texted voices over a tenor moving strictly in longs (3+1), such as the late thirteenth-century whole-chant setting *Salve mater* (*WF*, 64)[39] or the Worcester palimpsest *Inter choros*; second, motets in which the tenor is more active but not isoperiodic, such as *Ianuam quam clauserat* or *Salve sancta virgula*; third, motets in which the tenor articulates the basic modular number but is not yet isorhythmic, such as *Regi regum*; fourth, motets in which the

Figure 19. The Orthography of Isoperiodic Tenors

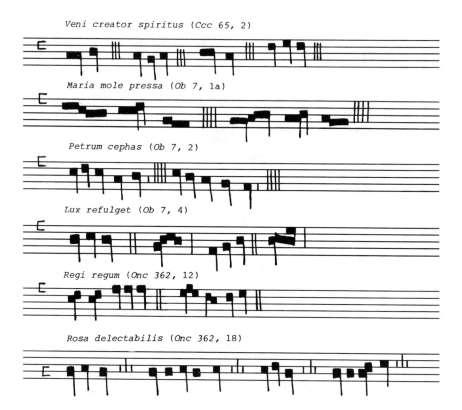

tenor is organized in a succession of identical rhythmic *taleae*, especially in longs and long- and breve-rests.

  Petrum cephas is a typical example of this last stage. It is in four voices, three of which (the two texted upper parts and the tenor) are isoperiodic; the quartus cantus does not participate in the numerical scheme. The modular number of this motet is 9, articulated in the upper parts as eight longs followed by a long-rest and in the tenor as four long-rests followed by five longs. Each texted phrase sets fourteen syllables, comprising two verses of a four-line stanza with syllable and accent pattern *8686pp*.[40] The even syllable count with *pp* stress usually invites treatment with an upbeat, but here the pickup has been stretched to a full bar. The first duplum phrase is offset from that of the triplum by seven bars of rest—its poem is, as a result, shorter than that of the triplum by one couplet—and the tenor is made to overlap with the triplum after three bars of rest. Since the tenor pattern itself begins with four bars of rest, the result is that the triplum sings an entire texted phrase supported only by the quartus cantus before the other two voices enter together. The effect is similar to that of the *introitus* that prefaces several isorhythmic motets by de Vitry and Machaut. This staggered pattern of entrances also (perhaps not merely incidentally) serves the purpose of creating tonal unity in *Petrum cephas*, which the cantus firmus does not provide, by allowing the piece to begin and end on D though the cantus firmus begins on F.[41]

While the motets like *Petrum cephas* are typified by the repetition of a consistent rhythmic figure in the tenor, two motets show more varied patterning. In *Lux refulget* there is a speeding up of declamation as a result of the quickening of tenor rhythms and shortening of the length of the modular unit in successive sesquialtera proportions (9:6:4). (See chapter 4, figure 49.) *Virgo sancta Katerina* demonstrates an even more complex response to the isoperiodic tradition. It takes as its tenor five statements of the *Agmina* melisma, each of which is patterned by the repetition of a different short rhythmic phrase. From the first to the last there is an acceleration in rhythmic values (from longs to breves and then to semibreves). The upper voices are cast in considerably longer periods than those of the tenor and are initially isoperiodic in units of 9L (tenor in 3L units) for the first *talea*, then in units of 8L (tenor in 2L units) for the second *talea*. Beginning with the third *talea* the tenor rhythms "infect" the upper voices and there is an acceleration in the rate of declamation, with a coincident shift in versification of the texts.

In general, isoperiodic motets show no prominent isomelic features because of the changing relationship of the isoperiodic module to the tenor *color*. However, some motets with strophic repeat of counterpoint are periodic, and there are some other interesting exceptions. In particular, two isolated motet voices, *Vas exstas* and *Dei preco*, have features of range and melodic cadencing that suggest they survive from motets in which they were the lowest voice, and they show not only the typical displacement of the modular unit found in single voices drawn from motets of isoperiodic design, but also unusual isomelic features. *Dei preco* is isoperiodic in 14L units which consist of two 7L units, each of which is a variation on a common melody. *Vas exstas* is more subtly designed. Its ten phrases are related melodically according to the scheme AA' BB' CC' DEFG (capital letters represent phrases setting two lines of poetry). Phrases A' and B share a common cadence figure, and so do B' and C. This in a sense ties together the first six phrases as a unit. D and E share a similar rhythmic figure at the cadence which is new, and this figure is picked up again at phrase G. The break between C' and D reflects the sense of the text, but not its versification, which remains the same.[42] (See figure 20.) *Dei preco* and *Vas exstas* share not only a 7L module, F final, and other features noted above, but also regularly recurring semibreve groups (in the b.4 of each module in *Dei* and b.4 and 7 in *Vas*) and regular motivic recurrences. They could well be from the same workshop.

Figure 20. Two Similar Isoperiodic Voices with Isomelic Features: *Dei preco* and *Vas exstas*

Vas ex-stas e-lec-ci-o-nis O Pau- le sa- cer- -ri- me

car-ne li- cet le- si- o- nis i- ctus sen- tis in-ti- me

per-se-quen-do gen-tem ma-gnus Chri-sti pri- us fu-e- ras

mi-tis e- ras ve- lud a- gnus post quan-do cor-ru-e- ras

lu- ce cir-ca te mi- can- te de ce- li pro-vin-ci- a

ti- bi vo- ce pro-cla- man- te ver- ba fan-te ta- li- a

Sau-le nunc et in fu- tu- rum qua- re me per-se-que- ris

ad cal-car est ti- bi du- rum si re- cal-ci-tra-ve- ris

ci- vi-ta- tem in- gre- di fe- sti- na tu ve-lo-ci- ter

me-e gen-ti te de-di con- ver-te-re per-hen-ni- ter.

Templum eya Salomonis is an isolated triplum with a regular periodic phrase structure in eight 9L phrases and impressive features of melodic correspondence and recurrence. The eight phrases define four pairs of melodic double versicles:

$$AxAy \; Bx'By \; Cx''Cy \; Dx'''Ey$$

where x and y are *ouvert* and *clos* cadential figures of length 4L that repeat (x in varied form, y literally) as refrains. The musical phrases are isodeclamatory, with one text stanza per phrase and an articulation of the melodic line into three segments by caesuras following the three verses of each stanza and their internal rhyme. Paralleling the melodic double versicles is a pairing of the stanzas by initial word ("intus," "foris," "ibi"). In effect, the motet text, written like a sequence, is set like a sequence; it mirrors its text musically to produce a hybrid with strict isoperiodicity whose isomelic features give it a close affinity to the refrain motets (see chapter 4, figure 48).

Finally, there is *Ut recreentur celitus*, which shows isoperiodicity in units of 10L for the first of its two sections and units of 12L for the second. This bipartite construction, with a coda at the end of each half, is unlike that of any other isoperiodic motet but rather recalls features of other freely composed motets a4 (2+2). *Ut recreentur* has some melodic repetition between alternate musical phrases (corresponding to alternate verses of text), but there does not seem to have been any consistent and strongly marked strophic repeat, nor do the adjacent phrases suggest any possibility for voice exchange. Because we lack the means to complete any of the fragments just described, they must remain tantalizing reminders of the creativity possible within the confines of isoperiodic phrase structures in the English motet.

The Duet Motets with Medius Cantus

In motets whose main units of declamation are the breve and semibreve, the increase in syllabic subdivision of the long leads to shorter phrases (as measured in longs) and to an increase in the variety of declamation patterns for the text. The most frequent isoperiodic module for these motets is one of 4L. The most important and numerous group of isoperiodic motets with such styling are the duet motets with *medius cantus*.[43] These are motets a3 in which a pair of texted voices of equivalent rhythmic activity and equal ambitus, lying an octave apart, encloses a cantus firmus that is in effect the middle voice of the three. Duet motets usually have a wide ambitus for each texted voice (a tenth or an eleventh) and for the motet as a whole (two octaves or more). They are, with the single exception of *Quare fremuerunt*, bitextual, and feature rapid semibreve patter where the outer voices utter text syllables homorhythmically in a counterpoint that often becomes simply a chain of parallel imperfect consonances, the style Harrison has dubbed "proto-faburden-parlando."[44] This parallel counterpoint is usually at the sixth. The duet motet is further distinguished by its subject matter, which turns away from more familiar topics (such as Mary, saints, and feast days of the church year) toward Jesus and devotional topics. By contrast, among the motets isoperiodic in long and breve there is a marked prevalence of motets on saints.

A number of motets and fragments prefigure what we may regard as the archetypal duet motet. First, a small group have a tenor that is either a middle voice by range or else shares its range with the duplum.[45] Among pieces in long-breve declamation, for instance, *Regina celestium* has a *medius cantus* (the tenor *Regina celi letare*, arranged in 4L phrases) but lacks any evident periodicity in the surviving texted voice. Two isolated voice parts just cited for certain isomelic features, *Dei preco* and *Vas exstas*, are most likely the lowest parts from duet motets with *medius cantus* in long-breve declamation. *Jhesu redemptor* is the only complete example of this type to survive, and it accommodates a text "too long" for its phrase module through recourse to bursts of declamation on semibreves without recurrent patterning.

Among motets with breve-semibreve declamation and a *medius cantus*, there are examples ranging from *Fusa cum silentio*, with its narrow range of only a thirteenth and texted outer voices that are not equal in activity,[46] to those whose outer voices are equally active but not regularly patterned with synchronized parlando, such as *A solis ortus*, or *Civitas nusquam*,[47] to motets such as *Jesu fili, Rosa delectabilis,* and *Quare fremuerunt*, with regularly recurring passages of semibreve patter in duo.

Jesu fili and *Rosa delectabilis*, in particular, show the strong impress of a common archetype. They both have an underlying mensuration in first mode, and their overall lengths and numerical structures are closely related (see figure 21). In each the initial displacement established between the outer parts is 1L, so phrases of 4L overlap by 3L. Where the parts coincide the declamation patterns are synchronized. This has been arranged to occur in both works so that the most rapid parlando is performed by the texted voices over the last two longs of the tenor phrase, especially while the tenor rests. The respective duet patterns may be seen in figure 22.

In both these motets the text in the upper voice of the duo is laid out so that verse and stanza endings correspond to musical phrase endings, while in the lower part musical phrase endings cut through the verses. At the end of each motet a line of verse has been added to the final stanza to stretch the last musical phrase into a sort of coda. The climactic effect is heightened in *Jesu fili* by having both voices sing the same text, "Reum munda nunc vicio." This technique of highlighting the text is also used several bars earlier on an equally significant line, "da mihi quod sicio."

Figure 21. *Jesu fili* and *Rosa delectabilis:* Related Phrase
Structures

Jesu fili		**Rosa delectabilis**
I	$64L = 5L + 13(4L) + 7L$	$60L = 5L + 12(4L) + 7L$
II	$= 16(4L)$	$= 15(4L)$
III	$= 6L + 13(4L) + 6L$	$= 6L + 12(4L) + 6L$

Figure 22. Duet Motet Parlando Patterns

Jesu fili

Rosa delectabilis

Quare fremuerunt stretches the duet concept in both music and text to its
practical limit. Here a single poem is sung simultaneously by both voices
throughout with additional troping in the lower voice that provides musical
continuity when the upper voice has a rest.[48] The text, unusually favored since
it may be heard with a clarity and emphasis not normally possible in an
isoperiodic motet, is an extraordinary poetic tour de force in which the incipits
of Psalms 2 through 12 are quoted in sequence and embedded in a regular
poetic matrix. Patter declamation in semibreves occurs where the tenor rests
(for two bars each time) and elsewhere as necessary to accommodate all the
words the clever rhymesmith has provided.

The tenor of *Quare fremuerunt* is also noteworthy. It does not have one of the simple tenor patterns of the other duet motets but rather is broadly patterned in longs, triple longs (here uniquely indicated by a three over the note-head),[49] and long-rests in the style of the tenors of motets like *Petrum cephas* (see figures 23 and 18). Appropriately, given the use of Psalms in the motet text, the tenor *color* is the incipit of a Psalm or Magnificat tone. It has been disposed in three rhythmic *taleae* of 8L (6L followed by 2L rests). In performance this tenor must be sung four times in all—forward, backward, forward, backward—to form a double palindrome. Retrograde performance is signaled by the last four pitches written out in the manuscript, which are a mirror image of the third *talea*, and by the initial rests, which are not sung when the tenor is read forward (the motet does not start with rests in the tenor) but are necessary to complete the retrograde statements.[50]

The stylistic parallel between the duet motets and English discant settings has been noticed by a number of scholars.[51] In a typical example of discant a3 the cantus firmus in the middle voice moves in even breves while the outer voices move around it in breves or shorter values in mainly homorhythmic patterns. Note values in the discant settings are reduced by a factor of two from those that appear in the duet motets (tenor motion in breves rather than in longs, with subdivision into semibreves and minims rather than into breves and semibreves) but the similarity in texture is obvious. Comparison is also apt between duet motets and the only two cantilenas that have Petronian-style syllabic semibreves and homodeclamatory patter, namely *Ave celi regina* and *Salamonis inclita*.[52] *Salamonis* is in three voices, with a predominance of contrapuntal motion in parallel 6-3 harmonies during semibreve patter passages. *Ave celi* is in two voices that often move together in parallel sixths. Its layout in both of its sources suggests the addition of a third (middle) voice.[53] In regard to the chronology of discant, cantilena, and duet motet, it seems simplest to suppose that motets such as *Jesu fili* and *Quare fremuerunt* are roughly contemporaneous with cantilenas like *Ave celi regina* and *Salamonis inclita* and that these predate the bulk of the English discant settings.[54]

Duet motets mainly appear in the younger English motet collections of the first half of the century such as *Lbl 1210*, *DRc 20*, and *Lwa 12185*. *Rosa delectabilis*, a palimpsest in *Onc 362*, is a significantly later entry to that earlier source and is written in an insular notational idiom. A few additional fragments may also be duet motets, including *Beatus vir* from *Lwa 12185*, *Zorobabel abigo*, which is a later entry in the front leaves of *Ob 7*, and *Radix Iesse* from *Ccc 65*. The first two of these use distinctive insular notations and the third, French Ars Nova notation. The composition *Astra transcendit* (*Llc 52, 2*) is a notable adaptation of duet-motet styling to a troped chant setting,

Figure 23.   Tenors of *Quare fremuerunt* and *Inter usitata*

Tenor of *Quare fremuerunt* (*Lbl 1210*, 9)

Tenor of *Inter usitata* (*Omc 266/268*, 2)

Hoc ter cantetur medio retro gradietur.

and it also uses an insular notational style. Thus the duet motet appears to be among the most persistent of all the English motet types of the first half of the century.

Other Isoperiodic Motets with Breve-Semibreve Declamation

Aside from the duet motets and fragments just mentioned, there are a few other strictly isoperiodic motets with declamation on breve and semibreve. Three of them, *Rex visibilium, Iam nubes*, and *Suffragiose virgini*, share an important formal trait: phrase displacement has been arranged to produce overlap by exactly one-half of the modular number (4L for the first two and 2L for the third). The underlying tenor pattern is either invariable (*Iam*) or varies only slightly (*Rex* and *Suffragiose*) between the two halves of the module; this permits exact rhythmic exchange between the upper parts within each module, and there is exact isorhythmic repetition between periodic modules in addition to isoperiodicity. (In this line of development isoperiodicity is necessarily prior to isorhythm.) See figure 24.

Rex visibilium carries out this design over just the first three-quarters of the motet. It uses its tenor, the low-lying whole-chant of the Gloria prosula *Regnum tuum solidum* (shaped ABBCCD), as the starting point for a structure that in several ways is very similar to that of a duet motet with *medius cantus*. Over phrases ABB of the tenor (28L=8L+2[10L]) the composer has fashioned an isoperiodic structure with declamation in overlapping chains of paired semibreves. Tenor phrases CCD are compressed into eight bars with an interruption of the isoperiodic phrase scheme and, simultaneously, abandonment of the previous regularly patterned declamation. *Iam nubes* is isoperiodic over the middle three of five 9L periods with a textless *cauda* over the first and a more irregular scheme over the last,

Figure 24. Isoperiodicity with Isorhythmicity

Rex visibilium

```
I    36L  =  1L  +  7(4L)  +  3L  +  4L
II        =  3L  +  7(4L)  +  2L  +  1L  +  2L
III       =  8L  +  2(10L)  +  8L  =  14(2L)  +  8L
```

Iam nubes

```
I    45L  =  4L  +  3L  +  7(4L)  +  2(3L)  +  4L
II        =  2L  +  3L  +  7(4L)  +  3L  +  4L  +  5L
III       =  5(9L)
```

Suffragiose

```
42L  =  2B  +  20(2L)  +  4B
```

when the text gives up the succession of lines beginning "iam." In *Suffragiose*, although the long is perfect, the initial displacement in the phrase scheme is 2B. After this, however, the module is 2L (6B). There is near rhythmic identity of the first 3B with the second 3B within the module and strict isorhythm between successive modules.

Other Periodicity

Motets with other kinds of periodic phrase schemes are fewer in number. Those with mixed periodicity are mainly from early in the century. Often their phrase schemes involve the use of consecutive or near consecutive integers. *Ade finit* is a good example of the general type. Its triplum has phrases of 11L and 13L, and the duplum has phrases of 9L, while the tenor moves in units of 4L. Triplum and tenor coincide, as a result, every 24L, the length of the tenor prior to repetition, and there is a marked degree of strophic repetition of counterpoint over each of the following two tenor statements. *Parata paradisi porta* is a more elaborate and probably later example. Its tenor proceeds in units of 14L while the texted voice has phrases of 6L, 8L, 9L, 12L, or 13L, for each of which there is a corresponding fixed declamation pattern and number of syllables (16, 25, 26, 31, and 35, respectively).[55] Both *Ade finit* and *Parata paradisi porta* have what will be called here "long-line" verse, in which lengthy lines of fixed syllable count and end rhyme span the musical phrase without marked metrical pulse or subdivision by internal rhyme or caesura.

The third form of periodic phrase construction mentioned at the beginning of this section, "subdivided-module periodicity," is the kind of periodicity seen in many Continental isorhythmic motets. Unipartite isorhythmic motets are usually simple isoperiodic motets with an elaborate scheme of mixed periodicity used to articulate phrases within the rather long module. Bipartite isorhythmic motets usually function similarly except that two such isoperiodic schemes are used, with a "joint" between them. Adjustments are made to the numerical scheme not simply at the beginning and the end, but also at the boundary between diminished and undiminished sections. Among the English motets "subdivided-module periodicity" occurs in three pieces from *Cgc 512*: *Mulier magni meriti, Princeps apostolice,* and *Orto sole.* The only other clear instance is found in a motet from *Lwa 12185, Beatus vir.* (See figure 25.) The development toward such fully worked out and consistent number schemes in isorhythmic motets can be observed in the motets of Philippe de Vitry from the 1320s and 1330s, following the chronology proposed by Sanders.[56] These kinds of scheme are found in all the fully isorhythmic motets of Machaut, which most likely are indebted in this respect to de Vitry. The English motets probably were composed before ca. 1340.

When considering the fourteenth-century motet in England, the question of French influence on notation, musical style, and form is primary, with regard to both chronology and the direction of influence. There can be no doubt that English musicians were fully aware of the Continental innovations of the musical Ars Nova by about 1350, for the author of the *Quatuor principalia* shows wide knowledge of Continental developments and in particular an admiration for Philippe de Vitry and a familiarity with his motets.[57] Of course, French motet style was already pressing against the native English musical idiom much earlier, to which insular examples of Petronian motets testify. As Levy has observed, "For a period around the beginning of the fourteenth century the well-developed English motet type represented [by *Thomas gemma*] must have held its own against an advancing French influence." Levy further posits that the sectional voice-exchange style of *Ave miles* and the isoperiodic design of *Petrum cephas* "would seem to represent a slightly later English conception of motet construction—a conception more rigid, more strongly influenced by French isorhythmic procedures."[58] More recently Sanders has argued for a position 180 degrees from that of Levy. Believing that "isoperiodicity is the English road to isorhythm,"[59] Sanders observes that a relative chronology of the development of large-scale sectional forms and isoperiodic phrase structures in English motets, in comparison to the evolution of these features in the motets of de Vitry, suggests the strong possibility of direct English influence on this innovative French musician.[60] Certainly there is no Continental counterpart to the extensive English repertoire of periodic motets in late Ars Antiqua notation.

Figure 25. Examples of Subdivided-Module Periodicity

```
Mulier magni meriti

I   54L = 3 + (6+3) + (6+4) + (5+4) + (5+2) + 4 + (3+2) + 4 + 3
II       = 7 + (2+7) + (2+7) + (2+7) + (2+3) + 6  +  3 + 6
III      = 3(18L) = 3(9+9)L


Princeps apostolice

I   52L = 6L + 3(5L) + (5+1)L + 5L + 4(5L)


Orto sole

I   60L = 4+4+4+(3+4)+4+4+(3+4)+4+4+(3+4)+4+4+3L
III      = 1+4+5+3+(2+1)+5+4+3+(2+1)+4+1+3+4+1+(1+1)+5+7+2L
IV       = 4(15L) = 4(3+4+4+4)L


Beatus vir

I   92B = 2(46B) = 2(20+20+6)B = 2( 2( 2(6B) + 8B) + 6B)
II       = 3B + 2(13B) + 7B + (10+3)B + 2(13B) + 7B + 10B
```

Other Insular Motet Types

Motets with Varied Rhythmic Patterning of the Tenor

Most of the English motets have a single consistent rhythmic pattern in the tenor. A few, however, have cantus firmi treated to rhythmic variation. Several of these have already been discussed, including the variation motet *Te domina*, the refrain motets *Suspiria merentis* and *Surgere iam est*, and the unusual periodic motets *Lux refulget* and *Virgo sancta Katerina*. Fragments of four further motets a4 are similar enough to each other to suggest they are of a motet type now represented by no surviving complete motets (see table 11). Their most distinctive feature is the rhythmic variation of tenor *taleae* of 4L units or occasionally, other multiples of 2L units. (See the lower voices of *Flos regalis* in figure 26.) These *taleae* are repeated a few times and then cast off in favor of a new pattern. In *Apello cesarem* and *Flos regalis* the change of tenor rhythm coincides approximately with repetition of the melodic *color*. This may also be the case in *Lingua peregrina*, judging from the part of the tenor that survives. In *Peregrina moror*, however, there are only two statements of a very long tenor *color*, and these are subdivided into roughly equivalent sections by internal shifts in tenor pattern.

Another feature held in common by all four is their second-mode

Table 11.   Other Insular Motet Types

Motets with Varied Rhythmic Patterning of the Tenor, esp. in units of 4L
Lingua peregrina
Peregrina moror
Apello cesarem
Flos regalis

Petronian-Style Motets with Stratified Levels of Activity
Inter amenitatis
Frondentibus
Rosa mundi
Triumphus patet

Patrie pacis
Caligo terre
Herodis in atrio

Duodeno sydere
Princeps apostolice

The Remainder
O crux vale
Augustine par angelis
Si lingua lota
Trinitatem veneremur
Hac a valle

---

mensuration and articulation of double-long feet. On account of their use of very large note-values, the two palimpsests from the Worcester fragments, *Lingua peregrina* and *Peregrina moror*, exhibit what Dittmer calls "larga-longa" notation (for a further explanation of which, see the section on "Binary Mensuration" in chapter 3). The surviving texted parts to these four fragments are not strictly periodic in phrase design, and their texts show a significant degree of irregularity in versification, although rhyme and some regular recurrence of syllable count help to define stanzas. There is actually, however, a high degree of coordination between the tenor and the texted voice. The upper part often matches or interlaces with the tenor rhythm and aligns its verses with the 4L units of the tenor. Most text lines are declaimed in one of the regular patterns that fits into 4L with declamation on long and breve (or can be explained in terms of a recognizable deviation from such a pattern if syllables are missing), and major text divisions (stanzas or groups of stanzas) coincide with shifts in tenor rhythm.

In *Apello cesarem* and *Lingua peregrina*, rests in the surviving vocal line sometimes appear to fall outside the 4L framework. Under these circumstances it cannot be said for certain just how the final motet design was

Figure 26. Rhythmically Varied Tenor *Taleae* in *Flos regalis*

Figure 26. (continued)

settled on, that is, whether it was the execution of some rigid scheme that was predetermined or whether as composition proceeded some influence may have been exerted by the phrase demands of the upper parts. *Peregrina moror* may represent the former case and *Apello cesarem* the latter. In the case of *Lingua peregrina* it is possible that those extra rests act to displace that voice in a periodic phrase structure that would have been perfectly regular in the missing triplum.

Petronian Motets

Of the remaining early fourteenth-century motets, the most significant group consists of those in the style of Petrus de Cruce, with stratification of activity between a fast-moving triplum engaged in the virtuoso declamation of a prose-like text, a slower moving duplum with considerably less text, and an unpatterned or very simply patterned tenor (see table 11).[61] This is the style of the majority of the newest motets in the *Roman de Fauvel*, for instance, although it should be noted that the *Fauvel* motets mostly set regular texts, while as a rule irregular phrases and lack of rhythmic patterning, coupled to syllabic declamation, result in irregularly versified texts in Petronian motets. *Inter amenitatis*, found in *Fauvel* as well as in an English source, is typical in its lack of regular phrase and verse structures. *Rosa mundi, Triumphus patet,* and *Frondentibus* are equally amorphous in musical facture. Given the English predilection for pattern and structure in the motet, it is not surprising to see how few motets and fragments there are of this type.[62]

Among stratified insular "Petronian" motets are three—*Caligo terre, Patrie pacis,* and *Herodis in pretorio*—with noteworthy elements of periodicity and striking duplum melodies. *Patrie pacis* has rigidly patterned semibreve declamation in the triplum and a melodious duplum with balanced phrase structure in long-breve declamation. The tunefulness of the duplum suggests that it is a single statement of a preexistent melody. This might account for the shortness of the motet as a whole, and also for the layout of the (unidentified) tenor, which moves in an uninterrupted series of eighteen undifferentiated longs (perhaps composed this way simply to support the duplum). *Caligo* uses the virelai "Mariounette douche" (the same tune found as the tenor of *Solaris ardor*) in the duplum and has a lowest written part (called "Tenor" in the manuscript) that is regularly patterned in rhythm without any repeating melodic *color*. It was evidently freely composed as a contrapuntal support to the actual *cantus prius factus*. The triplum is more irregular in phrasing (though it sets a regular text); the resulting three-voice counterpoint is sometimes awkward. Clumsy partwriting is also a feature of *Herodis in pretorio*. Here both tenor and duplum have highly repetitious melodic designs. The tenor, a French chanson in the form AAB, is stated three times to yield the overall shape AAB AAB AAB. The duplum has a series of double versicles with *ouvert* and *clos* cadences, suggesting that it, too, is a tune. Its form is AA′ x BB′ CC′ DD′ EE′ y. The elements x and y in this diagram were probably fabricated to help fit the duplum to the tenor (and the tenor itself may have been modified slightly from its monophonic form to help accommodate the duplum). The added triplum, like that in *Caligo*, does not have regular patterning, and again, as in *Caligo*, the counterpoint must be judged inexpert. In particular, the two lower voices do not fit well against one another.[63]

The Remainder

The remainder of the earlier fourteenth-century motets, mostly showing distinctively insular features of design, resist accommodation in the foregoing taxonomy (see table 11). Of these, three deserve to be singled out for particular attention: *O crux vale*, *Augustine par angelis*, and *Hac a valle*. *O crux* is a two-voice torso of what must have been a freely composed motet a4 (2+2) with the careful phrasing and melodic facture, sectional structure with coda, and sectionally-bounded changes of mensuration characteristic of the large-scale voice-exchange motets. However, though it exhibits some isomelic features in its second section, it shows no features of voice exchange.[64] *Augustine par angelis*, like *O crux*, survives as two voices of a four-voice original. Its counterpoint shows parallel sixths and open tenths that indicate the characteristic English harmony of the original, but there is no repetition of counterpoint corresponding to the threefold statement of the tenor, nor is there any hint of voice exchange despite the fact that the texted part alternates *cum* and *sine littera* passages. *Hac a valle* consists of one whole voice and part of a second (most likely voices I and III of a motet a4) that engage extensively in parallel counterpoint, mostly at the fifth or sixth. The second voice bears less text but is just as rhythmically active as the first, and both have quite wide ranges. It seems there was at least one other rhythmically active (upper) part, but the nature and level of rhythmic activity of the tenor appear to be impossible to judge. The insular notation and "progressive" counterpoint of this fragment (typical of all the motets in its source, *Lwa 12185*) suggest it is one of the newest motets in the earlier fourteenth-century corpus.

The Later Fourteenth Century

Ob 7 *and* DRc 20 *Rear Leaves*

Whatever the relative strength and direction of formative influence over the first third of the century or so, it is clear that few French pieces entered the English sources or vice versa.[65] This situation changes, however. The mature

French Ars Nova style is of great influence on English music from midcentury on, and the English repertoire comes to contain French pieces. It seems quite likely that the influx of motets represented by such collections as the rear leaves of *Ob 7* and *DRc 20* is in large part the result of many occasions for English exposure to recent French music on account of the activities of the Hundred Years' War. Not only were minstrels and domestic chapels of the English aristocracy brought over to France, but French chapels made the reverse trip across the channel with captured noblemen being held for ransom. The most important of all such occasions may well have been the period of captivity of the king of France, John the Good, who remained in England from 1357 to 1360 with his domestic court chapel.[66]

The bulk of the Ars Nova–style motets surviving from fourteenth-century England, most of them with Continental concordances and of probable Continental origin, are found in two sources, the rear flyleaves of *Ob 7* (six motets) and *DRc 20* (ten motets).[67] (See table 12.) In both manuscripts there are front flyleaves preserving insular motets in very different hands, and no incontrovertible links can be made between front and rear collections. The probability is strongest in both cases, however, that front and rear leaves were simply drawn from different gatherings of their dismembered parent codices. Both sets of rear flyleaves are written in what appear to be English text hands and show at least one characteristic English trait in their notation, the form of the perfect breve rest.[68] Hence they were copied in England. In regard to text content, the *DRc 20* motets "document . . . for the first time the importation unchanged of secular motets into Britain, where no indigenous examples survive,"[69] but all of the *Ob 7* motets are sacred in subject matter. In at least one case (*Ob 7*, 16) and possibly in others the sacred texts of *Ob 7* replace secular French love poetry.[70]

Harrison dates the *Ob 7* leaves to ca. 1340 and puts the *DRc 20* collection in the decade ca. 1350–60.[71] These dates are plausible, perhaps even slightly late, estimates for the age of the Ars Nova musical repertoires; they may be ten to twenty years too early for the ages of the sources themselves. If one judges by the ages estimated for the most important Continental manuscripts containing concordances to the repertoire of these English leaves, dates of copying in the 1360s or 1370s seem probable. *Ivrea* (*I-IVc 115*) is now thought to have been copied after 1365, with additions into the 1370s, either for the papal court in Avignon or for the court of Gaston Febus, count of Foix and Bearn (1343–1391).[72] *Trémoïlle* (*F-Pn 23190*) was copied in 1376, probably at the court of Charles V of France, by the king's chaplain Michael de Fontaine.[73] *Ivrea* and *Trémoïlle* have a strong affinity (29 concordances, mostly motets) and are clearly central sources of the repertoire from the greatest centers of the cultivation of polyphony in the French cultural orbit. The rear leaves of *DRc 20* have seven motets with concordances and of these,

Table 12.   Later 14th-Century Motets in England

Isorhythmic

Unipartite
Amer amours DRc 20, 11
Ad lacrimas DRc 20, 12
L'amoreuse DRc 20, 16
Apta caro DRc 20, 18
Mon chant DRc 20, 19

Tribum quem Lbl 28550, 5
Alme pater Lbl 40011B, 18
Deus compaignouns US-Wc 14, 3
Rex Karole US-Wc 14, 4
Degentis vita GB-YOX, 4

Bipartite
Omnis terra Ob 7, 12
Pura placens Ob 7, 15
Domine quis Ob 7, 16
Parce piscatoribus Ob 7, 17

Virginalis concio DRc 20, 10
Vos quid DRc 20, 13
O vos omnes DRc 20, 14
O canenda vulgo DRc 20, 15
Musicorum collegio DRc 20, 17

Firmissime fidem Lbl 28550, 4
Humane lingue Lbl 40011B, 17
Nec Herodis Ob 143, 3

Tripartite
Sub arturo plebs GB-YOX, 1

Motets with Insular Features

Cuius de manibus Ob 7, 11
Deus creator Ob 7, 14

Regne de pite Ob 143, 3

In ore te laudancium US-SM 19914, 1
Soli fines US-SM 19914, 3

Baptizas parentes Omc 266/268, 1
Inter usitata Omc 266/268, 2
Flos anglorum Omc 266/268, 3

Radix Iesse Ccc 65, 3

Ancilla Domini Lli 146, 6
Geret et regem TAcro 3182, 2
Rex piaculum TAcro 3182, 4

O dira nacio F-Pn 23190, 4

---

six (nos. 11, 13, 15, 16, 18, 19) are in both *Ivrea* and *Trémoïlle*, so in all likelihood *DRc 20* was once a comparable central (English) repository of Ars Nova polyphony. *Ob 7* has a similar relationship to the Continental sources, although with fewer concordances (no. 15 is in *Trémoïlle*, while no. 16 is in both *Trémoïlle* and *Ivrea*).[74]

Stylistic comparison suggests that most of the *unica* in the two English sources are also of Continental origin. *Omnis terra* (*Ob 7*, 12) and *Musicorum collegio* (*DRc 20*, 17) are bipartite isorhythmic motets a3 with diminution by one-half, notated in *tempus imperfectum maior*, with an overall range of a thirteenth. In this respect they are just like *Pura placens* (*Ob 7*, 15), *Domine quis* (*Ob 7*, 16), and other motets in *Ivrea* or by Machaut.[75] *Parce piscatoribus* (*Ob 7*, 17), *Virginalis concio* (*DRc 20*, 10), and *O vos omnes* (*DRc 20*, 14) are motets a4 with similar design features.[76] *Nec Herodis ferocitas* (*Ob 143*, 1), from a fragmentary insular source roughly contemporary with *Ob 7* and *DRc 20*, also belongs with this group.[77] These four are comparable in approach to *Vos quid admiramini* (*DRc 20*, 13) and *O canenda vulgo* (*DRc 20*, 15), both motets by Philippe de Vitry, and to other motets by de Vitry and Machaut.[78] Hence these fragments from English sources make an important contribution to the midcentury repertoire of motets a4.[79]

The only traces of an English origin for the motets in the rear leaves of *DRc 20* are in no. 10, whose duplum text ("Virginalis concio") also appears in the duplum of a later motet in the Old Hall manuscript, Byttering's *En Katerine solennia–Virginalis concio–T.Sponsus amat sponsum* (*Lbl 57950*, 145). The missing but restorable tenor of the Durham motet ("Virgo sancta Katerina") is used as a point of departure for a number of earlier English motet texts on Katherine but does not seem ever to have been used as a source of text or tenor for polyphony on the Continent, judging from a perusal of the text indices in RISM B/IV.

The situation in the rear leaves of *Ob 7* is different from that in *DRc*. Two *unica*, *Cuius de manibus* (*Ob 7*, 11) and *Deus creator* (*Ob 7*, 14), are quite likely to be either of English origin or written under strong English influence. The first of these has already been listed without particular comment in the foregoing typology as a five-section voice-exchange motet a4 (2+2) with coda. It is virtually a twin to *Ave miles* in terms of structure. *Cuius de manibus* and *Ave miles* have the same number of voices, the same overall length, the same comparative lengths of sections, similarly melismatic codas, and probably the same manner of texting continuously in successive paired stanzas of a single text. Two significant differences exist, however. First, *Cuius de manibus* is a free composition rather than one based on a cantus firmus (such as *Ave miles*), and second, it is notated in *tempus imperfectum maior* rather than in Franconian notation. The similarity of structure suggests that *Cuius de manibus* was deliberately modeled on the earlier *Ave miles*.

It is reasonable to turn the tables and ask whether *Cuius de manibus* shows any particularly English compositional features aside from gross aspects of form and structure. In fact, though it does not exhibit the smooth rhythmic flow, careful regard for declamation, neat phrasing, and tuneful melodic facture of the other motets of its type, it does have distinctive (and typically English) harmonic and local contrapuntal detail. To begin with, like most freely composed English motets, it is a tonally closed composition, here with a final on C, and has counterpoint that elaborates a very limited harmonic vocabulary. There is essentially just root motion by step from harmonies on C (and occasionally on E) to harmonies a step away on B♭ or D—the English supertonic and subtonic *pes* harmony so familiar from the Sumer canon and many other compositions.[80] The composition opens on a 10-8-5 sonority and frequent use of imperfect consonances is the norm, including extensive motion a3 in parallel 6-3 and 10-5 sonorities. One sees the constant employment of voice exchange not just as a formal device on the level of the section, but also on the most local scale between paired voices to animate a static harmonic environment. On the other hand, the elastic rhythms, alternating sustained motion in breves with lively stretches of semibreves and minims, along with occasional harsh dissonances in the four-part writing (characteristic and most prominent during the final cadence) indicate some indebtedness to the Continental Ars Nova idiom.[81]

Deus creator is the other motet from the Ars Nova gathering of *Ob 7* that demands consideration as an insular product. A description of this motet must begin with its tenor, which is fully equivalent to the upper voices in its degree of rhythmic activity, with motion predominantly in semibreves and minims and without any striking rhythmic patterning (apart from the short rhythmic sequence of bars 25–32) or internal melodic repetition. The tenor is stated in full three times, suggesting a relationship with unipartite isorhythmic motets, but *Deus creator* lacks the regularity and numerical coordination of phrase structure found in unipartite motets of midcentury (see figure 27). All triplum phrases begin on a downbeat; all duplum phrases, save for the first, on an upbeat.

The tenor of *Deus creator* is texted in *Ob 7* with the lines, "Doucement me reconforte / cele qui mon cuer ad pris." This text is known to be a couplet used by the trouvère Watriquet de Couvin (active in the 1320s and 1330s), for a *fatras*.[82] We are told, in fact, that Watriquet improvised the *fatras* to this distich in competition with another minstrel before Philip, the king of France (most likely Philip VI, who ruled 1328–50).[83] Another couplet on which Watriquet composed a *fatras* is "Presidentes in thronis seculi / sunt hodie dolus et rapina." These lines, the only Latin couplet Watriquet ever used for such a purpose, also occur as the incipit of the triplum of a motet in the *Roman de Fauvel*.[84]

Figure 27.   Numerical Structure of *Deus creator*

$$102B = 4(9B) + 8B + 2(9B) + 12B + 28B$$
$$= 4B + 2(10B) + 2(7B) + 8B + 10B + 9B + 13B + 24B$$
$$= 3(16B + 18B) = 3(34B)$$

The relationship between the couplet *Doucement* and the music of *Deus creator* is not entirely clear. Is the motet's tenor an ornamented version of a simpler monophonic setting of the couplet or the longer *fatras*, or could it be taken from a polyphonic setting of either of these? Could the motet itself in fact be a sacred contrafact of a musical setting made for one or the other? A recent discovery sheds some light on these questions. Charles Brewer has found a polyphonic setting of yet another couplet associated with Watriquet: "Amis loial vous ay trouvé / c'est drois qu'a vous me rende prise."[85] The setting (*PL-WRu I.Q.411,* 2) has the following features of present significance: it is in three voices, of which only the second bears text; the declamation is irregular and very melismatic; the setting is not tonally closed and there appears to be no cantus firmus, although the lowest voice moves in a lower range and with slower note values than those shared by the two upper parts; finally, the setting is written in *tempus imperfectum maior* and is divided into two sections, of 22B and 19B, by a single central cadence in all voices followed by rests and a double bar.

On the evidence of this new find, it seems likely that the tenor of *Deus creator* was drawn from a polyphonic setting of the couplet *Doucement* similar to that of *Amis loial*, which was also tonally open, divided into two sections (of 16B and 18B), melismatic in declamation, and written in *tempus perfectum maior*. The second, text-bearing voice was probably the one borrowed, and was likely transposed down to its present pitch level to serve as the motet tenor.[86]

Several features of this motet indicate English influence. The use of a French tenor supporting Latin upper parts, while not unknown on the Continent, is common in England. The assonance "Deus-Doucement" also suggests English tastes, as does the fact that the two upper parts take as their point of departure the *initia* of the two most highly ranked Kyrie tropes in the Salisbury rite. However, the irregularity of versification in the two texts and the manner in which they extend a short way into the concluding hocket suggest that they might be substitutes for another, perhaps secular French, pair of texts, a point in favor of a French origin for the piece.

More telling are certain features of style. A threefold statement of the tenor is relatively uncommon among Continental unipartite isorhythmic motets, which usually favor four, five, or six *taleae*.[87] The layout here recalls more strongly the English motets with strophic variation over a non-

Gregorian tenor. Indeed, tenor repetition in *Deus creator* is associated with considerable repetition of counterpoint, including exchange between the upper parts. Further, the tenor is rhythmically integrated with the upper parts, which tend to move homorhythmically with it in semibreves and minims. When one or another part rests, the remaining two move in parallel thirds, sixths, or tenths; when all three parts move together the counterpoint often is in parallel 6–3, 10–5, 10–6, 10–8, or 12–10 harmonies. This reliance on parallel imperfect intervals has no Continental equivalent, and in fact compares less with the parallel partwriting in duet motets, for instance, than with the expanded sonorities and partwriting of the later cantilenas in such sources as *US-NYpm 978, Occ 144,* or *LEcl 6120.*

On balance the factors just enumerated suggest that *Deus creator* is either the work of an English composer or has been modeled on fourteenth-century insular style features and motet practice. The presence of *Cuius de manibus* and *Deus creator* in a gathering with four motets typical of Continental Ars Nova developments is of great significance, demonstrating a more complex interaction of French and English musical culture around midcentury than has previously been recognized, most likely an English response to Continental developments.

English Isorhythm

After the rear leaves of *Ob 7* and *DRc 20,* there is no further sizeable body of isorhythmic compositions surviving in English sources until the Old Hall manuscript a half-century later. Hence it is difficult to write the history of the English assimilation of Continental isorhythmic techniques.[88] The isorhythmic motets and settings of the Gloria and Credo found in the first layer of Old Hall show a wide range of technique (and most probably of age as well) and may span most of the stylistic distance traversed in this era. A conservative benchmark for the native style in isorhythmic (hence "motet-style") mass movements is established by such similar pieces as the Gloria a4 (2+2) (by Pennard?) in the Fountains fragments (*Lbl 40011B*, 1), and a Gloria a4 (2+2) in a Bodleian Library source (*Ob 384,* 2).[89] These two Glorias are not at all far removed from the style of the isorhythmic motets a4 in *Ob 7* and *DRc 20.* They are both bipartite, with diminution by one-half in the melismatic "Amen" section. The first has four *colores* and twelve *taleae,* the second has two *colores* and six *taleae,* with strict isorhythm in all untexted lines. Both have a harmonically essential contratenor that is rhythmically equivalent to the tenor. In each there is also a distinctive phrase-by-phrase alternation of text between the upper parts, dividing the Gloria text into twelve segments (though the break points are not the same).[90]

What of English isorhythm in the motet? Returning to a consideration of later fourteenth-century sources, *US-Wc 14* and *GB-YOX* contain fragments of at least five isorhythmic motets that are certainly French in origin; there is a direct parallel to the rear leaves of *Ob 7* and *DRc 20*, though the repertoire of these less well-known sources is probably about a generation later.[91] The recent discovery of the concordance for *Sub arturo plebs* in *GB-YOX*, in notation employing the English *cauda hirundinis*, strengthens the probability of an English origin for this motet and brings it squarely within the scope of present concern. Much has been written about the dating of this well-known and controversial piece. Brian Trowell placed it in 1358, suggesting it was written for a gathering of Garter Knights at Windsor Castle. This early a date is less plausible on stylistic grounds than the 1360s, in the compositional milieu of the circle of Edward, the Black Prince, in Aquitaine (a suggestion of Günther), or the decade of the 1370s targeted by Roger Bowers's recent archival work and reading of the verse.[92] *Sub arturo plebs* would be relatively advanced in that time frame as well, given its tripartite structure, complex scheme of successive diminutions, and frequent syncopations, all of which are typical of much later fourteenth-century and early fifteenth-century motets.[93] Nothing links it to previous insular tradition.

Two motets from a very late fourteenth-century insular motet source without Continental concordances (*Lbl 40011B*, a source with close ties to Old Hall) perhaps reveal a little more about insular trends in isorhythm. *Humane lingue* shows the smooth rhythmic and melodic character of the stylistically advanced pieces in minor prolation and incorporates a sophisticated proportional diminution scheme.[94] *Alme pater*, a fragment, is a motet that may be dated through textual references (if these are being correctly interpreted) to the year 1384 or shortly thereafter, and so contributes valuable and scarce evidence for the chronology of style change.[95] It is a large-scale unipartite isorhythmic motet with *introitus*, probably not composed on a cantus firmus, with coloration in both surviving parts that in the upper one produces recurring passages of lively syncopation. Its counterpoint suggests that it is freely composed, as are many large-scale Continental isorhythmic motets of the last two decades of the century. *Sub arturo*, *Humane lingue* and *Alme pater*, as well as many examples surviving on the Continent, lack the subdivided-module periodicity that was the hallmark of the phrase structure of earlier isorhythmic motets.

The Indigenous Tradition

Are there traces of surviving indigenous traditions of motet composition in the same era as these later isorhythmic motets? Indeed, there are a few (see table 12), most of which are unfortunately so fragmentary that very little can be said about them. To be briefly noted are *Rex piaculum* (*TAcro 3182*, 2), which uses some voice exchange, *Radix Iesse* (*Ccc 65*, 3), which may possibly be a fragment of a duet motet with *medius cantus*, and *Baptizas parentes* (*Omc 266/268*, 1), whose counterpoint probably was very much like that of *Assunt Augustini* (*Llc 52*, 3) in appearance, with considerable rapid semibreve motion in parallel sixths.

However, about three motets more can be said. In them we see a fusion of native techniques with stereotypical features of Continental isorhythm. *Soli fines* (*US-SM 19914*, 3) is a case in point. Its tenor is a whole chant, a single statement of a *color* with embedded double versicle, disposed in four 24B *taleae*. Each *talea* consists of 12B in *modus minor* followed by 12B in *modus maior* (signaled by red coloration). Curiously, in the *modus minor* sections of *taleae* 2 through 4, the rhythmic pattern of *talea* 1 is retained but notes replace rests and vice versa. The two upper voices, in *tempus perfectum maior*, are too fragmentary to determine whether there was a regular phrase scheme (the triplum may have begun by alternating 16B and 14B phrases), but their counterpoint against the tenor occasionally demands a contratenor, which is satisfactorily supplied by reading the tenor in retrograde. Most typically English is the contrapuntal style—rhythmically active within rather static harmonies, emphasizing 5–3 and 6–3 sonorities both melodically and vertically (see figure 28).

Inter usitata is the second and most recoverable of the three motet fragments in *Omc 266/268*, and it is the only one written in a typical Ars Nova notation. Its tenor moves in breves and longs according to a simple second-mode pattern. A written instruction, or canon, specifies that the tenor be sung three times with the second statement in retrograde: "Hoc ter cantetur medio retro gradietur." (See figure 23 above.) Such canons are a feature of the tenors of many motets and motet-style mass movements of the late fourteenth and early fifteenth centuries and figure prominently in Old Hall. This canon is a very simple instruction, however, which suggests that the composition is either earlier than those in Old Hall or from a less sophisticated compositional milieu. The tenor is framed by rests of two breves. If the whole were to be repeated literally, then at the juncture of the first and second, or second and third, statements of the tenor there would be four breve-rests. Transcription reveals that only two are required, however; the set of rests belongs only at the end of each tenor statement, filling in a long-perfection after a breve. The initial rests are only necessary to be sung after the retrograde statement. However, since this requires that the tenor be notated with rests at the beginning, the upper two voices have also been given two breves worth of rest to start off with, so the entire motet begins (and incidentally, ends) with a moment of silence, a very curious situation indeed.

Inter usitata is not quite regular in its structure of mixed periodicity; the tenor phrases are in 12B units and the triplum is periodic in 16B units, while the duplum has 15B and 14B phrases. Nonetheless, the texts of triplum and

Figure 28.   Counterpoint in the *Tempus perfectum* Sections of *Soli fines* and *Regne de pité*

duplum are paired in length and versification. This is not normally the relationship between texts of an isorhythmic Continental motet, but it is typical of insular isoperiodic motets. A further markedly insular trait of this motet is its counterpoint, which features a great deal of note-against-note writing in parallel thirds and fifths, most conspicuously in the brief duet passages spanning rests in the tenor.

Regne de pité is a third example of the cross-fertilization of English and

Continental motet practice. It is preserved in *Ob 143* in the same music hand as a fragment of an isorhythmic motet a4 (*Nec Herodis ferocitas*) and an Agnus Dei setting in score that is also found in the earlier fourteenth-century English source *Ob 55*. *Regne de pité* is unusual in a number of respects. First, it is monotextual, setting a vernacular text; the upper voices sing (either homorhythmically, or separately) four stanzas of a widely preserved Old French poem attributed to Rutebeuf, following this poem's Anglo-Norman text tradition (see the section on "Vernacular Texts" in chapter 4). This unusual treatment of text is unknown in Continental motet repertoires but has precedents in the English repertoire, most immediately recalling the duet motet *Quare fremuerunt*.

The motet is divided into two parts in the proportional relationship 2:3, which is the durational relationship of breves under the mensurations in each section, *tempus imperfectum maior* and *tempus perfectum maior*, respectively.[96] Two lines are omitted from the second stanza of the original poem to provide 30 lines (rather than 32), which are divided by the structural midpoint into 12 and 18 lines, hence in the same proportion as the motet as a whole. The tenor is only written out once, in *tempus imperfectum*. After it is sung through, it must be read in retrograde with a change in mensuration paralleling that of the other parts. This is not specified in the manuscript, so performers must be guided by the instruction implicit in the last line of the text; that is, the tenor must be "besturné de vois et d'entendement," just as *EVA* becomes *AVE*. Regulation of the motet structure by proportion is not solely an English trait, but handled in this unique manner and with the unique method of text presentation, it can be taken as evidence for English authorship.

Several technical features of notation and counterpoint help to strengthen this surmise. In *Regne de pité* the *signum rotundum* is used in all parts to indicate the change of mensuration, and the *cauda hirundinis* indicates alteration of unligated semibreves under *tempus perfectum*. Perhaps most significantly, under *tempus perfectum* the first, rather than the second, of two semibreves must be altered in a binary c.o.p. ligature, a distinctively insular convention. Finally, although the amount of dissonance is high for an English piece, the amount of parallel motion in thirds and 6-3 harmonies is additional testimony for an insular origin (see figure 28).

One final piece must be brought into consideration in this chapter. The motet *O dira nacio* is not a "motet in England." It survives uniquely in the *Trémoïlle* manuscript, one of only four pieces to be preserved along with the index to this once impressive collection. The suggestion that *O dira nacio* is English has not to my knowledge been previously made, but deserves consideration. Text, form, and musical style all differ from the style and procedures of those motets named in the *Trémoïlle* index that are known through concordances, such as those found in *DRc 20*. Besseler has commented that the "conductus-like" phrasing of its upper parts points to an earlier date of composition.[97] Of course, that description might also be said to suggest the motet is not French in origin. To begin with, the text is on Thomas; most likely Thomas of Canterbury is meant, though here his bowels, not brains, are slashed. The two poems are stanzaic and paired in length and versification. The motet is built on an unidentified whole-chant with a single internal melodic repetition in its *color*. This tenor is laid out in longs and long-rests without any strict rhythmic patterning. The form of the motet is sectional, in twelve blocks of counterpoint defined by successive two-line units of the triplum text; the duplum text is usually declaimed simultaneously in the same pattern. The most frequent of the declamation patterns for these verses (a) and the most common alternative (b) are given in figure 29. The form of the motet may be diagrammed as follows:

A B A A C A B C A′ A′ A C

The A sections are built on declamation pattern (a) in both texted parts. Section B also uses (a) in both parts, though successively rather than simultaneously. Section C uses pattern (b) or some modification of it. The guiding principle behind this form seems to be variation, articulated through the text "from the top down."

The mensuration of *O dira nacio* is binary, with few minims (none set to a syllable), melismatic groups of binary c.o.p. ligatures, and declamation on long, breve, and semibreve. This is similar to the mensuration of *Tu civium, Virgo Maria*, or *Te domina*. The piece contains numerous imperfect consonances, including 5–3 harmonies and much parallel motion in thirds and sixths between the upper voices, especially in the rapid semibreve duet passages of the A sections when the tenor rests. All of the above points suggest the likelihood of the motet's English authorship. However, the identification of the chant used as the cantus firmus and confirmation that Thomas is the English saint are imperative if the question of origin is to be settled with any finality. Nonetheless, the kinship of *O dira nacio* in form and style to the three English variation-motets with binary mensuration just cited (or to *Thomas gemma*, to name another), suggests that the *Trémoïlle* motet came out of the same compositional milieu at about the same time as, or only a little later than, these pieces.

The English motet flourished in the early fourteenth century, carrying on well-established indigenous musical traditions. A number of distinct and persistent motet types were explored by English composers, including those using strict and varied voice exchange, strophic repeat with variation, refrains, and

Figure 29. 12- and 6-Syllable Declamation Patterns in *O dira nacio*

a. 12-syllable pattern

b. 6-syllable pattern

periodicity in many guises. Variation emerges as one of the most important means of compositional exploitation of musical ideas and structures. The Continent may have felt English influence especially through the impact that isoperiodicity and large-scale sectional structures may have had on de Vitry and his generation.

The particular directions in which the motet developed in the second half of the century are harder to follow, but what evidence there is suggests that native traits were not wholly erased, and that despite a taste for French notation there was not a capitulation in all quarters to French motet techniques. Isorhythmic composition in motets and mass movements takes its point of departure from motets such as those in the rear leaves of *Ob 7* and *DRc 20*, leading through motets such as *Sub arturo* and *Alme pater* to the motets of Old Hall and Dunstable. At the same time, motets such as *Deus creator, Cuius de manibus*, and a number of fragments reveal that purely insular types were sustained at least through the first three-quarters of a century or so. *Soli fines, Inter usitata, Regne de pité*, and *Humane lingue* show the impact of French notation and isorhythmic practices but preserve individualistic, insular approaches in respect to many details of their counterpoint and structure.

3

Motet Notations

The motets under consideration in this study were composed in an era in which musical notation was undergoing considerable change as new forms of mensural organization were being explored and codified. This rapid evolution of note forms and metrical structures in the late thirteenth and early fourteenth centuries has long been a primary interest of musicologists working on the medieval polyphonic repertoires of France and Italy. The notation of English polyphony in the same era has until recently, however, been *terra incognita*.[1] This lack of attention has been remedied by a few important contributions, most notably Ernest Sanders's "Duple Rhythm and Alternate Third Mode in the 13th Century," and Margaret Bent's "A Preliminary Assessment of the Independence of English Trecento Notations."[2] Thirteenth-century English notational practices are marginally better known, especially due to controversy over the rhythmic interpretation of the so-called English mensural notation (EMN) in the Sumer Canon and the Worcester fragments. This chapter will be prefaced with a short review of earlier practices to establish the background for a number of fourteenth-century insular conventions and also to clarify one important means of drawing the boundary line between thirteenth- and fourteenth-century motets and sources from England.

Writings on music by Englishmen are a significant source of reference for the notations to be discussed here, primarily the *Summa de speculatione musicae* of Walter Odington,[3] the *Regule* of Robertus de Handlo,[4] the *Summa* of Johannes Hanboys,[5] and the *Quatuor principalia* compiled by an anonymous Franciscan friar of Bristol.[6] They have long been available in the editions by Coussemaker and have been valued for their information about French practices from Franco to Philippe de Vitry. The fragmentary state of the English repertoire and the relative paucity of known sources until after the Second World War have made it difficult to evaluate and utilize these writers' comments on purely insular figures and practices. Empirical evidence of the sources and the testimony of the theorists are complementary and, as will be made clear below, only when they are brought together do many points made by the latter become clarified.

A study primarily devoted to the motets is a reasonable base from which to launch a discussion of fourteenth-century English notations because the motets span such a diverse range of notational practices. Table 13 is the focal point for this chapter. It groups the motets into large categories by features of notation, mensuration, and declamation; that is, the range of available symbols used to write the music down, the metrical organization of rhythmic values, and the primary durational units normally associated with a syllable of text. The critical distinction between groups 1, 2(i), and 2(ii) is the use of syllabic semibreves (none in group 1, duplets and triplets in group 2(i), and four or more per breve in group 2(ii)), with a further gradation by the number of melismatic semibreves providing ornamental subdivision of the breve.[7] Groups 3 and 4 list the motets with more innovative insular notations and those from later in the fourteenth century that exhibit French Ars Nova notation and mensurations. There are multiple entries for a number of motets, in particular for those with sectional changes of mensuration or those of group 2(ii) with innovative notations (entered also in group 3). A touch of the arbitrary inevitably enters into a categorization of this sort, for instance in the judgment as to whether m3 are rare, or in the fact that a single m3 in the midst of prevalent m2 is sufficient to shift a motet's location; the use of stems on semibreves is also not taken into account in groups 2(i) and 2(ii).

This means of tabulation was suggested by the approach of Frank Ll. Harrison to his discussion of "Division of the Brevis" in the introduction to PMFC XV. There he arranged his 36 motets into six groups differentiated by the division of the breve into two or three semibreves, the use of dots of division to clarify breve groups and the use of stems to clarify rhythm, the appearance of rapid parlando in semibreves, and the appearance of major prolation. Harrison's sensitivity to the problems of notation and rhythm has been a valuable impetus to the assembly of the data in table 13, which amplifies his approach without in large measure contradicting it.[8]

In the broadest view the notational development implicit in the organization of table 13 is chronological. However, it would be simplistic merely to equate the age of any motet with the age of its notation, which provides at best only an earlier terminus. Not all the motets in groups 1 or 2(i) are necessarily older than those in groups 2(ii), 3, or 4. Insular composers do not seem to possess the preoccupation with the codification of notation and mensuration that is the hallmark of the early French Ars Nova period. The English were notationally conservative because notation and syllabic declamation on long and breve, or breve and semibreve, were adequate for the kinds of musical form and patterned text setting with which they were preoccupied instead. In terms of sheer numbers, motets in Franconian notation predominate over those that are more innovative. Widespread adoption of Ars Nova mensurations after midcentury in motet and cantilena

Table 13. Notation, Mensuration, and Declamation in the Motet

Key: m2, m3 indicate melismatic semibreve duplets or triplets.
       s2, s3 indicate syllabic duplets or triplets.
       parentheses indicate the rare appearance of the semibreve group so designated.
       an asterisk before a motet indicates that it appears in more than one place in this table.
       An attempt has been made to put motets into an order indicative of increasing use of
       subdivision of the breve and increasing use of syllabic semibreves.
       First and second mode columns are roughly aligned horizontally.

Group 1:   *l* and *b* are primary units of declamation, with ornamental *s* in melismatic duplets and
       triplets.

First Mode		*Second Mode*	
Absorbet oris	m2	O homo considera	(m2)
*Alta canunt	"		
*Apello cesarem	"	Flos regalis	m2
Detentos a demonibus	"	Ade finit perpete	"
Ianuam quam	"	*Apello cesarem	"
Hostis Herodes	"	*O crux vale	"
O pater	"	*Ut recreentur	"
Quid rimari	"	Veni creator	"
Regi regum	"	*Hostis Herodes	"
Regina iam	"	*Rota versatilis	"
*Rota versatilis	"	*A solis-Ovet	" +(m3)
*Ut recreentur	"		
Venit sponsa			
Thomas gemma	(m2,m3)		
Excelsus in numine	(m3)		
Petrum cephas	m2,(m3)	*Lux refulget	m2,(m3)
Salve sancta parens	"		
Salve cleri	"		
Rex omnipotencie	"		
Barabbas dimittitur	(m2),m3		
*O crux vale	m2,m3		
Rex sanctorum	"		
Inter choros	"		
Candens crescit	"		
*Virgo sancta	"	*Virgo sancta	m2,m3

Table 13. (continued)

Group 2: s also used as a unit of declamation, with (i) up to 3s per *b* or 9s per *l* using dots of division; (ii) syllabic *s* in groups of 4 or more per *b*.

Group 2(i)

Genitricem	(s2)		
Regnum sine termino	(s2),m2		
Solaris ardor	(s2),m2,(m3)		
Si lingua lota	"		
Regina celestium	(s2),m2,m3		
Hostium ob amorem	"		
Dei preco	(s2),m2-4		
Iam nubes	(s2),m2-5		
		Suffragiose	s2
Maria mole pressa	s2,m2	Zelo tui	s2,m2
Vas exstas	s2,m2,(m3)	Doleo super te	"
Ave miles	"	Parata paradisi	"
Triumphat hodie	"	Fusa cum silentio	" +(m3)
		Templum eya	"
Balaam de quo	s2,m2,m3	*Alta canunt	
Trinitatem	"		
Jhesu redemptor	"		
*Lux refulget	" +(m4)		
*Virgo sancta	" +(s3),(m5)	Suspiria merentis	s2,(s3)
		Rex visibilium	" +m2,m3
Jesu fili	s2,s3,m2,(m4)	Rogativam potuit	s2,s3,m2
Quare fremuerunt	"	Surgere iam est	" +m4
Viri Galilei	s2,s3,m2,m3	A solis (Lwa)	s2-3,m2-3
Patrie pacis			" +(m4)
Civitas nusquam	" +(m4)		
Alma mater	"		
Caligo terre	s2,s3,m2-5		
De flore	s2,s3,m2-6		

Group 2(ii)

		Herodis in atrio	s2-4
Inter amenitatis	s2-4,m2,m3		
Mulier magni	s2-4,m2	Orto sole	s2-4,m2
Frondentibus	s2-4,m2-4	Duodeno sydere	" +m3
Laus honor	s2-5	Princeps	s2-4,m2-4
*Rosa delectabilis	s2-4,m2-5		
Rosa mundi	s2-6,m2,m3,(m4)		
		*Flos anglorum	s2-4
		*Beatus vir	s2-9
		*Triumphus patet	"
		*Hac a valle	"

Group 3: Innovative Insular Notations

Group 3(i): Circle-Stem Notational Complex

*Hac a valle (notation of Garlandia)
*Beatus vir (notation of Doncastre)

Firmissime fidem (intabulation)
Tribum quem (intabulation)

*Rosa delectabilis

(Triumphus patet)

Group 3(ii): Ternary Breve-Semibreve Notation

Ancilla Domini
Assunt Augustini
Baptizas parentes
Geret et regem
Nos orphanos
*Rosa delectabilis
*Thomas gemma (WF version)
Zorobabel abigo
*Flos anglorum

Group 3(iii): Forms of Binary Mensuration

(a) larga-longa notation

Lingua peregrina
Peregrina moror
*Rota versatilis
*Thomas gemma (long-breve version)

(b) binary long (and breve)

Syderea celi	s2,s3
Augustine par angelis	m2
Te domina	s2,m2
O dira nacio	s2,m2,(m3)
Tu civium	s2,m2,m4
Virgo Maria	s2,s4,m2,(m3)
*A solis-Ovet	s2,m2,m3
*Hostis Herodes	"
*Rota versatilis	"
*O crux vale	"

Table 13. (continued)

Group 4: French Ars Nova mensurations

circle-dot:	tempus perfectum maior
circle:	tempus perfectum minor
c-dot:	tempus imperfectum maior
c:	tempus imperfectum minor

Radix Iesse	Ccc 65, 3	circle-dot
Virginalis concio	DRc 20, 10	c-dot
Amer amours	DRc 20, 11	c-dot
Ad lacrimas	DRc 20, 12	c-dot
Vos quid	DRc 20, 13	c-dot
O vos omnes	DRc 20, 14	c-dot
O canenda	DRc 20, 15	c-dot
L'amoreuse flour	DRc 20, 16	c-dot
Musicorum collegio	DRc 20, 17	c-dot
Apta caro	DRc 20, 18	circle-dot
Mon chant	DRc 20, 19	circle-dot
Humane lingue	Lbl 40011B, 17	circle
Alme pater	Lbl 40011B, 18	c-dot
Cuius de manibus	Ob 7, 11	c-dot
Omnis terra	Ob 7, 12	c-dot
Deus creator	Ob 7, 14	circle-dot
Parfundement	Ob 7, 15	c-dot
Domine quis	Ob 7, 16	c-dot
Parce piscatoribus	Ob 7, 17	c-dot
Nec Herodis	Ob 143, 1	c-dot
Regne de pité	Ob 143, 3	c-dot/circle-dot
Inter usitata	Omc 266,268, 2	c-dot
*Flos anglorum	Omc 266/268, 3	circle-dot
Rex piaculum	TAcro 3182, 4	c-dot
Sub arturo plebs	GB-YOX, 1	c-dot
Degentis vita	GB-YOX, 4	c
In ore te	US-SM 19914, 1	c-dot
Soli fines	US-SM 19914, 3	circle-dot
Rex Karole	US-Wc 14, 3	circle
Deus compaignouns	US-Wc 14, 4	c-dot

is probably coincident with the relinquishment of a close text-music relationship in both genres and the abandonment of the cultivation of archetypes for motet construction that had persisted for several generations.

Three further tables form a coda to this introduction. The first of these, table 14, lists separately all those motets that exhibit changes in mensural organization. These shifts are, except in *Virgo sancta Katerina*, coterminous with strongly marked structural boundaries. *Virgo sancta* has a bar-by-bar alternation of first- and second-mode rhythms (*bllb* = 1+2+2+1) during the second statement of the tenor *color*; this kind of mixture is also found in the fourth section (*Katerina spe*) of *Rota versatilis*, where there is alternation of first and second mode with every phrase or half-phrase. Elsewhere the mingling of modes is seen only in passing details of rhythm, such as in the opening phrase of *Vas exstas*, the patterning of the tenor of *Suspiria merentis* (second mode, with one first-mode section), or in the rest-writing at the ends of phrases in *Parata paradisi porta* (where the cadence normally falls on a breve followed by a two-breve rest, but in one instance falls on an imperfect long followed by a single breve-rest). A change in mensuration often signals a shift in rhythmic activity and patterning of declamation. *Lux refulget* provides a dramatic example. Such a shift may also take place within the bounds of a single overall mensuration. *Orto sole* provides the best large-scale example, moving from semibreve duplets and breves to semibreve quadruplets, triplets, and breves after the structural midpoint (in effect, from group 2(i) to 2(ii) in table 13).

In regard to the use of stems on semibreves, see table 15 (and see also figure 34 below). Among the motets of group 2(i), stems only appear in *Dei preco* and *Jesu fili* from *DRc 20*, and in two *Ob 7* motets, *Templum eya salomonis* and *De flore martirum*.[9] Noteworthy is the fact that stems are not used to clarify the rhythm of the groups of four and five melismatic semibreves that occasionally appear in other motets of group 2(i). Stems are the rule within groups 2(ii), 3(i), and 3(ii); within group 2(ii) only *Rosa mundi* and *Inter amenitatis* lack them. A rough chronological development is apparent among those sources with at least occasional use of more than three semibreves per breve. The motets in one group of sources related among themselves by concordances—*Onc 362*, *Ob 652*, and *Lbl 24198*—lack stems. In a later group similarly related—*Cb 228*, *Cgc 512*, *Ob 7* (front leaves), and *DRc 20* (front leaves)—there is stemming.[10] *Lbl 1210* and *Lwa 12185* preserve examples of more elaborate and innovative insular practices that will be discussed below.

Finally, table 16 provides an overview of the cantilena repertoire grouped according to the same features as the motets. The cantilena repertoire sets poetry; it is in that respect related to the motet, whose means of setting verse are sometimes similar. For that reason the comparison afforded by table 13

Table 14.   Motets with Shifts in Mensuration

Motet	Division of the long
Rota versatilis	1st--2nd--binary--1st/2nd--binary
A solis-Ovet	2nd--binary-------2nd--binary
Hostis Herodes	2nd--binary--1st-------binary
O crux vale	2nd------------1st-------binary--1st
Ut recreentur	2nd------------1st
Apello cesarem	2nd------------1st
Alta canunt	2nd------------1st
Lux refulget	2nd------------1st
Virgo sancta	1st--1st/2nd------1st
Regne de pité	c-dot------circle-dot

and table 16 is instructive. The predominance of first mode over second mode in the motets is even more striking in the cantilenas. This is evident not just in groups 1 and 2(i) but also, more emphatically, in group 3, where breve-semibreve declamation is the rule and semibreve-breve rhythms are rarely encountered. The fact that group 2(ii) and all other group 3 categories are well supplied with motets but not cantilenas is indicative of the degree to which the cantilena is associated with regular declamation patterns, which are relatively rare in pieces in which there is rapid declamation on chains of semibreves. The two cantilenas in group 2(ii), *Salamonis inclita* and *Ave celi regina*, are exceptional pieces that were mentioned in chapter 2 for their similarity to duet motets. They do not have regularly and uniformly versified texts, but rather set varied pairs of stanzas to correspondingly varied musical double versicles. In neither cantilena is there a consistent organization of breves into perfect longs.[11]

In both long-breve and breve-semibreve cantilenas, the form can be understood as generated from the poetry through a consistent declamation scheme. Form is, in that sense, additive; hence the lack of a maximodus level of organization in long-breve pieces and of a modus level of organization in breve-semibreve pieces. One wonders why the two forms of "long-short" musical rhythm are then both necessary. The answer may lie in the ability to introduce melismatic elaboration in long-breve notation (breve-semibreve notation would have to introduce the minim) or in the more frequent use in breve-semibreve notation of declamation on the perfect breve (corresponding to the less commonly used perfect long). From a historical perspective breve-semibreve notation can be seen as supplanting older long-breve values, a process we can observe whether we know the reason or not.

Table 15.   Motets with More than 3 *s* per *b*, and Motets with Stems,
by Manuscript

Motets of Groups 1 and 2 with more than 3 s per b without stems, listed by source

Rosa mundi	Lbl 24198, 2
Surgere iam est	Lbl 24198, 4
A solis ortus	Lwa 12185, 5
Lux refulget	Ob 7, 4
Regina celestium	Ob 652, 3
Civitas nusquam	Onc 362, 5
Caligo terre	Onc 362, 9
Virgo sancta	Onc 362, 11
Iam nubes	Onc 362, 15
Inter amenitatis	Yc, 2

Motets with stemmed semibreves, listed by source

Mulier magni	Cgc 512, 1
Princeps	Cgc 512, 2
Laus honor	Cpc 228, 3
Herodis in atrio	DRc 20, 1
Jesu fili	DRc 20, 3
Princeps	DRc 20, 4
Dei preco	DRc 20, 5
Orto sole	DRc 20, 7
Triumphus patet	Lbl 1210, 2
Hac a valle	Lwa 12185, 2
Beatus vir	Lwa 12185, 3
Duodeno sydere	Ob 7, 5
Frondentibus	Ob 7, 6
De flore	Ob 7, 8
Templum eya	Ob 7, 9
Frondentibus	Ob 594, 1
Rosa delectabilis	Onc 362, 18

Table 16. Mensuration and Declamation in the Cantilena

Group 1: long-breve declamation

First mode		*Second mode*	
Ab ora summa	Lbl 1210, 14	Astrorum	Lbl 38651, 3
Ad rose titulum	Cgc 512, 13b	Gaude virgo	Lbl 3132, 1
Ave caro Christi	Cgc 512, 13a	Textless	Cfw, 4
Decora facie	Cpc 228, 6		
*Grata iuvencula	WF, 109		
In rosa primula	Lbl 1210, 12		
Lucerna syderis	Cjc 84, 3		
Mater Christi	Cgc 334, 4		
Missus Gabriel	Ob D.6, 1		
Psallens flecte	Cjc 84, 2		
Veni mi dilecte	Lbl 1210, 3		
Virga Dei generosa	Cgc 334, 9		

Group 2: breve-semibreve declamation

Group 2(i):

First mode		*Second mode*	
Ave mater summi	LEcl 6120, 7	Arbor Ade	Lbl 1210, 4
Gemma nitens	Cgc 512, 14		
*Grata iuvencula	WF, 109		
Virgo salvavit	Lbl 1210, 7		

Group 2(ii): lacking consistent modus level of organization

Ave celi regina	Cgc 512, 11
Salamonis inclita	Cgc 512, 10

Group 3: ternary breve-semibreve notation (an asterisk marks those with minims.)

A magnifica	Ob D.R.3*, 10/11
Beata es Maria	B-Br 266, 6
*Christi messis	LEcl 6120, 11
....filio Dei	Ob D.R.3*, 9
Includimur nube	Cgc 334, 6
*Jhesu Christe rex	GLcro 678, 2
*Letetur celi curia	GLcro 678, 1
Maria virgo	Ob D.R.3*, 13
....merenti modo	WF, 82
Mutato modo geniture	B-Br 266, 5
....numinis et rivos	Lbl 38651, 2
O ceteris preamabilis	Cgc 334, 8
Salve mirifica virgo	Ob D.R.3*, 7

Salve virgo singularis	Lbl 38651, 1	
.... solvisti criminis	Ob D.R.3*, 8	
Stella maris	Cgc 334, 7	
Virginis Marie	Cu 16, 1	
*Virgo decora	Ob 14, 4	

Group 4: French Ars Nova Mensurations (by source)

De spineto nata rosa	BERc 55, 3	c-dot
Virgo vernans velud	Cgc 230, 1	c-dot
...frangens evanuit	LEcl 6120, 1/2	c-dot/c
Ave mundi rosa	LEcl 6120, 5	c-dot
Hic quomodo	LEcl 6120, 9	c-dot
Christi messis	LEcl 6120, 11	c-dot/circle-dot/c-dot
O Maria laude	Lbl 57950, 41	c-dot/circle
... venie	Lbl 57950, 42	c
... et propitia	Lbl 57950, 45	circle-dot/c-dot
Pia mater salvatoris	Lbl 57950, 46	circle-dot
Salve porta	Lbl 57950, 54	c/c-dot/circle
Stella celi	Lbl 57950, 55	c-dot/circle
Singularis laudis	Occ 144, 1	circle-dot
Que est ista	Occ 144, 2	c-dot/circle-dot/c-dot
Fulgens stella	Occ 144, 3	circle-dot
... quod	Occ 144, 4	c-dot
... quod na rogaveris	Occ 144, 5	c-dot
Robur castis	Occ 144, 6	c-dot
Gaude virgo	US-NYpm 978, 2	c
Regem regum	US-NYpm 978, 3	circle-dot/c-dot/circle
Generosa Iesse	US-NYpm 978, 4	circle-dot/c-dot/circle-dot
Ut arbuteum	US-NYpm 978, 11	circle/c-dot/c

Later cantilenas in Ars Nova notation (most with sectional changes of mensuration) are relatively numerous, reflecting the flourishing of compositional activity in this genre to the very end of the fourteenth century. They have a text-music relationship less closely bound to patterning of declamation than the earlier pieces. Here declamation may be syllabic on the breve or regular only on a verse/stanza-to-phrase/section basis, or it may coordinate poetry to form without a neat isomorphism in structure (see the section "Versification" in chapter 4).

Thirteenth-Century English Mensural Notations

The notational practices in thirteenth-century English polyphony have not been much studied in comparison with Continental notations (the premodal and modal systems of the Notre Dame era, the early mensural systems of the first half of the thirteenth century, Franconian notation). The English go their own way in matters of notation. This is clear from the musical sources and also from the oft-cited testimony of a reporter of the 1270s, the Englishman Anonymous IV.[12] Early work in the field was done by Bukofzer, Levy, and Handschin, culminating in the editions and articles of the late 1950s by Dittmer.[13] Ernest Sanders addressed and corrected this body of work in his seminal article "Duple Rhythm." More recent contributions are the 1976 Oxford dissertation by Roger Wibberley, now summarized in the introduction to EECM 26, and a new edition of most of the recoverable pieces by Sanders in PMFC XIV (1979).[14]

Two notational styles must be distinguished in early English practice. The most important uses a rhomb (lozenge) to represent the breve; this notation is often referred to simply as English mensural notation (EMN). In the other style the breve is square, hence identical in appearance to the Continental variety. Square-breve notation may follow Continental precepts in its intended rhythmic realization, or it may embody rhythmic characteristics similar to those of rhomboid-breve notation. Table 17 lists all sources of thirteenth-century English polyphony, classified according to the style(s) of notation they exhibit and the approximate age(s) of their repertoire. It is difficult to say how old the rhomboid-breve convention is, but it goes back as far as the early thirteenth century. The oldest sources, marked A, mostly use Notre Dame–style nonmensural notation. Here declamation tends to fall exclusively on the long. Most breves are melismatic and hence occur either in ligatures or as part of coniunctura figures. In consequence few single breves or pairs of free breves occur and the rhomb, if it is being used, is hard to spot. In the later conductus and conductus-motets of group A, long-breve and long-breve-breve patterns begin to appear, and in these pieces the breve is always rhomboid. In group B sources, most of the notation is EMN. A few sources use the square breve, mostly in Continental fashion except within the Worcester fragments, *Ob 60*, and *US-Cu*. The youngest sources, group C, mainly use the square breve in Franconian fashion.

Idiomatic insular use of the breve (rhomb or square) can be separated into three categories:[15] (1) an alternation of single longs with single breves; (2) an alternation of single longs with pairs of breves; and (3) a succession of notationally undifferentiated breves (chains of paired breves). Most compositions show one type of notational idiom exclusively. A small number show predominantly one type while occasionally exhibiting features of

Table 17.   13th-Century Sources of English Polyphony

Key: 1 = non-mensural, Notre Dame type notation
2 = EMN with rhombs
3 = EMN with square breves
4 = Franconian

Sources by Sigla

Ccc 8	Ob 3
Ccl	Ob 18
Cgc 803	Ob 19
Cgc 820	Ob 25
Cjc 138	Ob 59
Cjec 1	Ob 60
Cjec 5	Ob 139
Ctc	Ob 257
Cu 29	Ob 343
CAc 128/1	Ob 400
CAc 128/6	Ob 489
	Ob 497
DRu	Ob 591
	Ob 1225
Lbl XVIII	Omec
Lbl XXI	Owc
Lbl 29	
Lbl 248	WF
Lbl 978	
Lbl 1580	D-Gu
Lbl 3132	F-Pn 25408
Lbl 5958	US-Cu
Llp 457	US-PRu 119
Lwa 33327	

Sources by Age

A. *Prior to 1260*

Cgc 803	1
Cjec 1	2
Ctc	2
Cu 29	1
CAc 128/1	1,(2)
Lbl XXI	1
Lbl 248	1
Lbl 978	1,2
Lbl 1580	1
Lbl 5958	(1),2
Llp 457	1,(2)
Ob 3	1
Ob 18	1
Ob 59	2
Ob 257	1
Ob 343	1
Ob 497	(1),2
Ob 1225	1
Omec	2
Owc	1
WF	1,2
F-Pn 25408	1,2

B. *ca. 1260-1280*

Cgc 820	2
Cjc 138	2
Cjec 5	3
DRu	2
Lbl XVIII	2
Lbl 29	2
Lbl 3132	4
Lbl 5958	2
Ob 19	2
Ob 25	2
Ob 60	2,3,4
Ob 139	(1),2
Ob 400	2
Ob 489	(1),2
Ob 497	1,2
Ob 591	(1),2
WF	1,2
D-Gu	2
US-PRuB,C	2

C. *ca. 1280-1300*

Ccc 8	4
Ccl	4
CAc 128/6	4
Lwa 33327	4
Ob 60	2,3,4
WF	2,3,4
US-Cu	2,3
US-PRu 119A	2,4

another, and in some there is a distinct shift, usually after an internal division, from one type to another (see table 18).

These notational idioms can be used to express several different mensurations. Compositions with notation of the first type, mainly alternating longs and breves, are unambiguously in first or second mode. Rhomboid-breve pieces in first mode are very numerous; mostly conductus-motets and troped chant settings, they make up the single largest subset of pieces in EMN. Rhomboid-breve pieces in second mode (breve-long) are, by contrast, extremely rare. Only three are known: *Nobili precinitur* (*Lbl 5958*, 1, an anglicized version of a Continental motet also preserved as *F-MO*, 58 (Rok 4.67)), *Fulgens stella* (*WF*, 74, an early piece with primitive two-voice counterpoint and a notation dependent on context and consistency of declamation for its rhythmic interpretation), and *O spes et salus* (*Ob 60*, fol. 104–104v, a fragment of a lengthy motet with a very highly developed form of EMN).[16] Square-breve pieces in first mode are rare and, along with square-breve second-mode pieces, occur mainly in the newest thirteenth-century sources (in Continental notation).

Compositions of the second type, with paired breves, may potentially indicate third mode, alternate third mode, or a binary third mode. Sanders has argued convincingly for an interpretation of paired English breves (and also, in some contexts, paired square breves) in trochaic rhythm, demonstrating the historical predominance of alternate third mode in the music of thirteenth-century England. He has further demonstrated that notation of the third type, chains of undifferentiated breves, ought to be read as a succession of trochaic pairs. In his analysis only a few pieces must be singled out for binary treatment of the long, primarily because of the complicating factor of the semibreve.

Wibberley's contribution to our understanding of EMN has been to call attention to the noticeable slant given note-heads in most of the sources of EMN so that square note-heads on longs and in ligatures become rhomb-like parallelograms with a distinct axis of orientation off the horizontal. It is Wibberley's thesis that this calligraphical feature of English scribal music hands is meant to facilitate the recognition of, and distinction between, long and breve, or between breve and altered breve, in binary and ternary ligatures. The longer value is indicated by slanting the note-head in the direction of melodic motion, and the shorter value is indicated by slanting the note-head in the direction perpendicular to the direction of melodic motion. By these means it is possible to indicate distinctions between third mode, alternate third mode, and binary third mode. Where note-head slant is pronounced, Wibberley's conjectures are compelling, but where note heads are rectangular and parallel with the staves, the argument from silence is not as strong. One needs somehow to establish that the scribe knew the slant convention and deliberately chose to write square instead of slanted note heads.[17]

Table 18. 13th-Century Pieces with Change of Notational Idiom

Pieces in EMN		
Felix namque Maria	WF, 4	Alt.3rd---1st
Fons ortorum	WF, 30	Alt.3rd---1st
Gaude Maria plaude	WF, 35	Alt.3rd---1st
Equitas in curia	Cgc 820, 1	Alt.3rd---1st
Virgo paris filium	WF, 14	1st---Alt.3rd
Pieces in Square Notation		
Christe lux mundi	WF, 1	1st---2nd
Kyrie fons pietatis	WF, 29	2nd---1st
Beata supernorum	WF, 26	1st---accel.
Alma iam ad gaudia	WF, 28	1st---accel.
Gloria: Spiritus et alme	Ob 60, 12	1st---binary

Some basic morphological features of EMN are given in figure 30. Particularly noteworthy are the use of the semibreve form with tail descending off to the left (especially in syllabic declamation), and the so-called English coniunctura (beginning with a tailed semibreve) that may replace the value of a long, imperfect long (altered breve), or regular breve.

Both Sanders and Wibberley have demonstrated the usefulness of comparisons between notations in pieces that survive both in EMN and in square-breve notation to establish the idiosyncratic features of EMN.[18] From among the small number of pieces that exist in both notational states, one is instructive to single out for comment here: *Salve sancta parens*, a troped chant setting (see figure 31). Two notational figures are of special interest in *Salve sancta*. First, chains of rhomboid breves, and some successions of longs and breves in alternation, translate into chains of square breves. The English coniunctura, when it stands in the place of a perfect long, is replaced by a ternary c.o.p. ligature *sine perfectione*. The stem on the first rhomb of the coniunctura indicates that it and the following rhomb are semibreves, each taking half the value of an altered breve (hence each equal to the third breve in duration). The ternary c.o.p. translates this meaning (1+1+1) directly into a Continental symbol without the rhythmic interpretation normally associated with it (i.e., 1+1+2); that is, the figure stands in the place of three equal regular breves rather than two. The conversion of the notation of a Gloria in EMN (*WF*, 88) into a square-breve version (*Ob 60*, 10) translates the coniunctura literally into two semibreves followed by a breve.[19]

Regis aula, a conductus-rondellus, provides further interesting examples of the transformation of ligatures. In its Franconian version, longs and rhombs have mostly been converted unproblematically into longs and square breves. A binary ligature *cum-sine* (breve-breve) is read 2+1 in EMN; in Franconian notation the same rhythm must be indicated by a ligature *sine-*

Figure 30. The Morphology of EMN

Simple Figures.

First and alternate third modes   Second mode

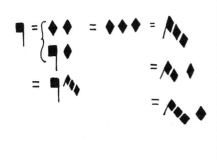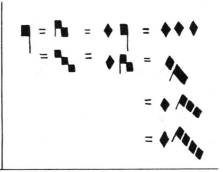

A stem descending laterally off the left shoulder of a rhomb marks the first of two or more semibreves, and may also be used to indicate syllable placement.

Do-mi-ni   De-us   Do-mi-ni   De-us

Binary Mensuration (in *US-Cu*)

   (4=2+2=1+1+2 = 1+1+1+1)

Binary Long and Ternary Breve in *Quam admirabilis* (*WF*, 16)

6 + 3+3 = 2+1+3

= 3+2+1

= 2+1+2+1

= 1+1+1 +2+1

Figure 30. (continued)

Ligatures:

Examples of the calligraphical distinction observed
by Wibberley (see EECM 26, pp. xxiv-xxv).

a. Single long and breve.

b. Ligatures for alternate third mode.

3 + ⌐2 + 1 + 3⌐ etc.

c. Ligatures for binary third mode.

2 + ⌐1 + 1 + 2⌐ etc.

2 + ⌐1 + 1 + 1⌐ + ⌐1 + 2⌐

sine (long-breve). A ternary ligature *cum-cum* (breve-breve-long) is read
2+1+2(or 3) in EMN; in Franconian notation the same rhythm must be
written with a ternary *sine-cum* (long-breve-long). As these examples show,
the EMN ligatures are not in direct conflict with the Franconian system's
manner of identifying the location of breves in ligatures; rather, their
translation is necessary because of the fact that the first of two paired breves is
the longer. To subdivide that first breve, as we saw above, one needs the
coniunctura or the c.o.p. shape whose upward stem indicates a halving of the
value of that larger breve.

A comprehensive survey of the thirteenth-century English repertoire
from the point of view of notation is still needed, growing out of the work that
has been accomplished in this area to date. A morphogenesis of EMN, with
special emphasis on the calligraphic slant convention, the semibreve, the
English coniunctura, and the forms of ligatures (particularly the c.o.p.) is a
top priority. Generic as well as chronological differences need to be explored.
Motets, in particular, because of their syllabic style and correspondences of
verse and musical phrase, bear the burden of the most elaborate notations and
the "complicating factor" of the semibreve. The longevity of the notation
needs to be established, as does the full implication of its norm of trochaic
rendition of paired breves for fourteenth-century English notations (a point to
be returned to shortly below).

Figure 31. Comparison of Thirteenth-Century Pieces in Two
Notational States

Salve sancta parens

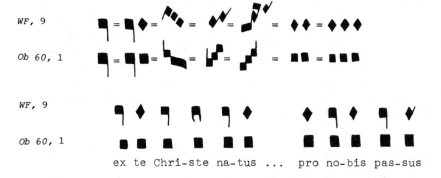

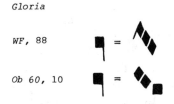

ex te Chri-ste na-tus ... pro no-bis pas-sus

Gloria

WF, 88

Ob 60, 10

Regis aula

US-PRu 119A, 1

Lb1 24198, 3

and

Franconian Notation and the Semibreve

The notation of the majority of the motets under consideration in this study is Franconian. That is, according to our conventional understanding, it follows the prescriptions codified ca. 1280 by a certain Franco of Cologne in his *Ars cantus mensurabilis.*[20] Early fourteenth-century English motets and cantilenas account for a significant part of the surviving Franconian corpus. Continental sources embodying its principles are relatively small in number, especially by comparison to the number of modal and early mensural sources of thirteenth-century French polyphony.

Franconian notation is fully mensural, with a relatively fixed rhythmical value for each notational symbol that is subject to modification through rules governing alteration and imperfection in only a limited number of contexts. The system has the inherent potential to erase all modal traits. Franco refers to this new freedom in the following way: "Observe also that the modes may run together in a single discant, for through perfections all are reduced to one. Nor need one attempt to determine the mode to which such a discant belongs, although it may be said to belong to the one in which it chiefly or frequently remains."[21] As we have seen above in our remarks on table 14, in practice there are only a very few pieces in which the modes can be said to be "run together," even briefly, in a single discant. Further, an underlying modal subdivision of the perfect long is clearly evident in the motets of groups 1 and 2 (and in some of those in group 3 as well).

The strongest force working to undo Ars Antiqua notational practice was the increasing subdivision of the breve, especially by syllabic semibreves.[22] Franco never discusses chains of semibreves occupying the duration of more than two regular breves. Since in his system a breve may be divided into two or three semibreves, the duration of two breves may be filled by four, five, or six semibreves, grouped 2+2, 3+2, 2+3, or 3+3. However, by extension Franco's rules allow, though nowhere demonstrate, the division of a perfect (ternary) long into as many as nine minor (syllabic) semibreves, with groupings clarified as necessary by the use of the *divisio modi*. Through the use of the *divisio*, therefore, a great variety of semibreve patterns is available.[23] As most widely disseminated, Franco's practice was modified by Petrus de Cruce, who introduced a dot or *punctus* in the place of Franco's *divisio* and used this dot consistently to distinguish all breve groups, a practice necessary because Petrus also permitted more than three (four to seven) semibreves per breve.

An important point can be made about subdivision of the breve, based on the evidence of the motet repertoire. This subdivision, whether highly patterned rhythmically or not, and whether syllabic or melismatic, tends to reflect the underlying modal foot of first or second mode by the location of the *fractio*, which occurs most frequently at the beginning of the longer part of the modal foot within the long-perfection. In first mode, the first breve is most likely to be divided, then (as the weight of examples shows) the third, and lastly the second. The most frequent subdivision of first mode is given in figure 32, example 1. This is a pattern so common that Lambertus accorded it a separate number in his expanded categorization of the rhythmic modes.[24] In the second mode the second breve is most frequently the one divided, then the third, and lastly the first. (Note that first and second modes differ in whether the imperfect long is fully subdivided before the "free" breve is.) Characteristic further subdivisions of first and second mode are given in figure 32, example 2.

The one important exception to the commonly encountered subdivisions just described involves the use of the three-note coniunctura figure given in figure 32, example 3, a breve followed by two descending semibreves. This replaces the value of two breves, more specifically replacing the imperfect long in a perfection filled long-breve or breve-long. Its usual interpretation in the present repertoire is just as it looks (*bss*); in essence it functions as a notational symbol in place of the awkward ternary ligature whose first element is a breve and whose second is a descending binary ligature c.o.p. There is occasional corroborative evidence for the *bss* interpretation when contrapuntal parallelism in another voice, or repetition of what must be intended as the same rhythm, associates this figure with a breve followed by a freestanding c.o.p. (see figure 32, example 4). Also, it is the rarer *ssb* figure that is directly

Figure 32. Subdivision of the Breve

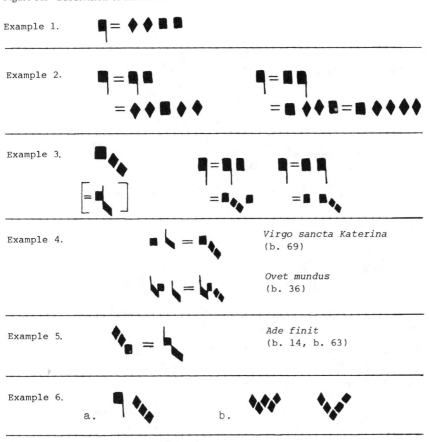

Example 1.

Example 2.

Example 3.

Example 4.

Virgo sancta Katerina
(b. 69)

Ovet mundus
(b. 36)

Example 5.

Ade finit
(b. 14, b. 63)

Example 6.

a.

b.

Figure 32. (continued)

Example 7. Unusual use of free syllabic and melismatic *s*.

a. Recurring patterns

(i) *Jhesu redemptor* (13 out of 14 phrases at the cadence)

in-si-   -ci-e   in- si-   -ci- e

(ii) *Vas exstas* (5 out of 10 phrases at the cadence)

sen- tis in-ti-me   sen-   tis in-ti-me

b. Occasional occurrences (selection)

(i) *O crux vale*

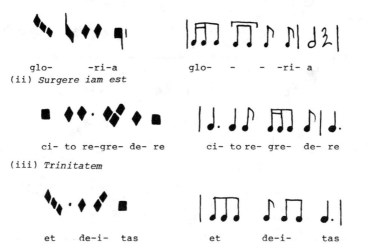

glo-   -ri-a   glo- - - -ri- a

(ii) *Surgere iam est*

ci- to re-gre- de- re   ci- to re- gre- de- re

(iii) *Trinitatem*

et   de-i- tas   et   de-i-   tas

---

equated with ternary c.o.p. ligatures.[25] The *bss* figure is more common in second-mode than in first mode, which can produce a mixture of two forms of *fractio* rather than one consistent pattern in motets with second-mode underpinning.

Another context in which free (i.e., conjoined but unligated) semibreves are sung melismatically involves coniunctura-like figures of three to six semibreves in the space of a breve. The descending figure given in figure 32, example 6a, is by far the most common of these and almost invariably replaces the third breve of a perfection following an imperfect long in first mode. Similar figures include those cited in example 6b. Much less common are those occasions when one or more of the semibreves replacing a breve are sung syllabically while the remainder are sung melismatically with a preceding or following syllable. This is indicated where it happens by very careful spacing of notational symbols. It is a regular feature of patterning at the approach to cadences in *Jhesu redemptor* and *Vas exstas* and appears unsystematically elsewhere. In contrast to the coniunctura figures, the free semibreves sung here do not emphasize descending melodic motion; instead, there may be pitch repetition or disjunct motion up or down (see figure 32, example 7).[26]

Rhythmic Interpretation of Semibreve Groups

Problems interpreting Franconian and Petronian notation mainly involve the intended rhythms for semibreve duplets, triplets, and larger groups that subdivide the breve. English notational styles and mensural practice in the fourteenth century raise many questions concerning the proper rhythmic interpretation of semibreves and introduce several systems (some showing Continental influence) for wholly or partially eliminating the ambiguity concerning their duration. This evidence will be considered below. First, however, the following discussion will briefly review some theoretical treatments of the semibreve in the thirteenth and fourteenth centuries and consider what has been said in the scholarly literature about English handling of these rhythmic problems.

In Franconian notation groups of two or three semibreves may replace the durational value of a breve, and no freestanding single semibreves are possible. Some compositions show the use of only duplets or triplets, while others may divide the breve both ways in the course of a piece. The most fundamental question regarding the rhythmic value of these semibreves is whether two are equal and three are not, or vice versa. It is never the case that two are equal (each a half of a breve) and that three are equal (each a third of a breve) in the same piece. (This point will be returned to below.) In the theory not yet reflecting the mensural practice of Franco's generation, paired semibreves are specified as equal and three as unequal (1+1+2); this is the position taken, for instance, by Amerus and Dietricus.[27] The scattered theoretical evidence supporting binary subdivision of the long refers mainly to contexts where the breve is also binary. For instance, Odington probably intends equal subdivision of the breve in remarks on binary versions of third and fourth mode, and the same association seems to be made in a discussion of these modes by Anonymous IV.[28] The unequivocal insistence of Franco and his generation that paired semibreves be unequal can be regarded as "a deliberate deviation" from the earlier tradition,[29] one that extends the relationships between long and breve to operate in much the same way between breve and semibreve. This innovation is tied to another, the systematic use of declamation on the semibreve.

For the period between Franco and de Vitry, what do theorists say about the subdivision of the breve by four or more syllabic semibreves? Petrus de Cruce, following Franconian precepts, interprets semibreve duplets unequally (1+2) and triplets equally; it is unclear from the testimony of our main reporter, Jacques of Liège, just how four through seven semibreves per breve were intended to be sung by Petrus. Modern scholars can have diametrically opposed views. Sanders, for instance, argues that the small semibreves must have been sung in a style of free virtuoso declamation, as fast as possible and hence for all practical purposes equal. Bent, on the other hand, assumes the faster semibreves of Petrus to be unequal according to one of the systems later codified.[30]

Then there is the doctrine of Petrus le Viser reported by Handlo. It is not easy to understand this Petrus or to associate his teaching with any surviving repertoire.[31] In his *mos mediocris*, "due semibreves equales sunt, et tres inequales, et quatuor equales, et quinque inequales" (CS I, p. 338). However, the *mos mediocris* encompasses two states of notation within its presumed medium tempo:

   (i)   with longs, semilongs, breves, and semibreves; semibreves (two to five per breve) are melismatic.
   (ii) with only semilongs, breves, and semibreves (two to five per breve); semibreves are syllabic in groups of two or three, melismatic in groups of four and five.

In addition to the recognition of a binary breve, applicable to both (i) and (ii), it is likely that the restriction to semilongs (i.e., imperfect longs, worth two regular breves) in (ii) also implies a binary modus (i.e., breves grouped by twos and no chains alternating semilongs with breves). It seems that for Petrus, syllabic semibreves make the tempo too slow if there are perfect longs. Hence only in (i) would there be binary breves as a level of subdivision of the perfect (ternary) long. He is silent on the exact means of rhythmic interpretation of the unequal groups of three or five semibreves per breve in the *mos mediocris*.

Walter Odington is more helpful. In his view, when a ternary breve is divided into four parts the first two are equal and twice as long as the last two.[32] (See figure 33, example a.) This specifies that *fractio* is applied at the end of the major semibreve, the longer part of the foot. The same is true in de Vitry's specification for *minimum tempus perfectum*, although the order of major and minor semibreve is reversed along with the specified location for subdivision.[33] By contrast, in de Vitry's *tempus imperfectum maior* four semibreves are interpreted as two pairs. (See figure 33, examples b and c.) Later fourteenth-century theorists tend to follow de Vitry in their

Figure 33. Rhythmic Conventions for Groups of Semibreves

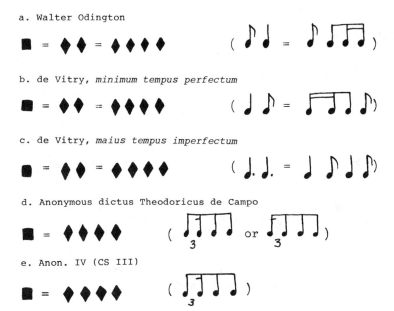

a. Walter Odington

b. de Vitry, *minimum tempus perfectum*

c. de Vitry, *maius tempus imperfectum*

d. Anonymous dictus Theodoricus de Campo

e. Anon. IV (CS III)

interpretation of four semibreves under *tempus perfectum*, including the Anon. dictus Theodoricus de Campo,[34] who interprets them in one of two ways, as in example d, at the pleasure of the singer, and the Anonymous IV of CS III,[35] who interprets them as in example e. In both cases the location of the *fractio* indicates that semibreve duplets would be read unequally as 2+1.

It is clear that to have firm criteria for the interpretation of semibreve groups one must know the character of the breve (binary or ternary) and the conventions in effect both for uneven duplets and for interpreting brevial subdivision by four or more semibreves. The theorists report a range of possibilities for what to do, but their immediate relevance to any particular motet or motet source is open to challenge. If stems are present to clarify semibreve conventions, then one may interpret from them the character of the breve on the basis of the location of the *fractio*. When stems are absent, one needs to make a few informed assumptions about possible rhythmic readings. We could assume that the rhythms specified in de Vitry's *Ars Nova* for *tempus imperfectum* and *perfectum* codify the unwritten conventions of the rhythmic language that had developed rapidly after the innovations of Petrus de Cruce. There may, of course, have been less widely favored alternative rhythmic idioms that he rejected (or was unaware of), and de Vitry's teaching and compositions may have been an influential point of departure rather than a codification of popular trends.

An anti-Franconian alternative. The specifically Franconian doctrine, widely disseminated, often copied, and carrying great authority, teaches that if the (ternary) breve is replaced by two semibreves, the first is minor and the second is major (1+2), and if by three, then all are equal minor semibreves. A few theoretical sources transmit an alternative rule concerning unequal paired semibreves in the same context, permitting the first to be major and the second to be minor (2+1). These sources include the following:

1. from the treatise of Magister Lambertus (Coussemaker's Pseudo-Aristotle):

    a. De recta breve...se ipsamque in duas diminuit partes non equales vel in tres tantummodo equales et indivisibiles, quarum prima pars duarum semibrevis minor appellatur, secunda vero major, et e converso. (CS I, p. 272)

    b. [speaking of a binary c.o.p. ligature:]...est ligatura duarum figurarum...prima autem minor semibrevis dicitur, secunda major, vel e converso. (CS I, p. 274)

2. from the 1279 treatise of the St. Emmeram anonymous (ed. Sowa), who reports on the doctrine of Lambertus concerning the binary c.o.p. ligature in order to take issue with it:

    a. et si inequales, utrum minus frustrum debeat precedere et maius sussequi necessario aut pro voluntate mutua et converso, sicut quam plures asserere sunt reperti. Deinde utrum pro maiore brevi in equipollentis possint supponere sicut quidam in suis artibus asserere non formidant, dicentes de ea [here 1b above is quoted]. (Sowa, p. 48)

    b. quidam dicunt in illa figura minorem semibrevem precedere et maiorem sussequi vel penitus e converso pro mutua cantantium voluntate. Et isti opinioni videtur maxima pars canentium adherere. Unde Magister Lambertus de tali figura dicit [again quoting 1b above]. (Sowa, p. 51)

3. from the *Ars Nova* of Philippe de Vitry:

    Minimum tempus posuit Franco. Unde notandum est secundum Magistrum Franconem...[quod] minimum tempus non est nisi tres continens semibreves, quae quidem adeo sunt strictae quod amplius dividi non possunt, nisi per semiminimas dividantur. Unde notandum quod, quando aliquis cantus temporis perfecti reperitur ubi non nisi tres continentur semibreves pro uno tempore, secundum minimum tempus pronuntiari debent (si sint quatuor, primae duae semiminimae, nisi aliter signentur). Item sciendum est quod, quando pro isto minimo tempore duae ponuntur semibreves, prima maior debet esse et nunquam secunda, nisi signetur, licet secundum artem veterem superius probaverimus quod secunda debet esse maior....(CSM 8, p. 29)

4. from an anonymous fourteenth-century *Compendium musicae mensurabilis artis antiquae*:

> Item quandocumque due semibreves pro recta brevi inveniuntur in unisono, id est in eadem linea vel in eodem spatio, ad voluntatem cantantis possunt fieri prima vel secunda maior; sed quando in diversis tonis inveniuntur, secundum maiorem concordantiam debet prima vel secunda semibrevis maior pronuntiari. (CSM 15, p. 69)

5. From the *Regule* of Robertus de Handlo:

> a. [in regard to binary ligatures:] si tractus autem ascendens, qui causat oppositam proprietatem, fiat curtus, tunc in hac obliquitate sine ligatura major semibrevis minorem precedit, ut hic patet: [example follows]. (CS I, p. 394)

> b. Quando due semibreves similes sunt in conjunctione, prima erit minor, alia major, ut supra in exemplo tertie huius rubrice. Nisi tractum obliquuum sit impedimentum, et tunc erit semibrevium dissimilitudo, et fiet prima major, altera minor, ut hic: [example follows]. (CS I, p. 396)

6. from the *Quatuor principalia*:

> Dividebat enim Franco longam in tres breves et brevem in tres semibreves, sed non minus quam in duas semibreves, quarum prima maior, secunda minor semibrevis ab eo nominatur, vel e contrario. (CS IV, p. 257; CS III, p. 337.)

7. from an anonymous midfourteenth-century Catalan treatise on the notation of the Ars Antiqua and Ars Nova, *De cantu organico* (ed. Anglés):

> In Cathalonia et aliquibus aliis locis observatur iste modus. In aliquibus, vero, terris, quando sunt due semibreves pro tempore, faciunt primam maiorem, secundam minorem. Et quando sunt tres, equales, ut patet hic superius. Et ista est doctrina quam omnes tenuerunt a .xxx. annis et citra.... Et ratione huius variationis dicam hic intellectum et traditionem predictorum magistrorum cantus organici primo, et postea modernorum. Magistri predicti dixerunt quod quando sunt due semibreves posite pro tempore imperfecto, sunt equales; quando, vero, de tempore perfecto, prima est maior, secunda minor. Dicitur, autem, maior, quia continet tantum de tempore quantum continent due prime semibreves trium positarum pro uno tempore. (Anglés, pp. 1352–53)

These examples hardly constitute proof of a vigorous tradition running counter to Franco's. Lambert is attacked by the St. Emmeram anonymous; the author of the *Quatuor principalia* may have in mind a different notational context from the one in question here;[36] the anonymous *Compendium* links the mensural choice to consonance; Handlo describes unusual note-shapes whose precise shapes are uncertain (but undoubtedly rarely, if ever, used), and the passage does not survive in Hanboys; de Vitry explicitly acknowledges Franco's way as the old way ("secundum artem veterem"). Nevertheless the possibility of reading a pair of semibreves as 2+1 rather than as 1+2 has some authority, and we must acknowledge that in certain otherwise "Franconian" repertoires or in certain geographical areas or musical centers, say in Catalonia or England, trochaism might be the norm.[37]

The assertion that there is a strong English preference for trochaic rendition of paired semibreves in the late thirteenth and early fourteenth centuries has in fact been made in recent years by scholars working on the repertoire. Sanders states that "it is likely that, contrary to Franconian practice, the English method of alteration (2+1) was applied to the semibreve in at least some English compositions of the time," and he cites some instances, including a number of pieces in which "the binary ligature cum opposita proprietate must be read 2+1."[38] Bent concurs and cites examples that cause her to propose "that trochaic interpretation of semibreve pairs might be taken much further than the cases noted by Sanders."[39] Wibberley reaffirms this point of view, arguing that for "those [notations] employing Petronian methods in which the semibreves are notationally undifferentiated . . . the traditional English preference for trochaically conceived rhythms" ought to be favored in the interpretation of semibreves, for "it hardly seems likely that a short-lived period of Petronian notation should have witnessed such a fundamental change in attitude towards performance as to admit the use of iambically conceived rhythms to any great extent."[40]

Aside from the theoretical testimony just cited, this position rests on certain assumptions and a particular body of evidence, both of which demand closer scrutiny. Sanders established firmly that there was indeed an English method of alteration in the thirteenth century, in which pairs of breves (rhombs or squares) must be read 2+1. There is no necessary reason for this relationship to devolve upon paired semibreves after the adoption of Franconian notation. One can, of course, hypothesize a rationale for what might have prompted such a transfer of rhythmic performance practice down one notational level. The Franconian system extends the relation between long and breve to that between breve and semibreve in several respects, including the interpretation of the second of a pair of the smaller values as the longer of the two. Following similar logic, some English musicians may have adopted a practice whereby, on account of the fact that traditionally the longer of two paired breves was the first, this relationship devolved upon the pair of semibreves. On the other hand, we know of no explicit English antipathy for iambic rhythms, there are exceptional examples of EMN in second mode (as well as binary rhythms, of course), and it seems perfectly reasonable to expect that if the English adopted features of Continental notational practice they could well have assimilated corresponding rhythmic idioms including iambic interpretation of semibreve pairs. There is no reason to assume a priori that because English mensural notation interprets paired breves trochaically that this convention must be followed for semibreves.[41]

The evidence cited by Sanders and Bent compels us to make an important distinction. They have not, in fact, proven that a trochaic preference applies to paired semibreves within a Franconian context. That problem remains open for the moment. Rather, they have shown evidence that the trochaic reading of paired semibreves applies to a small subset (those pieces with paired semibreves) of a class of compositions in what I shall call breve-semibreve notation (group 3(iii) in tables 13 and 16), a notation that will be discussed in detail shortly.[42] This sharpens the focus but at the same time narrows the field within which their evidence lies and within which their conclusions apply.

Harrison has also recently written on the problem of "the division of the brevis" in relation to the English motet repertoire. Regarding semibreve duplets he argues that "where a motet has only duple subdivision of the brevis ... no ambiguity about division of the brevis arises" and "the assumption is made here that subdivision is in notes of equal length." Further, "there is some warrant in the theoretical literature for unequal subdivision [but] in practice, however, this principle seems inapplicable in virtually all of the motets [of PMFC XV] to which it might be considered relevant."[43] As a result, he concludes not only that for those motets in which syllabic and melismatic duplets prevail they should be equal, but also that in those in which syllabic and melismatic triplets occur (frequently or infrequently), the duple or triple subdivision is always into notes of equal length (one-half or one-third of a breve, respectively). Both of these positions are subject to criticism. On the strength of the theoretical tradition outlined above, few modern scholars would follow Harrison in rejecting "the underlying axiom ... that the brevis is perfect, and hence all its subdivisions must be related to a basic triple subdivision" just because a composition has only semibreve duplets.[44] Moreover, it does not ever seem to have been acceptable to the thirteenth- and fourteenth-century theorists (Continental or English) on whom we rely that both semibreve duplets and triplets could divide the breve equally in the same piece.[45] Harrison does not raise the issue of the rhythm of semibreve duplets in those pieces in which he interprets them unequally; they are all transcribed iambically (1+2) with no reference to the school of thought that credits the possibility of a transcription trochaically (2+1).

Evidence of the musical sources. Empirical evidence provided by the English motets suggests the diversity of solutions available for the interpretation of semibreves in Franconian and Petronian contexts, including the anti-

Franconian (trochaic) interpretation of semibreve duplets. Contrapuntal evidence is perhaps the hardest to find and the most ambiguous in its analysis. To cite one example, *Civitas nusquam* provides a number of instances (eleven in all) where two semibreves in one voice are put against three in another. In only a small number of these does it seem to make any difference to the counterpoint whether the major semibreve is assumed to be the first or second of a pair; where it matters, the reading is better when the larger is first (arguing for 2+1 against 1+1+1, although a binary interpretation, 2+2 against 1+1+2, is not ruled out). The syllabic semibreve groups of figure 33, example 7, also suggest, in their distribution of notes, the intended rhythm of semibreve pairs. In most cases (*Trinitatem veneremur* being a distinct exception) the rhythm suggested is again anti-Franconian (2+1).

Not just the groupings of notes, but also the melodic shapes they outline, can suggest the underlying subdivision. This is particularly noticeable where repeated notes are found. In *Assunt Augustini* or *Alma mater*, for example, repeated notes are always the first two of an s3 or m3 group, suggesting that they subdivide a 2+1 figure. In the more progressive notation of the *Roman de Fauvel*, to cite a Continental counterpart, repeated notes in s4 or m4 groups are either the first two or last two, suggesting the subdivision 2+1+1 or 1+1+2 of a binary breve. Most motets fail to provide these kinds of clues, however.[46]

Semibreve stems clarify to a very important degree the problems inherent in the evaluation of semibreve groups. In the simplest case, the stem either ascends or descends from the center of the note-head. The descending stem lengthens value, normally identifying the major semibreve. An ascending stem shortens value, normally identifying the *semibrevis minima*, or smallest value. In contexts where stems are used it may be the case that all notational symbols have single, fixed values, or on the other hand, that (as in figure 33, example b) certain relationships still have to be understood by unwritten convention.

Although the most dramatic use of syllabic semibreves is in bursts of from five to seven or nine in the space of a breve, the most important expansion of Franconian practice in terms of frequency is the consistent use of four syllabic semibreves per breve. In the English motets (as in *Fauvel*) this is accompanied by the use of the downstemmed semibreve in almost every instance. (See figure 34, example a.) In these examples the breve is clearly binary; i.e., semibreve duplets are equal. Ambiguity remains in the rhythm of the four smaller semibreves. Some evidence suggests that the latter are unequal according to the convention specified by de Vitry in the *Ars Nova* for groups of two to four semibreves under *tempus imperfectum maior*. The evidence consists of a number of bits and pieces all pointing in the same direction: (1) in the motet *Dei preco* one semibreve triplet has an upward stem on the third rather than a downward stem on the first, presumably with

Figure 34. Some Stemming Practices in the English Motets

a. *Dei preco, Duodeno sydere, Frondentibus, Mulier magni meriti,*
   Orto sole, Princeps apostolice. (See also the *Alleluya confessoris,*
   D-W 499 (W3), no. 5.)

$$\blacksquare = \blacklozenge\blacklozenge = \text{\LARGE ♮} = \blacklozenge\,\blacklozenge\blacklozenge = \blacklozenge\blacklozenge\blacklozenge\blacklozenge = \left\lfloor \blacklozenge\blacklozenge\blacklozenge \right. = \blacklozenge \,\backslash\;(2+\overline{1+1'})\Big]$$

b. *Templum eya Salomonis (Ob 7)*

$$\text{♩} = \blacksquare\blacksquare\blacksquare = \blacklozenge\blacklozenge\,\blacklozenge\blacklozenge\;\blacklozenge\blacklozenge$$

c. *De flore martirum (Ob 7)*

$$\blacksquare = \blacklozenge\blacklozenge = \blacklozenge\,\blacklozenge\,\blacklozenge = \blacklozenge\blacklozenge\,\blacklozenge\,\blacklozenge = \blacklozenge\blacklozenge\blacklozenge\blacklozenge\,\blacklozenge = \blacklozenge\blacklozenge\,\blacklozenge\blacklozenge\blacklozenge\blacklozenge$$

d. *Jesu fili (DRc 20)*

$$\blacksquare = \blacklozenge\blacklozenge\;\;\blacklozenge\blacklozenge$$

e. *Laus honor (Ob 7)*

$$\blacksquare = \blacklozenge\blacklozenge = \blacklozenge\,\blacklozenge\,\blacklozenge = \blacklozenge\,\blacklozenge\,\blacklozenge\,\blacklozenge = \blacklozenge\,\blacklozenge\,\blacklozenge\,\blacklozenge\,\blacklozenge$$

equivalent meaning; (2) the *Ob 594* version of *Frondentibus* uses the downward stem exclusively but the *Ob 7* version, which originally had no stems, has had upward stems specifying de Vitry's rhythms entered by a later hand; (3) the motet *Inter amenitatis*, with groups of two to four syllabic semibreves, is not stemmed in *Yc* but is given de Vitry's rhythms by upward stems in *I-TR 87*, a much later source; (4) the cantilena *Salamonis inclita*, stemless in *Cgc 512*, is given de Vitry's rhythms by stems in *US-NYpm 978*, a later source; (5) the motet *Herodis in atrio*, with two to four syllabic semibreves per breve, has stemming following de Vitry in the hand of the original music scribe of *DRc 20*.

The cumulative impact of this evidence is to suggest that in any English composition with two to four syllabic semibreves per breve the breve is binary and each major semibreve is ternary (with pairs of minor semibreves read 2+1). This would apply, arguably, to the *Cgc 512* version of *Orto sole* or the original *Ob 7* version of *Frondentibus*, with later stems understood as a clarification, not modification of original intent.[47] It must be observed, however, that the English stemming patterns are slightly less limited than de

Vitry's (with the occasional position of the major semibreve as the last of three, and the appearance—admittedly rare—of the binary c.o.p. ligature in place of a major semibreve).

Other methods of stemming occasionally found among the motets specify a ternary breve, with either Franconian or anti-Franconian handling of semibreve duplets, in a few individual cases. In *Templum eya Salomonis* the downstemmed semibreve is used to specify the 1+2 rhythm of duplets (figure 34). In *De flore martirum* the upward stems on semibreves, more or less following the precepts of de Vitry for *tempus perfectum maior*, confirm by their pattern of *fractio* the iambic reading of duplets (figure 34). In *Jesu fili*, on the other hand, two short passages (see figures 33 and 34) unequivocally indicate the anti-Franconian reading of duplets. Finally, the use of downstems in *Laus honor vendito* should be noted for the record; the rhythms intended are not easy to interpret, but because there are no stems on either groups of two or three, two are probably unequal and three equal. The location of *fractio* may possibly indicate the trochaic reading of duplets.

Some of the motets of group 2(ii) show distinctive, innovative, and apparently insular stemming practices. Of these, only *Rosa delectabilis* is in first mode. The others are in second mode and may be considered examples of the second-mode tendency toward *fractio*. Two adopt for their subdivision of the breve the Ars Nova mensurations of de Vitry: in *Herodis in atrio, tempus imperfectum maior*, and in *Flos anglorum, tempus perfectum maior*. The others show features associated with insular fourteenth-century notations and will be be discussed below.

Fourteenth-Century English Notational Practices

A Notational Complex

A good number of fourteenth-century English compositions can usefully be thought of as belonging to a single notational complex unified by (1) the use of a dot (or *punctus*) to set off breve groups, (2) the use of the downward stem to mark the major semibreve, (3) either the use of a small circle (the *signum rotundum*) or minim stems to designate smaller values, and (4) the appearance of certain characteristic rhythmic patterns. The compositions included in this notational complex are listed in table 19, where they are arranged first by source and then by the primary and secondary divisions of the breve. The roughly equivalent French or Italian mensuration is indicated for purposes of orientation. In some of these pieces the smaller values are rarely used, while in others they are pervasive.

Bent has suggested that "If four was considered the basic Italian division of the breve and six the French, the English was nine."[48] This is certainly the

Table 19. The Circle-Stem Notational Complex

(i) *By source:*

Benedicta es celorum	BERc 55, 2
O ceteris preamabilis	Cgc 334, 8
Kyrie Cuthberte	DRc 11, 1
Astra transcendit	LIc 52, 2
Veni mi dilecte	Lbl 1210, 3
Et in terra	Lbl 1210, 5
Kyria christifera	Lbl 1210, 6
Virgo salvavit	Lbl 1210, 7
O lux beata	Lbl 1210, 8
(Dance)	Lbl 28550, 1
(Estampie)	Lbl 28550, 2
(Estampie)	Lbl 28550, 3
Firmissime fidem	Lbl 28550, 4
Tribum quem	Lbl 28550, 5
Flos vernalis	Lbl 28550, 6
Hac a valle	Lwa 12185, 2
Beatus vir	Lwa 12185, 3
Rosa delectabilis	Onc 362, 18

Note: Frangens evanuit (LEcl 6120, 1/2) is another possible candidate for inclusion. Its mensurations would be classified in Groups C and D(ii).

(ii) *By mensural practice:* (* indicates entry in two groups)

Group A   (tempus perfectum maior/ novenaria/ 9/8)

	circle	down-stem	stemmed minim
Lwa 12185, 2	x	x	
Lwa 12185, 3	x	x	-

Group B   (tempus perfectum minor/ senaria perfecta/ 3/4)

	circle	down-stem	stemmed minim
Cgc 334, 8	-	x	-
Lbl 1210, 8	-	x	-
Lbl 28550, 2	-	x	x
Onc 362, 18	-	x	-

Table 19.   (continued)

Group C   (tempus imperfectum maior/ senaria imperfecta/ 6/8)

*DRc 11, 1	x	-	x
Lbl 28550, 4	-	x	x
Lbl 28550, 5	-	x	x
*Lbl 28550, 6	-	x	x

Group D

D(i)   (tempus imperfectum minor/ quaternaria/ 4/8)
         (?= Hanboys: curta mensura)

Lbl 1210, 7	-	x	-
Lbl 28550, 1	-	x	-

D(ii)   (octonaria/ 8/ 16)
         (? = Hanboys: longa mensura)

BERc 55, 2	-	x	-
*DRc 11, 1	x	x	x
Llc 52, 2	x	x	x
Lbl 1210, 3	-	x	x
Lbl 1210, 5	x	x	-
Lbl 1210, 6	x	x	x
Lbl 28550, 3	-	x	x
*Lbl 28550, 6	-	x	x

case if one begins with theoretical testimony, which when describing insular techniques for breve subdivision concentrates almost exclusively on the ternary breve and semibreve. The extension of breve subdivision from seven to nine, the invention of the downstemmed major semibreve, and the use of a small circle to mark off the thirds of a ternary breve are all credited by Robertus de Handlo to a certain Johannes de Garlandia (whose nationality and further identity are unknown, although he is not to be confused wth an earlier theorist of the same name).[49]

One motet fragment, *Hac a valle*, survives in pure Garlandian notation (see figure 35, group A). In it the breve is divided into two to nine syllabic semibreves by a system in which breve units are set off by solid dots, ternary subdivisions of the breve are set off by small circles, the major semibreve (worth two-thirds of a breve) is a rhomb with a downstem, and all smaller values are simple rhombs whose values must be determined from context. The minor semibreve is worth one-third of a breve, the *minorata* is worth two-ninths of a breve, and the *minima* is worth one-ninth of a breve. The *minima*

Figure 35. Circle-Stem Notation in Practice

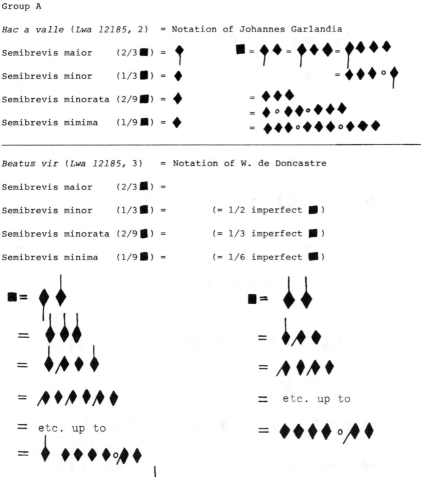

always precedes the *minorata* where two rhombs stand in place of the minor semibreve, establishing a predisposition toward iambic rhythms on the lowest level.

The only other piece clearly exhibiting a ninefold division of the breve is another motet fragment, *Beatus vir*, which uses the notational system attributed by Hanboys to the otherwise unknown W. de Doncastre.[50] (See

Figure 35.   (continued)

Group B

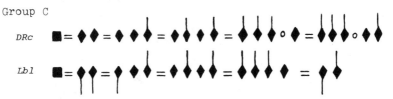

Group C

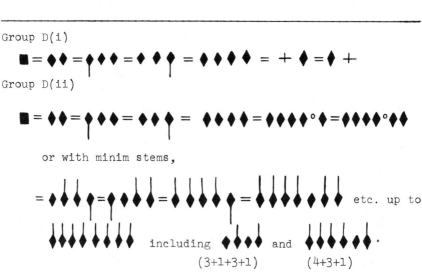

Group D(i)

Group D(ii)

or with minim stems,

etc. up to

including   and

(3+1+3+1)   (4+3+1)

again figure 35, group A.) Doncastre's system is very similar to Garlandia's in its resultant rhythms. However, the *minor, minorata,* and *minima* are distinguished by individualized note-shapes, and the customary division of the minor semibreve places the *minorata* before the *minima*, thus introducing a trochaic rather than iambic rhythm on the lowest level.[51] *Beatus vir* also effectively introduces the *semiminima* by using four minims in the place of a minor semibreve (some ambiguity remains in the rhythm of these groups of

4*m*) and introduces red coloration into both the tenor and texted voice to signal a recurring shift from perfect to imperfect modus and tempus. When the modus is perfect, an underlying second-mode foot is discernable, defined by the position of rests and full breves. When minim values are employed, the ternary or binary subdivision of the breve is clarified by the use of the *signum rotundum*. In many respects, therefore, the notation is an advance on Garlandia, and in all likelihood has felt French Ars Nova influence.

The rhythmic patterns characteristic of the other groups of this notational complex are listed in figure 35, groups B, C, and D. The circle makes its only other appearance where the breve is binary, in groups C and D. In the first line of group D(ii) the utility of the circle is clear, though in fact there is one characteristic rhythm that cannot be notated without using minim stems. In group C the circle is clearly superfluous, and Bent has very reasonably proposed as a historical process that "increasing use of minim stems eventually made the circle redundant and it died out."[52]

Relevant theoretical descriptions of duple divisions as they appear in Group D are confined to a reference by Hanboys to *curta* and *longa mensura*, terms that apply when the breve is divided into four or eight equal minor semibreves.[53] *Curta* and *longa mensura* may be the terms applicable to the forms of binary division of the breve seen above in groups D(i) and D(ii) of the circle-stem notational complex. They have a close kinship with *quaternaria* and *octonaria* in the Italian Trecento system of notation. Unfortunately, Hanboys gives no way to distinguish them from other possible kinds of binary division of the breve. When there are only four *s*, one is naturally faced with the problem of deciding whether they are equal (understood as in group D(i) or D(ii)) or else must be read unequally following some convention such as those of de Vitry. When seen in association with the other breve divisions of this notational complex such as appear in the two main sources of the notation, *Lbl 1210* and *Lbl 28550*, it seems reasonable to assume four *s* are equal. However, the same use of the downstemmed semibreve and two to four syllabic semibreves per breve also occurs in a number of motets discussed above whose source contexts and concordances rather strongly raise the possibility of an unequal interpretation. (See figure 34, example a.)

It is clear that in only a few examples, mainly motets and the *Kyrie Cuthberte*, is the use of these small note-values essential, i.e., integral to the conception of the piece (for instance, because of syllabic declamation or essential contrapuntal motion on these values). In the rest, the subdivision has a specifically ornamental character. In three instances, the two motets by Philippe de Vitry intabulated in the Robertsbridge codex (*Firmissime fidem* and *Tribum quem*) and the *Kyria christifera*, an unornamented version exists with which the present version may be compared. In the case of the motets, added rhythmic figuration leaves the basic contrapuntal structure intact,[54] while in the *Kyria* long-perfections have been pulled out of shape by the perhaps overenthusiastic addition of extra breves of precadential filigree (see figure 36).[55] The remaining pieces exhibit elaboration and diminution of rhythmic figures apparently also originating in simple long-breve and breve-semibreve notations.[56] As in the homorhythmic "protofaburden" of the duet motets or the similar activity in the outer voices of ornamented English discant settings written in Ars Nova mensurations, the ornamentation here is mainly neighbor-note motion and sequential figuration in parallel sixths or 6-3s.

This notational complex provides a securely English context for the mensural notation of the right hand in the Robertsbridge intabulations, whose apparent mix of French and Italian features has intrigued musicologists in the past. The association of this notational complex with instrumental music prompts the thought that the ornamental breve division might be at least partly instrumental in origin or character. Precedents in the vocal repertoire (motets and discant) have just been mentioned, but the virtuoso degree of diminution involved in the most elaborate of these settings is perhaps modeled on instrumental technique. The high degree of chromaticism employed in the Robertsbridge items is very likely also a sign of an instrumental idiom.[57] If so, it is even more interesting to point out that it is fully matched by the extravagant use of accidentals (producing dramatic departures from diatonicism) in the *Kyrie Cuthberte* and the cantilena *Stella maris*.[58]

On the basis of the sources we have, it would seem that this notational complex, and its associated ornamental style, flourished in England through the second and third quarters of the fourteenth century. It would have been current in the 1350s when, according to a suggestion made by Craig Wright, the Robertsbridge codex music might have been assembled for the pleasure of the French king John the Good, who was captive in England from 1357 to 1360.[59] And it may even be the case that we have here written examples of the kind of florid singing with "small breaking" that Wycliffe and his followers single out again and again in their castigations of church music over the last third of the century.[60]

Breve-Semibreve Notation

The notational complex discussed above originates in patterns of breve subdivision within a long-breve context, introducing smaller note-values into a Franconian long-perfection and then later, in all likelihood, introducing this style of subdivision into other mensurations. The next fourteenth-century insular notation to be discussed, breve-semibreve notation, stands in a very different relationship to Franconian tradition. From table 13 at the head of

Figure 36. Versions of the *Kyria christifera*

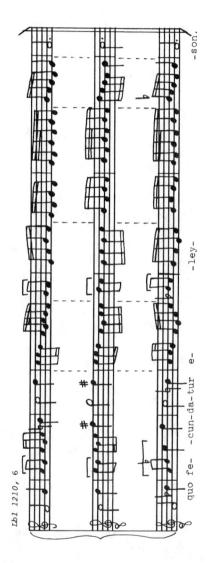

this chapter it can be seen that nine motets can be described as using breve-semibreve notation (group 3(ii)). The notation is, however, much more commonly found in the cantilena and discant repertoires. Therefore its main features will be dealt with from the point of view of its central corpus, and the motets will be returned to briefly for discussion at the end of this section.

There are two forms of English breve-semibreve notation, one in which the breve is ternary, which is very common, and one in which the breve is binary, which rarely occurs.[61] The following discussion will focus on the first kind. This notation is in many respects identical to the *tempus perfectum* of de Vitry, but certain notational and rhythmic idiosyncracies reveal it to be an independent, if closely related, system.

The fundamental unit of ternary breve-semibreve notation is the breve itself, which is shaped like a square. The next-smaller value, two-thirds of the ternary breve, is the major semibreve. In ten pieces, surviving in a total of eight different sources, this note-value is shaped like a rhomb, or in other words like the usual semibreve (see table 20).[62] The minor semibreve, worth one-third of a breve, also uses this shape. Thus the alternation of major and minor semibreves produces a chain of notationally undifferentiated semibreve pairs. Sanders and Bent must be credited with establishing that these paired semibreves are read trochaically (2+1), or in other words, with the major always preceding the minor semibreve.[63] Hence one can legitimately speak of an English preference for trochaic rhythms that is evident in thirteenth-century English mensural notation, in at least some of the pieces written in the nominally Continental-style notation adopted at the end of the thirteenth century, and here in the ternary breve-semibreve notation employed for much of the fourteenth century.

The paired-semibreve version of ternary breve-semibreve notation must certainly predate the adoption in England of one of the most important novelties of de Vitry's *Ars Nova,* namely the imperfect breve and its concomitant freestanding single semibreve. These introduce the capacity for transferring to the relationship between the breve and semibreve all the relationships existing between long and breve under the Franconian system. Under French influence the square replaces the rhomb as the form of the major semibreve so, as the *Quatuor principalia* puts it around midcentury, "maior autem semibrevis pro tanto dicitur, quia duas minores includit, et figurari debet ut brevis recta, quia equipollet brevi imperfecte."[64] It is in this fashion that breve-semibreve notation is found in the majority of fourteenth-century English sources. One piece, the cantilena *Includimur nube caliginosa,* is preserved in both versions, and the two *Angelus ad virginem* settings in the Dublin troper (*Cu 710*) show evidence of having been copied, using the square form of the major semibreve, from an exemplar in paired rhombs.[65]

In this notation the range of note-values is usually restricted to those three just described (perfect breve, major semibreve, minor semibreve) with

Table 20. Pieces in the Paired-Semibreve Version of Ternary Breve-Semibreve Notation

B-Br 266, 2	Spiritus et alme
B-Br 266, 5	Mutato modo geniture
B-Br 266, 6	Beata es Maria
Cgc 334, 5	Mutato modo geniture
Cgc 334, 6	Includimur nube caliginosa
Cgc 334, 7	Stella maris illustrans
Cgc 334, 8	O ceteris preamabilis
Cgc 512, 8	Mutato modo geniture
Lbl 1210, 8	O lux beata trinitas
Onc 362, 18	Rosa delectabilis
WF, 67 (Ob 20)	Thomas gemma
WF, 82 (WOc 68)	. . . merenti modo

no longs except as final longs and few or no minims. Ornamental figures occasionally may introduce more than three minor semibreves per breve, especially at cadences. When this happens, the rhythmic interpretation may be clarified through the judicious spacing of note-heads or the use of upward or downward stems; the implied subdivision of the minor semibreve in most cases is ternary.[66] There is usually no binary or ternary modus, i.e., no regular metrical grouping of breves by two or three, except in a few motets where breve-semibreve notation is introduced into a Franconian long-perfection as the means of division of the breve. On the other hand, rhythmic organization on the phrase level can often generate consistent larger groupings of breves, such as the groups of five and ten seen in the cantilena *Mutato modo geniture*.[67]

The two settings in English discant of the Latin song *Angelus ad virginem* will serve as an introduction to some of the idiosyncracies of breve-semibreve notation. Their notation of rhythm has been commented on by Bukofzer, Sanders, and Bent.[68] The breve is perfect and is subdivided either 2+1 (square-rhomb) or 1+1+1. The binary c.o.p. ligature occurs in two contexts. It either ligates the first two of three minor semibreves (i.e., taking the value of the major semibreve or altered breve), or it stands in place of the full perfect breve. Distinguishing between these contexts is a simple matter. The first is unambiguous in its rhythmic interpretation, but the second is problematic. How can we identify which of the two elements in the ligature is the larger value?

In a transcription of the first setting of *Angelus*, Bukofzer chose to render the rhythms of the ambiguous c.o.p. ligatures trochaically with the remark that "the unorthodox rhythmic interpretation of the ligature... is suggested by the context and by the middle voice at 'tu porta.' "[69] Bent points out that there is a curious piece of supporting evidence in the second *Angelus* setting. Here the ligature in the lowest voice at "Dominum" is an unusual stepwise descending form of the binary c.o.p. ligature with a *cauda hirundinis* attached to the second breve. The *cauda*, she posits, reinforces (and clarifies) the intended rhythmic interpretation of this ligature, which is iambic (1+2), suggesting thereby that the c.o.p. ligatures normally are trochaic.[70] There is additional internal evidence for this conclusion further along at the second "tu porta." Here the scribe began to copy out the tune in the middle voice as if for the fifth, rather than for the sixth and final phrase of the melody. The error was noticed and the incorrect pitches circled for deletion. At this point the scribe wrote two successive breve-perfections in which 2+1 rhythms were notated by paired semibreves, the first of which was given a downstem. This inconsistency in notation suggests that the exemplar from which the scribe copied was written in paired-semibreve notation in which the first of the pair, whether free or in ligature, was the larger value.

C.o.p. ligatures. Under the conventions just seen in *Angelus ad virginem* the binary c.o.p. ligature can have two different rhythmic meanings depending on context. It may either stand in place of the major semibreve (rhythmic value 2=1+1) or replace the ternary breve, standing for two semibreves the first of which is major and the second, minor (rhythmic value 3=2+1). A ternary c.o.p. ligature without perfection (*s-s-b*) must, as a result, be understood normally as having the value of two ternary breves (6=2+1+3). (See figure 37, example a.) In two exceptional cases, however, this note-shape is used to ligate three minor semibreves. In the first instance, a free setting of the Marian sequence *Virginis Marie laudes* (*Cu 16*, 1), this inference is drawn by comparison of the different notations of two otherwise identical cadences at the ends of both halves of a written-out musical double versicle on the words "plasma ex te nascentis" and "manet Iudea" (see figure 38).

/ This unconventional reading of a ternary c.o.p. is most likely also intended for the precadential ligatures in the Latin-texted Kyrie *Ob 14*, 1. Here there is a parallel in musical content to the counterpoint of free semibreves at the cadence in stylistically similar Kyries in breve-semibreve notation, and also a strong parallel to cantilena-style free pieces in long-breve notation such as the unornamented form of the *Kyria christifera* (*Ob 14*, 5). The latter has a strong resemblance to the other *Ob 14* Kyries in counterpoint and rhythm, but is notated one level of values higher, with precadential, stepwise-descending 6–3s written with ternary *cum-sine* (*bbb*) ligatures (see figure 38).[71]

Figure 37. Parallels in Ligature Formation

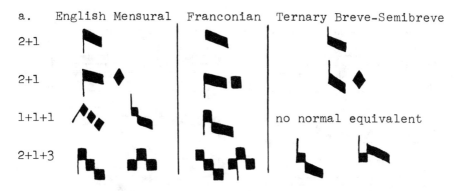

b. Hypothetical Derivation of the Abnormal Interpretation
of the Ternary C.o.p. Ligature

In general there is a parallel between the role of the ligatures in breve-semibreve notation and those used in the paired–square-breve form of thirteenth-century English mensural notation, as shown in figure 37, example a. The ternary c.o.p. is used in the square-breve version of EMN to ligate three equal values, the first two of which are conceptually semibreves (dividing the larger breve) though they have the same durational value as the third note, which is a breve. There is no normal means of ligating three semibreves in breve-semibreve notation. To explain the unusual use of the c.o.p. in the two special cases just mentioned (*Virginis Marie laudes* and the *Ob 14* Kyrie), it seems reasonable to propose a correlation with long-breve note-shapes in which an exact halving of values is indicated by the use of the upward tractus. This untraditional, hypothetical rationale is shown in figure 37, example b. It is offered as a means of explaining only the two special cases. The logic of figure 37, example a is posited as the normal reading of the c.o.p.

These observations suggest the following line of speculation: the introduction of breve-semibreve notation in England might have come about as a result of the decision to begin to write certain kinds of pieces (most notably at first, cantilenas and cantilena-style free settings) down one level of notation from their previously accustomed values, preserving the characteristic trochaic rhythms of these genres in new note-shapes. This proposed relationship of long-breve to breve-semibreve notation would be the

Figure 38.   Cadences in *Virginis Marie laudes* and Three Latin-
Texted Kyries

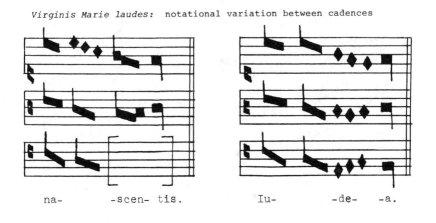

Virginis Marie laudes: notational variation between cadences

na-   -scen- tis.   Iu-   -de-   -a.

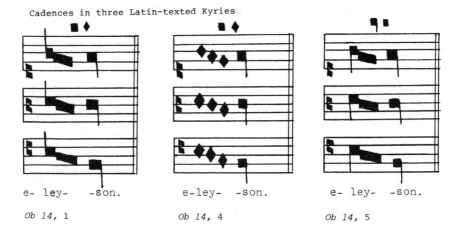

Cadences in three Latin-texted Kyries

e- ley-   -son.   e-ley- -son.   e- ley-   -son.

Ob 14, 1   *Ob 14, 4*   *Ob 14, 5*

clearest manifestation of a general shift to shorter values for which there
remain other pieces of evidence. For instance, the English discant setting of
Mater ora filium exists in two notational states, an earlier version in longs and
a later version in breves, as can be seen in figure 39.[72]

Two further examples speak directly to the question of the emergence of
breve-semibreve notation from long-breve notation through a direct
reduction of values. The first is the well-known motet *Thomas gemma*, which
survives in two sources in long-breve notation and in a third source in the early
paired-semibreve version of breve-semibreve notation.[73] A comparison of

Figure 39. Halving of Values in the Two Notational States of
Mater ora filium, *Thomas gemma*, and *Virgo decora*

Mater ora filium

Ob 3, 1   *Ob 55, 5*

Thomas gemma

a. *Cgc 512, 6*; *US-PRu 119A, 4*

b. *WF, 67* (*Ob 20*, fols. 35, 34)

Virgo decora

a. *Ob 25, 1/2*
b. *Ob 14, 8*

note-shapes, especially ligatures, shows the kinds of correlations proposed above. A second example is the composition *Virgo decora*, which has a rather unusual and illuminating history. It originated as a polytextual troped chant setting of *Virgo Dei genitrix* (the verse of the Marian gradual *Benedicta et venerabilis*), written in parts and notated in the long-plus-rhomboid-breve version of EMN. It was probably composed late in the third quarter of the thirteenth century.[74] The later version (in *Ob 14*, a source that has figured large in this entire discussion) has undergone a generic transformation into a cantilena by putting the parts in score, texting all voices with the words of the duplum, and cutting all note-values in half. If there were any intermediaries in this evolution they have not come to light; in any event, the association of EMN, and of the cantilena, with breve-semibreve notation is revealing.

Given that there were strong conventions in at least some English circles for the anti-Franconian interpretation of paired semibreves, it is little wonder that attempts would be made to invent unambiguous new notational symbols specifying the authentic Franconian doctrine. (English theoretical sources are among the best witnesses for Franco, after all.) According to Hanboys, this is precisely the contribution of Frater Robertus de Brunham, who originated the use of new forms of binary c.o.p. ligature to specify alteration of the second of two ligated semibreves, and introduced the swallow's tail, or *cauda hirundinis*, as a further tool to clarify the rhythms of paired semibreves, whether free or in ligature.[75] Hanboys and the author of the *Quatuor principalia*, as good Franconians, are offended by the introduction of these means of indicating alteration,[76] but the practicality of Brunham's notational devices caused their use to survive a few academic criticisms.

Brunham's ligature shapes are obviously closely related to familiar binary ligatures with propriety and perfection—the podatus and the clivis— except for the addition of an upward stem on the left hand side (see figure 40, example a). They appear in four musical sources.[77] In one instance, in the diminution section of the tenor and contratenor of the isorhythmic Gloria *Ob 384, 2*, Brunham's shapes occur precisely as the diminished counterparts of the standard binary ligatures just mentioned (see figure 40, example c), thus lending some credibility to the hypothesis that some Englishmen viewed the effect of the upward tractus as a direct halving of values (recall the unusual interpretation of the ternary c.o.p. just discussed).

The use of the *cauda hirundinis* is much more widespread. Its function is to label the major semibreve, or in the words of Hanboys, to assign alteration by a sign in the shape of a swallow's tail ("per duos tractulos ad similitudinem caude hirundinis").[78] Hanboys's examples of Brunham's device (figure 40, example b) show it attached to both free and ligated semibreves, always to signal the alteration of the second of two, or in other words to clarify by

Figure 40. Brunham's Ligature Shapes

a. Brunham's ligature shapes: *Lbl 8866*, fol. 78v (CS I, p. 431)

b. Hanboy's examples of the use of Brunham's "cauda hirundinis":
Lbl 8866, fol. 78v (CS I, p. 432)

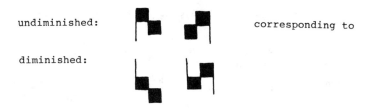

c. Ligatures in the tenor and contratenor of the Gloria, *Ob 384,* 2

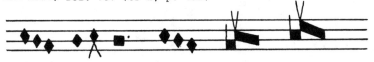

undiminished: corresponding to

diminished:

special means the normal Franconian convention. In actual practice (see table 21), it not only may mark the second of two free semibreves but may indicate the alteration of either the first or second of two ligated semibreves. In later fourteenth-century sources the *cauda* is used, independent of its original context and function, to alter a semibreve between two imperfect breves in *tempus perfectum maior*, to alter a semibreve between two minims, and to alter minims.

Motets in breve-semibreve notation. The use of ternary breve-semibreve notation in the motets is quite varied (see figure 41). *Thomas gemma* has been discussed above. *Ancilla Domini* and *Geret et regem* are similar in versification and apparent lack of regular patterning of declamation; they tantalize by the thought that they may represent an important direction for motet composition later in the century but are too fragmentary to allow of further comment. *Zorobabel abigo* and *Nos orphanos* are more substantial fragments. They put breve-semibreve notation to work in more varied textures than those found in discant and cantilena pieces; this is most noticeable in their diverse configurations of semibreves and rests. In

Table 21. Examples of the *Cauda Hirundinis* in Practice

Item	Source	Context
Latin-texted Kyrie	Ob 14, 1	to alter the first of two ligated *s*
Latin-texted Kyrie	Ob 14, 4	
Gloria	Lbl XXIV, 2	
Alma redemptoris	Ob 27, 2	
Sanctus	NWcro 299, 8	
Gloria	DRc Comm.Car., 1	
Gloria laus honor	WF, 82a (frag.xix)	
Angelus ad virginem	Cu 710, 2	to alter the second of two ligated *s*
Fulgens stella	Occ 144, 3	
Frangens evanuit	LEcl 6120, 1/2	
Credo	US-NYpm 978, 8	
Kyrie	I-PIca 176, 1	
Singulari laudis	Occ 144, 1	to alter the first or second of two ligated *s*
Numinis et rivos	Lbl 38651, 2	to alter the second of two single *s*
Christi messis	LEcl 6120, 11	
Humane lingue	Lbl 40011B, 17	
Regne de pité	Ob 143, 3	to alter the *s* between two *b*

Agnus	Ob 143, 1	♦♦♦	to alter the *s* between two *m*
Gloria	Ob 384, 1	♦♦♦ ♦	to alter one *m* in pairs of *m*
Gloria	Ob 384, 3	♦♦♦	"
Gloria	Ob 384, 4	♦♦♦	"
Credo	Lbl 40011B, 15	♦♪ (♩ ♫)	to alter the first of two ligated *s* across a perfection
Sub arturo plebs	GB-YOX		?

Zorobabel not a single breve-perfection is filled by three consecutive semibreves in any one voice-part. This is achieved, rather, by hocket between the surviving parts. It is also noteworthy that the rhythms of *Zorobabel* are consistently iambic (semibreve-breve). In *Baptizas parentes, Assunt Augustini,* and *Rosa delectabilis,* the long is perfect and rhythmic activity defines a first-mode underpinning. In *Rosa delectabilis,* the notation is a rhythmically ornamented version of paired-semibreve writing, with downstems added in the idioms of group B of the the circle-stem notational complex. In *Baptizas* and *Assunt,* breve-semibreve motion predominates with declamation falling in irregular fashion on long, breve, and semibreve values.

Ternary breve-semibreve notation is found in cantilenas, free cantilena-style settings, discant settings of plainchants, and motets—in other words, all the major genres of polyphonic music cultivated in fourteenth-century England—and seems to have been in use over about the same time period as circle-stem notation, i.e., the middle two quarters of the century. Some traces might arguably be said to remain in Old Hall.[79] Whereas the central French rhythmic language of the fourteenth century is that of *tempus imperfectum maior,* the English clearly have a preference for *tempus perfectum maior.* The dividing line between insular and French Ars Nova practice is elusive where the ternary breve (and square form of the major semibreve) is concerned. Hence the list of sources of this notation, offered as table 22, is necessarily only provisional.

Tempus perfectum, maior or *minor,* can be recognized (1) by the extensive use of minims in patterned and sequential rhythmic figuration, (2) by the consistent use of the minim as a unit of declamation, or (3) when sectional changes of mensuration introduce other Ars Nova prolations.[80] The

Figure 41.   Breve-Semibreve Notation in the Motets

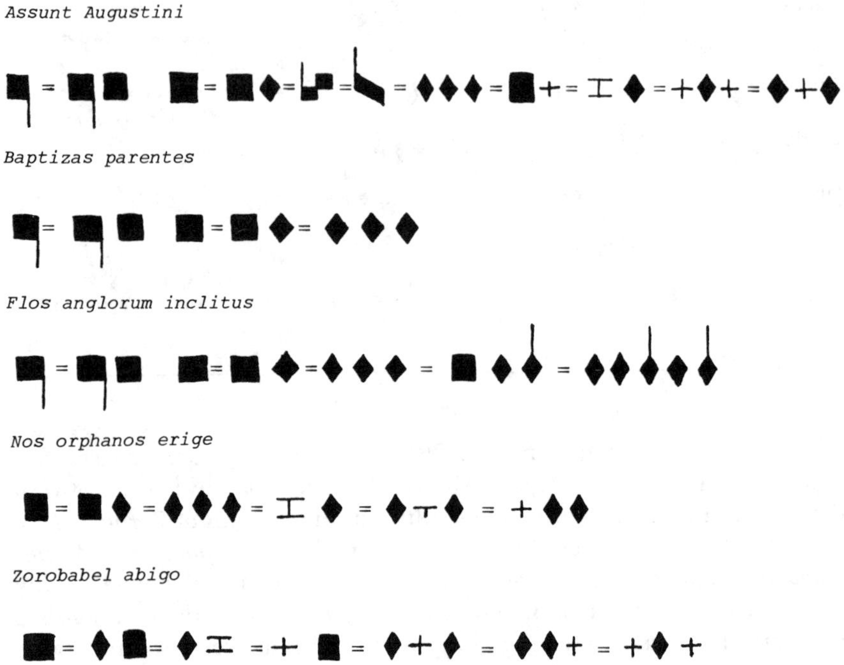

Assunt Augustini

Baptizas parentes

Flos anglorum inclitus

Nos orphanos erige

Zorobabel abigo

similarity (and compatibility) of English and French notational style seems to have led to a gradual merger for all practical purposes, especially through the proliferation of melismatic minims. There are examples where an English ternary breve-semibreve piece has accumulated enough minims in a late source to look Continental, which might reflect French influence or perhaps merely the English taste, in part improvisational at its root, for making settings more florid.[81]

Inevitably some ambiguity remains, especially in the interpretation of c.o.p. ligatures. Here context can often suggest a solution, as for example if melismatic c.o.p. ligatures are mixed with melismatic breve-semibreve motion, suggesting the Franconian (semibreve-breve) interpretation for the ligatures. A number of pieces in basically Continental notation exhibit some English notational traits, indicating the tenacity of certain aspects of the independent English tradition. For example, in the *tempus perfectum maior* section of the motet *Regne de pité* the *cauda hirundinis* makes an appearance and binary c.o.p. ligatures must be read trochaically.

Table 22. Sources of Breve-Semibreve Notation

Cgc 334	Ob D.R.3*
Cgc 512	Ob 14
Cu 16	Ob 27
Cu 710	Ob 55
CRc Communar's Cartulary	Ob 60
GLcro 678	Occ 144
LEcl 6120	Omc 266/268
Llc 52	TAcro 3182
Lbl XXIV	WF
Lbl 1210	B-Br 266
Lbl 38651	I-PIca 17
Lli 1	I-FOL
Lli 146	I-GR 197
NWcro 299	US-NYpm 978

Binary Mensuration

As was pointed out above, binary mensuration of the long and breve is rare in thirteenth-century polyphony and is scarcely mentioned by theorists describing Ars Antiqua practices. In the very late thirteenth and early fourteenth centuries it becomes more common in musical sources both on the Continent and in England.[82] The purpose of the following section is to discuss the rhythmic organization of the fourteenth-century English motets of group 3(iii), those with duple rhythm on one or more levels of mensural organization.

Only one English theorist, Hanboys, has directly relevant material. His treatise systematically discusses the use of eight species of simple figures that are used in mensural music. These are the *larga, duplex longa, longa, brevis, semibrevis, minor, semiminor,* and *minima*.[83] For each he provides an extensive presentation of its ligated and unligated shapes, the range of rhythmic values it can adopt, the notational configurations in which it can appear, and the other figures with which it can be mixed. The combinations and permutations of binary and ternary subdivision possible in Hanboys's system are considerable. At the extremes are the all-duple or all-triple mensurations, the cases of the *larga imperfecta ex omnibus imperfectis* and the opposite, the *larga perfecta ex omnibus perfectis*. Mensurations are characterized for Hanboys not only by the hierarchy of mensural organization but also by the range and frequency of occurrence of note values. Only a few consecutive simple figures in his descending series can be found together in any one voice-part.[84] Much of Hanboys's treatise can be taken as scholastic system building, especially his exhaustive treatment of the very largest and smallest simple figures.

In practice, the largest notated value used as the basis for metrical and rhythmical organization in the motets is the double long, but it occasionally occurs in contexts that demonstrate Hanboys's work to be grounded in more than mere speculation.[85] Two motet fragments found among the fourteenth-century palimpsests in the Worcester fragments, *Lingua peregrina* and *Peregrina moror* (*WF*, 44 and 47), are written using just three note forms: double long, long, and breve. (Their articulation of regular twice-2L units as a feature of mensuration and rhythmic language was mentioned in chapter 2.) Dittmer found the appearance of double longs and longs in the tenors (and the restriction to occasional double longs, single longs, and breves in the surviving upper parts) so distinctive that he coined for these pieces the label "larga-longa notation."[86]

It should be noted here that the "larga-longa" appellation has no medieval authority behind it, and an assertion by Dittmer that larga-longa notation is "discussed by R. Handlo and J. Hanboys" is in fact rather misleading.[87] Dittmer follows the fourteenth-century English theorist Torkesey and his school in using the name *larga* for the value known elsewhere as the *maxima* or *duplex longa*. It is the middle element in the trio *largissima, larga, longa*.[88] Handlo never uses the word *larga*, referring instead only to the *duplex longa*, which has the value of two simple longs (i.e., six breves).[89] This figure may stand by itself or be used in ligatures, and it may be imperfected to the value of five *tempora* (breves) by a preceding or following breve or breve-rest. Hanboys does refer to the *larga*, as we have seen. It is the largest in the trio *larga, duplex longa, longa*. In his system the *larga* cannot be ligated ("et simplex est, quia ligari non potest"), and it contains from nine to four longs.[90] The *larga perfecta* contains three double longs, each of which, curiously enough, consists of three (not two) perfect longs. The *duplex longa*, in turn, may consist of between nine breves (three perfect longs) and four breves (two imperfect longs). When it contains six breves (two perfect or three imperfect longs) it corresponds to the *duplex longa* of Handlo. Hence, the notation of *Lingua peregrina* might better be called *duplex longa–longa* notation. Although larga-longa notation arises out of the sorts of mensural organization implicit in Hanboys, it is not singled out for special mention there.

Concerning larga-longa notation as it is used in practice in the Worcester fragments, the following observation must be made. The large note-values have been employed to create a mensuration with two levels of binary and one level of ternary organization (double longs by twos, longs by twos, breves by threes). The archaic look of the notation is misleading. These large values are undoubtedly used to evade the problems inherent in the establishment of the same metrical hierarchy with smaller note-values (introducing paired semibreves or even minims while employing declamation that regularly falls on the smallest available rhythmic units).[91] The mensuration is akin to *modus imperfectus, tempus imperfectum, prolatio maior* notated two full levels higher than the note-values of de Vitry's prolation.

The two Worcester palimpsests have a second-mode subdivision of the long. Two further examples of larga-longa notation exhibit first-mode subdivision instead. These are the "long-breve" version of *Thomas gemma* and the first section of *Rota versatilis*.[92] We have seen in chapter 2 that *Thomas* is rigidly structured in 4L units that are divisible throughout into two 2L units. As in the Worcester pieces, rhythmic subdivision falls more often on the first two than on the second two longs—here most frequently setting a line of six syllables with penultimate (paroxytonic) accent, as in figure 42. The breve-semibreve version expresses these rhythms down one level in the metrical hierarchy, introducing a binary long and paired semibreves that must be read trochaically.

The first section of *Rota versatilis* stands in a kind of augmented notation with respect to the sections that follow. It is organized throughout into 2L units with declamation presumably on double longs and longs; in the two lower voices these units are mostly filled by double longs or equivalent rests. Further grouping into 4L units mainly follows fairly naturally (though one assumes it would be better defined if the upper voices had survived in full), but this section ultimately sacrifices regularity of mensuration in 4L groupings to a larger proportional scheme that requires it to have a total of 54 longs, a number not evenly divisible by four. Probably the "missing" bars are at the very end.[93]

It is highly likely on account of the mensural and rhythmic organization of the first section of *Rota versatilis* that the incipit of the top voice survives at all. It exists in an example quoted by Handlo to show notational figures and rhythmic values that may appropriately occur together, specifically illustrating the following remark: "Breves vero cum longis duplicibus misceri possunt, cum semibrevibus etiam et obliquis, ut hic patet."[94] The musical example that follows is obviously corrupt in our one source, and Bent sees a problem in associating it with the statement to which it is supposed to pertain.[95] However, it is possible to suggest a few plausible amendments to the incipit that bring it closer to a condition relevant to Handlo's remark, and at the same time allow it to fit more easily into the surviving lower parts than Bent's proposed alterations (see figure 43).[96]

A number of motets show some of the features of larga-longa notation without such a restriction in the range of note-values used or the rigid organization of mensuration and declamation around a succession of 4L (paired *duplex longa*) durations. These include the motets with varied rhythmic patterning of the tenor such as *Flos regalis*, and others with regularly articulated 2L units, like *Regnum sine termino*, *O crux*, *Inter choros*, and the

Figure 42. Declamatory Patterns for *6pp* Lines

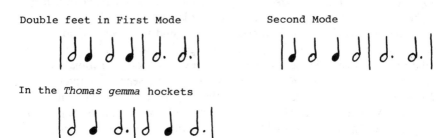

Double feet in First Mode   Second Mode

In the *Thomas gemma* hockets

Figure 43. Incipit of *Rota versatilis*

Incipit in *Lbl 4909*, p. 8 (fol. 4v)

Hypothetical original

Caius twin motets *Virgo Maria* and *Tu civium*. Here, too, we see not an archaic throwback to the rhythmic language of Perotin, but rather a notation with paired longs and syllabic breves corresponding to the more "modern" paired breves and syllabic semibreves of *tempus perfectum minor*.

The (b) motets under group 3(iii) of table 13 all exhibit a binary long. They present the inevitable question of how to subdivide the breve and semibreve. In Hanboys's discussion of the imperfect long ("longa imperfecta duorum temporum"), he does not explicitly consider the situation where it consists of two perfect breves, but he does make reference to the imperfect long that consists of two imperfect breves with a total value of four semibreves ("longa valet...quatuor semibrevium...quando longa constat de duabus brevibus imperfectis").[97] In his music example illustrating this situation, the semibreves are ternary (see figure 44). The motet most similar in notational behavior is *O dira nacio*, in which there are many chains of paired semibreves. In those few instances where the breve is divided by three, the final semibreve has been given an upward minim stem, thus clarifying at one stroke that the breve is binary and the semibreve is ternary. In *Augustine par angelis* semibreves are rare, never syllabic, and appear only as ligated duplets. Rhythmic equality for these duplets seems a reasonable assumption. The same conclusion also seems to be the most plausible for *Te domina*, where only semibreve duplets are written. In neither case, however, can the possibility that paired semibreves are read unequally (trochaically?) be entirely ruled out. In *Tu civium* and *Virgo Maria* the subdivision of the breve into two and four semibreves (with rare triplets in the latter) makes clear that the semibreve duplets are equal. It seems most likely that we have here an example of an all-binary mensuration, perhaps even an example of *curta mensura*, but again the possibility of the inequality of the smallest semibreves cannot be ruled out.

The large-scale voice-exchange motets with sectional changes of mensuration, i.e., *Rota versatilis*, *A solis–Ovet*, and *Hostis Herodes*, along with a stylistically related free composition, *O crux vale*, are the remaining motets exhibiting features of binary mensuration of the long and breve. Each has one or two sections where motion in longs and breves is replaced by motion in breves and semibreves with a shift to the smaller units for declamation (see table 14 at the head of this chapter). In the last section of *Rota* and in the third section of *O crux*, the new mensuration is clearly binary on the level of the long.[98] In *A solis–Ovet* and *Hostis Herodes* the mensural organization is more complex, and some evidence speaks for the possibility of a ternary long in the even-numbered sections. The situation is as follows. In sections two and four of these pieces the phrase structures span twelve or eighteen breves, articulated in two or three 6B subphrases. Ambiguity arises in the interpretation of the 6B units as two perfect longs or three imperfect longs. Most evidence favors a binary long, including melodic facture, rhythmic patterning, textual syntax, placement of harmonic change and internal cadences, and the writing of ligatures and rests (the latter, with some exceptions to be noted, are all written as single breve-rests). These are challenged, however, by the rest-writing in the melismatic interludes that occur at the ends of these sections in *A solis–Ovet* and after each of the 18B phrases in the relevant sections of *Hostis Herodes*. Here the alternation of long- and breve rests clearly indicates that the long is ternary (see figure 45a). Moreover, contradictory configurations of long- and breve-rests appear in the untexted voices during the second section of *Hostis (Hic princeps)*. In the lower two parts they support a ternary reading of the long, but in the top voice they support a binary reading (see figure 45b). I take the rest-writing to be accidental (perhaps scribal whim or the mistaken grouping of single breve-

Figure 44.   Hanboys's Example of Imperfect Long and Breve

Lbl 8866, fol. 70v

Figure 45.   Rest-Writing in *Hostis Herodes*

a. 18B phrase pattern in three 6B subphrases: 6x2B + 2x3B,
   according to the written constellation of rests.

b. Section 2 of *Hostis Herodes (Hin princeps)*.

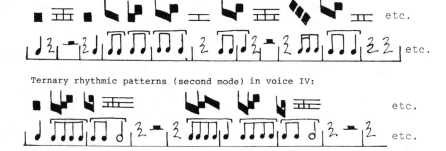

rests into imperfect long-rests) rather than essential to the character of the
mensuration, which rests on 6B subphrases that are to be understood
normally as consisting of three binary longs.[99]

The third section of *Rota versatilis (Rota Katerine)* is problematic in
another way. Here no two phrases are of the same length; the first two,
moreover, contain an even number of breves while the second two consist of
an odd number of breves (54B = 12B+14B+13B+15B).[100] No declamatory
pattern repeats on the phrase level. As a result, there is not much to

recommend an interpretation in binary longs over one in ternary longs. One can point out that the *signum rotundum* indicates a mensural shift at the start of this section, that the rests are single breve-rests grouped by twos (once, six are grouped by threes in *Lbl 24198*), and that the binary interpretation causes the form of the first two phrase endings to be the same (likewise for the second two), which would not be the case in a ternary reading.[101]

The method of division of the breve needs to be addressed here as well. In all of this last group, declamation is syllabic on semibreve duplets and melismatic on semibreve triplets. The frequency of appearance of triplets varies within each motet from section to section quite markedly, and also from motet to motet; triplets are considerably more numerous in *O crux vale* than in the others. As Bent has put it in regard to *Rota versatilis*: "Firm criteria for the interpretation of these semibreve groups are lacking."[102] She opts to render all semibreve duplets unevenly (2+1) in that piece. Given the characteristically insular form and counterpoint of these free compositions, the use of this insular method of breve subdivision seems plausible for all. As far as the relationship of note-values under changing mensurations in these sectional pieces is concerned, breve equivalency is incontrovertibly indicated. The shift in declamation and rate of general motion is therefore quite marked from section to section.

Other Insular Notational Peculiarities

The notation of Triumphus patet. *Triumphus patet* exhibits note-shapes in its triplum similar to some described by Hanboys. The varied and apparently inconsistent use of these shapes does not correspond to any of the practices cited by Hanboys or any other fourteenth-century theorist. Figure 46 details some of the configurations in which these note-shapes appear. Each configuration has the duration of a breve. It is clear, at the very least, that most semibreve shapes can adopt more than one value. It is likely that certain default rules are in operation for alteration and imperfection, and that by the use of some of these shapes such rules are overridden, perhaps creating shifts from a ternary to a binary division of the breve, or from a ninefold to a twelvefold subdivision.

Due to the near illegibility of the unique manuscript source, stems are hard to see and dots are hard to distinguish from dirt flecks. (Dots may possibly be used to subdivide some configurations as well as define breve units, though the latter is evidently their main function.) The correspondence between certain configurations with minims but no downstems and their counterparts with the oblique downward stem suggests, further, that the notation is not entirely consistent, and it certainly resists a fully consistent solution in transcription. Harrison, who devotes a paragraph to this notation

Figure 46. Configurations Equaling a Breve in *Triumphus patet*

The Note Shapes (in probable order from largest to smallest)

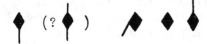

Notational Constellations Equaling a Breve (a selection)

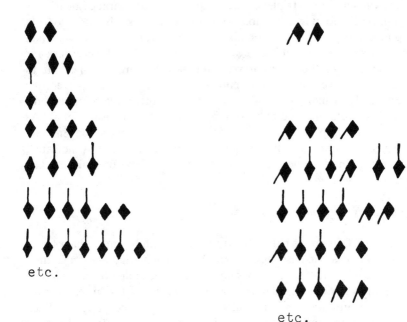

in the introduction to PMFC XV, concludes fairly that "though the rhythmic layout of the tenor and duplum (given an assumption about the perfection or imperfection of the brevis) provides a reasonably firm substructure, the details of the mensural rationale of the triplum must remain somewhat pragmatic."[103]

The signum rotundum. It will be useful to take a moment to explain the *signum rotundum* further. The little circle (*signum rotundum, figura rotunda, parvulum circulum*) has a variety of distinct uses in the theoretical and musical sources of late medieval England.[104] In roughly increasing order of significance these are as follows. (1) The circle (actually the sign ∅) is used as a "vide" symbol in the *Ob 652* version of *Rota versatilis* to indicate the correction of a scribal error (the RISM entry for *Ob 652*, and Wibberley in EECM 26, incorrectly call this a mensuration sign). (2) The circle indicates the pitch to which a plica must resolve in the music examples of *Lbl Royal 12.c.vi*, fol. 53v. (3) For some unknown purpose the circle is frequently placed over notes in the upper (mensurally notated) line of the compositions in the Robertsbridge codex (*Lbl 28550*). It may perhaps be a sign calling for some sort of ornamentation. (4) The circle is used to indicate a change of mensuration in *O crux vale, Rota versatilis,* and *Regne de pité*. Change of mode is coincident with change of section in these motets except in section four of *Rota versatilis,* where the change of mode from first to second between individual phrases is indicated this way.[105] (5) In Walter Odington's treatise, the circle replaces the *divisio modi* in its function of separating breve groups when (a) there are four to six semibreves per breve, or (b) when there are semibreve hockets where the *divisio* might be mistaken for a rest.[106] (6) Finally, the circle may be used to mark off each third of a ternary breve or each half of a binary breve, as in *Beatus vir* and *Hac a valle*. This is the use of the circle credited in Handlo and Hanboys to Johannes de Garlandia.

The brevis erecta. The *brevis erecta* is a form of the breve that is notated with an ascending left-hand tractus. It looks most like a plicated *brevis ascendens* that has lost its right-hand tractus. There are theoretical references to this note-shape in Handlo and Hanboys, who also report on the *longa erecta*.[107] Its use is to signal the temporary chromatic alteration of the note in question up a half-step.[108] In practice it is found on the pitches F and C, raising them to F# and C# as the leading tones to G and D in melodic cadences. The *brevis erecta* is relatively rare in surviving musical sources, and because it can be so easily mistaken for a misformed *brevis plicata* it may be that some awkward or otherwise inexplicable use of plicas on the leading tone at cadences (particularly in the discant and cantilena repertoires) may be a result of scribal confusion between the two symbols. The *brevis erecta* is unmistakably used in the motet repertoire only in *Tu civium* (*Cgc 512,* 4) and *Triumphus patet* (*Lbl 1210,* 2). Its appearance in conjunction with varied insular notational practices in these and other sources is striking.[109]

The notation of rests. The most important discussion of rests by an English theorist is found in Hanboys, who reviews a total of four different ways of writing them. He first presents the five rests of Franco as described in the *Ars cantus mensurabilis*.[110] Next to be covered are the eight rests according to the usage of the moderns: these are the familiar six shapes of de Vitry and Muris (including the semiminim form with hook to the right), augmented by one smaller value (with hook to the left) and a distinctive form of the perfect semibreve-rest (extending both above and below the line). As a general rule rests cannot be imperfected or altered, so there are not as many rests as note-values. The independent form of perfect semibreve-rest is therefore a useful addition to the standard complement. It is also found in the *Quatuor principalia* and the musical treatise of Petrus de Sancto Dionysio; representing the value of two-thirds of a perfect breve, it is found in the anonymous *De musica mensurabili* once attributed to Theodoricus de Campo.[111]

The third set of rests described by Hanboys is that of Robertus de Brunham. Brunham extends the "modern" concept of the perfect/imperfect pair of semibreve-rests to larger values—breve, long, and larga—thus increasing the total number of distinct rests to eleven.[112] The fourth and final set of rests we may take to be Hanboys's own. He provides a single rest-shape corresponding to each of the eight note-shapes proposed in his treatise, giving them no fixed value but rather taking the radical stand that each rest have the same nature as its corresponding note in respect to perfection and imperfection, alteration and diminution. For all four systems described by Hanboys, see figure 47.

What of these rest-shapes in the musical sources?[113] Brunham's form of the perfect long-rest is used in the motet *Veni creator spiritus* (*Ccc 65*, 2), otherwise notated in unexceptionable Franconian fashion, from a source all of whose other pieces are written in Ars Nova notation.[114] Among the motets in breve-semibreve notation, only the Taunton fragment *Geret et regem* uses the distinctive form of the perfect breve rest. *Nos orphanos* and *Zorobabel*, the only others that have considerable rest-writing, never rest for the duration of a perfect breve, but their forms for the imperfect breve-rest and perfect semibreve-rest correspond to those of Brunham.[115] Among motets in Ars Nova notation the number in *tempus perfectum maior* is small (see table 13, group 4) but significantly, the English rest-forms do appear, helping to establish that the rear leaves of *Ob 7* and *DRc 20* were copied in England. *Deus creator* (*Ob 7*, 14) is particularly rich in the variety of rests that it uses, but *Apta caro* (*DRc 20*, 18) and *Mon chant* (*DRc 20*, 19) also provide examples, especially of Brunham's perfect breve-rest. *Regne de pité* (*Ob 143*, 3) does not use the latter, but does employ the forms of the perfect semibreve-, imperfect semibreve-, and minim-rests. These distinctive forms are used as late as two English sources in void notation, *Lbl 40011B* (with its two motets) and *Cu 5943*.[116]

Taking the motet repertoire as a point of departure, it has been possible to establish a great deal about English notational practices in the fourteenth century. First, it is demonstrable that an English preference for the trochaic interpretation of undifferentiated paired semibreves holds both in Franconian ("ancient") and breve-semibreve ("modern") contexts, though not to the

Figure 47. Four Systems of Rests according to Hanboys

The Rests of Franco

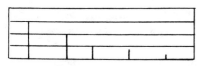

per.L imp.L B   maj.S min.S

The Rests of the Moderns

per.L imp.L B per.S. imp.S Mi SMi Ma

The Rests of Brunham

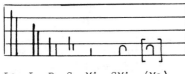

La L B S Mi SMi (Ma)   (per./imp. pairs)

Another Way of Writing Rests

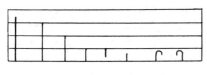

La DxL L B S Mi SMi Ma

La = larga
DxL = duplex long
L   = long
B   = breve
S   = semibreve
Mi = minor
SMi = semiminor
Ma = minima
per = perfect
imp = imperfect
maj = major
min = minor

exclusion of iambic practice in some pieces. A certain conservativeness in notation and rhythm evident in motets of the first quarter of the century is a result of an English preoccupation with musical forms and text setting that were possible using Franconian and Petronian notation.

The time of greatest innovation in English notational practice was in all likelihood the second quarter of the century, roughly between the completion of Handlo's essay (1326) and the compilation of the *Quatuor principalia* (1351), which already knows of, and complains about, the practices that Hanboys will link with the name of Frater Robertus de Brunham. Certain shadowy individuals named by Handlo and Hanboys, including Johannes Garlandia, W. de Doncastre, and Brunham, emerge as important innovators. Brunham, in particular, according to Hanboys, is responsible for the *cauda hirundinis*, special forms for rests, and special forms for c.o.p. ligatures. Though these are castigated by Hanboys and the author of the *Quatuor principalia*, they are found in many of the musical sources, testifying to their utility.

The most interesting motet source from the point of view of notation is *Lwa 12185*, with examples in the notations of Garlandia and Doncastre, a piece in breve-semibreve notation, and two others in Franconian and Petronian style. *Lbl 1210* and *Llc 52* are also important, the former for its juxtaposition of circle-stem notations with the unique notation of *Triumphus patet*, the latter for its juxtaposition of circle-stem and ternary breve-semibreve notations.

Insular notations have similarities to both French and Italian practices; the extent of influence and its direction are unclear. In general, however, the English notations show sufficient individuality and idiosyncracy to be regarded as insular responses to notational problems along lines of development parallel to those of the Continental musical cultures. All are responding to the same crisis, the need to codify and clarify rhythms when the breve is subdivided into four and more syllabic values, a practice inaugurated by Petrus de Cruce. French notational practices eventually are adopted in England, with an adherence to certain features of insular practice where possible (for instance, rest-writing in *tempus perfectum maior*). Milestones in the assimilaton of French practice are the introduction of the imperfect breve and freestanding single semibreve in *tempus perfectum*, the syllabic use of the minim, and eventually (in the later cantilenas), the appearance of the flagged semiminim.

4

The Texts of the Motets

The texts of the motets in the English repertoire constitute a relatively minor corpus of Latin poetry and heightened prose that is devoted almost exclusively to religious topics.[1] The motet is normally polytextual, so most complete compositions have a pair of texts with varying degrees of affinity in subject matter, length, and versification. Just as the polyphonic motet may be looked upon as a composite of melodies, so it may be considered a composite of texts, a polyphony of lyrics.[2] And just as music is expressed in number and sound, with *numerus* represented in the succession of melodic and harmonic pitch relationships, and in mensural structure and larger formal proportions as well, so the texts are governed by number (in syllable count and caesura, lengths of lines and stanzas, variety of stanzaic and strophic patterns) and sound (rhyme, assonance and alliteration, accent). As literary products of the late Middle Ages whose form and language are shaped by musical constraints and requirements as well as literary conventions, the texts—though mainly of unknown authorship and poorly understood provenance—perhaps deserve more attention than they have received until now.

The neglect of the texts of motets is not limited to the present repertoire, which has been virtually inaccessible even to specialists. Hendrik Van der Werf has recently made a call for more scholarly attention to the French texts of the well-known Montpellier codex, noting "it is still not known in what circles the [Parisian] motet, as a literary genre, originated." He goes on to observe that this ignorance extends to the Latin motets of the same manuscript, and that their contents, scrutinized for particular emphases, choices of words, and figures of speech, "may point to a certain period in the history of religion, devotion, or theology."[3] This holds equally well for the Latin texts of the English motets, which will require such expert scrutiny if they are to be brought out of isolation into a concrete literary and historical environment.[4] The present chapter will introduce the texts through a survey of general features of subject matter, content, and versification. Some consideration will be given to other repertoires of verse and music, with special emphasis on the thirteenth-century English motet and the devotional lyric.

Motet Subject Matter

The subject matter of the English motet[5] shows a heavy concentration on the lives of familiar saints, the Virgin Mary, and the greatest feasts of the church year—in effect, the highest ranking feasts of the *Sanctorale* and *Temporale* (see table 23). Secular texts, with the exception of *Sub arturo plebs*, are confined to the imported Continental motets that have not been provided with sacred Latin contrafacts. This emphasis on the sacred is apparent in the surviving contents of the most substantial collections of motet fragments from the first half of the century, which are given in table 24. (The late thirteenth-century source *Lwa 33327* is also included.)

In broadest terms, the motet lyrics are texts of praise and prayer. Some are simple prayers directed heavenward to God the Father, the Son, or the Holy Spirit, or sent through Mary or one of the saints as intercessor, for the well-being of the church or for individual salvation. The motet may speak of a saint or the significance of an occasion in the church year. These two approaches may be combined in a bipartite text that begins in expository fashion and then closes with a prayer, or a call for rejoicing or giving praise (for instance, put concisely—"Christ is risen; let us rejoice"). Often encountered is an ages-old tripartite form beginning with an invocation, following with a longer central section (enumerating complaints, recounting a saint's miracles), and closing with a petition for mercy or redress of grievances. The admonitory homily directed to an earthly audience is infrequently encountered. Nor is it usual to see a text that is cast as an individual's personalized statement of faith or contrition. The narrative voice is usually a communal one; the collective first person "nos" is much more common than the first person singular "ego."[6] A few texts are enlivened by the dramatic gesture of direct discourse, most often used during the narration of some story taken from the New Testament (Christ on the Cross, Mary Magdalene at the tomb, Paul on the road to Damascus).

While direct internal references to who is singing a motet are hard to find, references to musical performance are fairly frequent in the opening or closing verses. The participants are, however, usually specified only in the most general and commonplace terms:

psallat ergo plebs ovando	Ade finit
consonent omnia alleluia	Frondentibus
iubilando promat ecclesia sacra gaudia de virgine melliflua Maria	Orto sole
ergo pontifici solvant preconia clerus et layci cum diligencia	Salve cleri

Table 23. Subject Matter of Motets in England

	Saints	BVM	Feasts	Other	Total
Number	38	34	27	29	128
Percent	30	27	21	23	100%

Other =	God/Jesus	Admonitory	Secular	Problem
	9	7	10	3

Table 24. Contents of Selected Motet Sources, by Subject

Cgc 512	Lwa 12185
Katherine	Ascension
Common of Apostles	Nicholas
BVM	Trinity
Peter	Michael
Holy Spirit (Pentecost)	Christmas
Thomas	
Jonathan and Absalon	Lwa 33327
BVM	
BVM	BVM
	Christmas
DRc 20 (front leaves)	Easter
	Peter and Paul
Holy Innocents	Pentecost
contrition	Thomas
Jesus	Edward
Common of Apostles	Nicholas
John the Baptist	
Easter	Ob 7 (front leaves)
BVM	
	Mary Magdalene
Lbl 40011B*	penitence
	Peter
Katherine	God
Margaret	Benedict
Katherine(?)	Andrew
William	Easter
	Edmund
	Edmund
	Dedication of a church
	Easter

modulamina per totum celica	
canunt hodie colegia	
gaude dicencia	Tu civium
Laudes extollens martiris	
chorus hic letabundus	
salvatur nexu sceleris	
ut Deo fiat mundus.	De flore

Praise and rejoicing are the main themes of the foregoing quotations, to which a few more examples mentioning music but not participants can be added, including:

Ideo Christum colimus	
laudamus modulis musicis	
pro tot beneficiis.	Laus honor
adorant cum notulis modulis dulcissimis	
et canticis organicis plurimis.	Alma mater
preconia laudum	
cum melodia canora	
celebrant hodie.	Tu civium
Ipsum vocemus iugiter	
suspiriis suaviter	
per vocis laudem carminis.	Jhesu redemptor

These references sometimes invoke all Christian folk as participants in song; others refer just to the church, or to clerics and laymen, or more specifically to a choir: "nostri chorus ordinis" (*Ob 7*, 4) or "musicorum collegium" (*DRc 20*, 17). A most tantalizing reference of this type is to the "chorus monachorum" mentioned in the badly preserved lower part of *Baptizas parentes*. One further petition for aid makes a subtle reference to a cloistered order:

Hinc rogamus precibus	
ut serves a malis	
circumseptos menibus	
curie claustralis.	Parce piscatoribus

(Therefore we beseech in our prayers
that you may save from evils
those encircled by the walls
of the cloister-garth.)

An overt acknowledgment of narrative function is often expressed in the texts, underlining an account of a saint's life and death, miracles, or familiar emblems. Such statements include the following:

De flore martirum...canamus hodie	De flore
tabitam vivam legimus ex eius titulis	Petrum cephas
multiplex miraculum te canit hodie	Salve cleri
mult as des noms en prophetie	Regne de pité
Sic patent et rutilant Edwardi nec latitant vite mores et dogmata quam plurima	Civitas nusquam

and the impetus behind them all is expressed clearly in

facta fidem firmant relatui	Ave miles.

That is, these facts are intended, in their retelling, to strengthen faith. The lyrics make a lively tapestry akin to the stained glass, carvings, wall hangings, paintings, and inscriptions with which the interiors and exteriors of churches were ornamented. The reference to "titulis" in the line from *Petrum cephas* is instructive in this regard. A "titulus" could be in medieval usage a religious or moral verse, sometimes used in public inscriptions as a caption, i.e., a written accompaniment to illustrations on altars, walls, or windows, and the like. These motets similarly keep alive and renew the Christian stories.[7]

In view of the topical coverage and specific content of these texts, and the nature of those institutions known to have supported polyphony before the rise of collegiate and aristocratic chapels, it seems most probable that the texts are essentially liturgical rather than devotional, leaving open the question of where in the specific ritual of daily services the motet might have found a place. (On that vexed issue, see chapter 1.) This raises the question of how securely we can fix the occasion(s) in the church year for which a motet may have been intended. Many texts, readily identifiable as to subject, are not so specific in content that they are appropriate for a single day only; the correspondence between subject matter and liturgical calendar is not always explicit. However, most can be assigned to a particular feast through some reference or other in the language of the text. Two sets of motet fragments, *Onc 362* and *Lbl 24198*, still bear legible marginal rubrics that identify each item, e.g., "de sancto Edwardo" (see table 25). This style of rubrication, familiar from liturgical books, suggests that these two motet collections were intended as resources to be drawn upon for the celebration of certain feasts. In neither, though, were the motets in calendrical order according to the liturgical year. In *Lbl 24198* we happen to know the order was alphabetical instead.

Some evidence allows an estimate to be made of the size and means of organization of thirteenth- and fourteenth-century English collections. From the thirteenth century, fragments in *Lbl 5958* are from an alphabetically

Table 25.   Rubrics in *Lbl 24198* and *Onc 362*

Lbl 24198: rubric usually split between verso and recto

motet	rubric	original foliation
Rota	(de sancta) katerina	(R) VI
Rosa mundi	de sancta (maria)	R (VII or VIII?)
*Regis aula	de sancta (maria)	
Trinitatem	de sancta trinitate	T II
Te domina	de sancta maria	T (III or IV?)
Triumphat	de sancto (laurencio)	

Onc 362: rubric entire on one margin (on verso if motet laid out across an opening)

motet	rubric	original foliation
Ianuam	de sancto thoma cantuarie	LXXv
Triumphat	de sancto laurencio	LXXIv
Civitas	de sancto edwardo	LXXVIv
Excelsus	de sancto thoma cantuarie	LXXVII
Ade finit	de resurrectione	LXXVIIv
Solaris	de sancto (augustino)	LXXXII
*Fulget	de sancto petro	LXXXVIIIv
*Sanctorum	(too worn to read)	XC

organized codex (items from B survive, two of which are numbered X and XII); the famous Harleian index (*Lbl 978 (LoHa)*, fols.160v–161) preserves textual incipits for 164 items in a lost codex that was arranged by musical genre (see below); *Ccc 8* has paginations up to 558; Dittmer's Worcester volume I has foliations up to cxxxviii; *Lwa 33327* has headings for "quadruplices" and "triplices." From the fourteenth century, *Onc 362* has foliations up to xc; *Ccc 65* has foliations up to c; *Llc 52* and *Ob 652* may come from alphabetically arranged collections; and *Lbl 24198* (an alphabetically arranged codex with items extant from R, S, T) has numerations for each letter implying either eight compositions per letter, or eight pages per letter. A book with 100 or more compositions may reasonably be extrapolated.[8]

What we can tell of motet codices from the extant fragments suggests that the majority were devoted exclusively to motets or else had large integral gatherings of motets. Some sources mix motets with discant and cantilena settings; these are mainly from later in the century. Most were manuscript books but a number were *rotuli* (*Ob 652, Lpro 261*, and *BERc 55* are the only ones identified as such to date).[9] Some, such as *Ccc 8*, were large anthologies of several hundred pieces. Others, perhaps the majority, were reasonable working collections of perhaps 60 to 100 pieces. Some sources were certainly smaller than that, with fewer pieces. In a few cases motets were entered onto blank pages of a book (*Yc*) or entered into what amounts to a commonplace book of music and other materials (*Cgc 512*, which may in fact represent a "complete" collection). From the earlier to the later fourteenth century there may also be a historical trend away from large working collections (of 60 to 100 motets) to smaller collections (on the order of 10 to 15). If this is eventually verifiable, then it probably reflects either a change in motet function, a change in the institutions cultivating the motet, or both.

The failure of even a single English motet collection of any size to survive in full deprives us of ready means by which to determine the normal number of motets in such a book, the usual distribution of subject matter, and the internal ordering (if in fact there were norms for any of these). The lack of an integral collecton is made up in part by the survival in *Lbl 978 (LoHa)* of the index to a now lost book of English polyphony from the later thirteenth century (ca. 1290). The primary contents of this lost codex consisted of a series of 37 Alleluias, 38 conductus, and 81 motets (see table 26).[10]

The *LoHa* Alleluias form a series of feasts from the *Sanctorale* and *Temporale* running in chronological order from Christmas to December 6 (Saint Nicholas), hence spanning the church year and conveniently defining for some institution those occasions on which festal polyphony was provided at mass.[11] It seems reasonable that the conductus and motets that follow provided a repertoire to draw from on the same occasions, if not in fact more often, whether they were music for mass or office. They are grouped into gatherings defined by musical criteria. A few of the motets in the index can be identified with surviving compositions, but the greater number are unfortunately known only through their *LoHa* incipit, which means some ambiguity must inevitably remain in the determination of their subject matter. Nonetheless, it is clear that Marian subjects predominate, as the BVM can be associated with over half the incipits. (Among the Alleluias, by contrast, only about a third (12 of 37) of the total are Marian.) A fair number of the remainder are on saints.

We need to ask to what degree we can learn about the typical subject matter of a single motet collection from the surviving corpus. On the basis of two assumptions—(1) that the makeup of most contemporaneous motet collections was basically the same and (2) that the survival of motets is basically random—the surviving specimens as a group ought to constitute a reasonable approximation of the contents of a motet codex in regard to distribution of subject matter. In fact, the correlation between subject matter coverage in the *LoHa* index and surviving thirteenth-century English motets is gratifying. If the latter are canvassed for their subject matter, we find 50 percent on the BVM and nearly all the rest devoted to Jesus or the saints.[12] This gives us confidence that the percentages in table 23 provide a reasonably accurate picture of an "idealized" fourteenth-century collection of medium size.

Table 26. The *LoHa* Index

Ordo libri W. de Winton

1.1 Spiritus et alme. R. de Burgate
1.2 Rex omnium lucifluum.i.Regnum tuum solidum
1.3 Item Regnum tuum solidum
1.4 Virgo decora. Virgo dei genitrix
1.5 All. Virginis inviolate. Virga Iesse
1.6 All. Gaude mundi domina. Gaude virgo
1.7 All. Salve virgo domini. Salve virgo
1.8 All. Virga ferax

Postea Responsoria W. de Wicumbe

2.1	All. Dies sanctificatus	Dec. 25 Christmas
2.2	All. Video celos apertos	Dec. 26 St. Steven
2.3	All. Hic est discipulus	Dec. 27 St. John
2.4	All. Te martirum	Dec. 28 Holy Inn.
2.5	All. Gloria et honore	Dec. 29 St. Thomas
2.6	All. Multiphariam	Dec. 31 Circum.
2.7	All. Vidimus stellam	Jan. 6 Epiphany
2.8	All. Adorabo	Feb. 2 Purif.
2.9	Item All. Adorabo	Pur. or oct.
2.10	All. Pascha nostrum	Easter
2.11	Item Pascha nostrum	Easter
2.12	All. Dulce lignum	May 3 Inv.Holy Cross
2.13	All. Ascendens Christus	Ascension
2.14	Item Ascendens Christus	Ascen. or oct.
2.15	All. Paraclitus	Pentecost
2.16	All. Benedictus es Domine	Trinity
2.17	All. Inter natos	June 24 John Bapt.
2.18	All. Tu es Symon Bariona	June 29 Peter, Paul
2.19	All. Non vos me elegistis	July 25 St. James
2.20	All. Levita Laurencius	Aug. 10 St. Lawr.
2.21	All. Hodie Maria virgo	Aug. 15 Assump.
2.22	All. Nativitas gloriose	Sept. 8 BVM Nat.
2.23	All. In conspectu	Sept. 29 St. Michael
2.24	All. Judicabunt	Nov. 1 All Saints
2.25	All. Hic Martinus	Nov. 11 St. Martin
2.26	All. Veni electa	Nov. 25 St. Kath.
2.27	All. Dilexit Andream	Nov. 30 St. Andrew
2.28	All. Tumba Sancti Nicholai	Dec. 6 St. Nicholas
2.29	All. Justus germinabit	St. Nicholas

2.30 All. Ave Maria
2.31 All. Salve virgo
2.32 All. Gaude virgo
2.33 All. Porta Syon

Table 26. (continued)

4   Motetti cum una littera et duplici nota

4.1   Gloriemur crucis in preconio
4.2   Mundialis glorie
4.3   Salve virgo que salvasti
4.4   Reges Tharsis et insule   Epiphany
4.5   Radix Iesse
4.6   Nimis honorati sunt   apostles
4.7   Omnis sexus gaudeat
4.8   Ave pater inclite   ?saint
4.9   Christi miles rex Edmundus   Edmund
4.10 Zelo crucis innocens
4.11 Veritatis vere testis
4.12 Ad gloriam deice
4.13 Homo quam ingratus

5   Motetti cum duplici littera

5.1   Quem non capit
5.2   Super te Ierusalem
5.3   Precipue mihi dant
5.4   Presul ave flos presulum   Nicholas
5.5   De stirpe Davitica
5.6   Plausit sterilis
5.7   Sancte Dei preciose   Steven
5.8   Anima mea liquefacta est
5.9   Descendi in ortum meum
5.10 O felicem genitricem
5.11 Mira federa
5.12 Salve gemma virginum
5.13 O Maria vas mundicie
5.14 Maria laudis materia
5.15 Benedicta sis lucerna
5.16 In Domino gaudeat   Easter
5.17 Epulemur et letemur   Easter
5.18 Resurgente salvatore   Easter

6   Item moteti cum duplici nota

6.1   Claro paschali   Easter
6.2   Mira virtus Petri   Peter

7   Item cum duplici littera

7.1   In sanctis est mirabilis   saint
7.2   In te martir patuit   martyr

It is noteworthy that in the early fourteenth-century repertoire, Marian motets drop from 50 percent to nearer 25 percent of the total number, with an increase in the proportion of motets on saints and those assignable to particular feasts of the *Temporale*.[13] If the shift in subject matter is real rather than merely a fiction of faulty data, there may be cumulative historical and liturgical reasons for it, constituting the sum of many changes within specific liturgical institutions. A thirteenth-century model for these changes may be the enhancement of the liturgy at the Royal Abbey of St. Denis in Paris in the years 1234 through 1259, when many new feasts and new processions to chapels in the chevet were added, and many established feasts were dramatically elevated in rank, especially affecting saints.[14] Though the emphasis on Mary in English polyphony remains considerable, the drop in the percentage of motets devoted to her is significant. It is possible that the composition of Marian cantilena settings affected the total number of new Marian motets being composed, not replacing the motet directly but substituting a different form of polyphony for the celebration of her feasts.

A medium-sized motet collection with a distribution of subject matter equivalent to that suggested by the fourteenth-century remains would be not unlike a sequentiary in size and topical coverage. In terms of the liturgical calendar, there is a direct congruence between the saints and holidays for which a sequence is provided and feasts of highest rank (in both secular and monastic calendars). Therefore a sequence repertoire, like the *LoHa* Alleluia series, would define a certain body of feasts that might require motets. In both the sequence and motet repertoires, concordances between surviving sources are high in number; most of the repertoire was held in common by many institutions, with few pieces of local origin or pertaining to a local saint. In addition there are pieces for the Common of Saints and for the Proper of Time, such as for the anniversary of the dedication of a church. (This point will be developed below with respect to the motet.) As in major sequentiaries, some of the motet sources have more than one motet on a saint. In the case of the motets, this might be explained in part simply as the preservation of popular pieces from an earlier repertoire when the present source was compiled. But of course, the more highly ranked saints might have more pieces because they have more feasts requiring adornment with a sequence or motet.

A point needs to be made about the noticeable lack of liturgical order in the fragments of motet collections that survive. A certain disorderliness from a calendrical point of view in a given book does not necessarily speak against the hypothesis of a liturgical function for its motets. It could merely indicate that convenience of access to any specific piece was either not a high priority or not considered a problem (most collections would have had indices). Also, this attitude toward organization may be indicative of the volatile or transitory nature of the collection in the contemporary view—in other words, that polyphony was seen as a fluid body of material subject to additions or deletions in part or in whole over a relatively short time span. By contrast, a chant book transmitted a rather stable repertoire and could be expected to serve, if well made and conveniently organized, for a very long time.

Table 27 provides a systematic listing of the fourteenth-century motets by subject, beginning with a calendrical series from Christmas through Advent in parallel with the ordering of the *LoHa* Alleluias (i.e., with an interruption after the Purification of the BVM for the movable feasts of the Easter season). The list has been augmented by the inclusion of relevant thirteenth-century items (enclosed in parentheses) and relevant nonmotet items (given an asterisk) to give as complete a picture as present knowledge permits of the saints for whom polyphony survives in England through the fourteenth century. Where subject matter is not explicit about the particular occasion of use (as in some compositions in honor of a saint, for instance) the motet has been placed in the highest possible feast (and when a name might apply to a number of saints, the most likely identity has been adopted). Marian motets, and others whose subject matter is not readily assignable to any date in the church year, are separately listed afterwards.

Saints appearing as the subjects of motets include such long-established and internationally popular figures as Nicholas, Katherine of Alexandria, Thomas of Canterbury, Peter, Lawrence, Margaret, and various of the apostles. They are joined by saints of the religious and monastic orders such as Benedict, Augustine of Hippo, Martin of Tours, and Augustine of Canterbury, as well as other British saints of varying degrees of renown such as Edmund of East Anglia, Edward (King and Confessor), William of York, Augustine of Canterbury, and two minor Anglo-Saxon women, Eadburga and Wenefreda. If no mechanism skewed the extant distribution of subject matter, then chance survival ought to insure a spread of subjects favoring motets on the more common and highly ranked saints of the church (represented in most collections with one or more pieces) over those dedicated to more local figures.[15] This is pretty well borne out, as table 27 demonstrates, especially by the numbers of motets on Thomas, Katherine, and Nicholas.[16]

Regarding the motets of the *Temporale*, there is a predictable concentration on the holidays of the Christmas and Easter seasons. We find pieces for Christmas Day, Holy Innocents, Saint Thomas, and Epiphany (with Marian motets on the Annunciation and Nativity perhaps augmenting the number for Christmas as motets simply "de nativitate"), and there are motets for Easter, Ascension, Pentecost, and Trinity Sunday. The Easter motets can be divided into three distinct groups, Passion motets (*Barrabas dimittitur*, *Laus honor*, and *Mons olivarum*), Resurrection motets (e.g., *Ade finit*, *Frondentibus*), and motets on Mary Magdalene at the tomb (*Maria mole pressa* and *Valde mane diluculo*). Within the first and third of these groups the similarity of approach and language is striking.

Table 27. Systematic Listing of Motets by Subject Matter

Motets of the Temporale and Sanctorale

Date	Occasion (LoHa Alleluia)	Motet (13th C. bracketed) (* for non-motet item)
Dec. 25	Christmas LoHa 2.1	A solis-Salvator A solis-Ovet mundus Rogativam potuit (O nobilis nativitas) *In exclesis gloria BVM motets "de nativitate"
Dec. 26	St. Stephen LoHa 2.2	(Sancte Dei pretiose LoHa 5.7)
Dec. 27	St. John, Ap. LoHa 2.3	
Dec. 28	Holy Innocents LoHa 2.4	Herodis in pretorio
Dec. 29	St. Thomas LoHa 2.5	Excelsus in numine Ianuam quam clauserat O dira nacio Thomas gemma (O mores perditos) (Opem nobis) (Pastor gregis LoHa 3.31) (Salve Thomas flos LoHa 3.32)
Dec. 31	Circumcision LoHa 2.6	
Jan. 6	Epiphany LoHa 2.7	Balaam de quo Hostis Herodes Surgere iam est (Reges Tharsis LoHa 4.4)
Jan. 25	Conv. of St. Paul	Vas exstas eleccionis
Feb. 2	BVM Purification LoHa 2.8 LoHa 2.9	
Mar. 21	St. Benedict	Lux refulget monachorum

Apr. 29	St. Peter of Verona	(O decus predicantium)
	Easter	Barrabas dimittitur
	LoHa 2.10	Laus honor vendito (+Holy Cross)
	LoHa 2.11	Mons olivarum
		Maria mole pressa (+Mary Magd.)
		Valde mane diluculo
		*Felix Magdalene LoHa 3.25
		Ade finit perpete
		Alta canunt assistentes
		Frondentibus
		Parata paradisi porta (+BVM)
		Si lingua lota (+BVM)
		(O mors moreris)
		(In Domino gaudeat LoHa 5.16)
		(Epulemur et letemur LoHa 5.17)
		(Resurgente salvatore LoHa 5.18)
		(Claro paschali LoHa 6.1)
		(O Iudee nepharie LoHa 7.16)
		*Ave caro Christi LoHa 3.9
		*Resurrexit Dominus LoHa 3.38
	Ascension	Viri Galilei
	LoHa 2.13	
	LoHa 2.14	
	Pentecost	Suspiria merentis
	LoHa 2.15	Ut recreentur spiritus
		Veni creator spiritus
		(Domine celestis rex)
		(Dona celi factor)
		*Veni sancte spiritus LoHa 3.10
		*Veni creator spiritus LoHa 3.1
		*Veni creator spiritus LoHa 7.12
	Trinity	Beatus vir
	LoHa 2.16	Deus creator omnium
		Firmissime fidem
		Trinitatem veneremur
May 3	Inv. of Holy Cross	Laus honor (+Easter)
	LoHa 2.12	Ma insuper et tymiata
		O crux vale
		Triumphus patet hodie
May 26	Augustine of Cant.	Augustine par angelis
		Solaris ardor

Table 27.   (continued)

June 8	William of York	Hostium ob amorem
June 15	St. Eadburga	(Virgo regalis fidei)
June 24	Nat. John Bapt. LoHa 2.17	Dei preco (+Decap. Aug. 29) (Zacharie par helie LoHa 7.22) *Zacharie filius LoHa 3.29
June 29	Peter and Paul LoHa 2.18	Petrum cephas Tu civium primas (Pro beati Pauli) (Pro beati Pauli) (Tu capud ecclesie) (Mira virtus Petri LoHa 6.2) (Roma felix decorata LoHa 7.43) *Fulget celestis *Quem trina polluit
June 30	Commem. St. Paul	Vas exstas (+Conv.) ?Inter usitata (+BVM) ?(O spes et salus) (+BVM)
July 20	St. Margaret	Absorbet oris faucibus *Virgo vernans velud rosa
July 22	Mary Magdalene	Maria mole pressa (+Easter) Valde mane diluculo *Felix Magdalene LoHa 3.25
July 25	St. James LoHa 2.19	Parce piscatoribus Nec Herodis ferocitas (Senator regis curie)
Aug. 4	Simon de Montfort	(Miles Christi gloriose) (Salve Symon Montisfortis)
Aug. 5	St. Dominic	?*In celesti ierarchia LoHa 3.2
Aug. 10	St. Lawrence LoHa 2.20	Triumphat hodie Christi
Aug. 15	BVM Assumption LoHa 2.21	
Aug. 20	St. Bernard	Detentos a demonibus Regina iam discubuit Venit sponsa de Libano
Aug. 24	St. Bartholomew	O pater excellentissime (O sancte Bartholomee)

Aug. 28	Augustine of Hippo	Assunt Augustini
		Jhesu redemptor omnium
Sept. 8	BVM Nativity	
	LoHa 2.22	
Sept. 29	St. Michael	Nos orphanos erige
	LoHa 2.23	(Te Domine laudat)
Oct. 4	St. Francis	*Alleluia. Hic Franciscus
Oct. 13	St. Edward	Civitas nusquam
		(Ave miles de cuius)
		*Regem regum
Nov. 1	All Saints	
	LoHa 2.24	
Nov. 3	St. Winifred	Inter choros paradisicolarum
Nov. 6	St. Leonard	*Alleluia. Fit leo fit Leonardus
Nov. 11	St. Martin	Baptizas parentes
	LoHa 2.25	
Nov. 20	St. Edmund	Ave miles celestis
		De flore martirum
		Flos anglorum inclitus
		(Christi miles rex Edmundus LoHa 4.9)
Nov. 25	St. Katherine	Flos regalis
	LoHa 2.26	Mulier magni meriti
		Rota versatilis
		Virginalis concio
		Virgo sancta Katerina
		(Virgo ...manet lux)
		(Virgo regalis fidei)
		(Virgo sancta Katerina)
		(Virgo sancta Katerina LoHa 7.26)
		(Katerina lex divina LoHa 7.27)
		?(Clericorum sanctitate LoHa 7.28)
		*Katerina progenie LoHa 3.36
		*O laudanda virginitas
Nov. 30	St. Andrew	Duodeno sydere
	LoHa 2.27	(In odore)
		*Andreas celici LoHa 3.7
		*Dux Andrea LoHa 3.8
Dec. 3	St. Barbara	(Barbara simplex animo)

Table 27.   (continued)

Dec. 6   St. Nicholas   Hac a valle
              LoHa 2.28   Salve cleri
              LoHa 2.29   (Psallat chorus)
                                    (Salve gemma confessorum)
                                    (Sospitati dedit)
                                    (Presul ave flos presulum LoHa 5.4)
                                    (Salve gemma confesorum LoHa 7.29)

Motets to the BVM

Annunciation/Nativity of Christ

Ancilla Domini
Caligo terre
Candens crescit
Exulta Syon filia
Geret et regem
Orto sole
Quid rimari
Syderea celi cacumina
Zelo tui

Nativity of the BVM

Iam nubes
Rosa delectabilis

BVM Assumption

Alma mater
Detentos a demonibus (and St. Bernard)
Regina iam (and St. Bernard)
Venit sponsa de Libano (and St. Bernard)

General Texts to the BVM

Ad lacrimas flentis
Apta caro plumis
Corona virginum
Cuius de manibus
Lingua peregrina
Peregrina moror
Pura placens
Patrie pacis
Radix Iesse
Regina celestium
Regne de pite[a]
Rex omnipotencie
Rosa mundi

Salve sancta virgula
Te domina
Virgo Maria
Vos quid admiramini

Exceptional BVM texts

Inter usitata (Immaculate Conception and St. Paul)
Parata paradisi porta (BVM memorials during Eastertide)
Si lingua lota (+Easter)
Soli fines (mention of Carmelites)
Suffragiose virgini (setting of rhymed Marian legenda)

Other Topics

Common of Apostles (some specific apostle?)

Princeps apostolice

Dedication of a Church

Templum eya

Jesus/God

Domine quis
In ore te laudancium
Humane lingue
Jhesu fili Dei
Omnis terra
Quare fremuerunt
Regi regum enarrare
Regnum sine termino
Rex invictissime

Homiletic, Contrition or Admonition

Apello cesarem
Degentis vita
Fusa cum silentio
Inter amenitatis
O homo considera
Vide miser
Zorobabel abigo

Secular

Amer amours
Alme pater

Table 27.   (continued)

Deus compaignouns
L'amoreuse flour
Mon chant
O canenda vulgo
Musicorum collegio
Rex Karole
Sub arturo plebs
Tribum quem

Problems

Doleo super te (liturgical or non-liturgical?)
O vos omnes (dedication, admonition, or secular)
Rex piaculum (tropic chant setting of Alleluia?)

Viewed as a whole, though, the motets of Christmas and Eastertide do not form as large a percentage of the total repertoire as might be expected from their central position in the liturgical year. Perhaps it is the wealth of ritual unique to these feasts that precludes a larger number of motets; the more elaborate the liturgy, the less necessity there was for its augmentation with this form of polyphony, if the motet is limited to liturgical functions. Hence a single motet might suffice for either Christmas Day or Easter Sunday just as one would suffice on the feast of Saint Lawrence or John the Baptist.[17]

The motets on Mary are mainly less specific in their content than those for saints and high holidays. Most cannot be clearly associated with any particular Marian feast, but rather are very general in nature. Some were presumably votive motets, just as there were votive sequences.[18] A number of these more general Marian texts are primarily catalogues of her epithets. As it is put in *Regne de pité*, "mult as des noms": many are her names. She is the reembodiment of Judith and Esther, the antithesis of Eve, the withered branch that flowered, a sweet remedy, a healer, a guide along the path to Heaven, a blossom surpassing all others in fragrance and appearance, and so on. *Rosa mundi, Te domina,* and *Virgo Maria* show how easily this cataloguing is adaptable to situations in which musical considerations such as variable phrase structures and declamation call for irregular texting.

Some motets on Mary are clearly most appropriate for her Nativity, Annunciation and the Christmas season, or Easter. *Inter usitata* is on her Immaculate Conception, and in this motet (as well as in the thirteenth-century motet *O spes et salus*) her name is linked with that of Saint Paul. In two or three more (the motets of *CAc 128/2*) she is associated with Saint Bernard, whose feast day (August 20) falls within the octave of her Assumption (August 15).

The most remarkable BVM texts in terms of subject matter are those of *Suffragiose virgini*, which narrate two Marian *legenda* in verse. The texts are hard to read, but appear to be miracles of Our Lady similar in approach to the sorts of tales told in prose or verse in a multitude of later medieval sources, both in Latin and the vernacular.[19] Collections of such *exempla* and *fabulae* proliferated rapidly in the later Middle Ages, so much so that they are roughly comparable in quantity even to that other popular genre, saints' lives. No search has yet found a concordance to either story set in the motet.

Determining subject matter is normally not a problem but some decisions are unavoidably interpretive and, consequently, arbitrary to some degree. Two motets whose assignment to Trinity Sunday is fairly certain show the sort of analysis that is occasionally required. *Deus creator* has as its text incipits the initial lines of two Latin-texted Kyries, *Deus creator omnium* and *Rex genitor*. Both have the often-encountered Trinitarian format in which the first three acclamations concern God the Father, the second three God the Son, and the final three God the Holy Spirit. The motet triplum goes on to concern the three persons of the Trinity, though not in the specific language or content of the Kyrie text, while the duplum deals with the life of Christ from His conception to His ascension. Both motet texts are thus, in their own ways, appropriate to Trinity Sunday, though no internal reference explicitly and unambiguously calls for the use of the motet on that day. The assignment of *Beatus vir* to Trinity Sunday is similarly hypothetical. It is suggested by text content ("unum in trinitate sed trinum in unitate"), but since only one text survives, doubts can still be entertained. An association with Trinity Sunday is strengthened, though, by the following: many Proper chants for Trinity begin with some version of a blessing for the Lord, for instance "Benedicta sit Deus," "Benedictus es Domine," or "Benedicimus Deum." The tenor of *Beatus vir* is perhaps the most familiar such formula, "Benedicamus Domino." The duplum is assonant with this tenor, and it is likely that the missing triplum was also assonant, perhaps even through the citation of some blessing formula. Hence the entire motet, resonant with verbal associations to Trinity chants, would have been especially apt for performance that day.[20]

Another miscellaneous class of pieces that presents difficulty in liturgical assignment is that small number about the moral conduct of life grouped together in table 27 under the heading "Contrition or Admonition."[21] On account of its tenor, one late-thirteenth-century example of this textual genre, *O mores perditos-O gravis confusio-T.Opem nobis*, has been assigned a place within the calendrical section of table 27 on the feast of Saint Thomas of Canterbury. Its tenor is a well-known chant from Thomas's office, and the texts appear to be suitable moral commentary for his commemoration. This kind of assignment, based in the first place on the source of the tenor, is less convincing in cases such as those presented by *Apello cesarem* and *Fusa cum silentio*. Their tenors are drawn from graduals for Christmas and Saint John's

Day (December 27), respectively, but are traditional cantus firmi frequently used for the tenors of motets from the days of the earliest clausula and motet repertoires of Notre Dame. The very popularity of these tenors calls into question the direct association of motet and feast on their account. Neither are the subjects of the motets obviously suitable: *Apello* rues the temptations and pitfalls awaiting a good man in this world, and *Fusa cum silentio* deals with a theme common to the friars' preaching handbooks, the too-noisy prayer or *oratio clamorosa*.[22] Another dimension needs to be considered, however. *Vide miser* is set to a tune named "Wynter," and if this tenor was chosen not merely for its symbolic associations but also because of the time of year in which the motet was sung, then it may be that "homiletic motets" were traditionally sung during the cold months, perhaps specifically between Christmas and Epiphany.[23]

Only three motets present truly insoluble problems in assignment. Too much of the text of *Rex piaculum* (*TAcro 3182,* 2) is illegible to allow determination of subject matter beyond the fact that the piece is probably a tropic chant setting of an Alleluia. *O vos omnes*, the duplum text of an imported motet, voices a tone of cynical, secular complaint against the worldliness of the church which is closer to that of the lyrics of de Vitry than to any insular motet texts save perhaps those of *Trinitatem veneremur*. It is impossible to say whether the lost triplum may have had more political overtones or conversely, that it spoke in friendlier fashion of the dedication of some church building, an occasion that might have called forth a musical sermon with elements of both chastising and rejoicing.

The third problematic piece, *Doleo super te*, presents a different sort of dilemma for both of its texts are preserved, perfectly legible, and are well known. They are ultimately derived from the Bible, but the composer's more immediate source was two antiphons for the Magnificat drawn from a series provided for a stretch of Sundays after Trinity.[24] (The motet's cantus firmus is also drawn from one of these two antiphons.) The texts describe David grieving for his son Absolom and for Jonathan. The use of antiphons for two different occasions seems a barrier to liturgical employment, and Sanders claims "there can be little doubt that the motet is unliturgical."[25]

Two further motet fragments, each merely an isolated voice (*Templum eya Salomonis* and *Princeps apostolice*), provide further interesting testimony on the subject matter orientation of the English motet. They suggest that there might be such a thing as a motet belonging to the Common of Time or Saints and made Proper to suit the needs of individual institutions and their calendars. The text of *Templum eya Salomonis* makes the traditional association of the new celestial Jerusalem with Solomon's temple. This tradition further associates both of these with the Christian sanctuary on earth, particularly (and most familiarly) in the words of the dedication rite.[26]

Double-versicle couplings of melodies with text stanzas in the surviving part are strikingly suggestive of the sequence tradition (see figure 48). One sequence, in particular, which functions "in dedicatione ecclesie," may have been a direct source of influence: *Rex Salomon fecit templum.*[27] Its seventh stanza, emphasizing the trinity:

> sed tres partes sunt in templo
> trinitatis sub exemplo
> ima summa media

may have inspired the threefold "intus, foris, ibi" device that so markedly structures *Templum eya.* A dedication poem by Walter of Chatillon that begins:

> Templum veri Salomonis
> dedicatur hodie
> Deus trinus in personis
> unius essentie

has a striking resemblance to *Templum eya* in its opening line, but the motet text and Walter's poem do not prove to be any more closely related. The poem, in fact, is much more closely dependent on the sequence than the motet text is.[28]

Given these associations it is likely that the motet was in fact meant for performance in celebration of the anniversary of the dedication of a church, one of the feasts of highest rank in its calendar. Since the provenance of its source is Bury St. Edmunds, it was probably intended for festivities in honor of the abbey church. It may never be known whether the motet was written initially for Bury or whether instead it was borrowed and altered to be suitable, or whether indeed its missing text may have been so general in reference that it was suitable for any number of institutions. There are motets extant that show how this last possibility might work. The most unequivocal example is the thirteenth-century motet *Virgo regalis fidei*, which is more or less appropriate for any virgin-martyr with a four-syllable name. In its single source the name provided is Katerina, but a marginal note provides for the substitution of Eadburga.[29] For another example, the language of the texts of *Jhesu redemptor* is very general, being made proper to Saint Augustine solely in two paired stanzas (6 lines out of 25) of the duplum. With a minimum of emendation the motet could be made usable by a skilled rhymester for any feast "de communi unius confessoris" or "in natali unius confessoris." This possibility is lent additional credence by the function of the motet tenor, *Jhesu redemptor omnium*, which in the Use of Salisbury was the hymn for the Common of a Confessor.[30]

Figure 48. Sequence Style in *Templum eya salomonis*

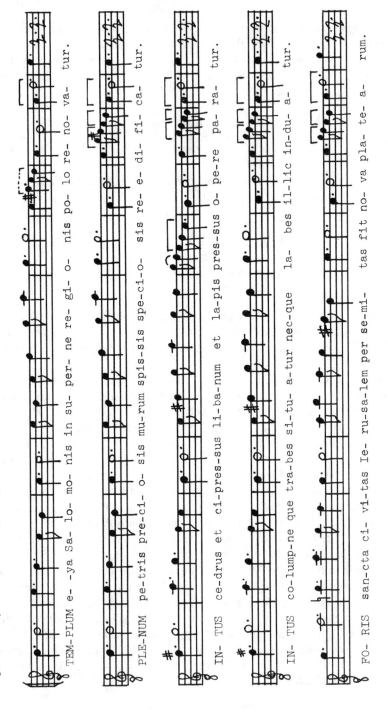

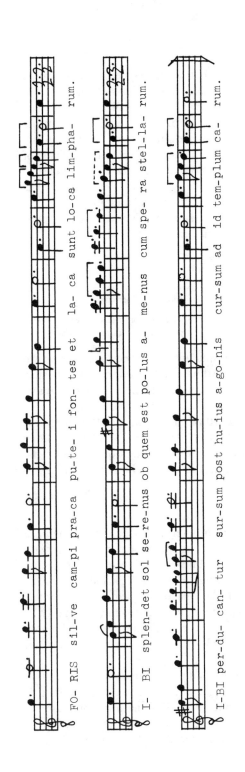

FO- RIS sil-ve cam-pi pra-ca pu-te- i fon- tes et la- ca sunt lo-ca lim-pha- rum.

I- BI splen-det sol se-re-nus ob quem est po-lus a- me-nus cum spe- ra stel-la- rum.

I-BI per-du- can- tur sur-sum post hu-ius a-go-nis cur-sum ad id tem-plum ca- rum.

The fragment *Princeps apostolice* further fuels the speculation that some motets may have been composed for a broad spectrum of feasts by an orientation toward the Common rather than the Proper of Saints. The surviving text names all the apostles with a brief description or capsule comment on the evangelizing activity or martyrdom of each. This topic was a favorite one, and many such texts may be found under the rubric "Common of Apostles" in the *Analecta Hymnica.*[31] *Princeps apostolice* is in fact clearly modeled on one of these, the sequence *Alleluya nunc decantet*, which is classified as "in die unius apostoli" in the Sarum Missal and given the rubric "in festis plurimorum apostolorum" in the Hereford Missal.[32] Correspondences between motet text and sequence are close:

Motet	Sequence
Indis vite dogmata	Bartholomeus dat
dat Bartholomeus	Indis vite dogmata
Thomam fossum lancea	Thomas confossus lancea
Indi contestantur	cursum consummat in India

These similarities suggest the motet was suitable for performance on the same occasions as the sequence, that is, on those feasts of one or more apostles where the rubrics for the sequence at mass direct one to the *Commune Sanctorum*. In the Use of Salisbury this included James and Philip (May 1), Barnabas (June 11), James (July 25), Bartholomew (August 24), Symon and Thaddeus or Jude (October 28), and Thomas (December 21). The loss of one text for this motet prevents any more certain determination. Some of the saints just named have one or more motets in the surviving repertoire.

Textual Evidence for Provenance

Texts on saints provide our most important internal clues to the provenance of sources and pieces. Provision for local saints and holidays in an otherwise normative liturgical calendar can often nail down very securely the specific institution for which that calendar was intended. Since few local saints are honored by the very highest rank of feast, a collection of sequences or motets containing a piece dedicated to a relatively minor figure can reasonably be assigned its provenance. Unfortunately it is the local saint, venerated highly enough to require a motet in only a limited region, whose survival in a motet text is least likely.

As things stand, the lack of extensive and readily available comparative data limits the effectiveness (though not the potential) of the motet data.[33] Usually it is merely confirmatory, if nonetheless illuminating. For example, front and rear flyleaves of music have been bound into a book (*Ob 7*) known to have been in the library of the major Benedictine abbey of Bury St. Edmunds in the thirteenth and fourteenth centuries. The front flyleaves contain two motets on Bury's patron, Edmund of East Anglia, and there is also a fragment of a motet on Saint Benedict whose surviving text makes direct reference to the three primary vows of the monastic vocation, namely poverty, chastity and obedience, and speaks of the "nostri chorus ordinis" (see figure 49). In the rear leaves is a fragmentary motet on Saint James with a subtle reference to the enclosed life worked into its final petition for aid (quoted above). The association of the musical leaves with the abbey is incontrovertible.

Another source, *Omc 266/268*, preserves a motet on Edmund along with motets on the BVM and Paul, and on Martin of Tours. The motet on Martin emphasizes his traditional image as a founding father of Christian monasticism, an association made clear by references to Abraham (regarded as the Biblical forefather of monastic movements), to Martin not only as "sacer presul" but also as "neophitus primus," and to a "chorus monachorum" over which he apparently presides.[34] There is no external evidence of provenance for the music leaves or their former host manuscript (*GB-Omc lat. 7*), and despite the distinctiveness of the constellation of subjects it has not been possible to pinpoint where the music might have been assembled. Bury is certainly a prime candidate, but the presence of a motet on Edmund cannot be regarded as conclusive.[35]

Two different saints Augustine occur among the motet texts. Augustine of Hippo, doctor of the church and patron of the regular Augustinian canons, is celebrated in a motet, *Jhesu redemptor*, from a source (*Cfm*) for which independent, external evidence establishes an origin in the Augustinian priory at Coxford in Norfolk.[36] However, a second piece on this Augustine, *Assunt Augustini*, has not been helpful in tracing a medieval provenance for its source, *LIc 52,* now at Lincoln Cathedral.[37] Augustine of Canterbury is remembered in two motets as the refounder of the English church and the founder of monasticism at Canterbury. One of these motets, *Solaris ardor romuli*, survives in a source of uncertain provenance, *Onc 362.* Hohler proposes a London origin for *Onc 362*, mainly because of the presence of a text on Saint Edward ("A composition in S. Edward's honour is hardly thinkable except in or near Westminster or a Royal chapel"),[38] but the source also has two motets on Saint Thomas of Canterbury. Surely for a codex with motets on two Canterbury saints (Thomas and Augustine), an origin in Canterbury at Christ Church or St. Augustine's must be held more plausible than London.[39] The second motet on the English Augustine, *Augustine par angelis*, sets a text that is known elsewhere only from an early fourteenth-century hymnal of St. Augustine's, Canterbury. Curiously the motet source, *Ob D.6*, is from a house dedicated to the other Augustine (St. Augustine's, Daventry).[40] The text, or even the motet in its entirety, may have been borrowed with no regard for the confusion of saints.

In at least three other instances, motets on saints tend to confirm the testimony of external evidence for general source provenance. It is certainly appropriate, for instance, to find a motet on William of York among fragments, *Lbl 40011B**, that can be associated with the Cistercian abbey at Fountains in Yorkshire. A late thirteenth-century bifolio wrapping early sixteenth-century Westminster accounts, *Lwa 33327*, preserves motets on Peter, the patron saint of the church, and on Edward, King and Confessor, who is buried there. Then there are the two Anglo-Saxon women. Doubts have been raised by Hohler about the identification of Eadburga with the Pershore saint (June 15) and of Wenefreda with the Shrewsbury saint (November 3); these doubts are appropriately cautionary but on balance I do not believe they survive the test of Ockham's razor.[41] In other words, it still seems most natural that these local saints would turn up among the varied remains we call the Worcester fragments, since Pershore and Shrewsbury are relatively nearby houses in the Severn valley.

External References in the Motet Texts

In general the English motets do not refer to the current events of their day and therefore cannot be placed in a historical context that way. A few instances may be cited from the thirteenth-century repertoire, in none of which do we have an "occasional" piece that contradicts the essentially religious and cloistered nature of the motet genre.[42] The early fourteenth-century repertoire includes just two relatively overt contemporary references. *Thomas gemma* celebrates the monk Thomas of Dover, martyred in 1295,[43] and the stylistically archaic *Trinitatem veneremur* alludes in its duplum to the depredations of "rex et papa." This is probably a reference to the dissatisfaction of the clergy over taxation and the loss of prerogatives to king and pope during the reign of Henry III, a dissatisfaction so profound that it was one of the leading causes of the Baron's Revolt.[44] The complaints against the corruption of the church in *Petrum cephas*, or even the struggle of a good man against a deceitful enemy in *Apello cesarem* ("Apello cesarem qui non habet comparem in iudicio nam sepe sedicio") seem more stereotyped.

Among the later fourteenth-century motets are some, mostly of apparent Continental origin, that make fairly specific references to the contemporary scene. *Musicorum collegio* is one of a number of "musicians motets" that we know of.[45] From the contents of the text it would appear that it is a salutation from the author to a musical chapel he has visited; the function is even responsible for the choice of tenor: "avete" (greetings). The triplum directly names the seven individuals of the collegium: Hugo, Robert of Huy, Johannes, Nichasius, J. Pallart, J. Anglici, and Stephen, while the duplum makes reference to them in the following manner: "vidi septem... quorum nomina sunt scripta tripli pagina." No chapel records yet searched preserve this group of names. Perhaps an English connection can be construed from the presence of "Joe the Englishman" in the choir. It can be said, however, that the "curia gallicorum" to which they belong is not the royal French court, though it may possibly be another aristocratic chapel.[46] One line of the triplum can be read to say either that the men sing their offices "out of holy desire" or that they belong to a chapel of Saint Desiderius (Saint Didier). The parish church of Saint-Didier in Avignon that was raised to the collegiate level in 1385 is a possible candidate, but there are a number of towns by that name and even more churches.[47]

Several musical details in the text are of interest. First, the choir is said to perform the Lady Mass four times a month; this is probably a reference to the Saturday Lady Mass, which was part of the widely observed commemorative office for the Virgin on that day.[48] Further, the music of this chapel is described as in three parts that avoid the vice of dissonance. This is an apt description of English cantilena and discant styles, and in fact much of the repertoire in these styles was intended for Marian services. Certainly, though, the description fits conservative conductus-style (simultaneous-style) Continental mass music as well,[49] so there is not necessarily a reference to purely English practices here.

One or two other motets of this genre survive in fourteenth-century English sources. *Sub arturo plebs*, perhaps the only "native" secular motet, is securely in the Continental tradition of the musicians motet. Its triplum names and praises fourteen English musicians; the duplum gives a brief history of music, mentions the motet's composer J. Alanus by name, and explains the proper mensural interpretation of the tenor.[50] The striking similarity between the texts of *Sub Arturo plebs* and *Musicorum collegio* (the triplum gives a catalogue of musicians, while in the duplum the author identifies himself and speaks of the art of music in more learned and recondite language) indicates a common tradition for this *topos*.[51] Music and musicians are honored by a means usually reserved for popes and great princes. *Deus compaignouns* (*US-Wc 14*, 3), with its praise of generous, companionable friends who sing well, and its reference to at least two individuals by name (one of whom is a Gwillelmus nicknamed Malcharte), projects a tone much like that in *Musicorum collegio*. Since the text is not burdened with musical erudition, however, there still must remain some doubt about the audience to whom it is addressed.

Two further motets concern themselves with political problems of the last third of the century. *Rex Karole* is dedicated to Charles V, king of France from 1364 to 1380. On the basis of a detailed analysis of its text, Günther argues for a date of composition in 1375, possibly originating at the French royal court. The motet may have been introduced to the English during negotiations with the French at Bruges in the winter of 1375–76.[52]

The subject matter of *Alme pater* is more difficult to pin down in detail due to ambiguities in its language.[53] Apparently the text has to do with the problems of the papacy and the control of Naples in the years immediately following the Great Schism (late 1370s or 1380s). The pope referred to in the text could be either Urban VI, the Roman pope to whom England was allied, or Clement VII, the Avignon pope allied with the French. The poem seems to make the most sense if the pope is assumed to be Urban. In that case, the events referred to are likely those of 1384, when Charles of Durazzo (who had taken Naples from its Queen Joanna for Urban in 1381–2) turned against his pope. Urban's campaign to establish control over Naples failed, and he was besieged for many months by Charles in a castle at Nocerno (Luceria Christianorum). The English cardinal Adam Easton was a member of Urban's party during this ordeal, and English attention to the siege would naturally have been as intense as medieval lines of communication allowed.[54] It is difficult to imagine a composer in the Avignon or French royal circles setting the text; it is equally difficult to believe that it could have been written in Italy in a style so foreign to that distinctive musical culture. The possibility must be considered, then, that the work is English—that such musical knowledge and skill, in imitation of French models, was possessed by some English composers, probably in the employ of aristocratic chapels, in the 1380s.[55]

Two final texts from the later fourteenth-century motets make unconventional references that may prove to be of significance for the purpose of establishing provenance. First, *Inter usitata* refers not just to the BVM, but also to Saint Paul and a "novelle structure."[56] This slim piece of evidence may point to a specific institution with important new construction in the general time period we are concerned with, but no identification can be proposed here. Lastly, the Marian text *Maria diceris* (*US-SM 19914*, 3) refers to Mary as "carmeli flosculus." This appellation is not unusual, but a further line, "iam carmelitis porrigetis manum," reemphasizes the association with Carmel and prompts the suggestion that the poem is a specifically Carmelite song of praise to Mary. The Carmelite friars were an order "de Beata Virgine" and they are well known (on the Continent) for their cultivation of music from the midfourteenth century on. One of the central events in this order's early history occurred in thirteenth-century England where, according to tradition, Simon Stock had the vision in which Mary gave the scapular to the order.[57] The bestowal of this distinctive cloak of office may be referred to in the following lines of *Maria diceris*: "repereras o domina sub tuo quando clamide te [. . . don]ans hiis solamina." The identification of the tenor of this motet someday may provide more information about the music's provenance.[58]

Other Repertoires

For some perspective on the significance of the distribution of subject matter in fourteenth-century English motets, comparison with other repertoires of Latin motets and sacred literature is illuminating. Earlier and later motets in England are a natural starting point for such an examination.[59] It has already been observed that the thirteenth-century English motet is similar in its range of topics though oriented more toward the BVM. Early fifteenth-century English isorhythmic tenor motets show continued devotion to a variety of sacred subjects, especially saints. The motets preserved in Old Hall (*Lbl 57950*) have topics including Saint Thomas of Canterbury, Saint Katherine, Saint George (two motets), the BVM, and Pentecost. There are also two *Deo gratias* substitutes. Margaret Bent has assembled scraps of a codex (*H6*) that, if reconstructed, would be comparable to Old Hall in size and contents. Some eight motets can be counted among the fragments. Loss of text makes identification of the subject matter tentative in almost every case, but evidently there were motets on the Holy Innocents (or other young martyrs), Saint Nicholas, a confessor, a musician or musical subject (possibly sacred, and the topic of two items), and Edward (either the recent king or traditional English saint), as well as the same two *Deo gratias* substitutes that appear in Old Hall.[60] A third repertoire, the twelve surviving isorhythmic motets of John Dunstaple, includes six on saints: Saint Alban, Saint Michael, Saint Germanus, Saint Anne, Saint John the Baptist, and Saint Katherine. Three further motets are on the BVM, two are on Pentecost, and one survives untexted.[61] Surviving with most of Dunstaple's motets in *I-MOe 1.11 (ModB)* are motets by Benet on Saint Alban and Saint Thomas of Hereford and by Forest on Saint Oswald; an anonymous motet probably on Saint Bartholomew survives with Dunstaple's *Preco preheminencie* in the English fragment *CAc 128/3*.[62]

Continental motets. In Parisian music circles ca. 1200 Latin was the language of the motet as it first developed out of the discant *clausula*. The earliest motet texts bore strong assonant and tropic relationships to the text of their tenors, but they soon began to "depart altogether from the tenor's words and their connotations"; a vogue for the use of French texts instead of Latin, a radical innovation of around 1215, led to the dominance of the genre by secular lyrics "by the third decade of the century."[63] However, "the intrusion of the vernacular was a French specialty, [and] elsewhere—including, surely, large areas of France—Latin as well as some degree of tropic textual relationship between the Tenor and the upper part(s) were generally retained."[64]

In her discussion of the texts of *F-MO*, Rokseth identified four categories that together encompass the themes of nearly all thirteenth-century Latin motets, distinguishing those that comment on the major feasts of the Christian year, those devoted to the Virgin Mary, those that concern the corruption of morals of the clergy, and those that give moral advice for the conduct of life.[65] In *F-MO* about three-fourths of the Latin texts (86 of 117) are devoted to Mary, with the remainder divided fairly evenly between those about feasts (texts of nos. 60, 70, 306, 310, 331, 340–41), the clergy (texts of nos. 37, 52, 286, 287) and moral conduct (texts of nos. 47, 65, 264, 328). Significantly, the latter three categories contain motets believed by scholars to be of non-Parisian origin.[66]

Hans Tischler has published various statistical surveys of the subject matter of the Continental Latin-texted motets of the thirteenth century. He identifies four similar categories as primary: Mary, Jesus, other holy persons, and various religious subjects and criticism[67]—and summarizes the trends in text-content from the very earliest days of the motet as follows:[68]

> The main balance shifts from an emphasis on Jesus to one on Mary as early as about 1210; and Mary's predominance becomes nearly exclusive at the end of the century. Other holy persons are addressed less and less often as time goes on. Religious subjects, on the other hand, particularly moral sermons and criticisms, regain ground in the last decades of the century after a total eclipse during the midcentury.

This summary encompasses a diverse range of sources, and in its generality tends to obscure regional differences. However, a perception of geographical variation in motet-text preference sharpens the outlines of these trends in Tischler's most recent essay.[69] Significantly, for several non-Parisian manuscripts he observes that the proportion of Marian texts drops in relation to those concerning moral sermons, scriptural verses and stories, various feasts, and Jesus.

In the early fourteenth century the trend in Parisian circles was back to the use of Latin in motet texts. Trouvère-related secular love poetry was abandoned for political or polemical texts with strong overtones of the *admonitio*, especially in the motets of the *Roman de Fauvel* and in the output of de Vitry (Machaut's courtly French motet lyrics are the outstanding exception). Texts of a purely religious nature are few.[70] In the later fourteenth century the motet in both France and Italy became a vehicle for propaganda and political ceremony, honoring the kings of France, the doges of Venice, popes and antipopes, and other great rulers and patrons, such as Gaston Febus, the Count of Foix and Bearn. With regard to the themes treated in its texts, then, the English motet may be sharply distinguished from the Latin motets written within the French or Italian traditions in the thirteenth and fourteenth centuries. It has, instead, affinities with other "peripheral" sources.

However, an important distinction remains there as well, in the relative preponderance of texts on saints and feasts in England over those on homiletic topics.

The carol and the devotional lyric. The question of subject matter cannot be left without some comparison of the motet with better-known contemporaneous repertoires of short religious lyric verse, the carol and the devotional poem. The carol thrived in England in both Latin and the vernacular. Though its history as a polyphonic musical genre belongs primarily to the fifteenth century, texts in carol form[71] are traceable back at least as far as the early fourteenth century. From their inception they were meant for singing, and some monophonic tunes for carols survive. Greene has published approximately 500 carol poems in English,[72] while Stevens has published over 130 musical settings, mostly polyphonic, of carols in English and Latin.[73] Since carols were written over a span of 200 years any classification by subject matter, such as the order of presentation in Greene, must be approached with some caution as a basis for generalization; nonetheless the broad outlines are clear and transcend any relative fluctuations in the popularity of topics. Carols treating events of the Christmas season from Advent through Epiphany, and carols on the Virgin and Child or on the Annunciation (which are of course both appropriate to Christmas) far outweigh any other topics. Though the carol is by no means associated exclusively with the Christmas season, it appears to have been understood most frequently as such. There is a distinct lack of emphasis on the next important liturgical season, Easter: "until the early Tudor period, English carols on themes of the Passion and Resurrection are very rare."[74] Harrison's tabulation of the subjects treated in three fifteenth-century polyphonic carol manuscripts makes this point clearly.[75]

What[ever] kind of institution they may have been used in, at least three of these [carol] sources have a presumably complete carol repertoire for their particular place. In the Ritson manuscript there is written beside all but one of its 44 carols the day or content for which it was intended. Applying this information by analogy to the carols in the Selden and Egerton manuscripts—with Ritson a total of about 105 carols including concordances—the following occasions and subjects appear to be represented:

Christmas Day (in die nativitas)	22 carols
St. Stephen's Day (December 26th)	2
St. John's Day (December 27th)	4
Holy Innocents' Day (December 28th)	4
St.Thomas of Canterbury's Day (December 29th)	3
The Circumcision (January 1st)	2
Epiphany (January 6th)	8
de nativitate, (which [Harrison takes] to mean suitable over the whole season of 12 days)	32

The Virgin Mary	4
St. George's Day (April 23rd)	1
Those shown as ad libitum in Ritson, which divide into four categories:	
a) Moral	14
b) Convivial	1
c) Nationalistic	5
d) Agricultural-Ritual	1

total   103

A fourteenth-century repertoire closely related to the carol is the group of 60 Latin hymns preserved in the *Red Book of Ossory*.[76] These were written sometime during the period from 1320 to 1360 by the English Franciscan Richard Ledrede, Bishop of Ossory, for his clerics to sing in place of secular lyrics with more worldly sentiments. All but one of the poems is stanzaic, and over half of them exhibit the burden and verse structure of the carol. The assignment of the first four poems to a specific feast is given by rubrics:

Cantilena de nativitate Domini
Alia cantilena de eodem festo
De eodem festo
De eodem festo

Though the rubrics then cease, it is clear that there is at least a rough ordering of all the contents in accordance with the liturgical calendar, beginning with Christmas, proceeding to Easter, and then going on to more miscellaneous subjects, in particular the BVM. Greene enumerates 25 songs on the Nativity and Christmas season, 11 on Easter and the Resurrection, 1 on the Annunciation, and 23 more diverse pieces.[77] Colledge's count includes 13 on Christmas and 10 on Epiphany, 10 on Easter, 8 on the BVM, 5 on Christ, and 2 on the Holy Spirit.[78] The varying totals reflect the ambiguity inevitably encountered in such subject matter; most of the poetry on the Virgin is suitable for Christmas, for instance. In my opinion 29 texts can be counted for the Christmas season and perhaps 15 more for Easter. However, the rest of the poems—on God, Jesus, Mary, or some more general moral topic—are less specifically tied to single occasions.

Greene has remarked on the unusually high emphasis on Easter in the poems of the *Red Book*, by comparison with the English carol.[79] Otherwise the two types of verse are remarkably similar and equally distinct from the motet in the coverage of subject matter, in verse form, and presumably, in performance context.[80] A well-known marginal entry that appears in the *Red Book* after the first four hymns sheds some light on their origin:[81]

Nota: Attende, lector, quod Episcopus Ossoriensis fecit istas cantilenas pro vicariis Ecclesie Cathedralis, sacerdotibus, et clericis suis, ad cantandum in magnis festis et solaciis, ne guttera eorum et ora Deo sanctificata polluantur cantilenis teatralibus, turpibus et secularibus; et cum sint cantatores, provideant sibi de notis convenientibus secundum quod dictamina requirunt.

This is remarkable testimony not only to the kinds of song a cleric might sing (or be asked not to sing), but also to the times of year when such clerics might be most inclined to raise their voices in song. Ledrede specifies that his verses are "for singing on the great feast days and at times of recreation." For 12 of the 60 hymns the scribe has noted an incipit of vernacular verse that presumably identifies the secular tune to which the Latin text was to be sung (and on whose versification the Latin lines were presumably modeled). One must wonder whether these were precisely the tunes with objectionable lyrics to which Ledrede refers. In any event, impromptu singing on occasions of communal conviviality, especially on the most joyous and music-filled holidays of the Christian year, was apparently seen by Ledrede as an opportunity to check ribaldry and instill a little devotion in his clerics.

Devotional poetry flourished concurrently in Latin, Anglo-Norman, and English during the thirteenth and fourteenth centuries. New developments in the vernacular lyric, particularly in English poetry during the latter half of the thirteenth century, may be understood as deriving from and parallel to the Latin tradition.[82] English lyrics, now thought to be almost exclusively the product of clerics, at least before 1350 or so, came mainly from the pens of Franciscans.[83] The intended audience for their devotional verse was primarily an uneducated laity; the poet sought to capture the listener's attention through a simple, even humble style and powerful visual imagery, and strove to evoke an immediate, personal response. The tone is intense and subjective, infused with affective piety and direct emotion that are aimed at stimulating or renewing a simple, unquestioning faith and evoking contrition and repentance. Jeffrey emphasizes that "the performance context of certain varieties of Middle English lyric" was in preaching evangelical sermons to the populace; the typical poem might even be said to be "a gospel song."[84]

The Latin motet, by contrast, is less intimate, more objective and more formal. Except for those few texts of contrition or admonition, the motet seldom exhibits a sermon-like stance with man rather than God as the intended recipient of its message. There is, however, a little common ground between the devotional Latin lyric and motet texts.[85] For instance, excerpts of the *Dulcis Jhesu Memoria* were set polyphonically at least half a dozen times in the thirteenth century on the Continent and in England; one setting survives in the Worcester fragments (*WF*, 75).[86] Saint Bernard, the beloved central figure of Cistercian and Franciscan devotion, is memorialized in motets setting hymn texts from a widely-known, rhymed office in his honor.[87] The Franciscan Saint Bonaventure is associated with the English motet repertoire through the use of the refrain stanza *Laus honor Christo* from his famous office on the Holy Cross, *In passione Domini*,[88] as the tenor of *Laus honor vendito*. The language of the surviving text of this Passion motet, and the very similar language in another, *Barrabas dimittitur*, are closer than that of any other insular Latin motet to the kind of intense concentration on the Passion of Christ that characterizes the most familiar devotional poetry.[89]

Vernacular Texts

Medieval Latin was the preeminent language of the English motet; its near-exclusive use in the repertoire (instead of either Middle English or Anglo-Norman) is a significant feature of the genre, as has already been mentioned. In general, avoidance of the vernacular was a feature of the motet outside a narrow but prolific Parisian orbit. There are almost no pieces with Flemish/Germanic texts, for instance, or Provençal.[90] Nonetheless, each music culture may have had its own reasons for the stance it took with regard to the use of its native language(s). The strong English preference for Latin-texted motets is stated directly in the testimony of a late-fourteenth-century witness:[91]

> Practicus insignis gallicus sub gallicis hemus hunc discantavit cantum sed post reformavit latini lingua anglis sepius fit amena reddendo deo gratias.

> The distinguished French practitioner composed this song on French melodies [texts] but after he revised it with the Latin language it is once more made pleasing to the English for reciting *Deo gratias*.

At least two reasons suggest themselves for this predilection: (1) Latin was the preferred medium for the presentation of the sacred subject matter dealt with by English motets, and (2) it was the appropriate language for the context in which they were usually performed. The surviving examples of the motet using the vernacular help shed some light on these suggestions.

The appearance of vernacular lyrics in motet tenors is a phenomenon associated with the increasing proportion of non-Gregorian tenors in Continental motets of the generation represented by the seventh and eighth fascicles of the Montpellier codex.[92] Judging by the surviving numbers of pieces, the English were more taken with this development than the French, not surprising given the well-established English propensity for using non-Gregorian *pes* tenors. Propriety was apparently not offended by the juxtaposition of the sacred with the secular (sometimes perhaps even obscene) sentiments of these lyrics.[93] Only two tenors have come down to us with

Middle English incipits. The older is in a motet from the third quarter of the thirteenth century, *Veni mater gracie–T.Dou way Robin*, whose tenor is a short but closed tune, perhaps a refrain, that is stated thirteen times as a kind of *pes*.[94] The tenor text seems not to be related to the text of the surviving upper part. The younger example is *Vide miser*, whose tenor, identified only as "Wynter," is a more extended melody that is stated in full three times.

French-texted tenors are a richer source of vernacular lyrics and melodies that are neither liturgical nor courtly. Most are from motets in *Onc 362* and *F-TO 925* that seem to be roughly contemporary with the later Montpellier motets.[95] (The *fatras* setting used as the tenor of *Deus creator* is a much later nod to this tradition.) Their tenors are all intact tunes (though there may have been some tampering with the end of *Hey hure lure*), but only two—*Hey hure lure* and *Trop est fol*—preserve more than just a textual incipit. However, a fuller text for *A definement*, a strophic pastourelle, does survive elsewhere.[96] None of the melodies is otherwise known, so these tenors afford an important glimpse into the style and rhythmic language of lighter French verse forms in the early fourteenth century. The melodies in *F-TO 925* are mainly simple couplets with double-versicle styling and *ouvert-clos* cadences. *Mariounette douche* is a virelai (form ABBAA), *Hey hure lure* is a ballad-like AAB, *Trop est fol* has the simple scheme AA BB AA BB AA, and *A definement* has the form AB B′C B′C′ (=ABB′). The textless tenor of *Alma mater* (*BERc 55*, 1) is in the form of a rondeau, i.e., AB AA AB AB.

Use of the vernacular is even less frequent in upper parts than in tenors. Leaving aside the Sumer Canon (a rota on a *pes*), Middle English is found in just one extant motet, *Worldes blisce*. This late thirteenth-century work is transmitted solely in an unusual source, *Ccc 8*, whose leaves and binding stubs of music are the scraps from a manuscript that once ran to several hundred folios. Its surviving contents show a remarkably wide range of musical genres, including a number of French motets in parts (some known from the Montpellier codex), settings in score of both English and French texts, and textless three-voice *clausulae*. This was a remarkably diverse anthology rather than a homogeneous collection of motets.[97]

Worldes blisce survives in two parts and may possibly be complete a2, an assumption not contradicted by its counterpoint. If this is so, then the unusually thin texture may represent the deliberate avoidance of polytextuality in the interest of the clear presentation of a single poem. The text, which is in the mainstream of the devotional lyric (judging from its graphic description of the suffering of "sweet Jesus" on the Cross), exists in part in a much later source, Franciscan friar John Grimestone's commonplace book of sermon materials, dated 1372.[98]

French texts on both sacred and secular subjects are not unknown in the thirteenth-century English motet repertoire,[99] but are distinctly more uncommon in the fourteenth-century. Surviving examples, all from later in the century, are mostly from imported isorhythmic motets, mainly in fact from the rear leaves of *DRc 20*. Additionally, *Deus compaignons de cleremunde* (*US-Wc 14*, 3) bears text that is bilingual, alternating French and Latin, and Reaney judges it to have originated in northeastern France.[100] A further text, *Parfundement plure*, is in the duplum of the *Ob 7* motet *Pura placens*. There are references to Continental sources for this piece, and the text is most likely of Continental origin. However, since these reference cite only the duplum incipit, it is of some interest to ask whether the triplum's Latin text is original or a contrafact. Just possibly the triplum could be an Englishman's Latin replacement for secular French verses. Speaking for this is the sacred subject matter, the high degree of alliteration in the first line ("Pura, placens, pulchra, pia"), and the assonance of the two text incipits. It should be noted that the duplum can be read either in reference to the BVM or as a courtly reproach to some contemporary lady of virtue. Its references are not so explicitly secular that it would have been necessary to make a substitution for it in a rewriting to English taste.

Regne de pité, the final example of French lyrics in the English motet, occupies a position in the repertoire curiously similar to that of *Worldes blisce* though it was written perhaps 75 years later. *Regne* is no contrafact. The motet was designed as a setting of the single text it bears, and this text has an independent tradition of transmission that is associated with Franciscans and devotional poetry.

The text of *Regne de pité* comprises 4 stanzas of a 26–stanza poem known as *Les neuf joies Nostre Dame* or *Li diz proprietez Nostre Dame* that is customarily attributed to the thirteenth-century French poet Rutebeuf. The stanzas used in the motet are I, II, XIX, and XX of the widespread version in Old French. However, they also occur as stanzas I through IV in the version of the poem transmitted in a small group of Anglo-Norman sources including *Ob 143*.[101] The first two lines of the second stanza of the original are omitted in the motet, providing 30 lines to be set. These are divided by the structure of the motet into two unequal parts of 12 and 18 lines, respectively.

At least one of the Anglo-Norman sources of this text has an important Franciscan connection: *Lbl Add 46919* (*olim Phillipps MS 8336*), which belonged to the friar William Herebert (d. 1333). In this collection the poem is falsely attributed to the Anglo-Norman friar Nicholas Bozon (or Bohun).[102] Perhaps the unusual collection of items in *Ob 143* will prove to have Franciscan associations.[103] It is worth noting, in any event, that the stanzas of the poem that were used for *Regne* suit the world of the motet more closely than the world of private devotion. Mary is not cuddling the Christ child and singing him a lullaby, taking him to the temple or greeting the Magi. Nor is she lamenting at the Cross or tomb. Rather, her epithets are Biblical and theological.

Text Contents: Sources and Models

Content and language of the motet texts are not an issue wholly separable from subject matter, as the foregoing has repeatedly demonstrated. Here I would like to draw together some more specific observations about sources and models for text language. The lyrics are indebted to many different sources and are rarely wholly original in thought or expression. At the same time, few are borrowed in their entirety from elsewhere. Rather, they are mostly written specifically for the motet with which they are now found. The medieval author accepted and utilized traditional genres, topics, and idioms in the fashioning of a sacred text. He sought to say again what had already been said before. It was not originality that was prized but rather a demonstrable grasp of conventional means to a common end, emphasizing familiarity and continuity in text and expression. As a consequence for the motet, its texts are rich in "allusions to and manipulations of" familiar liturgical and Biblical passages.[104] Manipulation takes place by two basic processes: (1) expansion through tropic elaboration, paraphrase, and variation, or (2) contraction through what one might call a "lyrical abridgment" of material.[105]

The few directly borrowed texts are listed in table 28. Most are from hymns, taking over several stanzas intact. In the cases of *Ut recreentur* and *A solis–Salvator*, hymn text is used as a framework for additional verses, alternating either pairs of lines or individual lines with newly written material. In at least three other motets, *Caligo terre*, *A solis–Ovet*, and *Hostis Herodes*, a single stanza of a hymn, not an entire text, is used similarly.

Two pairs of motet texts that are set elsewhere turn up in *Onc 362* in motets that are among the most archaic preserved in that source. The *Onc 362* setting of *O homo–O homo* is probably not much later than the thirteenth-century English setting in *Lbl 5958, 2*, and the two settings of *Iam nubes–Iam nubes*, one most likely English and the other Continental, are comparable in age and technique.[106] This kind of resetting of texts is seen in two further pairs in the English thirteenth-century motet repertoire and seems to be a practice of that era rather than of the fourteenth century.[107]

Motets with exact Biblical quotations or very near paraphrases embedded in their texts are listed in table 29. No claim for completeness in this regard can be made. The New Testament passages are mainly drawn from the Gospels, and the Old Testament passages mainly come from the Psalms. Systematic quotation is taken farthest in *Quare fremuerunt*, where the incipits of Psalms 2 through 12 are embedded in a poetic matrix so constructed that they not only make sense but contribute to a rhyme scheme as well. The allusions in the triplum of *Civitas nusquam* and the duplum of *Fusa cum silentio* to parables from Matthew are examples of the use of familiar Biblical passages in a slightly less "sophisticated" fashion. Of course the proximate

Table 28.   Directly Borrowed Texts

Motet	*Text*
	Devotional poetry
Candens crescit	Candens lilium columbina
Radix Iesse	Ortum floris
Regne de pité	Regne de pité
	Older Paired Motet texts
Iam nubes	Iam-Iam
O homo considera	O homo-O homo
	Antiphon
Doleo super te	Doleo super te
	Rex autem David
	Hymn
A solis-Salvator	A solis ortus
	& Salvator mundi
Augustine par angelis	Augustine par angelis
Detentos a demonibus	Bernardus doctor inclitus
Regina iam discubuit	Iam regina discubuit
	& Venit sponsa de libano
Veni creator spiritus	Veni creator spiritus
Ut recreentur spiritus	Veni creator spiritus

source for Biblical language may be the liturgy, as is the case with the motet *Doleo super te*. In a different approach, the language of *Excelsus in numine* is infused with phraseology and imagery taken from Luke via the *Benedictus* at lauds.

The condensation or abridgment of material is most apparent in texts on saints, which tend to cover similar ground in similar language in every text on the same individual. This is due to the fact that the same sources are drawn upon every time such texts are written, using the familiar language of saints' lives and of the liturgy: sequences and proses, antiphons and responsories, and matins lessons.[108] Texts for Katherine are often taken from the antiphons and responsories of her rhymed office (in particular the chants *Virgo sancta Katerina* and *Virgo flagellatur*), or as in the motet *Mulier magni meriti*, from her *legenda*. The pair of Marian stories abbreviated in *Suffragiose virgini* provide a similar example; as was mentioned above, they are probably drawn from the vast stock of such tales, condensed and versified to be accommodated to the medium of the motet.

Table 29.   Use of Biblical Quotation or Paraphrase

Motet	Biblical reference
Texts of the Sanctorale	
Civitas nusquam	Matthew 5:14-15; 14-30
Dei preco	Matthew 11:11; 14:1-12
Excelsus	Luke 1:68-79; Psalms 4:4, 7
Maria mole pressa	Matthew 28:1-10
Petrum cephas	Matthew 4:19-20; 16:18-19
Vas exstas	Acts 9:15-16; 26:14
Texts of the Temporale	
A solis-Ovet mundus	Luke 2
Barrabas dimittitur	Matthew 27:46; John 19:28
Hostis Herodes	Matthew 2:1-12
Herodis in pretorio	Matthew 2:13-18; Isaiah 1:6; Proverbs 1:17
Laus honor vendito	Matthew 27:46
Viri Galilei	Acts 1:11
Other Motet Subjects	
Beatus vir	Psalm 1, etc. (common incipit)
Doleo super te	2nd Samuel 1:22, 26; 18:33
Domine quis habitabit	Psalm 14(15)
Fusa cum silentio	Matthew 25:1-12
Inter amenitatis	Matthew 12:25
Musicorum collegio	Revelation 1:12-2:1
O vos omnes	Lamentations 1:12
Omnis terra	Psalm 103(104); Matthew 13:12; Isaiah 61:11
Quare fremuerunt	Psalms 2-12 (incipits)

Note: Where there is a more proximate source in the liturgy this is noted in the critical report.

A number of examples will show some of the kinds of textual manipulation of sources and models discoverable in the motet corpus; some of these have been noted above in this chapter or in chapter 2. The two large-scale voice-exchange motets *A solis–Ovet* and *Hostis Herodes* quote and then paraphrase both text and melody of hymns for Christmas and Epiphany. *Princeps apostolice* has been modeled directly on the sequence *Alleluya nunc decantet.* Stanzas of *Salve cleri* paraphrase successive verses of the Saint Nicholas prose *Sospitati dedit egros. Viri Galilei* is constructed textually as a series of variations on the familiar Ascension Day text that is quoted as its last stanza. *Domine quis habitabit* expands on the language and imagery of a psalm. In the case of *Barrabas dimittitur* the language of the upper parts is indebted to a matins responsory for Good Friday. The incipit of *Zelo tui* ("Zelo tui langueo virgo regia") is identical to the explicit of a famous poem by Richard Rolle of Hampole. The relationship (if any) of the motet text(s) to the Yorkshire mystic is unknown.[109] Table 30 gives these textual relationships along with a few that have been discovered but not listed or discussed above.

Assonance

The motets setting whole chants usually show a strong tropic relationship to their tenors throughout the texts of the upper voices; in the weaker cases this may be expressed just through quotation at the beginning and end of the motet. A relationship weaker still, yet distinctive, links incipits of the several texts of a motet by the same word or word-root, consonant-vowel cluster, or merely the same consonant. This is the relationship I have been calling assonance, using the word in its most general sense (i.e., likeness/similarity/correspondence or resemblance of sounds in words or syllables).[110] Assonance at the beginning and end of a motet text is a device common to the very earliest European motets on account of their tropic relationship to the tenor but is seen less and less in the course of the thirteenth century outside of England. Its numerous occurrences in later thirteenth- and fourteenth-century English motets testifies to a particularly English preoccupation with the motet as a complex of interrelated texts.[111]

A typical example of an English motet with texts linked by assonance and subject matter is *Petrum cephas–Petrus pastor–T.Petre (amas me)*. In some instances the tenor seems to have been chosen out of the desire for assonance, or the upper parts have been made assonant with a given tenor, without any particular regard for relationship in content. This is likely the case in such combinations as *Barrabas–Barrabas–T.Babilonis flumina* or *Frondentibus florentibus–T.Floret*. However, the expression of lamentation in the psalm paraphrase implied by the incipit *Babilonis flumina* might be considered appropriate to Good Friday. Similarly, *Floret* sounds as if it might be the incipit of some spring song (such as those in the *Carmina Burana*), so if there was no immediate connection to Easter at least the imagery of flowering and renewal would be appropriate. Examples using French secular ditties as tenors, e.g., *Ade finit–Ade finit–T.A definement d'este*, *Triumphat hodie–T.Trop est fol*, and *Herodis–Herodis–T.Hey hure lure*, give clear evidence for the full severing of sound and sense. It is rare to find no assonance relating the texts to the tenor.[112] This lack usually signals that the tenor is freely composed, as in *Candens–Candens*, *Mulier–Multum*, *Orto sole–Origo viri–O virga*, *Te domina–Te domina*, or *Thomas–Thomas*.[113] Because the probability of intended assonance is high, it can occasionally be of help in finding a missing or unidentified tenor.[114]

Table 30. Other Discovered Textual Relationships

Motet	*Text*
	Hymn
A solis-Ovet mundus	A solis ortus
Caligo terre	Nox et tenebre et nubila
De flore martirum	Deus tuorum militum
Hostis Herodes	Hostis Herodes impie
Humane lingue	O gloriosa domina
Jhesu redemptor	Jhesu redemptor omnium
	& Eterne rerum conditor
	Sequence
O crux vale	Salve crux sancta
Princeps apostolice	Alleluya clare decet
Templum eya	Rex Salomon fecit
	Antiphon
Orto sole (O virga Iesse)	O radix Iesse qui stas
Virgo sancta Katerina	Virgo sancta Katerina
	Responsory
Barrabas dimittitur	Barrabas latro
	Metrical litany
Rex sanctorum	Rex sanctorum angelorum
	Rhymed Matins invitatory
Assunt Augustini	Assunt N

Some mention ought to be made of the phenomenon of alliteration in individual motet texts. It is most noticeable in long-line verse, which lacks fairly regular metrical accents, and in the heightened prose of the more irregularly versified lyrics. Alliteration is most common in the first line of a text, or is at least sustained for a longer stretch there (for example: "Parata paradisi porta protoplausto patuit / Que nutu creatoris omnia creantis claruit," or "Multum viget virtus marcet vicium"). Within the body of a text it is likely to be seen only for a word or two; like echo rhymes, it enhances the sonic qualities of the text while allowing the author greater flexibility than regular verse in adapting words to rhythms of breves and semibreves (for example, from *Rosa mundi purissima*: "cuncta pellens pericula / per secula salutis / unda virtutis viola / febrem fugans fervorie").

Versification

The relationship of text and music in the medieval motet is in its nature fundamentally quantitative, not qualitative. Whether a text is taken and set to music or a piece is composed and then given a newly fashioned text, the affective character that the text may possess will not be reflected in the setting, nor will musical word-painting illustrate individual words or images in special fashion.[115] Rather, the musical lines of a motet are an abstract, neutral vehicle for the delivery of the words, and the relationship of one to the other will be concerned with questions of declamation, syntax, and structure. And here the potential interplay of word accents and naturalistic speech rhythms with melodic accent, metrical accent, or rhythmic accent is not normally a consideration either. A motet "presents" a text or texts, but does not "project" them, or read the way an actor would in a naturalistic way; rather, a verse form is set out.

In describing the word-music relationship one needs to deal with three aspects that are interdependent variables: text structure, the style of declamation, and musical form. Texts may be regular or irregular in structure, lying somewhere on the continuum between regular verse and flat prose. Regular verse is constructed by means of versification schemes normal for the rhymed, accentual, strophic Latin poetry of the later Middle Ages.[116] Irregular texts show a variable degree of heightening of prose by the use of assonance, alliteration, echo-rhyme and end rhyme, the placement of stress accent and caesura, and the recurrence of uniform line lengths, defining stanzaic structures. A composer may begin with the decision to set a certain text (a poem or an irregular text such as that of an antiphon or Mass Ordinary movement), or be constrained by the musical fabric of a piece just composed to add a text of a certain structure.

The predominance of regularly versified texts in the early fourteenth-century English motet confirms in a general way a process from irregular to regular texts that was for Continental motets in Latin "the historical trend in motet verse structure for over a century."[117] However, the nearly exclusive appearance of regularly versified texts in the most modern Latin motets of the *Roman de Fauvel* and the Latin motets of de Vitry and Machaut is not paralleled in England, where it is often in the most "progressive" motets that one finds irregular verse.

Characterizing the style of declamation in any given piece involves a number of considerations. To start with, declamation may be syllabic or melismatic from pitch to pitch. More significant is whether declamation is syllabic in consistent rhythmic units. In the latter case, declamation might be isochronic on the long or the breve, or proceed in alternating units (typically, longs and breves, or breves and semibreves), with or without ornamental, melismatic subdivision of these values. Instead of regular patterning of declamation in one or two units of declamation, there may be lengthier patterns that incorporate more syllables before replicating (especially common when declamation is on breve and semibreve), where the pattern may repeat every bar or two bars, or from one musical phrase to the next. One may find regular declamation of an irregular text, or the opposite—irregular declamation of a regular text.

Lastly one must examine the musical fabric itself, in particular its sectional divisions and phrase structure, but also on a more local level its variety of rhythmic surface features, for the degree to which they can accommodate a regular text. In the English motet of the early fourteenth century two trends are apparent. On the one hand motet structures present a regular text in a regular setting (for instance, the isoperiodic motets with long-breve declamation), and on the other some are texted syllabically "after the fact," resulting in an irregular text that may nonetheless be isomorphic with the musical structure, as a result of the fit of syllables to note-values at the lowest level and the coordination of textual syntax on a higher level with the musical morphology of phrase or section.

The degree of correspondence or equivalence of text and musical structures—whether these are entirely autonomous or there is an isomorphism (i.e., direct parallel in structure) between the two—is an interesting parameter to examine. In rare cases one may find no equivalence at all. More commonly there is at least the association of a unit of text (line, couplet, stanza) with a musical phrase or section. When the syntactical or verse units correspond directly in length to the musical sections or phrases, a relationship usually effected through syllabic and/or regularly patterned declamation, then one can speak of isomorphism with a fixed and predictable correlation (the degree of precision depends on declamation).

The most obvious relationship, as has been said already, is that between regular musical structures and regular poetry, as for example in *Lux refulget* (see figure 49). A number of instances where regular poems are set with lesser, varying degrees of equivalency will show the kind of variation likely to be encountered. *Radix Iesse* has an equivalence of stanza to musical phrase, but phrases are irregular in length and declamation is also irregular; the situation is similar though not taken to such an extreme, in *Virgo sancta Katerina*. In *A solis ortus* and *Princeps apostolice* phrase lengths are regular but details of declamatory rhythm vary. In *Mulier magni meriti, Hac a valle* (triplum), and *Beatus vir,* syllabic declamation sets up an isomorphism between text and music, but varied phrasing and variable rhythmic detail lead to small-scale irregularities. The prose texts are articulated by end rhyme, alliteration, and the like, and syntactical units so demarcated are coincident with musical boundaries. Here parallel formations in musical construction lead to parallel formations in text that are noticeable even without precise regularity. (See *Mulier* in figure 49.)

Figure 49. Poetry and Structure in *Lux refulget* and *Mulier magni meriti*

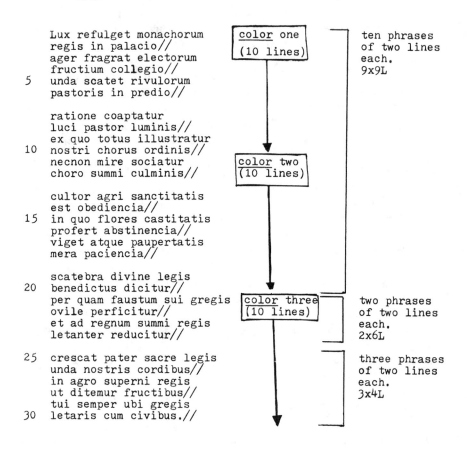

	Lux refulget monachorum	color one	ten phrases

Lux refulget monachorum
regis in palacio//
ager fragrat electorum
fructium collegio//
5 unda scatet rivulorum
pastoris in predio//

ratione coaptatur
luci pastor luminis//
ex quo totus illustratur
10 nostri chorus ordinis//
necnon mire sociatur
choro summi culminis//

cultor agri sanctitatis
est obediencia//
15 in quo flores castitatis
profert abstinencia//
viget atque paupertatis
mera paciencia//

scatebra divine legis
20 benedictus dicitur//
per quam faustum sui gregis
ovile perficitur//
et ad regnum summi regis
letanter reducitur//

25 crescat pater sacre legis
unda nostris cordibus//
in agro superni regis
ut ditemur fructibus//
tui semper ubi gregis
30 letaris cum civibus.//

color one
(10 lines)

color two
(10 lines)

color three
(10 lines)

ten phrases
of two lines
each.
9x9L

two phrases
of two lines
each.
2x6L

three phrases
of two lines
each.
3x4L

9L phrase

6L phrase

4L phrase

		Syll.	Musical Phrase and Subphrase	Paired Strophe
	Mulier magni meriti//	8	3L(6 syll.)	A
				3L+6L
	iubar Alexandrie	7)		32 syll.
	arguit Maxencium	7)		
	sine misericordia	8)		
5	perse--quentem	4)	9L(33 syll.)	A'
	Christianum populum//	7)	14+19	
				37 syll.
	dum fidem ecclesie	7)		
	odit sacre falsum	6)		
	coli iussit ydolum	7)		
10	sed virgo gracilis	6)		
	Cate--rina	4)	10L(37 syll.)	B
	ydolis contraria//	7)	20+17	4L+5L
				36 syll.
	Christi legem tenuit	7)		
	docuit et habuit	7)		
15	in memoria	5)		
	unde Maxencius	6)		
	furi--bundus	4)	9L(35 syll.)	B'
	evitat talia//	6)	19+16	
				36 syll.
	O virgo candida	6)		
20	fulgida graciosa	7)		
	linque hunc errorem	6)		
	et Deo nostro	5)	7L(29 syll.)	C
	prebe favo--rem//	5)	19+10	
				2+3+4L
	aut retores ab omni mundi	9)		33 syll.
25	climate parabo	6)		
	tuum ad honorem//	6)	4L(21 syll.)	
	quos convertebat	5)		
	Christo dantes hono--rem//	7)	5L(12 syll.)	C'
				28 syll.
	post machinatam totam rotam	9)		
30	in incredulorum	6)		
	vertendo dolorem//	6)	4L(21 syll.)	
	martiris fert florem.//	6	3L(6 syll.)	

Note: The way the text has been laid out in lines, syllable count looks quite irregular. Counting larger groups of words by following the subphrases and phrases reveals more consistency. So does counting the syllables in each musical strophe; there are slight variations in declamation in the first and third pairs (A and C) but in B there is strict regularity.

The relationship of word to music can be described by the same principles in the fourteenth-century Continental-style isorhythmic motets. The phrase structures of these motets are periodic, usually in fairly elaborate schemes with mixed periodicity. Essentially, though, they may be regarded in the large as fairly simple strophic structures with a high potential for correspondingly simple isomorphic textual structures. As a rule, this happens in practice.[118] Both triplum and duplum are normally regular in versification but differ in length and verse structure. The triplum text is longer and organized into a number of stanzas. The duplum is considerably shorter and often consists of a single stanza with uniform line length and rhyme. (The two texts of *Pura placens* are a typical pair in these regards.) This is a direct result of the typical phrase patterns, in which the triplum is normally constructed with more (shorter) phrases and the duplum has fewer (longer) phrases. The amount of text is directly proportional to the number of phrases. Hence the customary difference in length (and corresponding difference in declamation, which must be considerably more rapid in the triplum).[119]

The degree of equivalence between text and music can vary from distant to close in a voice of an isorhythmic motet. Two examples taken from *Ob 7* show some of the variation found in practice. (See figure 50.) The triplum text of *Parce piscatoribus* is written in six eight-line stanzas that are linked in a complex rhyme scheme (stanzas I and VI by one rhyme, stanzas II and III by both rhymes used, stanzas III to VI by one rhyme (la/ra), and stanzas II to V by the final vowel sound *a*). As the figure shows, the coordination of this text to the numerical phrase scheme and 2:1 proportional diminution are only approximate. Phrase endings fall regularly within the first four stanzas but do not coincide with stanza breaks, and constantly shift position in regard to stanza structure in the diminution section.

In *Domine quis*, on the other hand, there is an elaborate versification scheme (not quite entirely regular in details of syllable count) that stands in very close equivalence to the musical phrase scheme. Here phrases end consistently at line and stanza endings, and there is a distinct shift in versification at the diminution section. The short phrases of 4B and 3B in the first section are articulated by rhyming couplets, and the last stanza (lines 34 through 36) is extended in syllable count to fit the final musical phrase, which is extended from 9B to 12B.

The tenor of *Domine quis* ("Concupisco," i.e., "I desire") is manifestly more appropriate to the French texts that survive with the music of this motet in Continental sources than to its Latin texts in *Ob 7*, which are surely contrafacted. Whoever wrote the Latin, most probably an Englishman, was intimately familiar with the structure of the motet and took it into careful account in his shaping of the poetry. (This was not, as comparison reveals, simply a matter of mimicking the versification of the French, which though

Figure 50. Relation of Isorhythm to Text in Two *Ob 7* Motets

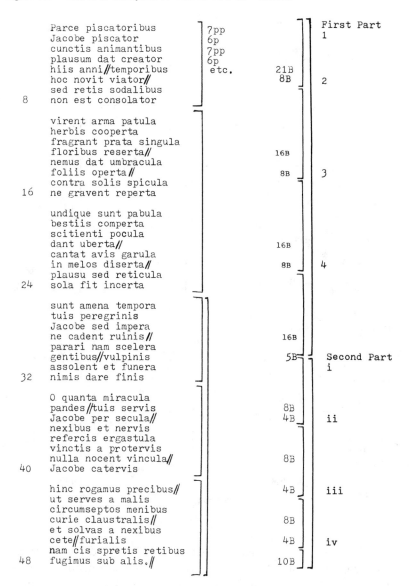

Figure 50.   (continued)

				Musical Phrases
	Domine quis habitabit	8p		First Part
	aut quis te digne laudabit	8p		1
	in tuo sanctissimo tabernaculo	12pp		
	quod operatus est			
6	sine quovis auxilio//	14pp	16B	
	aut quis est qui requiescet/	8p	4B	2
	et nunquam senescet/	6p	3B	
	in arduo tui cacumine montis excelsi	15p		
	in quo habitare			
12	ipse te crevisti//	12p	11B	
	Domine hic habitabit//	8p	4B	3
	et digne laudabit//	6p	3B	
	qui iuste ingreditur	7pp		
	ullis sine maculis	7pp		
	minime qui leditur	7pp		
18	pravitatis iaculis//	7pp	11B	
	et qui semper operatur//	8p	4B	4
	atque delectatur/	6p	3B	
	facere iusticiam	7pp		
	modernis temporibus	7pp		
	dignus est leticiam	7pp		
24	capere cum civibus //	7pp	11B	
	qui verum in corde fatur	8p		Second Part
	et non adulatur	6p		i
27	habebit tabernaculum/	8pp	8B	
	qui malum non operatur	8p		ii
	montem hic lucratur	6p		
30	sanctum et habitaculum//	8pp	9B	
	Domine glorie rex eterne	8p		iii
	lucisque superne	6p		
33	nos mundes a piaculo/	8pp	9B	
	et da sic graciam operari	10p		iv
	ut tecum letari	6p		
36	possimus in tuo sancto tabernaculo.	13pp	12B	

carefully tailored to the motet itself sacrifices the last detail of correspondence to a more regular verse structure.) It has been remarked already that there is good testimony for the English propensity to retext Continental compositions. Other motets from *Ob 7* (especially *Domine quis*, but also *Parce piscatoribus* and *Omnis terra*) may be contrafacts of motets that originally had secular French texts. Until the texts of these motets have been fully understood and their tenors all identified (or until Continental concordances emerge), it will be difficult to say whether the motets are compositions by Englishmen (writing in Continental style), contrafacts made palatable for English tastes, or directly imported Continental Latin motets.

Verse Types and Declamation

Table 31 summarizes some features of versification in the regularly versified texts of the English motets. Where a regular text is mixed in versification, the various stanzas are entered separately. Texts are grouped according to the standard units of declamation, and here separate entries are made when a uniformly versified text undergoes acceleration to a faster pace of declamation. Texts are then subdivided by verse form, and an observation is made of the prevailing rhythmic mode of the setting.

In the rhymed, accentual, stanzaic Latin poetry of the later Middle Ages the primary formal features of the individual line are the number of syllables and the stress accent at the end of each verse. The stress accent in table 31 has been designated by *p* (standing for paroxytonic, the penultimate falling or feminine accent) or by *pp* (proparoxytonic, the antipenultimate accent).[120] As the texts are analyzed here, line breaks are usually defined not just by rhyme but by the caesura.[121] This reveals the poetic structure of the text at a glance, with the disadvantage that it deemphasizes the longer unit of verse, regarded as the proper line by many analysts,[122] that corresponds to the musical phrase (for instance, *15pp=8p7pp*). The term "long-line verse" is introduced here to cover those few texts whose line length, corresponding to the musical phrase, is not regularly articulated into smaller units (e.g., the 35–syllable lines of *Parata paradisi porta*).

A line of verse that has an even number of syllables and *pp* stress (even *pp*) or an odd number of syllables and *p* stress (odd *p*) may in fact possess a regular iambic stress pattern (weak-strong). Similarly, a line of odd *pp* or even *p* may possess a regular trochaic stress pattern (strong-weak). It can be convenient to use iambic and trochaic as a shorthand for these combinations of accent and syllable count, but in the use of this metrical terminology some caution must be exercised, for two reasons. First, the strictly regular recurrence of metrical feet is seldom rigorously adhered to in a line of medieval Latin poetry, and the modern reader must beware the imposition of a "bounce" on the text where it is not present. Second, the possibility exists of confusion with the long-breve and breve-long divisions of the perfect long (sometimes referred to as trochaic and iambic rhythms—long-short and short-long), which (as we shall see below) do not correlate with trochaic and iambic verse in the relation of musical declamation to poetic rhythm.

From table 31 a number of observations and generalizations can be made. To begin with, *pp* lines are more common than *p* lines, and trochaic

Table 31. Declamation in Regularly Versified Motet Poetry

Note: (1) An asterisk indicates that rather than having a pick-up, an extra syllable is handled in some other fashion, usually by being absorbed into an accelerated declamation pattern or being stretched over a whole bar. (2) Incipits beginning with a hyphen belong to the same motet as the first non-hypenated motet incipit above. (3) If only a duplum is intented, the citation is to the incipit, with the first word of the duplum text in brackets following, e.g. Rota versatilis (Katerine).

I. *Regular poems set regularly on long and breve*

A. *Even pp/ odd p (iambic)*

  4x8pp

Absorbet oris faucibus	1st mode with pick-up
Detentos a demonibus	"
Regina iam discubuit	"
Venit sponsa de libano	"
Solaris ardor Romuli	"
-Gregorius sol seculi	"
-Petre tua navicula	"
Virgo materque filia	1st mode*
A solis ortus (Ob 81)	2nd mode with pick-up
Veni creator spiritus eximie	"
Hostis Herodes impie	1st/2nd mode with pick-up
Ut recreentur spiritus	"

  2x8pp7p (=15p)

De flore (Deus tuorum)	1st mode*

  8686pp

Petrum cephas	1st mode with pick-up
-Petrus pastor	"
Caligo (Virgo materque)	1st mode*

  6666pp

Rota versatilis	1st mode (?*)
Regi regum	1st mode with pick-up
Salve cleri	"
Maria mole pressa	" (and *)

  10pp (= 4p+6pp)

Ave miles	1st mode with irreg. accel.

9p (or 3x9=27p)

    Dei preco   1st mode with pick-up

B. *Even p/ odd pp (trochaic)*

    13, 11, 9pp

    O pater excellentissime   1st mode

    9997pp

    Ave miles   1st mode with irreg. accel.

    4x8pp (+10p, 8p)

    Dei preco   1st mode

    2x8p7pp (=15pp)

    Absorbet oris faucibus   1st mode
    Regi regum ennarare   "
    Vas exstas eleccionis   "

    Alta canunt   2nd mode
    Lux refulget   "
    Ovet mundus   "

    Virgo sancta Katerina   1st and 2nd modes
    -De spineto rosa   "
    Rota versatilis (Katerina)   "

    8p8p7pp (Victorine sequence)

    Maria mole pressa   1st mode
    Rex sanctorum   "

    Virgo sancta Katerina   1st and 2nd modes
    -De spineto rosa   "

    8686p

    Thomas gemma   1st mode
    -Thomas cesus   "

Table 31. (continued)

2x8p5pp (=13pp)

O crux vale	2nd mode

2x7pp6p

Excelsus in numine	1st mode
-Benedictus Dominus	"
Herodis in atrio	2nd mode
Rota versatilis (Orbis)	"

2x76pp (=13pp)

Salve cleri speculum	1st mode
Ianuam quam clauserat	"
-Iacinctus in saltibus	"

776pp

De flore (Deus tuorum)	1st mode*
Salve sancta virgula	"

777pp

Quid rimari cogitas	1st mode
Fusa cum silentio	2nd mode
-Labem lavat	"

2x75pp

Zelo tui langueo	2nd mode
-Reor nescia	"

77557pp

Patria gaudencium	1st mode

7557557pp

Rex omnipotencie	1st mode

7pp7pp6p

Maria mole pressa	1st mode

8p6pp8p5pp, 7pp7pp6pp/5pp

Candens lilium columbina	1st mode

C. *Long-Line Verse*

    26, 21, 17p

        Ade finit perpete   2nd mode
        -Ade finit misere   "

    10pp+8p

        Inter choros   1st mode
        -Invictis pueris   "

II. *Regular poems set regularly on breve and semibreve*

A. *Even pp/ odd p (iambic)*

    4x8pp

        Patrie pacis lucide   1st mode
        Suffragiose virgini   "
        -Summopere sanctam   "

        Hostis Herodes impie   binary

    2x68pp

        Rota versatilis (Virgo)   binary

    6pp

        Balaam de quo (Huic)   1st mode

        Rex visibilium   2nd mode
        -Rex invictissime   "

        O dira nacio   binary
        -Mens in nequicia   "

B. *Even p/ odd pp (trochaic)*

    2x8p7pp

        Jesu fili   1st mode
        -Jesu lumen   "

        Lux refulget   2nd mode

Table 31. (continued)

8p8p7pp

Balaam de quo	1st mode
A solis-Ovet	binary

8p8p6p

Templum eya Salomonis	2nd mode

2x7pp8pp (=15pp)

Rosa delectabilis	1st mode
-Regalis exoritur	"

2x7p8pp

Vas exstas eleccionis	1st mode

7776pp, 2x8p7pp

Surgere iam est	2nd mode

C. *Long-Line Verse*

31, 26, 25, 16pp

Parata paradisi porta	2nd mode

24pp

Viri Galilei	1st mode

3x11p+10pp, 998pp

Orto sole serene	2nd mode

8p8p14pp

Surgere iam est	2nd mode

III. *Regular poems irregularly set on long and breve*

76pp

O crux vale (O crux arbor)	1st mode

10pp

Ave miles	1st mode*

4x8pp

Augustine par angelis	binary

IV. *Regular poems irregularly set on l, b, and s*

A. *Even pp/ odd p (iambic)*

3x or 4x 8pp

Caligo terre	1st mode
Jhesu redemptor	1st mode with pick-up
-Jhesu labentes	"
A solis ortus (Lwa)	2nd mode
-Salvator mundi	"
Rogativam potuit	"

4x or 5x 6pp

De flore martirum	1st mode
Maria mole pressa	"

3x4p+6pp

O crux vale (O beata)	binary

B. *Even p/ odd pp (trochaic)*

7pp6p

Princeps apostolice	2nd mode

2x6p5pp

Rota versatilis (Rota Kat.)	binary

C. *Long-Line Verse*

18, 17, 14, 13p

Suspiria merentis	2nd mode

17, 12, 10pp

Suspiria (Meroris)	2nd mode

Figure 51. Formulas for the Handling of *p* and *pp* Lines

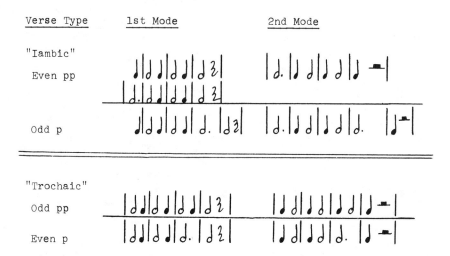

verse (even *p* or odd *pp*) is more common than iambic (even *pp* or odd *p*). Though second mode is less common overall than first mode, it appears with about the same frequency in settings of trochaic and iambic verse. The most significant means of musical differentiation between these verse types is the association of iambic verse with upbeat phrase beginnings and of trochaic verse with downbeat patterns. The differentiation of *p* from *pp* stress accent is effected by different formulas for cadential rhythms at the end of the line. (See figure 51.)

Modifications to the alternation of long and breve as units of declamation most often occur in the stereotyped extension of the penultimate (stressed) syllable in a *p* line and the extension of the pickup in iambic verse to a full bar anacrusis. Alternatively, the pickup may be absorbed into the first full bar, now containing three breves rather than an imperfect long and a breve. This is perhaps the simplest example of the type of accommodation that must be made when the musical phrase is shorter than the length required for regular declamation of the verse on long and breve. Such a situation demands acceleration of declamation to breves or to breves and semibreves, which may be patterned or fitted in ad hoc. For instance, this quickening is handled as an opportunity for patterning in *Templum eya* and *Parata paradisi porta*, but is dealt with more inconsistently in *Jhesu redemptor*. In another sort of case, the varying lengths of the sections of exchange in *Ave miles* provide an opportunity for setting in different ways the *4p6pp=10pp* line, with occasional recourse to semibreve declamation. *Candens crescit* shows a similarly unrigorous regard for exact patterning. In its duplum the verse is often in excess of the declamatory norm by one syllable. The musical phrase provides an ideal pattern for verse of *8p5pp=13pp* per line with a refrain of *7pp7pp5pp*, but often the lines are *9p6pp 8pp8pp6pp*, requiring the subdivision of the imperfect long into two breves somewhere in the phrase.

One of the most interesting questions for the student of later medieval music is the relation between musical declamation and poetic rhythm for regularly versified texts. The most common verse forms include the hymn stanza (*4x8pp*) and lines of *6pp*[123] among the iambic types, and the Victorine-sequence form *8p8p7pp* among the trochaic types.[124] Table 31 shows that verse forms in this repertoire were handled in various ways. The *4x8pp* strophe, for example, is regularly set in long and breve or breve and semibreve values, and also occurs irregularly set in breve and semibreve. The mensurations of these settings include first mode, second mode, and binary meter. Lines of *6pp* receive similarly diverse treatment. However, if one looks solely at the regular poems regularly set in long and breve units, familiar conventions for the metrical patterning of common verse types emerge, which are summarized, for lines of six or seven syllables, in figure 51.

5

Conclusion

The vigorous musical life of fourteenth-century England spawned distinctive genres of polyphony and indigenous notational systems that yielded only gradually to the encroachment of the French Ars Nova over the course of the century. The woefully fragmentary remains of insular motets reveal not only a remarkable number of distinct archetypes for motet construction, but also a number of other consistent traits of musical thought that recur throughout this time period—an interest in four-part writing and counterpoint saturated with imperfect intervals; an interest in the processes of musical variation and motivic work; an interest in selecting unusual tenors and exploiting the potential of tenor design; an interest in numerical proportion, whether expressed in phrase lengths, the spans of larger sections, or the relationships between mensurations.

Despite the fact that there are important superficial resemblances to French and Italian practice in the English notational systems, Bent wisely cautions us against too readily seeing a foreign influence of any sort here. All three music cultures evolved notational and mensural systems in the late thirteenth and early fourteenth centuries in response to nearly the same sets of circumstances. Without a single unified theoretical system propounded by a Guido Frater or Marchettus, a de Vitry or Muris, the English explore several lines of notational development, and we must struggle to piece together a picture of these diverse musical practices from the notoriously fragmentary English sources and the few relevant references that the theorists leave us. The insular notations that survived longest in use—the circle-stem notations and ternary breve-semibreve notation—testify to the vitality, individuality, and continuity of approaches to musical notation in late medieval England.

It is through further work on the texts and the issues they raise that substantial progress can be made in relating the motets to the musical life and social history of fourteenth-century England. This is not to deny that more research is needed into the evolution of style, or that the sources need reexamination, or that the chronology of notational developments in England

and on the Continent needs more careful study along with related music theory and theoretical circles. The most underdeveloped areas of research, however, involve the institutions that performed the motet, and the circumstances of its performance. An assessment of the roles of the Black Death and the Wycliffites, the Franciscans and Dominicans, and the universities, will be critical to a future understanding of the origins and paths of circulation of this music. Finally, we will need to look more closely into the patterns of survival for evidence as to whether there was a shift in the use of the motet over the course of the fourteenth century, and if so, whether the rise of new choral institutions, their new patrons, and their liturgies played any role in this trend.

Appendix 1

List of Manuscripts Cited

B-Ba 758	Brussels, Archives Ecclésiastiques, 758
B-Br 266	Brussels, Bibliothèque Royale, II.266
B-Br 19606	Brussels, Bibliothèque Royale, 19606
CH-Fc 260	Fribourg, Bibliothèque Cantionale et Universitaire, Z 260
D-BAs 115	Bamberg, Staatliche Bibliothek, Lit. 115 (*olim* Ed.IV.6) (Ba)
D-DS 3471	Darmstadt, Hessische Landes- und Hochschulbibliothek, 3471 (Da)
D-Gu 220	Göttingen, Niedersächsische Staats- und Universitätsbibliothek, Theol.220g
D-Mbs Clm 5362	Munich, Bayerische Staatsbibliothek, Clm. 5362
D-Mbs Kasten D IV ad (31)	Munich, Bayerische Staatsbibliothek, Kasten D IV ad (31)
D-ROu 100	Rostock, Universitätsbibliothek, Phil.100/2
D-W 499 (W3)	Wolfenbüttel, Herzog-August-Bibliothek, 499
D-W 677 (W1)	Wolfenbüttel, Herzog-August-Bibliothek, 677
D-W 1099 (W2)	Wolfenbüttel, Herzog-August-Bibliothek, 1099
E-GER	Gerona, Archivo de la Catedral, uncat. leaves
E-MO 1	Monserrat, Biblioteca, 1 (Libre Vermell)
E-Sco 5-2-25	Seville, Biblioteca Colombina, 5-2-25
F-CA 1328	Cambrai, Bibliothèque Communale, B.1328
F-CH 564	Chantilly, Musée Condé, 564 (*olim* 1047)
F-MO	Montpellier, Faculté de Médecine, H.196
F-Pa 135	Paris, Bibliothèque de l'Arsenal, 135
F-Pn 67	Paris, Bibliothèque Nationale, Coll. de Picardie, 67 (Pic)
F-Pn 146	Paris, Bibliothèque Nationale, fonds fr. 146
F-Pn 2444	Paris, Bibliothèque Nationale, nouv. acq. lat. 2444
F-Pn 2605	Paris, Bibliothèque Nationale, nouv. acq. lat. 2605

F-Pn 23190	Paris, Bibliothèque Nationale, nouv. acq. fr. 23190 (*olim* Trémoïlle; *F-SERRANT*)
F-Pn 25408	Paris, Bibliothèque Nationale, fonds fr. 25408
F-Sm 222	Strasbourg, Bibliothèque Municipale, 222 C.22 (STRASS)
F-TO 925	Tours, Bibliothèque Municipale, 925
GB-BERc 55	Berkeley Castle, Muniments, Select Roll no. 55
CAc 128	Canterbury, Cathedral Library, Additional 128
Ccc 8	Cambridge, Corpus Christi College, 8
Ccc 65	Cambridge, Corpus Christi College, 65
Ccc 410	Cambridge, Corpus Christi College, 410
Ccl	Cambridge, Clare College, binding fragment without shelf mark
Cfm 47-1980	Cambridge, Fitzwilliam Museum Library, 47-1980 (*olim* 34-3)
Cgc 230	Cambridge, Gonville and Caius College, 230/116
Cgc 334	Cambridge, Gonville and Caius College, 334/727
Cgc 512	Cambridge, Gonville and Caius College, 512/543
Cgc 803	Cambridge, Gonville and Caius College, 803/807
Cgc 820	Cambridge, Gonville and Caius College, 820/810
Cjc 23	Cambridge, St. John's College, 23 (B.1)
Cjc 84	Cambridge, St. John's College, 84 (D.9)
Cjc 138	Cambridge, St. John's College, 138 (F.1)
Cjc 262	Cambridge, St. John's College, 262 (C.7)
Cjec 1	Cambridge, Jesus College, QB 1
Cjec 5	Cambridge, Jesus College, QB 5
Cpc 228	Cambridge, Pembroke College, 228
Ctc	Cambridge, Trinity College, O.2.1
Ctc 29	Cambridge, Trinity College, O.9.29
Cu 11	Cambridge, University Library, Hh.vi.11
Cu 16	Cambridge, University Library, Ff.vi.16
Cu 29	Cambridge, University Library Ff.ii.29
Cu 710	Cambridge, University Library, Additional 710
Cu 5943	Cambridge, University Library, Additional 5943
DRc 11	Durham, Cathedral Library, A.III.11
DRc 20	Durham, Cathedral Library, C.I.20
DRc Comm. Cart.	Durham, Archives of the Dean and Chapter, Prior's Kitchen, Communar's Cartulary
DRu 13	Durham, University Library, Bamburgh Collection, Sel.13

En 18.7.21	Edinburgh, National Library of Scotland, Advocates MS 18.7.21
GLcro 149	Gloucester, Country Record Office, D.149
GLcro 678	Gloucester, Country Record Office, D.678
H6	fragmentary choirbook reassembled from numerous sources by Bent; see Bent, "More Progeny."
I-MOe 1.11	Modena, Biblioteca estense, α X.1.11 (*olim* lat. 471) (ModB)
Lbl 7.A.vi	London, British Library, Royal 7.A.vi
Lbl 12.C.vi	London, British Library, Royal 12.C.vi
Lbl XVIII	London, British Library, Cotton, Vespasian A.XVIII
Lbl XXI	London, British Library, Cotton, Titus A.XXI
Lbl XXIV	London, British Library, Cotton, Titus D.XXIV
Lbl 29	London, British Library, Cotton, Fragment 29
Lbl 248	London, British Library, Arundel 248
Lbl 978	London, British Library, Harley 978 (LoHa)
Lbl 1210	London, British Library, Sloane 1210
Lbl 1580	London, British Library, Sloane 1580
Lbl 3132	London, British Library, Harley 3132
Lbl 3307	London, British Library, Egerton 3307
Lbl 4909	London, British Library, Additional 4909
Lbl 5958	London, British Library, Harley 5958
Lbl 8866	London, British Library, Additional 8866
Lbl 24198	London, British Library, Additional 24198
Lbl 28550	London, British Library, Additional 28550
Lbl 38651	London, British Library, Additional 38651 (F)
Lbl 40011B	London, British Library, Additional 40011B
Lbl 40011B*	London, British Library, Additional 40011B*
Lbl 40725	London, British Library, Additional 40725
Lbl 46919	London, British Library, Additional 46919 (*olim* Phillipps 8336)
Lbl 57950	London, British Library, Additional 57950 (OH)
Lbl 59846M	London, British Library, Additional 59846 M
Lbl 62132A	London, British Library, Additional 62132A (*olim LEcl 6120; SR 23*)
LEcl 6120	see *Lbl 62132A*
LIc 52	Lincoln, Library of the Dean and Chapter, MS 52, binding fragments
Lli 1	London, Lincoln's Inn, Misc. 1 (Misc. 45)
Lli 146	London, Lincoln's Inn, Hale 146 (Misc. 26)
Llp 457	London, Lambeth Palace, 457
Lpro 23	London, Public Record Office, E/149/7/23 (dorse)

Lpro 2/261	London, Public Record Office, LR 2/261
Lrcp 777/65	London, Royal College of Physicians, 777/65
Lwa 12185	London, Westminster Abbey, 12185
Lwa 33327	London, Westminster Abbey, 33327
Mr 24	Manchester, John Rylands Library, Lat. 24
NWcro 299	Norwich, Norfolk and Norwich Record Office, Flitcham 299
Ob D.R.3*	Oxford, Bodleian Library, Dep. Deeds, Christ Church C. 34/D.R.3*
Ob D.6	Oxford, Bodleian Library, Dep. Deeds, Christ Church C. 34/D.6
Ob 3	Oxford, Bodleian Library, Rawlinson liturg.d.3
Ob 7	Oxford, Bodleian Library, E.mus.7
Ob 14	Oxford, Bodleian Library, Arch.Selden B.14
Ob 18	Oxford, Bodleian Library, Rawlinson G.18
Ob 19	Oxford, Bodleian Library, Lat.liturg. b.19
Ob 20	Oxford, Bodleian Library, Lat.liturg. d.20
Ob 25	Oxford, Bodleian Library, Seville 25
Ob 27	Oxford, Bodleian Library, Fayrfax 27
Ob 55	Oxford, Bodleian Library, Barlow 55
Ob 59	Oxford, Corpus Christi College, 59
Ob 60	Oxford, Bodleian Library, Mus.c.60
Ob 72	Oxford, Bodleian Library, Lyell 72
Ob 81	Oxford, Bodleian Library, Hatton 81
Ob 139	Oxford, Bodleian Library, Douce 139
Ob 143	Oxford, Bodleian Library, Mus.d.143
Ob 257	Oxford, Bodleian Library, Bodley 257
Ob 308	Oxford, Bodleian Library, Douce 308
Ob 343	Oxford, Bodleian Library, Bodley 343
Ob 384	Oxford, Bodleian Library, Bodley 384
Ob 400	Oxford, Bodleian Library, Rawlinson C.400*
Ob 489	Oxford, Corpus Christi College, 489
Ob 497	Oxford, Corpus Christi College, 497
Ob 548	Oxford, Bodleian Library, Bodley 548
Ob 591	Oxford, Bodleian Library, Wood 591
Ob 594	Oxford, Bodleian Library, Laud misc. 594
Ob 652	Oxford, Bodleian Library, Bodley 652
Ob 1225	Oxford, Bodleian Library, Rawlinson D.1225
Occ 144	Oxford, Corpus Christi College, 144
Omc 266/268	Oxford, Magdalen College, 266/268
Omc 267	Oxford, Magdalen College, 267

Omc lat. 7	Oxford, Magdalen College, Latin 7
Omec 248	Oxford, Merton College, 248
Onc 57	Oxford, New College, 57
Onc 362	Oxford, New College, 362
Owc 213*	Oxford, Worcester College, 213* (*olim* 3.16(a)*)
TAcro 3182	Taunton, Somerset County Record Office, DD/WHb 3182
WF	the Worcester fragments; see *WOc 68* or *Ob 20*
WOc 68	Worcester, Cathedral Library, Additional 68
Yc	York, Minster Library, xvi.N.3
YOX	Yoxford, private possession
I-Bc Q15	Bologna, Civico Museo Bibliographico Musicale, Q 15 (*olim* 37)
I-FOL	Foligno, Biblioteca Comunale, fragment of music
I-GR 197	Grottaferrata, Biblioteca dell'Abbazia, collocazione provisoria 197
I-IVc 115	Ivrea, Biblioteca capitolare, 115
I-Ma 71	Milan, Biblioteca Ambrosiana, R71 sup.
I-MOe 1.11	Modena, Biblioteca estense, α.X.1.11 (*olim* lat. 471) (ModB)
I-MOe 5.24	Modena, Biblioteca estense, α.M.5.24 (*olim* lat. 568) (ModA)
I-PIca 176	Pisa, Biblioteca Cateriniana del Seminario Arcivescovile, 176
I-TR 87	Trent, Museo Provinciale d'Arte, 87
PL-WRu I.Q.411	Wrocław (Breslau), Biblioteka Uniwersytecka, I.Q.411
US-Cu 654	Chicago, University of Chicago Library, 654 appendix
US-NYpm 978	New York, Pierpont Morgan Library, 978
US-PRu 103	Princeton, Princeton University Library, Medieval and Renaissance Manuscripts, 103
US-PRu 119	Princeton, Princeton University Library, Garrett 119
US-SM 19914	San Marino, Huntington Library, HM 19914
US-Wc 14	Washington, Library of Congress, M 2.1.C 6a.14

Appendix 2

Critical Reports

The musical materials necessary for the study of the motets found in the fourteenth-century English repertoire are distributed in a wide range of modern sources, including PMFC volumes I, V, and XIV through XVII. Provision here of an exhaustive critical report on each piece together with its text, and transcriptions of all unpublished fragments, would have led to the unchecked growth of an already substantial appendix. As a result, while critical reports have been provided for each motet or fragment, they vary in their level of detail depending on how substantial a piece of music survives, how much is said about it in the foregoing chapters, and whether there exist other modern editions with substantial commentary. The fullest reports include not only source information, but also a bibliography of the literature on a piece (editions, facsimiles, commentary, recordings); observations on the cantus firmus, formal design, notation, and text; and general remarks on features of interest not otherwise covered.

Two "finding lists" provide the necessary means of access to appendix 2. The first arranges the motets alphabetically by the incipits of their short titles, with a reference to the source under which the critical report has been entered. The second presents the motets by source, in an alphabetical arrangement by RISM-style *sigla*. This is the order of presentation followed in appendix 2, so the second list serves as its detailed table of contents. Both lists have been annotated for quick reference with an indication whether a transcription of the motet is available in a volume of PMFC or was provided in the appendix of this author's 1983 thesis for Columbia University (see the bibliography). The latter is indicated by an asterisk.

The Motet Repertoire by Short Title

Motet	Source	Transc.
A solis ortus	Ob 81, 1	XVI, 94
A solis ortus	Lwa 12185, 5	*

Absorbet oris	Lbl 40011B*, 1*	*
Ad lacrimas	DRc 20, 12	XV, 34
Ade finit	Onc 362, 7	XV, 4
Alma mater	BERc 55, 1	*
Alme pater	Lbl 40011B, 18	*
Alta canunt	Onc 362, 8	*
Amer amours	DRc 20, 18	V, 19
Ancilla Domini	Lli 146, 6	*
Apello cesarem	Onc 362, 1	*
Apta caro	DRc 20, 18	V, 4
Assunt Augustini	LIc 52, 3	*
Astra transcendit	LIc 52, 2	*
Augustine par angelis	Ob D.6, 2	*
Ave miles celestis	Ob 7, 7	XV, 20
Ave prolem parienti	LIc 52, 1	—
Balaam de quo	Onc 362, 4	XV, 2
Baptizas parentes	Omc 266/268, 1	*
Barrabas dimittitur	BERc 55, 1	XV, 32
Beatus vir	Lwa 12185, 3	*
Caligo terre	Onc 362, 9	XV, 5
Candens crescit	Cpc 228, 4	XIV, 60
Civitas nusquam	Onc 362, 5	XV, 3
Corona virginum	F-TO 925, 6	XVII, Suppl. 3
Cuius de manibus	Ob 7, 11	XVI, 103
De flore martirum	Ob 7, 8	XV, 21
Degentis vita	GB-YOX, 4	V, 23/23a
Dei preco	DRc 20, 5	*
Detentos a demonibus	CAc 128/2, 1	*
Deus compaignouns	US-Wc 14, 3	—
Deus creator	Ob 7, 14	XV, 23
Diex coment	Lpro 2/261, 2	—
Doleo super te	Cgc 512, 7	XV, 27
Domine quis	Ob 7, 16	V, 16a
Duodeno sydere	Ob 7, 5	*
Excelsus in numine	Onc 362, 6	XVI, 99
Exulta Syon	F-TO 925, 1	XVII, Suppl. 1

Firmissime fidem	Lbl 28550, 4	I, 30
Flos anglorum	Omc 266/268, 3	*
Flos regalis	Lbl 40011B*, 2*	*
Frondentibus	Ob 7, 6	—
Fusa cum silentio	DRc 20, 2	XV, 30
Genitricem personantes	Lbl 40011B*, 3*	*
Geret et regem	TAcro 3182, 2	*
Hac a valle	Lwa 12185, 2	*
Herodis in pretorio	DRc 20, 1	XV, 29
Hostis Herodes impie	Ob 81, 3	XVI, 96
Hostium ob amorem	Lbl 40011B*, 5*	*
Humane lingue	Lbl 40011B, 17	XV, 36
Iam nubes	Onc 362, 15	XV, 8
Ianuam quam clauserat	Onc 362, 2	XV, 1
Jesu fili	DRc 20, 3	XV, 31
Jhesu redemptor	Cfm, 2	XVII, 13
In ore te laudancium	US-SM 19914, 1	*
Inter amenitatis	Yc, 2	I, 22
Inter choros	WF, 79	XIV, App. 26
Inter usitata	Omc 266/268, 2	XVII, 56
L'amoueuse flour	DRc 20, 16	V, 21
Laus honor	Cpc 228, 3	*
Lingua peregrina	WF, 44	*
Lux refulget	Ob 7, 4	*
Ma insuper	F-TO 925, 4	—
Maria mole pressa	Ob 7, 1a	*
Mon chant	DRc 20, 19	V, 15
Mons olivarum	F-TO 925, 7	—
Mulier magni meriti	Cgc 512, 1	XV, 25
Musicorum collegio	DRc 20, 17	XV, 35
Nec Herodis ferocitas	Ob 143, 1	*
Nos orphanos erige	Lwa 12185, 4	*
O canenda vulgo	DRc 20, 15	I, 14
O crux vale	Onc 57, 2	*
O dira nacio	F-Pn 23190, 4	XVII, 55

O homo de pulvere	Onc 362, 17	XV, 9
O pater excellentissime	Onc 57, 1	*
O vos omnes	DRc 20, 14	*
Omnis terra	Ob 7, 12	XV, 22
Orto sole	Cgc 512, 9	XV, 33
Ovet mundus	Ob 81, 2	XVI, 95
Parata paradisi porta	Lpro 2/261, 1	*
Parce piscatoribus	Ob 7, 17	*
Patrie pacis	Cgc 512, 12	XV, 28
Peregrina moror	WF, 47	*
Petrum cephas	Ob 7, 12	XV, 18
Princeps apostolice	Cgc 512, 2	*
Pura placens	Ob 7, 15	XV, 24
Quare fremuerunt	Lbl 1210, 9	XV, 13
Quid rimari cogitas	CAc 128/2, 2	*
Radix Iesse	Ccc 65, 3	*
Recita formosa	Lbl 40011B*, 6*	*
Regi regum enarrare	Onc 362, 12	*
Regina celestium	Ob 652, 3	*
Regina iam discubuit	CAc 128/2, 3	*
Regne de pite	Ob 143, 3	XVII, 57
Regnum sine termino	WF, 80	*
Rex Karole	US-Wc 14, 4	V, 26
Rex omnipotencie	WF, 48	*
Rex piaculum	TAcro 3182, 4	*
Rex sanctorum	Ob 652, 2	*
Rex visibilium	Ob 7, 3	XV, 19
Rogativam potuit	Ob 652, 5	*
Rosa delectabilis	Onc 362, 18	XV, 10
Rosa mundi	Lbl 24198, 2	*
Rota versatilis	Lbl 24198, 1	*
Salve cleri	Ob 81, 4	XV, 11
Salve sancta virgula	Ob 652, 4	*
Si lingua lota	US-PRu 119A, 5	*
Solaris ardor	Onc 362, 10	XV, 6
Soli fines	US-SM 19914, 3	*
Sub Arturo	GB-Yoxford, 1	V, 31
Suffragiose virgini	Cfm, 3	XVII, 54

Surgere iam est	Lbl 24198, 4	*
Suspiria merentis	Cgc 512, 5	XV, 26
Syderea celi	F-TO 925, 3	—
Te domina	Lbl 24198, 6	XV, 16
Templum eya	Ob 7, 9	*
Thomas gemma	Cgc 512, 6	XIV, 61
Tribum quem	Lbl 28550, 5	I, 27
Trinitatem veneremur	Lbl 24198, 5	XV, 15
Triumphat hodie	Lbl 24198, 7	XV, 17
Triumphus patet	Lbl 1210, 2	XV, 12
Tu civium	Cgc 512, 4	XVI, 98
Ut recreentur	WF, 78	*
Valde mane	F-TO 925, 5	XVII, Suppl. 2
Vas exstas	Cpc 228, 1	*
Veni creator	Ccc 65, 2	*
Venit sponsa	CAc 128/2, 4	*
Vide miser	F-TO 925, 9	XVII, Suppl. 5
Virginalis concio	DRc 20, 10	*
Virgo Maria	Cgc 512, 3	XVI, 97
Virgo mater salvatoris	Cfm, 1	XVII, 14
Virgo sancta Katerina	Onc 362, 11	XV, 7
Viri Galilei	Lwa 12185, 1	*
Vos quid admiramini	DRc 20, 13	I, 7
Zelo tui langueo	Lbl 1210, 13	XV, 14
Zorobabel abigo	Ob 7, 1b	*

The following, listed separately, may belong together (see critical reports for details):

1) A solis ortus–Ovet mundus	Ob 81, 1/2
2) Absorbet oris–Recita formosa	Lbl 40011B*, 1*/6*
3) Genitricem–Hostium	Lbl 40011B*, 3*/5*
4) Regina iam–Venit sponsa	CAc 128/2, 3/4

The Motet Repertoire by Source

Source	Transc.

BERc 55

1	Alma mater	*
4	Barrabas dimittitur	XV, 32

Ccc 65

2	Veni creator	*
3	Radix Iesse	*

Cfm

1	Virgo mater salvatoris	XVII, 14
2	Jhesu redemptor	XVII, 13
3	Suffragiose virgini	XVII, 54

Cgc 512

1	Mulier magni meriti	XV, 25
2	Princeps apostolice	*
3	Virgo Maria	XVI, 97
4	Tu civium	XVI, 98
5	Suspiria merentis	XV, 26
6	Thomas gemma	XIV, 61
7	Doleo super te	XV, 27
9	Orto sole	XV, 33
12	Patrie pacis	XV, 28

Cpc 228

1	Vas exstas	*
2	Virgo Maria (see *Cgc 512*, 3)	
3	Laus honor	*
4	Candens crescit	XIV, 60

CAc 128/2

1	Detentos a demonibus	*

2 Quid rimari cogitas   *
3 Regina iam discubuit   *
4 Venit sponsa   *

DRc 20

 1 Herodis in pretorio   XV, 29
 2 Fusa cum silentio   XV, 30
 3 Jesu fili Dei   XV, 31
 4 Princeps apostolice (see *Cgc 512*, 2)
 5 Dei preco   *
 6 Barrabas dimittitur (see *BERc 55*, 4)
 7 Orto sole (see *Cgc 512*, 9)
10 Virginalis concio   *
11 Amer amours   V, 19
12 Ad lacrimas   XV, 34
13 Vos quid   I, 7
14 O vos omnes   *
15 O canenda vulgo   I, 14
16 L'amoreuse flour   V, 21
17 Musicorum collegio   XV, 35
18 Apta caro   V, 4
19 Mon chant   V, 15

LIc 52

1 Ava prolem parienti   —
2 Astra transcendit   *
3 Assunt Augustini   *

Lbl 1210

 2 Triumphus patet   XV, 12
 9 Quare fremuerunt   XV, 13
13 Zelo tui   XV, 14

Lbl 24198

1 Rota versatilis   *
2 Rosa mundi   *
4 Surgere iam est   *
5 Trinitatem veneremur   XV, 15

| 6 | Te domina | XV, 16 |
| 7 | Triumphat hodie | XV, 17 |

Lbl 28550

| 4 | Firmissime fidem | I, 30 |
| 5 | Tribum quem | I, 27 |

Lbl 40011B

| 17 | Humane lingue | XV, 36 |
| 18 | Alme pater | * |

Lbl 40011B*

1*	Absorbet oris	*
2*	Flos regalis	*
3*	Genitricem personantes	*
4*	Rota versatilis (see *Lbl 24198*, 1)	
5*	Hostium ob amorem	*
6*	Recita formosa	*

Lli 146

| 6 | Ancilla Domini | * |

Lpro 2/261

| 1 | Parata paradisi porta | * |
| 2 | Diex coment | — |

Lwa 12185

1	Viri Galilei	*
2	Hac a valle	*
3	Beatus vir	*
4	Nos orphanos	*
5	A solis ortus	*

Ob D.6

| 2 | Augustine par angelis | * |

Ob 7

1a	Maria mole pressa	*
1b	Zorobabel abigo	*
2	Petrum cephas	XV, 18
3	Rex visibilium	XV, 19
4	Lux refulget	*
5	Duodeno sydere	*
6	Frondentibus	—
7	Ave miles celestis	XV, 20
8	De flore martirum	XV, 21
9	Templum eya Salomonis	*
10	Barrabas dimittitur (see *BERc 55,* 4)	
11	Cuius de manibus	XVI, 103
12	Omnis terra	XV, 22
14	Deus creator	XV, 23
15	Pura placens	XV, 24
16	Domine quis	V, 16a
17	Parce piscatoribus	*

Ob 81

1	A solis ortus	XVI, 94
2	Ovet mundus	XVI, 95
3	Hostis Herodes	XVI, 96
4	Salve cleri	XV, 11
5	Fusa cum silentio (see *DRc 20,* 2)	

Ob 143

1	Nec Herodis ferocitas	*
3	Regne de pité	XVII, 57

Ob 594

1	Frondentibus (see *Ob 7,* 6)

Ob 652

1	Rota versatilis (see *Lbl 24198,* 1)	
2	Rex sanctorum	*
3	Regina celestium	*

4   Salve sancta virgula   *
5   Rogativam potuit   *

Omc 266/268

1   Baptizas parentes   *
2   Inter usitata   XVII, 56
3   Flos anglorum   *

Onc 57

1   O pater excellentissime   *
2   O crux vale   *

Onc 362

1   Apello cesarem   *
2   Ianuam quam clauserat   XV, 1
3   Triumphat hodie (see *Lbl 24198,* 7)
4   Balaam de quo   XV, 2
5   Civitas nusquam   XV, 3
6   Excelsus in numine   XVI, 99
7   Ade finit   XV, 4
8   Alta canunt   *
9   Caligo terre   XV, 5
10 Solaris ardor   XV, 6
11 Virgo sancta Katerina   XV, 7
12 Regi regum ennarare   *
15 Iam nubes   XV, 8
17 O homo de pulvere   XV, 9
18 Rosa delectabilis   XV, 10

TAcro 3182

2   Geret et regem   *
4   Rex piaculum   *

WF

44 Lingua peregrina   *
47 Peregrina moror   *
48 Rex omnipotencie   *

53	Candens crescit (see *Cpc 228*, 4)	
67	Thomas gemma (see *Cgc 512*, 6)	
78	Ut recreentur	*
79	Inter choros	XIV, App. 26
80	Regnum sine termino	*

Yc

1	Zelo tui (see *Lbl 1210*, 13)	
2	Inter amenitatis	I, 22

GB-Yoxford

1	Sub arturo	V, 31
2		—
3		—
4	Degentis vita	V, 23/23a

F-Pn 23190

4	O dira nacio	XVII, 55

F-TO 925

1	Exulta Syon	XVII, Suppl. 1
3	Syderea celi	—
4	Ma insuper	—
5	Valde mane	XVII, Suppl. 2
6	Corona virginum	XVII, Suppl. 3
7	Mons olivarum	—
8	Ade finit (see *Onc 362*, 7)	
9	Vide miser	XVII, Suppl. 5

US-NYpm 978

12	Candens crescit (see *Cpc 228*, 4)	

US-PRu 119A

4	Thomas gemma (see *Cgc 512*, 6)	
5	Si lingua lota	*

US-SM 19914

1	In ore te laudancium	*
3	Soli fines	*

US-Wc 14

3	Deus compaignouns	—
4	Rex Karole	V, 26

Critical Reports

BERc 55

Berkeley Castle, Muniments, Select Roll 55 (BERc 55) was identified as a source of fourteenth-century English polyphony by Andrew Wathey in 1981. It is a rotulus with weekly household accounts for an aristocratic Yorkshire family in the years 1302 and 1303. Four musical items have been added on the reverse, including two motets. Andrew Wathey and William Summers have kindly shared information about this source with me, and Wathey is preparing a report about it for publication.

Alma mater digna virgula
Ante thorum virginis
Tenor de Alma mater and Ante thorum

Source: BERc 55, first musical item.
C.f.: identified by the rubric given above and also by a similar rubric under an erased statement of the tenor that was begun below voice I, reading: "Pes de Alma mater et de Ante thorum." The designation "Tenor" or "Pes" in any case apparently hides a short rondeau with the traditional alternation of musical elements AB A'A' AB AB.
Form: very high degree of strophic repetition, with some variation, following the design of the tenor.
Notation: semibreve duplets must be read 2+1.
Text: on the Assumption of the BVM.

Barrabas dimittitur dignus
Barrabas dimittitur inmerito
T. Babilonis flumina

Source: BERc 55, fourth musical item; *DRc 20,* fol. 3 (RISM no. 6); *Ob 7,* fol. VIv (RISM no. 10), voices II and III only.

Literature: Ed. in PMFC XV, no. 32; Wibberley, "English Polyphonic Music," pp. 364–68. Facs. in EECM 26, pl. 153 (*DRc*) and pl. 53 (*Ob*). Harrison, "Ars Nova," pp. 82–83.

C.f.: non-Gregorian; called "Pes de Barrabas dimittitur" in *BERc,* identified in *DRc* as "Babilonis flumina," and unlabeled in *Ob 7.* The Latin incipit probably derives from a rhymed version of Psalm 136(137) that was set monophonically to the tenor tune. Sung three and one-third times, the last statement probably for purposes of ensuring tonal closure.

Form: motet a3 with varied voice exchange and strophic repeat with variation; irregular mixed periodicity.

$$\begin{array}{lll} \text{I} & 60\text{L} & = 7+3+4+4+4+4+8+4+8+4+4+6 \text{ L} \\ \text{II} & & = 2+6+8+8+4+4+8+4+8+4+4 \text{ L} \\ \text{III} & & = 20(3\text{L}) = 3(3(6\text{L})) + 6\text{L} \end{array}$$

Text: on Christ's Passion; the texts expand on the language of a matins responsory for Good Friday, *Barabas latro dimittitur et innocens Christus occiditur* (*Brev. Sar.* I, p. dccxci; *AS,* pl. 226). The text of *Laus honor* (*Cpc 228,* 3) is similar in content and tone.

Remarks: The varied voice exchange between sections one and two is straightforward. In the third tenor statement, the restatement of the material of the first period is very free; striking are the rising and falling fifths in b. 37 and 39, which may be an attempt at affectively setting Christ's last words on the Cross, and the direct canonic imitation between voices I and II at b. 47–51 and 49–53, and b. 52–55, 53–57, and 55–58. The leap of a seventh to "clamans" in II (b. 32–33) may also be deliberately affective. Note that for a voice-exchange motet the range (a fifteenth) is wide and the counterpoint, with its intervals of twelfths and tenths, is also wide. Though notation and rhythms of declamation are conservative, the final cadence is a progressive 10–6 to 12–8.

Ccc 65

Veni creator spiritus eximie
T. Veni creator

Source: Ccc 65, fol. 135v (RISM no. 2).

Literature: Facs. in EECM 26, pl. 106. Sanders, "English Polyphony," pp. 223–24; Fenlon, *Manuscripts,* pp. 76–77.

C.f.: whole-chant setting of the Pentecost hymn *Veni creator spiritus;* the melody is more melismatic here than in the version in *LU,* p. 885, and has been extended by three notes to provide tonal closure for the motet on F (rather than on the chant final, G).

Form: triplum and tenor of an isoperiodic motet a4 (2+2) with broadly patterned tenor:

$$\text{I} \qquad 115\text{L} = 8(12\text{L}) + 19\text{L}$$
$$\text{II} \qquad\qquad = 1\text{L} + 19(6\text{L})$$

Notation: mensuration sign reverse-C-dot in front of both voices; if interpreted (as seems reasonable) as specifying *tempus imperfectum maior,* its only practical effect is to clarify that the breve is binary, so paired semibreves are equal. Perfect-long rests are written in the manner attributed to Robertus de Brunham (see chapter 3, figure 47).

Text: sets five consecutive stanzas of the Pentecost hymn, with an additional four syllables added at the end of each odd-numbered line except the last, to provide successive couplets with twenty syllables that are set regularly in 12L phrases; the final four lines are set to the last (19L) phrase.

Remarks: overall range was originally at least a fourteenth (E–dd) and perhaps a double octave (D–dd).

Radix Iesse

Source: Ccc 65, fol. 136 (RISM no. 3).

Literature: Facs. in EECM 26, pl. 107; Fenlon, *Manuscripts,* p. 76. Fenlon, op. cit., p. 77.

C.f.: none survives; perhaps it was related to the melody with which the text is found in *Cul Hh.vi.11* (see below in *Text*).

Form: an isolated voice-part whose range and style of melodic cadencing suggest it is the lowest voice of a motet, possibly a duet motet with *medius cantus.* There is considerable small-scale melodic and rhythmic repetition that, in conjunction with the phrase lengths, indicates a regular grouping of three breves into a perfect long. Phrase lengths are mainly in multiples of 3B, but are not entirely regular in the second half:

$$\text{I} \qquad 120\text{B} = 18 + 12 + 9 + 15 + 13 + 20 + 18 + 8 + 7.$$

The text is half sung by b. 67.

Notation: tempus perfectum maior with few minims. The note-heads are carefully spaced for declamation. The long is probably perfect; most minim activity falls on the third breve of a perfection, though this is not invariably the case. Rhythms of semibreve duplets and imperfect breve followed by semibreve are both written, so it seems that the duplets ought to be read unequally in the order 1+2.

Text: to the BVM, topically appropriate for the Annunciation and Christmas season. The verses set here are the third and final stanzas of *Ortum floris,* a poem found in *Cul Hh.vi.11,* fol. 69v–70, where it is set to a monophonic tune. Very probably the motet set the first two stanzas of this poem in one missing upper voice. The text is listed twice by Chevalier (nos.

31387 and 39809) and it is edited from *Cul* twice in the *Analecta hymnica* (*AH* 20, pp. 51–52; *AH* 45b, pp. 23–24). The poem is also listed in Anderson, "Notre Dame and Related Conductus—A Catalogue Raisonné," as no. L81, and it is discussed in Gennrich, *Die Kontrafaktur im Liedschaffen,* pp. 21 and 76–78, where reference is given to a musical concordance with a Provençal text, *Quant voi née (Milan, Bibl. Ambrosiana, MS R71 sup.,* fol. 143: Rayn. 534). Gennrich gives a comparative transcription of Latin and Provençal settings on pp. 229–30.

Remarks: The motet is not tonally closed, and the frequent sounding of low B♭ is remarkable. Overall range may have originally been as great as a double octave (B♭–bb♭).

Cfm

Virgo mater salvatoris
Virgo pia vite via
T. [Kyrie]

Source: Cfm, fol. 1–1v (no. 1).
Literature: Ed. in PMFC XVII, no. 14. Facs. in EECM 26, pl. 143–44. Lefferts and Bent, "New Sources," pp. 286–89.
C.f.: unlabeled in the MS; whole-chant setting of Kyrie melody (related to Vat XII ("Pater cuncta") and also to Sarum 22) whose present version is found only in insular sources (see, for instance, *Paris, Bibliothèque de l'Arsenal, MS 135,* fol. 233v).
Form: motet-like troped chant setting in nine sections with considerable contrapuntal repetition following the repetitions in the chant melody. Similar in approach to troped Kyrie settings found in the Worcester fragments and concordant sources (see PMFC XIV, App. 21 and Lefferts and Bent, "New Sources," pp. 277–81). Perhaps slightly later in date of composition than these, though surely still a thirteenth-century composition.
Text: Kyrie trope addressing Father, Son, Holy Ghost, and the Virgin Mary. The assonance of incipits and some later simultaneous correspondences of vowel sounds and whole syllables suggest that the texts are expanding upon a Latin Kyrie text previously associated with the plainchant. None, however, is known at present from surviving sources.

Jhesu redemptor omnium labencium
T. Jhesu redemptor omnium
Jhesu labentes respice

Source: Cfm, fol. 2 (no. 2).

Literature: Ed. in PMFC XVII, no. 13. Facs. in EECM 26, pl. 145; Fenlon, *Manuscripts,* p. 71. Lefferts and Bent, "New Sources," pp. 289–91; Fenlon, op. cit., p. 72.

C.f.: hymn for the Common of a Confessor; written once, to be sung four times in full.

Form: isoperiodic duet motet a3 with *medius cantus;* declamation mostly on longs and breves:

$$
\begin{aligned}
\text{I} \quad & 80L = 1L + 7(10L) + 9L \\
\text{II} \quad & = 4(20L) = 4(4(5L)) \\
\text{III} \quad & = 12L + 7(10L) + 8L
\end{aligned}
$$

Acceleration of declamation in the middle of a musical phrase is both common and relatively unpatterned in *Jhesu redemptor,* where 24 syllables *(3x8pp)* must be compressed into the space that would accommodate only 19 syllables if regularly declaimed on long and breve.

Text: to Jesus and Saint Augustine of Hippo, on the feast *in natale* of the latter. Voice I borrows only the incipit of the tenor hymn. Voice III begins on a variation of the seventh stanza of the Ambrosian hymn *Eterne rerum conditor* to provide an apt incipit, and borrows some vocabulary from the tenor hymn in succeeding lines.

Remarks: unusually wide range of voice parts: I and III span a tenth and an eleventh, respectively, and the motet spans a seventeenth overall.

Suffragiose virgini
Summopere sanctam Mariam
T.

Source: Cfm, fol. 2v (no. 3).

Literature: Ed. in PMFC XVII, no. 54. Facs. in EECM 26, pl. 146. Lefferts and Bent, "New Sources," pp. 291–94.

C.f.: unidentified; probably a chant melisma. Stated seven times with a constantly shifting relationship between *color* and *talea.*

Form: isoperiodic, with strict isorhythmic repetition of a module of 2L (= 6B). See chapter 2, figure 24.

Text: miracles of the BVM, in part illegible due to heavy wear on the MS. See the discussion of texts to the BVM in chapter 4.

Cgc 512

Mulier magni meriti
Multum viget virtus
T.

Source: Cgc 512, fol 246v–247 (RISM no. 1).

Literature: Ed. in PMFC XV, no. 25; Wibberley, "English Polyphonic Music," pp. 263–67. Facs. in EECM 26, pl. 120–21; dipl. facs. in Apfel, *Studien* II, pp. 66–67. Apfel, *Studien* I, p. 29; Harrison, "Ars Nova," p. 75; Sanders, "English Polyphony," pp. 201–3; idem, "Tonal Aspects," pp. 24–26; idem, "England: From the Beginnings," p. 288.

C.f.: freely composed as a tuneful double-versicle *pes* in two 9L-phrases with *ouvert* and *clos* cadences; stated three times.

Form: paired strophic variation with quasi-refrain over the final five notes of the tenor's *clos* cadence:

AA′x BB′x CC′x.

Subdivided-module periodicity on a module of 9L; see chapter 2, figure 25.

Notation: use of downstemmed major semibreve and dots of division; see figure 34 in chapter 3. The edition in PMFC XV does not resolve the occasional rhythmic conflicts in *s* groups, and treats occasional groups of three *s* without downstem differently from those with such stems.

Text: to Saint Katherine, in language similar to that of her legend as printed, for example, in *Brev. Sar.*

Remarks: acceleration to faster rhythmic values and rise in tessitura as motet progresses; very little homorhythmic patter of texted voices on *s,* though. Harrison has observed ("Ars Nova," pp. 75–76) that *Mulier magni meriti* and another *Cgc 512* motet, *Suspiria merentis* (no. 5), share in common a distinctive melodic device—falling fifths in semibreves—that generates melodic-rhythmic activity within a single harmony. Similar rocking fifths, in breves, can be seen in *Barrabas dimittitur* (*BERc 55,* 4).

Princeps apostolice

Source: Cgc 512, fol. 247v (RISM no. 2); *DRc 20,* fol. 2v (RISM no. 4).

Literature: Facs. in EECM 26, pl. 142 (*Cgc*) and pl. 152 (*DRc*).

C.f.: lost, but repetition of phrase scheme and melodic material after 26L indicates it was stated twice.

Form: isolated triplum of a motet a3 with stratification of rhythmic activity. Subdivided-module periodicity; see chapter 2, figure 25.

Notation: both sources use the downstemmed semibreve as the first in groups of three *s.* See chapter 3, figure 34.

Text: for the Common of apostles, related in language to the sequence *Alleluya nunc decantet* for that class of feasts. See the discussion in chapter 4.

Virgo Maria
O stella marina
Virgo Maria
Flos genuit

Source: Cgc 512, fol. 248v–249 (RISM no. 3); *Cpc 228,* fol. iv (RISM no. 2), I and II only.

Literature: Ed. in PMFC XVI, no. 97; Wibberley, "English Polyphonic Music," pp. 268–74. Facs. in EECM 26, pl. 122–23 (*Cgc*) and pl. 203 (*Cpc*); dipl. facs. in Apfel, *Studien* II, pp. 68–69. Apfel, *Studien* I, p. 29; Harrison, "Ars Nova," pp. 76–77; Sanders, "English Polyphony," pp. 92, 197.

C.f.: freely composed.

Form: motet a4 (2+2), repeated in its entirety with voice exchange within upper and lower pairs of voices; more complex internal structure. See chapter 2, figures 9 and 10.

Notation: binary long and breve; probably binary semibreve.

Text: to the BVM.

Tu civium
O cuius vita
Tu celestium
Congaudens

Source: Cgc 512, fol. 252v–253 (RISM no. 4).

Literature: Ed. in PMFC XVI, no. 98; Wibberley, "English Polyphonic Music," pp. 275–81. Facs. in EECM 26, pl. 124–25; dipl. facs. in Apfel, *Studien* II, pp. 70–71. Apfel, *Studien* I, pp. 20ff, 29, 52; Sanders, "English Polyphony," p. 92. Recorded on disc Harmonia Mundi France HM 1106.

C.f.: freely composed.

Form: as in *Virgo Maria,* above; see chapter 2, figures 9 and 10.

Notation: as in *Virgo Maria,* above.

Text: to Saint Peter.

Suspiria merentis
Meroris stimulo
T.

Source: Cgc 512, fol. 253v–254 (RISM no. 5).

Literature: Ed. in PMFC XV, no. 26; Sanders, "Tonal Aspects," pp. 28–30; Wibberley, "English Polyphonic Music, pp. 282–88. Facs. in EECM 26, pl. 126–27; dipl. facs. in Apfel, *Studien* II, pp. 72–73. Apfel, *Studien* I, p. 29; Harrison, "Ars Nova," p. 76; Sanders, "English Polyphony," pp. 209–13, 215; idem, "Tonal Aspects," pp. 26–27; idem, "England: From the Beginnings," pp. 287–88.

C.f.: a presumably freely-chosen six-pitch series (DGFCDC) stated nineteen times; the ostinato recurs in one of four rhythmic configurations (abcd) repeated thus:

aa bb aa bb cc bb dd bb d bb.

Form: refrain motet a3 in five sections, with simple periodic phrase scheme and melodic repeat with *ouvert* and *clos* cadences over each tenor double versicle. See chapter 2, table 9 and figure 16. Sanders calls it a "variation motet."

Text: to the Holy Spirit at Pentecost.

Remarks: refrain only written out once in each voice; see the discussion in chapter 2. See also the remarks on *Mulier magni meriti* (*Cgc 512*, 1) above.

Thomas gemma cantuarie
Thomas cesus in doveria
Primus tenor
Secundus tenor

Source: Cgc 512, fol. 254v–255 (RISM no. 6); *US-PRu 119A,* fols. 4, 3v, 2, 5v (RISM no. A4); *Ob 20,* fol. 35, 34v (RISM no. 67 = *WF,* 67), I and IV only.

Literature: Ed. in PMFC XIV, no. 61; Dittmer, MSD 2, no. 67; Levy, "New Material," pp. 234–39; Stevens, *Music in Honour of St. Thomas,* no. 6; Wibberley, "English Polyphonic Music," pp. 289–301. Facs. in EECM 26, pl. 128–29 (*Cgc*), pl. 210–11 (*US-PRu*), pl. 212 (*Ob 20*); Dittmer, *Oxford, Latin Liturgical D 20,* pp. 43–44 (*Ob 20*). Apfel, *Studien* I, p. 52; Dalglish, "Variation," pp. 46–47; Dittmer, MSD 2, pp. 46–47; Harrison, MMB, pp. 144–45; idem, "Ars Nova," p. 77; Hughes, WMH, p. 105; Levy, "New Material," pp. 224, 228, 230; Sanders, "English Polyphony," pp. 207–9; Stevens, "St. Thomas," pp. 341–42. Recorded on discs Expériences Anonymes EA-0024; Nonesuch H-71292; Harmonia Mundi France HM 1106.

C.f.: freely composed and varied *pes.* The designations P(rimus tenor) and (S)ecundus tenor are found only in *Ob 20.*

Form: motet a4 (2+2) in periods of varied voice exchange punctuated by a refrain; an "ostinato variation," as Dalglish puts it. See chapter 2, figure 11.

Notation: long-breve notation in *Cgc* and *US-PRu;* breve-semibreve notation (with paired semibreves) in *Ob 20.* See chapter 3, figure 39.

Text: on Thomas of Dover (martyred 1295) and Thomas of Canterbury. On its versification see chapter 2, figure 12.

Doleo super te
Absalon fili mi
T.

Source: Cgc 512, fol. 255v (RISM no. 7).

Literature: Ed. in PMFC XV, no. 27; Handschin, "Sumer Canon II," pp.

89–90; Wibberley, "English Polyphonic Music," pp. 302–5. Facs. in EECM 26, pl. 130. Apfel, *Studien* I, p. 29; Handschin, op. cit., pp. 88–91; Sanders, "English Polyphony," pp. 204–7; idem, "Motet," pp. 547–49. Recorded on disc Harmonia Mundi France HM 1106.

C.f.: lowest voice, patterned 2(4(4L)) with two *colores,* is actually freely composed. The duplum consists of a transposed and rhythmicized version of the second half of the antiphon *Rex autem David* (*AS,* pl. 297), which has the musical shape ABC A′B.

Form: motet a3 with strophic repeat and variation, exploiting the varied repeat in the duplum's *cantus prius factus.* At the end of the second half, where the chant breaks off, there is a texted coda with homorhythmic declamation (mostly in unison) of similar texts by the upper voices.

Text: The origin of these texts is in the Old Testament (triplum from 2 Sam. 1 : 26, 22 and duplum from 2 Sam. 18 : 33) but the proximate source for the motet is as Magnificat antiphons for Saturdays during the summer months when the *historia* at matins is the *Hist. Reg.* (see *AS,* pl. 296–97 and *Brev. Sar.* I, p. mclxxii).

The motet's point of departure was clearly the duplum text (David lamenting Absalom), and the triplum text was chosen to be complementary. The liturgical function of this motet (if any) is unknown; Sanders regards it as unliturgical ("English Polyphony," p. 204). Note that both the chosen texts are cast as direct speech.

Remarks: duplum and pseudo-tenor were composed as a pair, to which the triplum was added; the duplum is often the highest voice by range, and is only slightly less active rhythmically than the triplum; further, it cadences to the octave over the final at the end, while the triplum takes the fifth. Note that there is often an unusually wide distance between the upper voices and the pseudo-tenor (for instance, a 15–12 harmony in b. 12).

Orto sole serene
Origo viri
O virga Iesse
Tenor

Source: Cgc 512, fol. 256v–257 (RISM no. 9), voices I, III, IV; *DRc 20,* fol. 3v–4 (RISM no. 7), all four parts.

Literature: Ed. in PMFC, no. 33 (*DRc*); Wibberley, "English Polyphonic Music," pp. 309–15 (*Cgc*) and pp. 369–76 (*DRc*); and in Sanders, "English Polyphony," pp. 244–48 (*Cgc*). Facs. in EECM 26, pl. 132–33 (*Cgc*) and pl. 154–55 (*DRc*); dipl. facs. in Apfel, *Studien* II, pp. 74–75 (*Cgc*). Apfel, *Studien* I, p. 30; Harrison, "Ars Nova," pp. 83–84; Sanders, "English Polyphony," pp. 242–43.

C.f.: freely composed, tuneful *pes* with four phrases; stated four times.

Form: a motet a3 with stratified activity, to which *DRc 20* adds a fourth voice ("Origo viri") that parallels the activity of the top part. Original three parts demonstrate subdivided-module periodicity in 15L units, but the added voice does not participate in this phrase scheme. See chapter 2, figure 25.

Notation: the downstemmed semibreve is used on the first of groups of three *s* in *DRc* but not in *Cgc*.

Text: to the BVM at Christmas time. The incipit of voice III is "Virga Iesse" in *DRc;* however, though "virga" is the first word visible in *Cgc*, the initial letter is not capitalized and there is the possibility that a syllable has been lost in the inner margin. Wibberley makes the plausible proposal that the incipit was originally "O virga Iesse." This attractive suggestion is adopted here not only because it restores assonance but also because it brings the incipit closer to its likely model, the Advent antiphon beginning "O radix Iesse, qui stas in signum populorum."

Remarks: A structural division into two halves is articulated by a shift to faster units of declamation in the third tenor statement. The original motet a3 has progressive 10–5 harmonies and nearly no homorhythmic patter. The added voice is written in homorhythm now with I, now with III, and is often rather crude in counterpoint, with parallel octaves and fifths. Its text is also rather crudely written.

Patrie pacis
Patria gaudencium
T.

Source: Cgc 512, fol. 259v (RISM no. 12).

Literature: Ed. in PMFC XV, no. 28 and in Wibberley, "English Polyphonic Music," pp. 328–30. Facs. in EECM 26, pl. 138; dipl. facs. in Apfel, *Studien* II, p. 76. Apfel *Studien* I, p. 30 and Sanders, "English Polyphony," p. 217.

C.f.: unidentifed, apparently a whole chant; perhaps freely composed pseudo-tenor, with *cantus prius factus* in voice II.

Form: motet a3 with stratification of activity, perhaps with "double structure" (see the discussion of Petronian motets in chapter 2).

I	$18L = 3 + 3 + 3 + 3 + 6L$
II	$= 4 + 4 + 3 + 3 + 4L$
III	$= 18L$

Text: to the BVM.

Cjc 23

This source is discussed by Mark Everist and Margaret Bent in Lefferts and Bent, "New Sources," pp. 306–14 with full facsimiles. The four extant items are motetlike settings a4 (2+2) of textual tropes of liturgical items, apparently freely composed. The first two items are for the Purification of the BVM (February 2) and the second two are for Easter. The first three are all in second mode and show periodicity in 10L; the last is in first mode and shows periodicity in 6L.

Dominum benedixit

> *Source: Cjc 23,* recto (item no. 1).
> *Form:* duplum and one lower voice.
> *Text:* paraphrases the *Nunc dimittis* and doxology, perhaps based on the BVM antiphon for Purification (*AS,* pl. 404).

Spectabili de genere

> *Source: Cjc 23,* recto (item no. 2).
> *Form:* duplum and one lower voice.
> *Text:* paraphrases a short BVM responsory, verse, and doxology for the Purification, *Speciosa facta* (*AS,* pl. 404).

Quis queso precabilium

> *Source: Cjc 23,* recto-verso (item no. 3).
> *Form:* triplum and one lower voice.
> *Text:* paraphrase of short responsory(?) (illegible), verse, and doxology.

Crucifixus surrexit

> *Source: Cjc 23,* verso (item no. 4).
> *Text:* paraphrases the responsory *Crucifixum in carne* and the antiphon verse *Dicant nunc iudei.*

Cpc 228

Vas exstas eleccionis

> *Source: Cpc 228,* fol. i (RISM no. 1).
> *Form:* a lowest voice by range and form of melodic cadence; isoperiodic, perhaps from a duet motet a3 with *medius cantus* in long-breve declamation:
> $$70L = 8L + 8(7L) + 6L.$$

Phrases tend to be paired either by musical rhyme at the incipit or at the cadence, producing the design:

AA'BB'CC'DEFG,

where A'B and B'C share identical cadences. See figure 20.

Text: the conversion of Saint Paul, as told in Acts 9 : 1–22, 22 : 4–16, and 26 : 9–18 (with close correspondence of text lines 1 through 4 to Acts 9 : 15–16 and of text lines 13 through 16 to Acts 26 : 14). The final two stanzas (set to phrases DEFG, the ones not musically linked) have direct speech, and the last stanza changes the style of versification. Note the acceleration to *b-s* declamation on the final couplet.

The language of Acts 9 used in this motet is also drawn on extensively for the services on January 25; it is likely that the missing c.f. was taken from a chant proper to that day, perhaps even one setting the words "vas eleccionis" or "tu es vas eleccionis."

Remarks: this voice begins in second mode (distorting the melodic similarity between the first two phrases) to stretch the phrase from 7L to 8L for isoperiodic offset.

Laus honor vendito
T. Laus honor Christo

Source: Cpc 228, fol. ii (RISM no. 3).

Literature: Sanders, "English Polyphony," pp. 240–42, with transcription.

C.f.: text and melody for the last stanza of the matins hymn that serves as the refrain in Saint Bonaventure's office on the Holy Cross, *In passione Domini* (see *AH* 50, pp. 568–71); sung twice.

Form: the surviving parts are probably triplum and tenor of a motet a4 (2+2) with strophic repeat and variation.

Notation: up to five syllabic semibreves per breve, with the use of the downstemmed semibreve.

Text: for Easter. The text begins as a variation and expansion on the text of the tenor. Succeeding lines closely recall the language of *Barrabas dimittitur* (*BERc 55,* 1) and the closing lines recall a similar formula in *Zelo tui langueo* (*Lbl 1210,* 13).

Remarks: Sanders observed the correspondences in musical content between the first and second halves of the motet. Superposition of one over the other shows a very high degree of repetition, and also occasionally the way in which the missing voice must have interwoven with its surviving counterpart. Further, there is repetition of counterpoint within each tenor statement over similar tenor phrases. On the basis of this sort of examination it is clear that a fourth (lower) voice is necessary for contrapuntal reasons (unsupported fourths).

Candens crescit lilium
Candens lilium columbina
Tenor primus
Quartus cantus

Source: Cpc 228, fol. iiv (RISM no. 4); *Ob 20*, fol. 28v (RISM no. 53 = *WF*, 53); *US-NYpm 978*, fol. 7v–8 (no. 12).

Literature: Ed. in PMFC XIV, no. 60; Dittmer, MSD 2, no. 53; Stevens, TECM I, no. 8. Facs. in EECM 26, pl. 192–193 (*US-NYpm*), pl. 204 (*Cpc*), and pl. 205 (*Ob 20*). Apfel, *Studien* I, p. 53; Dittmer, MSD 2, p. 43; Hughes, WMH, p. 94; Sanders, "English Polyphony," pp. 214–16.

C.f.: voices III and IV function in effect as a single, freely-composed, harmonic part made to support voice II.

Form: refrain motet a4 (2+2), apparently fashioned as a polyphonic setting of the rondo-like melody in voice II, which is likely a *cantus prius factus*. See chapter 2, figure 17. The form of voice II—paired strains with *ouvert* and *clos* cadences—is reflected in the other voices:

$$96L = 16 + 12 + 12 + 16 + 12 + 12 + 16L$$
$$\text{AA' BCC' BCC' AA' DCC' DCC' AA'}$$

Text: to the BVM. Since voice I acts as a filler part that sustains melodic activity, its text is fairly irregular.

CAc 128/2

This source was first brought to light by Nicholas Sandon in "Fragments of Medieval Polyphony at Canterbury Cathedral," pp. 39–44, where it is designated *Cant 2*. I prefer to cite it as above, where *CAc 128* is the guard box of fragments in which the leaf may be found and "2" refers to Sandon's designation. The reader must be warned, however, that this item is not the second numbered fragment in the box.

Three important additions can be made to Sandon's remarks. First, another music fragment found in the cathedral library has been added to the box (*CAc 128/6*, preserving a thirteenth-century English troped chant setting; a report on this source by Dr. Robert Ford is forthcoming). Next, concerning *CAc 128/2*: (i) items 1, 3, and 4 have well-known and often anthologized texts on Saint Bernard that also concern the Assumption of the BVM, within the octave of which (August 15 through 22) his primary feast is usually observed (August 20); and (ii) the one piece not about Bernard, item 2, is a four-section voice-exchange motet a4 with coda, apparently for the BVM.

Items 3 and 4 are linked by their texts, as they set at least six consecutive verses of a hymn for Saint Bernard. The untexted voice surviving for each of these motets has a rubric reading "...s de primo puncto" and "...de secundo puncto," respectively. Sandon plausibly suggests that the missing words in each case are "Quartus cantus." Another alternative might be "Tenor primus" or "Tenor secundus." The expressions "de primo puncto" and "de secundo puncto" suggest the possibility that we have here a motet in two parts (the "primus" and "secundus punctus") setting one text.

In all probability the Bernard motets were a4 (2+2). The counterpoint made by the surviving voices and the rubric "[sec]undo tenore" in the lower voice of the first item point to an accompaniment by two untexted lower parts. Some counterpoint in the fourth item seems to require another upper part. Missing upper and lower voices may, as Sandon notes, have been either on facing pages or in an adjacent column on the same page, now very much cut down. (It is not entirely ruled out, however, that these are pieces with a single texted voice and two supporting parts.)

The reconstructible counterpoint of the pieces on Saint Bernard seems similar to that of the cantilenas in long-breve notation, with generally conjunct melodic lines and frequent parallel motion in 6–3 harmonies. Since, in addition, these motets show uniform declamation and regular periodicity of phrase structure, they seem at least a stylistic generation later than the motets of *Lwa 33327* with which Sandon compared them. (I would like to thank Dr. Sandon for the opportunity to go over my transcriptions of this source with him.)

Detentos a demonibus
Secundo tenore

> *Source: CAc 128/2,* recto (no. 1).
> *C.f.:* probably freely composed.
> *Form:* perhaps duplum and supporting voice of a motet a4 (2+2) with mixed periodicity:
> $$\text{I} \quad 51L = 2(17L) + 16L$$
> $$\text{II} \qquad\;\; = 3L + 6L + 6(7L)$$
> *Text:* the last three stanzas of a nine-stanza hymn to Saint Bernard of Clairvaux and the BVM that begins *Bernardus doctor inclitus* (listed as Chev. 2473; ed. in *AH* 52, pp. 131–33 and *Mone* III, p. 233). In this hymn, every fourth line is itself the incipit of a well-known hymn.
> *Remarks:* perhaps this motet is the final third of a larger setting of the hymn *Bernardus doctor inclitus* (see the relationship suggested between nos. 3 and 4). Of course, if there was a second upper voice, now missing, it may have set more of the text from this hymn.

Quid rimari cogitas
Tenor primus

Source: CAc 128/2, recto (no. 2).

C.f.: freely composed.

Form: triplum and tenor of a four-section voice-exchange motet a4 (2+2) with melismatic coda; counterpoint is mostly restorable from these two parts:

$$72L = (11+12)L + 2(5L) + 2(8L) + 2(8L) + 7L.$$

Text: to the BVM.

Regina iam discubuit

...s de primo puncto

Source: CAc 128/2, verso (no. 3).

C.f.: probably freely composed.

Form: the surviving parts show mixed periodicity:

$$\text{I} \quad 68L(?) = 4(17L)$$
$$\text{II} \qquad\quad = 13(5L) + 3L$$

Text: to Saint Bernard and the BVM; possibly the first part of a larger composition with the piece that follows, setting the first four stanzas of a hymn to Bernard and the BVM that begins (in most sources) *Iam regina discubuit* (listed as Chev. 9365; ed. in *AH* 52, pp. 131–33 and *Mone* III, pp. 233–34).

Venit sponsa de Libano

...de secundo puncto

Source: CAc 128/2, verso (no. 4).

C.f.: probably freely composed.

Form: the surviving parts show mixed periodicity:

$$\text{I} \quad 33L(?) = 17L + 16L$$
$$\text{II} \qquad\quad = 3(11L)$$

Text: sets the succeeding two stanzas of the hymn identified in the motet above. *Venit sponsa* is a fragment, and it is possible that a further two stanzas may have been set. This motet may be simply the second part of *Regina iam discubuit.*

DRc 20

Herodis in pretorio

Herodis in atrio

T. Hey hure lure

Source: DRc 20, fol. 1 (RISM no. 1).

Literature: Ed. in PMFC XV, no. 29 and in Wibberley, "English Polyphonic Music," pp. 353–57. Facs. in EECM 26, pl. 149. Harrison, "Ars Nova," p. 78.

C.f.: a little French ditty whose rather obscure lyrics are most likely either onomatopoetic nonsense (Harrison, op. cit.) or perhaps obscene (a suggestion of the present author in his edition of the text for PMFC XV, where "hung" is a misprint for "hug"). For onomatopoetic refrains, see van den Boogaard, *Rondeaux et refrains,* pp. 260–62.

Form: motet a3 with stratified levels of activity; apparently constructed by adding the duplum, which appears to be a *cantus prius factus* in its own right with melodic shape AA′xBB′CC′DD′EE′y, over three statements of the tenor, and then writing a triplum.

$$\text{I} \qquad 51L = 2(8L) + 4L + 5L + 4L + 10L + 5L + 7L$$
$$\text{II} \qquad\quad = 2(6L) + 4L + 4(2(4L)) + 3L$$
$$\text{III} \qquad\quad = 3(17L) = 3(6+6+5)L$$

What emerges is a rather awkward, early Petronian-style piece not unlike *Caligo terre* (*Onc 362,* 9). There is repetition of motivic material in the triplum and a high degree of dissonance.

Notation: duplum and triplum have signature F♯ throughout; stemming on semibreves is in the hand of the original scribe and follows de Vitry. The G-tonality with signature F♯ is also seen in *Suffragiose virgini* (*Cfm,* 4). See the remarks by Bowers in Lefferts and Bent, "New Sources," p. 293.

Text: for Holy Innocents Day, December 28. The triplum text is closely modeled on Matt. 2:1–18, especially in lines 13 through 18, and the duplum text quotes from Isa. 9:6 and Prov. 1:17.

Remarks: The final word of the tenor text ("moy") is not underlaid to the music in *DRc 20*; rather, it has been added at the foot of the page. Harrison attributes this to a scribal oversight, and restores it to the tenor melody in his PMFC edition. The possibility must be raised, however, that the omission was deliberate, in which case it probably indicates that the original tune was modified slightly to be accommodated to the polyphonic context (perhaps to a preexistent tune in the duplum).

Fusa cum silentio
T. Medius cantus. Manere
Labem lavat criminis

Source: DRc 20, fol. 1v (RISM no. 2); *Ob 81,* fol. 2v (RISM no. 5).

Literature: Ed. in PMFC XV, no. 30; Wibberley, "English Polyphonic Music," pp. 258–62. Facs. in EECM 26, pl. 68 (*Ob 81*) and pl. 150 (*DRc*); dipl. facs. in Apfel, *Studien* II, pp. 64–65 (*Ob 81*). Apfel, *Studien* I, p. 29; Harrison, NOHM III, p. 91; idem, "Ars Nova," p. 79; Sanders, "English Polyphony," pp. 222–23.

C.f.: labeled "medius cantus" in *DRc* and unlabeled in *Ob 81*. It is the melisma on "manere" from the verse of the gradual *Exiit sermo* for the feast of Saint John the Apostle and Evangelist, December 27. Sung almost two and one-half times.

Form: duet motet a3 with *medius cantus;* periodic in modules of 8L, 4L, and 2L:

$$
\begin{array}{rl}
\text{I} & 58\text{L} = 7\text{L} + 5(8\text{L}) + 11\text{L} \\
\text{II} & = 29(2\text{L}) = 2(24\text{L}) + 10\text{L} \\
\text{III} & = 1\text{L} + 13(4\text{L}) + 5\text{L}
\end{array}
$$

Text: homiletic, decries the "oratio clamorosa" (see chapter 4, p. 176 and note 22). The tone is reminiscent of that in *O homo considera* (*Onc 362,* 17), especially at line 21 ("homo nunc considera"). Line 18 ("rigetur omnis arida") recalls a verse from *Veni sancti spiritus* ("riga quod est aridum"). Lines 10 through 14 of the lower texted voice are drawn from Matt. 25 : 1–12.

Remarks: the texts are not of the same length and are sung at unequal rates, with regular long-breve declamation in the lower texted voice and irregular declamation on long, breve, and semibreve in the upper. Perhaps one of the earliest examples of a duet motet; if so, that might explain why it was transmitted with the tenor specifically labeled *"medius cantus."*

Note the following corrections to the readings in PMFC XV: declamation in III: 6 through 8 ought to have rhythm *bl-bl-bl-b*.

Jesu fili Dei patris
T. Jhesu fili virginis
Jesu lumen veritatis

Source: DRc 20, fol. 2 (RISM no. 3).

Literature: Ed. in PMFC XV, no. 31; Wibberley, "English Polyphonic Music," pp. 358–63. Facs. in EECM 26, pl. 151. Harrison, "Ars Nova," pp. 79, 82.

C.f.: unidentifed; however, the text underlaid to the tenor ("Jhesu fili virginis. rex celestis agminis.") is identical to the initial two lines of a Latin devotional sequence found uniquely in *Cul 710,* fol. 123 (p. 178), and Harrison has shown that there is some melodic similarity between the sequence melody and the motet tenor. It is highly implausible that the c.f. was derived directly from the sequence tune by some systematic, if drastic, reshaping; the relationship is certainly less direct. The tenor is written out once and must be sung twice, except for the omission of the last two 4L phrases the second time.

Form: duet motet a3 with *medius cantus* and isoperiodic phrase structure; very similar to *Rosa delectabilis* (*Onc 362,* 18). See chapter 2, figure 22.

Text: prayer to Jesus. The two texts are not only identical in versification, but share lines 28 ("da mihi quod sicio") and 31 ("reum munda nunc vicio") and are divided into 16+15 lines by the -*cio* rhyme.

Dei preco

> *Source: DRc 20,* fol. 3 (RISM no. 5).
> *Literature:* Facs. in EECM 26, pl. 153.
> *Form:* a lowest voice by range and form of melodic cadence; perhaps from an isoperiodic duet motet a3 with *medius cantus* in long-breve declamation. See chapter 2, figure 19.
> $$56L = 17L + 14L + 14L + 11L$$
> $$= 3L + 7(7L) + 4L$$
> *Notation:* use of the downstemmed semibreve. One occurrence of the upstemmed semibreve on the fourth note (E) of b. 28 creates an *ssm* rhythm that may be an alternate equivalent for *major-s ss,* in which case groups of three *s* ought all to be transcribed with the rhythms of de Vitry.
> *Text:* on John the Baptist and his beheading. Text lines 1 through 4 are derived from Matt. 11 : 11 and lines 8 through 10 from Matt. 14 : 1–12.
> *Remarks:* inconsistent declamation tends to end a *p* line with the rhythm *lb* rather than *perfect-11.* Note the recurrence of a melodic figure *ssbb* (EFGF).

[Virgo sancta Katerina]
Virginalis concio
[T. Virgo sancta Katerina]
Contratenor. de virgo sancta Katerina

> *Source: DRc 20,* fol. 336* (RISM no. 10), voices II and IV only.
> *Literature:* Facs. in EECM, pl. 157. Harrison, "Ars Nova," p. 77; Hughes and Bent, *Old Hall Manuscript* III, p. 43.
> *C.f.:* none survives, but the Saint Katherine antiphon *Virgo sancta Katerina* (*AS,* pl. W), which is suggested as a likely candidate by the wording of the contratenor, can in fact be made to fit well with the surviving counterpoint.
> *Form:* surviving parts are the duplum and contratenor of a bipartite panisorhythmic motet a4 with *introitus,* coda, and diminution by one-half; two *colores* and eight *taleae.*
> $$126B = 7(18B)$$
>
> | | |
> |---|---|
> | I | $= ?$ |
> | II | $= 3B + 16B + 7(9B) + 6B + 3(9B) + 11B$ |
> | III | $= 13B + 4(12+6)B + 4(6+3)B + 5B$ (as reconstructed) |
> | IV | $= 13B + 9B + 3(18B) + 14B + 4(9B)$ |

Notation: contratenor is in *modus perfectus* (*tempus perfectum* upon diminution) with second-mode rhythms; the tenor, as reconstructed, is in *maximodus perfectus, modus imperfectus* (*modus perfectus, tempus imperfectum* upon diminution).

Text: to Saint Katherine, November 25. The text in I probably began "Virgo sancta Katerina," judging by the wording of the contratenor. The text in voice II survives elsewhere in the duplum of a later motet in Old Hall, *En Katerine solennia–Virginalis concio–T. Sponsus amat sponsum* (*Lbl 57950,* 145) by Byttering.

Amer amours est la choison
Durement au cueor
T. Dolor meus

Source: DRc 20, fol. 336* (RISM no. 11), part of I and all of II and III; *F-Pn 67,* fol. 67 (RISM no. 1); *F-Pn 23190 (Trém),* index vii; *I-IVc 115,* fol. 56v–57 (RISM no. 72).

Literature: Ed. in PMFC V, no. 19. Facs. in EECM 26, pl. 157 (*DRc*).

Form: unipartite isorhythmic motet a3 with *introitus;* two *colores* and six *taleae.*

$$120B = 12B + 6(18B)$$

I	$= 32B + 2B + 4(16+2)B + 14B$
II	$= 12B + 21B + 4(18B) + 15B$
III	$= 12B + 6(6+12)B$

Text: courtly French love poetry.

Ad lacrimas flentis
O speculum spericum
T. Dulcis virgo tenor.

Source: DRc 20, fol. 336*v–337 (RISM no. 12); *CH-Fc 260,* fol. 86 (RISM no. 2).

Literature: Ed. in PMFC XV, no. 34. Facs. in EECM 26, pl. 158 (*DRc*). Harrison, "Ars Nova," p. 84; Sanders, "Motet," pp. 549–50; Zwick, "Deux motets inédits."

C.f.: verse of an Alleluia to the BVM known only from an English source, *F-Pa 135,* fol. 209. (Not listed in *GS* indices.)

Form: unipartite isorhythmic motet a3; three *colores* and six *taleae.* Just prior to the restatement of each *talea,* voice I splits into two parts for one musical phrase, then reunites. In the following number scheme the split phrase is indicated by an apostrophe:

$$108B = 6(18B)$$

I $106B = 16B + 3(9'+9)B + 2(10'+8)B$

II $= 20B + 4(18B) + 14B$

III $= 5(6+12)B + (6+10)B$

Text: to the BVM.

Remarks: The form is articulated by the use of hocketing and change of phrase length in voice I for *taleae* five and six, and also by the rhyme scheme and stanzaic structure of the texts, which articulate three larger sections of two *taleae* each. Further, there is a recurring pattern of declamation (*smsmss*) and either voice exchange or imitation when voice I splits: "the periodic twinning of the Triplum is marked by initial *Stimmtausch* or some other imitative device" (Sanders, "Motet," p. 549).

Vos quid admiramini
Gratissima virginis species
Tenor. de vos quid admiramini [Gaude gloriosa]
Contratenor de vos quid admiramini

Source: DRc 20, fol. 336*v–337 (RISM no. 13); *B-Ba 758*, fol. 67 bisv (RISM no. 4); *F-CA 1328*, fol. 11 (RISM no. 47); *F-Pn 23190 (Trém)*, index xxiii; *I–IVc 115*, fol. 8v–9 (RISM no. 13).

Literature: Ed. in PMFC I, de Vitry motets no. 7; Marrocco and Sandon, *Oxford Anthology*, no. 58. Facs. in EECM 26, pl. 59 (*DRc*). Leech-Wilkinson, "Compositional Procedure," pp. 50–67, 265–66.

Form: bipartite isorhythmic motet a4 with two *colores*.

$$162B = 6(15B) + 8(9B) \text{ (idealized scheme)}$$

I $157B = 18B + 2(11+19)B + 14B + 3(18B) + 11B$

II $= 21B + 2(30B) + 13B + 3(18B) + 9B$

III $= 5(5+10)B + (5+11)B + 7(9B) + 3B$

IV $= 2B + 5(15B) + 13B + 7(4+5)B + 4B$

Text: to the BVM; critical ed. in Dronke, *Medieval Latin*, ii, pp. 406–10.

Remarks: written in the 1330s, according to Sanders ("Early Motets," p. 37).

O vos omnes
T. Introitus tenoris. Locus iste. tenor.

Source: DRc 20, fol. 337v (RISM no. 14).

Literature: Facs. in EECM 26, pl. 160.

C.f.: beginning of the gradual for the dedication of a Church; see, for example, *GS* pl. 175 or *LU*, p. 1251.

Form: duplum and tenor of a bipartite isorhythmic motet a4 with melismatic *introitus* and diminution by one-half; diminution section is melismatic with hocket. The *introitus* has four *colores* and four *taleae*, while the main body of the motet has a tenor of two *colores* and eight *taleae*.

$$180B = 4(18B) + 4(18B) + 4(9B)$$

$$I = (10+36+18+8)B + (20+2(18)+16)B + (8+2(9)+10)B$$

$$II = 4(8+6+4)B + 4(5+13)B + \tfrac{1}{2}(4(5+13))B$$

Text: complaint on the present state of the Church. The incipit ("O vos omnes") recalls the Lamentations of Jeremiah (Lam. 1: 12).

O canenda vulgo
Rex quem metrorum
T. Rex regum tenor.
Contratenor

Source: DRc 20, fol. 337v (RISM no. 15), voices II and III only; *CH-Fc 260,* fol. 86v (RISM no. 3); *F-Pn 2444,* fol. 48v (RISM no. 2); *F-Pn 23190 (Trém),* index no. xx; *I-IVc 115,* fol. 55 (RISM no. 69).

Literature: Ed. in PMFC I, no. 14 with further commentary in PMFC V, p. 207. Facs. in EECM 26, pl. 160 *(DRc).* Leech-Wilkinson, "Compositional Procedure," pp. 33–49, 262–64.

Form: bipartite isoperiodic motet a4 with diminution by one-half; three *colores* and twelve *taleae.* Diminution section melismatic with hocket.

$$120B = 8(12B) + 4(6B)$$

$$I = 14B + 6(12B) + 9B + 3(6B) + 7B$$

$$II = 15B + 6(12B) + 9B + 4(6B)$$

$$III = 8(6+6)B + 4(3+3)B$$

$$IV = 1B + 7(3+9)B + 3B + 8B + 4(6B)$$

Text: in praise of Robert of Anjou (1278–1343), king of Naples and Sicily.

Remarks: written in the 1330s, according to Sanders ("Early Motets," p. 37).

L'amoreuse flour
En l'estat d'amere
T. Sicut fenum arui

Source: DRc 20, fol. 338 (RISM no. 16), I only; *F-Pn 23190 (Trém),* index xvi; *I-IVc 115,* fol. 59v–60 (RISM no. 75).

Literature: Ed. in PMFC V, no. 21. Facs. in EECM 26, pl. 161 *(DRc).*

Form: unipartite isorhythmic motet a3; two *colores* and six *taleae.*

$$144B = 6(24B)$$

I	$= (11+15)B + 4(9+15)B + 9B + 13B$
II	$= 4B + 5(10+14)B + (10+10)B$
III	$= 6(7+10+7)B$

Text: courtly French love poetry.

Musicorum collegio
In templo Dei posita
T. Avete. Tenor.

Source: DRc 20, fol. 338v–339 (RISM no. 17).

Literature: Ed. in PMFC XV, no. 35. Facs. in EECM 26, pl. 162–63. Harrison, "Ars Nova," p. 85.

Form: bipartite isorhythmic motet a3 with diminution by one-half; two *colores* and eight *taleae.*

$$144B = 4(24B) + 4(12B)$$

I	$= 7B + 3(4+7+13)B + (4+7+12)B + 3(12B) + 6B$
II	$= 8B + 3(4+8+12)B + (4+8+8)B + 3(12B) + 8B$
III	$= 4(10+5+9)B + \frac{1}{2}(4(10+5+9))B$

Text: a musicians motet. See discussion of musicians motets in chapter 4.

Apta caro plumis
Flos virginum
T. Alma redemptoris mater

Source: DRc 20, fol. 338v–339 (RISM no. 18), where it is complete without the contratenor found in some other sources; *F-CA 1328,* fols. 1v, 17 (RISM nos. 2a, 37); *F-CH 564,* fol. 60v–61 (RISM no. 101); *F-Pn 23190 (Trém),* index xxii; *I–IVc 115,* fol. 5v–6 (RISM no. 7); *I-MOe 5.24 (olim 568),* fol. 18v–19 (RISM no. 29).

Literature: Ed. in PMFC V, no. 4 and in CMM 39, no. 3. Facs. in EECM 26, pl. 162–63 (*DRc*). Leech-Wilkinson, "Compositional Procedure," pp. 156–68, 279–80.

Form: unipartite isorhythmic motet a3 (a4) with *introitus;* two *colores* and three *taleae.*

$$90B = 9B + 3(27B)$$

I	$= (3+12)B + 2(13+14)B + (13+8)B$
II	$= (17+15+3)B + (9+15+3)B + (9+15+4)B$
III	$= 9B + 3(27B)$

Text: to the BVM.

Mon chant en plaint
Qui dolereus
T. Tristis est anima mea

> Source: DRc 20, fol. 339 (RISM no. 19), voice I only; F-Pn 23190 (Trém), index xliii; I–IVc 115, fol. 22v–23 (RISM no. 37).
> Literature: Ed. in PMFC V, no. 15. Facs. in EECM 26, pl. 164 (DRc).
> Form: unipartite isorhythmic motet a3; three colores and five taleae.
> 120B = 5(24B) (idealized scheme)
> I   115B = 25+3(24)+18B = (8+3+10+4)+3(7+3+10+4)+(7+3+8)B
> II   = 20+3(24)+23B = (9+3+8)+3(13+3+8)+(13+3+7)B
> III   = 4(24B) + 19B = 4(10+3+2+9)B + (10+3+2+4)B
> Text: courtly French love poetry.

LIc 52

LIc 52 consists of binding strips and flyleaves taken from Lincoln, Library of the Dean and Chapter, MS 52 when this volume was rebound in 1977. It is described by Susan Rankin in Bowers and Wathey, "New Sources," pp. 137–53 with full facsimiles of the fragments and partial transcriptions of items 2 and 3. (I would like to thank Dr. Rankin for providing me with photocopies of the fragments and a copy of her report prior to publication.) The fact that all texts begin with A is noteworthy, suggesting either an alphabetically ordered music manuscript or a gathering exclusively devoted to troped-chant settings of Alleluias, such as one also sees in the earlier D-W 499 (W3) (Wolfenbüttel, Herzog-August-Bibliothek, MS 499).

Ave prolem parienti

> Source: LIc 52, fol. 1r (item no. 1).
> Notation: tempus imperfectum maior.
> Remarks: fragment of one or two voices of a composition a3 or a4 dedicated to the BVM.

Astra transcendit
T. Alleluya V. Assumpta est Maria
Astrorum celsitudinem

> Source: LIc 52, fol. 1v–2 (item no. 2).
> C.f.: the soloist's portions of the Alleluya, not as found in LU, p. 1603 but closely following the reading in GS, pl. 195. Note that the final two tenor taleae are not written out in the MS; a custos on the pitch C indicates a return to the beginning of the verse.

Form: troped whole-chant setting a3 with bipartite division following the Alleluya/Verse form of the chant. The layout is as a duet motet with *medius cantus,* including a regularly patterned tenor and some periodicity in phrase structure:

$$\text{I} \quad 58L = 6L + 8L + \ldots$$
$$\text{II} \qquad = 20L + 38L = (5 + 3(4) + 3)L + (7(5) + 3)L$$
$$\text{III} \qquad = (10 + 10)L + (7 + 5 + 6 + 4(5))L$$

Notation: circle-stem notation with minim stems and at least one appearance of the *cauda hirundinis* (I:11). Almost all breves are plicated.

Text: tropic to the chant and designed mainly as a series of salutations to Mary. Rankin has observed that the duplum begins with two three-line stanzas very similar to the language of a fragmentary cantilena found in *Lbl 38651,* fol. 2 (RISM no. 3).

Motet   **Cantilena**

Astrorum celcitudinem   Astrorum altitudinem
omnemque celi aciem   totamque poli aciem
David concendit filia   transcedit virgo regia

Sedet iuxta trinitatem   Iuxta sedem propaginem
ob inmensam castitatem   immensam plenitudinem
in regis gloria.   h . . .

Assunt Augustini
T.

> *Source: LIc 52,* fol. 2v (item no. 3).
> *C.f.:* freely composed?
> *Form:* voices I and III of a motet or motet-like setting a4 (2+2). The form is bipartite, suggesting that the piece might be a setting of a chant like the Alleluia and verse of *LIc 52,* 2.
>
> $$60L = 12L + 48L (= 5(12L)), \text{ plus final long.}$$
>
> *Notation:* ternary breve-semibreve notation.
> *Text:* to Saint Augustine of Hippo. The verses begin with a formula familiar from the matins invitatory of a number of rhymed offices:

Motet   **Offices**

Assunt Augustini   Assunt Dominici   Assunt Thome
leta solempnia   leta sollemnia   martiris solennia
instantque celici   laude multiplici   virgo mater
viri festalia.   plaudat ecclesia.   iubilet ecclesia.

See the *Analecta Hymnica: Register* for these and further examples.

Remarks: There is some musical rhyme, as in bars 1–2 and 7–8 or bars 37–38 and 54–55. No regular intervals of systematically repeating counterpoint have been discovered, however. Note that hocketing in semibreves must have been a remarkable feature of the lower two parts.

Lbl 1210

Triumphus patet hodie
... genuflectere
T.

> *Source: Lbl 1210*, fol. 1v–1* (RISM no. 2).
> *Literature:* Ed. in PMFC XV, 12. Facs. in EECM 26, pl. 24–25.
> *C.f.:* unidentified 39-note, 19L melody in F, sung three times; carefully shaped rhythmically into two 6L and one 7L phrase. Harrison views it as an 18L melody that is modified in the third *talea*.
> *Form:* Stratified motet a3 with rapidly sung upper voice and two voices of slower, nearly equal rhythmic activity. No regular patterns of phrasing or declamation. The duplum appears to be a well-shaped melody with melodic sequences, some repetitions, and carefully controlled use of its range.
>
> I $57L = 5+6+10+8+6+8+5+9$ L
> II $= 4+2+3+5+4+4+3+6+6+4+6+5+5$ L
> III $= 3(19L) = 3(6+6+7)L$
>
> *Notation:* unique notation of triplum. See chapter 3, figure 46.
> *Text:* to the Holy Cross.
> *Remarks:* seems most similar in approach to *Herodis in atrio* (*DRc 20*, 1).

Quare fremuerunt gentes
T.
Quare fremuerunt gentes

> *Source: Lbl 1210*, fol. 140v–141 (RISM no. 9).
> *Literature:* Ed. in PMFC XV, no. 13. Facs. in EECM 26, pl. 32–33; dipl. facs. in Apfel, *Studien* II, pp. 76–78. Apfel, *Studien* I, p. 30; Sanders, "English Polyphony," pp. 234–38 with partial transcription.
> *C.f.:* tone for the psalm *Quare fremuerunt* as sung with the antiphon *Dominum dixit ad me* on Christmas Day at first mass, according to Harrison in PMFC XV, citing a Cistercian gradual, *Paris, BN lat.n.a. 2605*, fol. 27. Another interpretation must be considered. The c.f. is a palindrome, and up to the point of reversal it is identical to the beginning of the eighth Magnificat

tone in the use of Salisbury (see Frere, *The Use of Sarum* II, p. lxxi.) Explanation as a palindrome accounts for why the c.f. is not written out in full and why it begins with seemingly unnecessary rests (necessary for retrograde statement), a technique seen also in the tenor of *Inter usitata* (*Omc 266/268*, 3). Depending on one's interpretation, then, the tenor is sounded either two or four times. See chapter 2, figure 23.

Form: duet motet a3 with *medius cantus;* isoperiodic in a module of 8L:

    I   96L = 10L + 10(8L) + 6L
    II   = 12(8L)
    III   = 5L + 6L + 10(8L) + 5L

Notation: a small figure 3 is written over each *longa triplex* in the tenor. See chapter 2, figure 23.

Text: incipits of Psalms 2 through 12 embedded in a poetic matrix; the single text is shared by both voices and declaimed simultaneously except when one or the other voice rests. At these points the text varies slightly between voices.

Remarks: The rhythm is slightly awry in bars 51–55 of the PMFC edition.

Zelo tui langueo
T.
Reor nescia

Source: Lbl 1210, fol. 142v–143 (RISM no. 13); *Yc,* fol. 10v (no. 1), I and II only.

Literature: Ed. in PMFC XV, no. 14. Facs. in EECM 26, pl. 36–37 (*Lbl*) and pl. 213 (*Yc*); dipl. facs. in Apfel, *Studien* II, pp. 78–81 (*Lbl*). Apfel, *Studien* I, p. 30; Bowers, "Performing Ensembles," pp. 188–92; Caldwell, "Review," p. 470; Harrison, EECM 26, pp. xiv–xv; Lefferts and Bent, "New Sources," pp. 359–60; Sanders, "English Polyphony," pp. 231–34; idem, "Motet," pp. 544–46.

Cf.: unidentified; sung four times.

Form: duet motet a3 with *medius cantus;* isoperiodic in a module of 8L, with a rhythmic caesura in the third or fourth bar of each 8L phrase, thus articulating 8 as 3+4+1 or 4+3+1. The unaccompanied beginning is unusual—the tenor has 2L of rest and voice III has 4L of rest. For another instance, see *Doleo super te* (*Cgc 512*, 7).

    I   130L = 15(8L) + 10L
    II   = 2L + 32(4L)
    III   = 4L + 15(8L) + 6L

Text: to the BVM (not to the Holy Cross, as is misprinted in PMFC). The incipit of the triplum is identical to the final line of a poem by Richard Rolle, the *Canticum Amoris* (see chapter 4, p. 196 and note 109). John Caldwell has also observed the relationship to Rolle's poem (op. cit), though he notes only the similarity of the first line of the *Canticum* to the incipit.

On the basis of a translation provided by me for PMFC XV, it would seem that the motet expresses the thoughts of a woman. In EECM 26, Harrison argues from this that the motet provides further evidence for the nunnish provenance of *Yc,* and further, that it establishes that nuns sang motets. One could add, in addition, that on account of Rolle's association with the Cistercian nunnery of Hampole the possibility might be entertained that the motet was originally composed for or by the Yorkshire nuns.

However, I now read the texts slightly differently, with the result that they no longer seem to support the above speculations. What I now believe to be a more sensible punctuation and syntax for the last lines of the triplum is as follows:

non meroris	[but for Mary, we sinners] would not
a miseria	feel relief from
sentiret remedium.	the misery of sorrow.
Ergo, David	Therefore, dear daughter
cara filia	of David,
que laudum preconia	may it be that the praises of praises
tibi condecent	are rightly fitting to be said to you
apte dici	for all those kindnesses.
ob tot beneficia.	

And as for the duplum text, it seems to begin with direct speech on the part of Eve, then move into a narrative of the result of her crime, which is the main topic of the triplum also. Direct discourse is not unknown in the motet texts, nor is this the unique instance where a woman speaks (see lines 22 through 29 of *Maria mole pressa* [*Ob 7,* 1a] where the works are spoken by Mary Magdalene). Hence I do not see the necessity of associating the texts of *Zelo tui* with nuns. (See also the recent comments of Bowers, op. cit., where the above points are made independently and at greater length.)

Remarks: unusually wide range (a sixteenth), with wide ambitus of the outer voices (an eleventh and a thirteenth).

Lbl 24198

Rota versatilis
Rota versatilis
T.
Q.C.

Source: Lbl 24198, fol. 132 (RISM no. 1), II and IV only; *Lbl 40011B*,* 4*, I and III only, fragmentary; *Ob 652,* fol. i, iiv, 69, 70v (RISM no. 1), II and IV, fragmentary.

Literature: Transcribed, with text edition, facsimiles, and extensive discussion of the sources, in Bent, "Rota versatilis"; see also Bent, *Fountains Fragments* (forthcoming). Facs. in EECM 26, pl. 1 (*Lbl 24198*) and pl. 208–9 (*Ob 652*). Sanders, "England: From the Beginnings," p. 289; idem, "Motet," pp. 546–47.

C.f.: freely composed.

Form: large-scale voice-exchange motet a4 (2+2) in five sections of varying length and mensuration. See chapter 2, table 7 and figure 7, and chapter 3, figure 43. Due to the fragmentary nature of the surviving materials, only sections III and V can be fully reconstructed. Sanders observes that if one takes the long in section III as ternary and in section V as binary, then the numerical proportions between the sections as measured in longs (108:76:36:80:54) stand very nearly in the simpler numerical ratios 12:8:4:9:6 (e.g., 108:72:36:81:54).

Text: on Saint Katherine.

Remarks: The incipit of voice I survives uniquely as a musical citation in the treatise of Robertus de Handlo (*Lbl 4909,* fol. 4v = p. 8). This treatise was completed in 1326, according to its explicit, providing a terminus for composition that accords well with Sanders's judgment that the motet could have been composed no later than the first two decades of the fourteenth century. An entry in a fifteenth-century index in *Lbl Royal 12.C.vi* reads "Modus componendi rotam versatilem."

Rosa mundi purissima

Source: Lbl 24198, fol. 132v (RISM no. 2).

Literature: Facs. in EECM 26, pl. 2.

Form: isolated triplum of a motet a3 with stratification of rhythmic activity; irregular phrase structure and no readily apparent repetition of melodic material that might indicate underlying tenor structure:

71L(72L?) = 5+6+4+3+4+5+3+3+4+6+5+8+3+6+2+4(5?)L.

Notation: groups of up to six syllabic semibreves per breve, with no stems.

Text: to the BVM.

Remarks: thirteen of sixteen phrases cadence to F.

Surgere iam est hora
T. Surge et illuminare

Source: Lbl 24198, fol. 133 (RISM no. 4).

Literature: Facs. in EECM 26, pl. 3.

C.f.: incomplete and unidentified in the MS; three rhythmically varied statements (only the latter two of which are preserved) of the beginning of the verse *Surge et illuminare* of the Epiphany gradual *Omnes de Saba.*

Form: refrain motet a3 in three sections with double-versicle melodic facture. See chapter 2, table 9 and figure 16.

Text: likely for Epiphany; mixed in versification. The increasing length of stanzas leads to accelerating pace of declamation.

Remarks: RISM no. 4a is an isolated fragment that does not belong with *Surgere* and may possibly be part of an untexted voice of a motet now lost with the facing page to fol. 133.

Trinitatem veneremur
Trinitas et deitas
Trinitatis vox
T. Benedicite Deum celi

Source: Lbl 24198, fol. 133v, 1 (RISM no. 5).

Literature: Ed. in PMFC XV, no. 15. Facs. in EECM 26, pl. 4–5. Apfel, *Studien* I, p. 30; Bowers, "Performing Ensemble," p. 172.

C.f.: unidentified in the MS; whole-chant setting of the verse *Benedicite Deum celi* of the gradual for Trinity Sunday *Benedictus es Domine.* Due to its ambitus, the c.f. is not always the lowest sounding voice.

Form: motet a4 (3+1) with fairly irregular phrase structure, always in multiples of 2L:

$$I \quad 48L = 18L + 8L + 8L + 4L + 10L$$
$$II \quad\quad = 10L + 18L + 10L + 10L$$
$$III \quad\quad = 2L + 4L + 4L + 6L + 14L + 12L + 6L$$
$$IV \quad\quad = 12(4L)$$

Voices I and II generally paired in parallel declamation on *b* and *s.* Voice III has a well-crafted melodic profile.

Notation: rhythmic-melodic figures of threes, and counterpoint of twos against threes, suggest 1+2 reading of duplets.

Text: to the Holy Trinity (marginal note: "de sancta trinitate"); reference is made to depredations of "rex et papa."

Remarks: variants to PMFC edition include II: 39 *ss(b)* (EE E). III: 21 *lsss* (E EDC); 22 *ss b sss* (DCBCBA).

Te domina regina
Te domina Maria
T.

Source: Lbl 24198, fol. 133v, 1 (RISM no. 6).

Literature: Ed. in PMFC XV, no. 16. Facs. in EECM 26, pl. 4–5.

C.f.: varied version of a *pes* tenor found in the thirteenth-century English repertoire. See figure 14.

Form: motet a3 built in loose periods of varied voice exchange; double-texted throughout. See chapter 2, figure 14.

Notation: binary long and breve.

Text: to the BVM (marginal note: "de Sancta Maria"). For its form, see chapter 2, figure 13.

Remarks: wide overall range (a sixteenth) and ambitus of individual voices (a twelfth and a tenth). Harrison in PMFC XV calls it a "dialogue motet."

Triumphat hodie

. . . .

T. Trop est fol

T. Si que la nuit

Source: Lbl 24198, fol. 1v (RISM no. 7), voices I and III; *Onc 362,* fol. 85v (RISM no. 3), voices I and IV.

Literature: Ed. in PMFX XV, no. 17; partial ed. in Sanders, "England: From the Beginnings," pp. 284–86; partial ed. in *History of Music in Sound* II, pp. 58–60. Facs. in EECM 26, pl. 6 (*Lbm*) and pl. 83 (*Onc*); dipl. facs. in Apfel, *Studien* II, p. 42 (*Onc*). Apfel, *Studien* I, p. 28; Harrison, "Ars Nova," p. 71; Dom A. Hughes, NOHM II, pp. 398–99, 403; Sanders, "English Polyphony," pp. 195–97. Recorded on disc RCA LM-6015 (History of Music in Sound, II).

C.f.: French chanson, divided between the two lower voices. Its musical form (AA BB AA BB AA) was readily adaptable to this division, phrase by phrase. Harrison suggests a virelai as the original poetic type (critical notes in PMFC XV).

Form: voice-exchange motet a4 (2+2) on a c.f. in five sections plus hocketing coda. The motet is incomplete in both sources, but between them the entire two-voice supporting structure and one of the two upper voices can be reassembled. The missing upper part can mostly be reconstructed through varied voice exchange with the surviving part; it is demanded by MS layout, the hocketing counterpoint (including a textual hocket with missing syllables), and the implausibility of a 1+2 texture with so many other surviving examples a4.

Text: to Saint Lawrence (marginal note: "de sancto Laurencio"). Original was probably continuously double-texted throughout. For assonance, Sanders suggests missing voice began with some form of the Latin word "tropaeum."

Lbl 28550

Firmissime fidem teneamus
Adesto sancta trinitas
T. Alleluya Benedictus

   Source: Lbl 28550, fol. 43v–44 (RISM no. 4), in tablature; *B-Br 19606*, rotulus (RISM no. 4); *F-Pn 146*, fol. 43–43v (RISM no. 29).
   Literature: Ed. in Apel, CEKM I, no. 4 (*Lbl*); EEH II, pp. 96–100 (*Lbl*); PMFC I, no. 30 (*F-Pn*). Facs. in EEH I, pl. 43–44 (*Lbl*).
   Form: motet a3; two *colores* and sixteen *taleae* with mensural diminution (not exact) to one-third, and corresponding shortening of phrase lengths:

   I   96L = 6+9+9+12+9+8+14+7+7+7+5+3L
   II   = 12+9+9+12+18+19+7+5+5
   III   = 8(9L) + 8(3L)

   Notation: originally *modus* and *tempus imperfectum*, with minor prolation (Apel in CEKM) or major prolation (Schrade in PMFC I). *Lbl* version is intabulation, probably for keyboard, using notational symbols for mensural upper line reflecting English practice (see chapter 3, figure 35) and alphabetical notation for lower part. For a fuller description of the details of this notation, see the critical reports for PMFC XVII, nos. 59–61.
   Text: for the Holy Trinity.
   Remarks: Sanders, "Vitry, Philippe de," sets date of composition no later than mid-1314; the *Lbl* version may date to the 1350s. See the discussion of the insular form of notation in chapter 3.

Tribum quem non abhorruit
Quoniam secta latronum
T. Merito hec patimur

   Source: Lbm 28550, fol. 44–44v (RISM no. 5), in tablature; *B-Br 19606*, rotulus (RISM no. 3); *D-Mbs Kastner D IV, ad 31; D-Mbs clm 5362; D-ROu 100*, fol. 43 (RISM no. 2); *F-Pn 146*, fol. 41v–42 (RISM no. 26); *F-Sm 222*, fol. 71 (RISM no. 115).
   Literature: Apel, CEKM I, no. 5 (*Lbl*); EEH II, pp. 101–5 (*Lbl*); PMFC I, no. 27 (*F-Pn*). Facs. in EEH I, pl. 44–45 (*Lbl*); Besseler and Gülke, *Schriftbild*, pl. 18a–b (*Lbl*).
   Form: isoperiodic motet a3 (in effect a unipartite isorhythmic motet) with *introitus* of 6L; two *colores* and twelve *taleae*.

   I   78L = 9L + 2(12+12)L + 12L + 9L
   II   = 3L + 12L + 2(11+13)L + 15L
   III   = 6L + 3(24L) = 6L + 12(6L)

Notation: see comments on motet above.

Text: comment on the French political situation suggesting a date of composition shortly after April 1315. Date of *Lbl* version as in remarks on motet above.

Lbl 40011B

Humane lingue organis
Supplicem voces percipe
Tenor [Deo gratias]
Contratenerem
Solus tenor et cantetur pro Deo gratias

Source: Lbl 40011B, fol. 14 (RISM no. 17).

Literature: Ed. in PMFC XV, no. 36. Facs. in Bent, *Fountains Fragments* (forthcoming); dipl. facs. in Apfel, *Studien* II, pp. 121–22. Bent, "Transmission," p. 78; Bukofzer, SMRM, pp. 91, 110–11; Harrison, NOHM III, pp. 105–6; Hughes, "Reappraisal," pp. 104–5, 125–26; Sanders, "Motet," pp. 565–66.

C.f.: whole chant sung twice; the remark given with the *Solus tenor* indicates that it is a *Deo gratias,* and the melody is identical to the third melody for *Benedicamus Domino* in *GS,* pl. 19*.

Form: bipartite isorhythmic motet a4 (2+2) with diminution in the ratio of 8:3 (result of 3:1 under O and 2:1 under C); two *colores* and four *taleae.* No periodic phrase structure:

$$44B = 2(16B) + 2(6B).$$

Notation: tempus perfectum, prolatio minor in the upper voices; alternation of *tempus perfectum* and *imperfectum* in tenor and contratenor, with the use of mensuration signs and coloration. The *cauda hirundinis* in voice I alters a semibreve. Bukofzer notes several features of this motet that may show the scribe's unfamiliarity with certain conventions of isorhythmic treatment. (See also Bent, "Transmission.")

Text: prayer to God; a *Deo gratias* substitute. The text of voice I quotes from an interior stanza of the Marian hymn *O gloriosa domina.* There seems to be in both texts an attempt to fashion *4x8pp* hymn stanzas rhyming abba.

Remarks: Hughes thinks *Humane lingue* is French, in the French tradition of *Deo gratias* substitutes such as is represented by the last two motets in Old Hall (nos. 146 and 147). Sanders thinks it is English on account of its interesting proportional relationships.

Alme pater pastor vere
Tenor de Alme pater

Source: Lbl 40011B, fol. 14v (RISM no. 18).

Literature: Facs. in Bent, *Fountains Fragments* (forthcoming). Bent, "Transmission," p. 82, n. 54; Bukofzer, SMRM, pp. 91, 111; Hughes, "English Sacred Music," II, 2, p. 29.

C.f.: apparently free, with no evident *color.*

Form: triplum and tenor of an unipartite isorhythmic motet a4 (2+2) with *introitus;* three *taleae:*

$$181B = 11B + 2(57B) + 56B.$$

In each of the tenor *taleae,* 57B = 5(3B) + 15(2B) + 12B. Coloration makes the long perfect over the first part of each *talea;* then it reverts to imperfect, and there is melismatic hocketing over the last 12B.

Notation: void black, with the use of black coloration.

Text: refers to events surrounding the papacy during the early 1380s; see the section on "External References" in chapter 4.

Remarks: Bukofzer suggests the possibility of canon in the *introitus,* with a second entrance after 6B. This motet shows a high degree of compositional control over local detail, not just by the hocketing and nervous rhythms of the upper voice (introduced through coloration) that recur in each *talea,* but also by the rhythm *sms* that ends many phrases, the stepwise movement shared between the extant voices (as in bars 109–112), the frequent melodic recurrences in the lower voice, and by the interesting use of thirds between these two parts.

Lbl 40011B*

Lbl 40011B, the so-called Fountains fragments, consists of six pages of music from a paper manuscript of the late fourteenth or early fifteenth century and eight small parchment strips from a manuscript of early fourteenth-century English motets. I will use an asterisk to designate the parchment as *Lbl 40011B*.* These eight strips are not unrelated, but rather fit together to form larger fragments in the manner in which they have been bound on pages by the British Library, as follows:

Item		Fragment	Strips
1*	...absorbet oris faucibus	A	1,2,3/a,b,c
2*	...flos regalis triumphalis	Av	1,2,3/d,e,f
3*	...genitricem personantes	B	4,5/g,h
4*	Rota versatilis	Bv,Cv	4,5,6,7/i,k,n,o
5*	...hostium ob amorem	C	6,7/l,m
6*	...recita formosa	D	8/p
blank staves		Dv	8

The original dimensions of a page (for twelve five-line staves) may be roughly estimated as:

page:	30 x 24 cm
music block:	24 x 18 cm
staff gauge:	1.2–1.3 cm

Further associations can be made between the fragments. B and C are linked immediately by item 4*. It is possible that they are from a single leaf with C cut from near the top and B cut from approximately the middle. If that is so, then items 3* and 5* could be two voices of another motet, a possibility strengthened by the fact that they are similar in notation, declamation, and irregularity of versification. Fragments A and D are linked by music hand and ink, the use of red rubrics, and the occurrence of erasures that emend the notation. Possibly they were cut from the same page, with A above D. Since item 2* is the end of a piece, it is perfectly within reason to find Dv blank beneath it. This juxtaposition naturally suggests that items 1* and 6* form a single composition.

The entry in RISM B/IV/4 on the parchment strips of *Lbl 40011B* is unsatisfactory. Bent, *Fountains Fragments* (forthcoming) will have facsimiles and descriptions of this source; see also Bent, "Rota versatilis," pp. 71–74, which has facsimiles of Bv and Cv.

. . . absorbet oris faucibus
. . . recita formosa

Source: Lbl 40011B*, 1*/6*.

Form: probably triplum and tenor of a motet a4 (2+2) with large-scale sectional voice exchange along the lines of *Rota versatilis* or *Hostis Herodes*. The extant poetry indicates that each section had two four-verse strophes, with different versification schemes for each section. The text clearly comes to its conclusion before the last *sine littera* section of the upper voice, so we can judge that (1) the text would have been repeated, and (2) the extant voice is the triplum rather than the duplum.

Text: to Saint Margaret (she is not named, but the text is clearly based on her legend). The extant rubrics instructing repetition in the lower part ("recita formosa" and "recita christiana") probably preserve the first word of two otherwise missing stanzas of text.

. . . flos regalis
[Conditor] Kyrie. Tenor primus
Kyrie seconde

Source: Lbl 40011B*, 2*.

C.f.: four statements of the first acclamation of *Conditor Kyrie.* The beginning of the rubric for the "tenor primus" is illegible, but probably read "Conditor." However, the c.f. is actually found in the "Kyrie seconde." These two voices, without the short fragment of surviving upper part, are given in figure 26.

Form: fragments of the duplum and the two lower supporting voices of a motet a4 (2+2) with rhythmic patterning of the tenor in repeated and varied 4L units.

Text: to Saint Katherine (?); about one-quarter survives.

... hostium ob amorem
... genitricem personantes

Source: Lbl 40011B*, 5*/3*.

Form: if from the same page, then judging from the layout of item 4*, item 5* ought to appear above 3*. This puts a voice of lower range above a voice of higher range, suggesting that perhaps these voices are not from the same piece. Item 3* begins with text and moves into a melismatic section. The alternation of *cum* and *sine littera* may indicate voice exchange, or perhaps merely the start of another voice. In the left margins of both 3* and 5* there are tails of initials now cut off. In the case of 3* the letter was apparently an A.

Text: in 5*, to Saint William, probably William of York.

Lli 146

Ancilla Domini

Source: Lli 146, fol. Bv (no. 6).

Literature: Lefferts and Bent, "New Sources," pp. 329–32 with facsimile.

Notation: English ternary breve-semibreve notation, possibly with a perfect long.

Text: to the BVM.

Remarks: isolated single voice, presumably of a motet. In versification, declamation, and notation this fragment is most similar in appearance to *Geret et regem* (*TAcro 3182,* 2).

Lpro 2/261

Parata paradisi porta
T. Paradisi porta

Source: Lpro 2/261, fol. iv (recto of music leaf).
Literature: Lefferts and Bent, "New Sources," pp. 332–37, with facsimile.
C.f.: whole-chant setting of an antiphon for memorials of the BVM at Easter (see *AS,* pl. 252); stated one and four-fifths times.
Form: duplum and tenor of a motet with mixed periodicity, showing small amount of clear repetition and variation of counterpoint on restatement of the tenor. Probably there was homorhythmic patter on semibreves between the surviving texted voice and the lost triplum. The wide range suggests a motet a4, but the counterpoint of the surviving voices never implies a missing lower part.

  I   126L $= 4(6L) + 2(12+8)L + 2(13+9+8)L + 2L$(final long)
  II $= 9(14L)$

Text: tropic expansion on the antiphon text, in long-line verse with elaborately patterned declamation. See Lefferts and Bent, op. cit. There is noteworthy alliteration in the opening lines.

T. Diex coment

> *Source: Lpro 2/261,* fol. 1 (verso of music leaf).
> *Literature:* as for no. 1.
> *C.f.:* unidentified; only text incipit visible.
> *Remarks:* page carefully erased of music; ultraviolet illumination reveals only stray staff lines, note-heads, and stems. Just the tenor rubric is visible to the naked eye.

Lwa 12185

Viri galilei
T.

> *Source: Lwa 12185,* fol. 1 (RISM no. 1).
> *Literature:* Facs. in EECM 26, pl. 169.
> *Form:* voices II and III of a freely-composed motet a4 (2+2) in sections of voice exchange that repeat strophically with variation, followed by a coda: AA BB CC CC AA BB D.
>
> $$100L = 6(2(8L)) + 4L.$$
>
> Voice I can be reconstructed through exchange with II, and IV is in large part recomposable. The last two bars of each 8L section are identical, acting as a refrain.
> *Text:* on Ascension; six strophes, the first five of which are all variations on the last, which is from the liturgy for Ascension (used in the Introit and elsewhere). The ultimate source for the lines is Acts 1 : 11.

Hac a valle lacrimosa
Hostem vicit crucis signaculo

> *Source: Lwa 12185,* fol. 1v (RISM no. 2).
> *Literature:* Facs. in EECM 26, pl. 170–71; Bent, "Preliminary Assessment," p. 81.
> *Form:* two upper voices of a motet a4 (a3?); the uppermost has periodicity of phrase structure, while the lower voice is not so regular. Not counting the final long, and normalizing a slight irregularity in the fourth and fifth phrases (13B and 14B rather than 12B and 15B, respectively), that structure is:
> $$I \quad 40L = 24L + 16L = (6+4+5+4+5)L + 4(4L).$$
> *Notation:* only known example of the notation of Johannes de Garlandia as described by Robertus de Handlo. See chapter 3, figure 35. The long is perfect, with the underlying impress of second mode.
> *Text:* on Saint Nicholas. Text stanzas are prosish, with some internal alliteration and rhyme, linking *-ibus* end rhyme, and some tendency toward fifteen-syllable line lengths.
> *Remarks:* hard to say whether motet has c.f. or was free; the two voices span a very wide range (a sixteenth) with wide individual ranges (a tenth and an eleventh), suggesting the motet was probably a4. There is parallel motion on the smallest rhythmic values in fifths, sixths (most frequent), octaves, and tenths. At least one more rhythmically active voice seems called for, which could be an upper part if there were a slower-moving tenor underlying the occasional fourths that appear now.

T. [Benedicamus Domino]
Beatus vir

> *Source: Lwa 12185,* fol. 2 (RISM no. 3).
> *Literature:* Facs. in EECM 26, pl. 172–73; Dittmer, *Robert de Handlo,* p. 21 (with an unreliable edition on pp. 22–24). Sanders, "English Polyphony," p. 251.
> *C.f.:* unlabeled in the MS; it is a *Benedicamus Domino* melody (see, for instance, *Manchester, John Rylands Library, Lat. 24,* fol. 14, col. 2, staff 17). The whole chant is sung twice.
> *Form:* tenor and lowest voice of a duet motet a3 with *medius cantus;* phrase structure of subdivided-module periodicity. See chapter 2, figure 25.
> *Notation:* only known example of the notation of W. de Doncastre as described by Hanboys. See chapter 3, figure 35. Long and breve are normally both perfect, within an underlying scheme of second mode; red coloration is used in both voices to imperfect long and breve.

Text: for Trinity Sunday.

Remarks: range may originally have been a fifteenth or even a sixteenth (Bb–cc) overall.

Nos orphanos erige
T. [Veni creator spiritus]

> *Source: Lwa 12185,* fol. 2 (RISM no. 4).
>
> *Literature:* Facs. in EECM 26, pl. 172–73; Dittmer, *Robert de Handlo,* p. 21.
>
> *C.f.:* unlabeled in the MS; RISM correctly identifies as the familiar melody for the hymn *Veni creator spiritus,* though the RISM incipit incorrectly reads F3 clef as C3.
>
> *Form:* lower two voices of a motet a3 (or possibly a4) exhibiting strophic repeat with variation (see chapter 2, figure 15); ten *taleae* and three and one-third *colores.* Final tenor statement probably to provide tonal closure (see also *Barabbas dimittitur, BERc 55,* 1).
>
> $$98B = 3(30B) + 8B.$$
>
> *Notation:* English ternary breve-semibreve notation; no perfect-breve rests, but the forms for imperfect-breve rest and perfect-semibreve rest correspond to those of Brunham. See chapter 3, figures 41 and 47. The tenor uses red coloration to imperfect the long, as in *Beatus vir.*
>
> *Text:* to Saint Michael.

A solis ortus cardine
[T.]
Salvator mundi Domine

> *Source: Lwa 12185,* fol. 2v (RISM no. 5).
>
> *Literature:* Facs. in EECM 26, pl. 174.
>
> *Form:* outer voices of a duet motet a3 with *medius cantus;* isoperiodic with a module of 4L:
>
> $$\text{I} \quad 50L = 2L + 12(4L)$$
> $$\text{II} \qquad\;\; = ?$$
> $$\text{III} \qquad = 3L + 11(4L) + 3L$$
>
> *Text:* for Christmas; in each text the odd-numbered lines quote a total of three stanzas from a well-known Christmas hymn.
>
> *Remarks:* The c.f., not extant, was probably a hymn tune or other appropriate seasonal melody, laid out in a simple second-mode pattern of longs and breves. An additional voice at the bottom of the page, labeled "Tenor secundus," does not belong to this motet.

Ob D.6

Augustine par angelis
T. Summe presul Augustine

    Source: Ob D.6, fol. 11 (RISM no. 2).
    Literature: Facs. in EECM 26, pl. 45. Hughes, "New Italian and English Sources," pp. 174–75.
    C.f.: an unidentified tune laid out in 59 even longs followed by a long rest; labeled "Summe presul Augustine certus cantus. triplex." These 60L are to be sung three times ("triplex"); "certus cantus" most likely indicates simply that this is "the given voice" on which the motet was constructed. The tenor melody, possibly a fairly neumatic tune associated with some hymn text for Augustine, may have set words beginning "Summe presul Augustine," but it is more likely that this is simply the incipit of the missing triplum.
    Form: duplum and tenor of a motet a4 (2+2). Two missing voices may be inferred by the range of the surviving voices (a fourteenth overall, often sounding a tenth or twelfth apart) and counterpoint (with many imperfect intervals and occasional unsupported fourths); the harmony of the original must have been very "English." Alternation of *cum* and *sine littera* sections in the texted voice also points to the loss of an upper part, though there is no apparent use of voice exchange or periodic phrase structure.
    Notation: binary mensuration of the long and breve. Though the counterpoint moves mainly in longs, there seems to be no higher-level organization of these values.
    Text: to Saint Augustine of Canterbury. It also survives in a fourteenth-century hymnal from Saint Augustine's, Canterbury (*Cambridge, St. John's College MS 262*, fol. 74v–75, text only), where it is the second of three hymns to the local saint. See P.M. Korhammer, "The Origin of the Bosworth Psalter," p. 178 and M.R. James, *Descriptive Catalogue,* p. 304 (the hymns are not indexed in Chevalier, Walther, or the *A H*). The hymnal preserves an additional stanza between stanzas 3 and 4 of the motet text.
    Remarks: This motet was copied into empty pages of a fourteenth-century cartulary preserving late thirteenth-century charters of the chapel of Saint Mary at the Cluniac priory of St. Augustine's, Daventry (which was apparently functioning by the thirteenth century as a free Benedictine house with a close relationship to the Benedictine priory nearby at Coventry). The motet obviously raises questions about the transmission of texts (and music) between Canterbury and Daventry, as well as about the puzzle of its presence at a house dedicated to the "other" Augustine.

Ob 7

Maria mole pressa
T.

> *Source: Ob 7,* fol. III (RISM no. 1a).
> *Literature:* Facs. in EECM 26, pl. 46.
> *C.f.:* unidentified; sung three times.
> *Form:* duplum and tenor of an isoperiodic motet a4 (2+2) with broadly
> patterned tenor. Module is 15L, only loosely expressed in the phrase structure
> of the upper part, and the final long is not part of the scheme:
>
> I   90L = 15L + 17L + 30L + 13L + 15L
> II   = 3(30L) = 6(15L)
>
> *Text:* on Mary Magdalene and Easter. The text makes the traditional
> association of Mary Magdalene with the incidents in Luke 7 : 37–38 and 8 : 2
> and then brings in the Gospel narrative of her participation in the
> Resurrection, as in Matthew 28 : 1–10 or Mark 16 : 1–8.
> *Remarks:* some small amount of strophic repeat of counterpoint;
> irregular declamation of a fairly regularly versified text, not coordinated with
> phrase structure. RISM incorrectly identifies the two voices at the bottom of
> the leaf as part of this motet (see *Ob 7,* 1b).

Zorobabel abigo
Zorobabel actibus

> *Source: Ob 7,* fol. III (RISM no. 1b).
> *Literature:* Facs. in EECM 26, pl. 46.
> *Form:* two similarly active parts lying a fifth apart in range; width of
> counterpoint, hocketing, and occasional unsupported fourths suggest a motet
> a4 with another voice in each register. Possibly c.f. was a *medius cantus,*
> perhaps a *Benedicamus Domino* melody judging from the incorporation of a
> variant on this formula at the end of the text. There is a fair amount of
> repetition of melodic material.
> *Notation:* ternary breve-semibreve notation unusual in its 1+2
> subdivision of the breve. See chapter 3, figure 41.
> *Text:* a prayer renouncing evil.
> *Remarks:* entered in a later hand; RISM incorrectly identifies these two
> voices as part of *Ob 7,* 1a.

Petrum cephas ecclesie
Petrus pastor potissimus
T. Petre
Quartus cantus

Source: Ob 7, fol. IIIv–IV (RISM no. 2).

Literature: Ed. in PMFC XV, no. 18 and in EBM II, pp. 24–31. Facs. in EECM 26, pl. 47–48 and in EBM I, pl. X–XI. Apfel, *Studien* I, p. 30; Harrison, NOHM III, pp. 93–94; Lefferts, "Motet," p. 74, n. 7.; Levy, "New Material," p. 231; Reese, MMA, p. 404; Sanders, "English Polyphony," pp. 219–20; idem, "Motet," p. 544; idem, "England: From the Beginnings," p. 286.

C.f.: the opening melisma on "Petre" from the responsory *Petre amas me* (see *AS*, pl. 444); stated four times (not two, as incorrectly stated in PMFC).

Form: paradigmatic isoperiodic motet a4 (2+1+1) with broadly patterned tenor; rhythmic module of 9L. See the discussion of this motet in the section on isoperiodicity in chapter 2.

$$
\begin{array}{ll}
\text{I} & 108\text{L} = 12(9\text{L}) \\
\text{II} & = 7\text{L} + 10(9\text{L}) + 11\text{L} \\
\text{III} & = 10\text{L} + 10(9\text{L}) + 8\text{L} \\
\text{IV} & = \text{irregular}
\end{array}
$$

Text: to Saint Peter; the triplum is drawn from the Bible, especially Matt. 4 : 19–20 and 16 : 18–19, while the duplum draws on the Apocrypha, especially the story about Simon Magus.

Remarks: important early use of "precadential protofaburden" while tenor rests.

Rex visibilium
Rex invictissime
T. Regnum tuum solidum

Source: Ob 7, fol. IIIv–IV (RISM no. 3).

Literature: Ed. in PMFC XV, no. 19. Facs. in EECM 26, pl. 47–48; EBM I, pl. X–XI. Apfel, *Studien* I, p. 30; Lefferts, "Motet," pp. 59–60.

C.f.: whole-chant setting of the *Regnum* prosula for the Gloria. The full text is underlaid, though highly abbreviated.

Form: essentially isoperiodic motet a3; module of 4L over the first 28L, then more irregular to the end. Tenor's melodic design is ABBCCD and design is regular on ABB, while for CCD the tenor melody is compressed into fewer bars on faster note-values. Tenor *taleae* not consistent in 4L because patterning is coordinated with melodic repetition in the tenor. See chapter 2, figure 24.

Text: prayer to God, vaguely tropic to the tenor text.

Remarks: range of a sixteenth. In general, this motet has attributes of a duet motet with *medius cantus* except for the relative ranges of the voices. It is a later addition to the MS, probably contemporary with *Ob 7,* 1b.

Variants to PMFC XV edition: III:17 ought to be identical to III:7, i.e., *bssb* (CDCD).

Lux refulget monachorum
T.

> *Source: Ob 7,* fol. IVv (RISM no. 4).
> *Literature:* Facs. in EECM 26, pl. 49. Lefferts, "Motet," p. 60.
> *C.f.:* unidentified; disposed in three and one-fifth *colores.*
> *Form:* triplum and tenor of an isoperiodic motet a4 in three sections with
different rhythmic modules:

$$114L = 90 + 12L + 12L$$
$$I = (10L + 8(9L) + 8L) + 2(6L) + 3(4L)$$
$$II = (8L + 9(9L)) + 6(2L) + 3(3L) + 4L$$

The first 90L set two *colores* and two-thirds of the text (twenty lines) on long-
breve declamation in second mode. The remaining one-third of the text (ten
lines) is declaimed more rapidly over the final 24L on breve and semibreve in
first mode. The shift of mode, marked acceleration of declamation (in two
stages), and rise in tessitura of the texted voice create an effect similar to
diminution in an isorhythmic motet, with a strong sense of formal
demarcation and drive to a climax.

> *Text:* on Saint Benedict, with reference to his rule. See chapter 4, figure
50.
> *Remarks:* range of a sixteenth; use in voice I of C1 clef with signature b-
natural above.

Duodeno sydere

> *Source: Ob 7,* fol. V (RISM no. 5).
> *Literature:* Facs. in EECM 26, pl. 50.
> *Form:* triplum of motet a3 with stratification of rhythmic activity; some
periodicity on the phrase level but no patterning of declamation or replication
of phrases over the tenor.

$$63L = 4(6L) + 7L + 5L + 5L + 9L + 5L + 8L$$

Through examination of the melody and its permissible counterpoint, it can
be shown that the tenor was 21L, stated three times.

> *Notation:* downstemmed semibreve on the first in groups of threes.
Underlying second mode, as evidenced by subdivisions of the breve and rest-
writing at cadences.
> *Text:* on Saint Andrew and the apostles.
> *Remarks:* range of an eleventh; use of C1 clef with signature b-natural
above.

... alleluya
Frondentibus florentibus
T. Floret

Source: Ob 7, fol. V (RISM no. 6), voices II and III; *Ob 594,* front board (no. 1), a badly worn mirror image of all three voices.

Literature: Facs. in EECM 26, pl. 50 (*Ob 7*); facs. (*Ob 594*) and transcription in Lefferts and Bent, "New Sources," pp. 342–47.

C.f.: identified only by the textual incipit "Floret" in *Ob 7.* Certainly a non-Gregorian melody, with tuneful balanced phrases (four phrases of 5L) and a degree of rhythmic ornamentation that suggest its possible derivation from a polyphonic setting, perhaps of a cantilena beginning with the same incipit. Sung three times.

Form: motet a3 with stratified levels of activity, lacking regular phrase structure; a small degree of varied strophic repetition is evident in the duplum alone.

Text: a spring song on Easter. The duplum text has had fairly wide distribution following its transcription in the *Bodleian Quarterly Record* 5 (1926), pp. 22–23. See Gaselee, *Medieval Latin Verse,* no. 73; Raby, *Medieval Latin Verse,* no. 275; Spitzmüller, *Poésie latine chrétienne,* p. 1404. Presumably for better scansion, the Oxford publications amend line 5 to begin "surgens die tercia" rather than "die tercia surgens."

Ave miles celestis
Ave rex patrone
T. Ave rex gentis
Tenor ii

Source: Ob 7, fol. Vv–VI (RISM no. 7).

Literature: Ed. in PMFC XV, no. 20; Bukofzer, SMRM, pp. 30–33; Stevens, TECM, no. 15; partial ed. in Besseler, *Musik des Mittelalters,* p. 172; Reese, MMA, pp. 401–3. Facs. in EECM 26, pl. 51–52. Apfel, *Studien* I, p. 30; Bukofzer, SMRM, pp. 23–29; Harrison, MMB, p. 146; Sanders, "English Polyphony," pp. 199–201; idem, "Motet," p. 543. Recorded on disc EMI (Odeon) CSD 3504 (HMV CSD 3504).

C.f.: whole-chant setting of the Magnificat antiphon at first vespers on the feast of Saint Edmund; setting of the first Psalm tone with its second termination in the motet coda.

Form: paradigmatic five-section voice-exchange motet a4 (2+2) with coda. See chapter 2, table 1. Paired stanzas sung successively in all sections except the second, which is the shortest and therefore divides a single stanza between the voices.

Text: to Saint Edmund. Edmund fulfills the works of the predicted Messiah, just as Jesus did. See Matt. 11 : 2–5 or Luke 4 : 18–19 with reference to Isa. 29 : 18–19; 35 : 5–6; 61 : 1. "Benedicamus Domino" incorporated in final stanzas.

De flore martirum
Deus tuorum militum
T. Ave rex gentis

Source: Ob 7, fol. Vv–V (RISM no. 8).
Literature: Ed. in PMFC XV, no. 21 and Bukofzer, SMRM, pp. 29–30.
Facs. in EECM 26, pl. 51–52. Apfel, *Studien* I, p. 31; Bukofzer, SMRM, pp.
20–23; Dalglish, "Variation," pp. 40–41; Harrison, MMB, p. 146; Dom A.
Hughes, NOHM II, p. 396; Sanders, "English Polyphony," pp. 214–15, 216.
Recorded on disc Expériences Anonymes EA-0024.
C.f.: same antiphon as in *Ave miles,* but using only first 30 pitches, not
whole chant; disposed in two *colores* and six *taleae.*
Form: strophic repeat with variation and some voice exchange in motet
a3; moderately regular mixed periodicity:

$$\text{I} \quad 42L = 9 + 6 + 2 + 6 + 2 + 9 + 2 + 6 \ L$$
$$\text{II} \qquad = 4 + 4 + 8 + 8 + 8 + 10 \ L$$
$$\text{III} \qquad = 2(21L) = 2(3(7L))$$

Text: to Saint Edmund. The duplum begins as a paraphrase of the hymn
Deus tuorum militum, which is sometimes sung in a version beginning
melodically like the antiphon used as the motet c.f. See Bukofzer, SMRM, p.
21 and Sanders, "English Polyphony," p. 214, n. 54.

Templum eya Salomonis

Source: Ob 7, fol VIv (RISM no. 9).
Literature: Facs. in EECM 26, pl. 53. Lefferts, "Motet," p. 60.
Form: isolated triplum with isoperiodic phrase structure (72L = 8(9L));
phrases paired as double versicles with *ouvert* and *clos* cadences, the cadence
figure itself recurring as a refrain. See the discussion of isoperiodic motets in
chapter 2, and see chapter 4, figure 48.
Notation: second mode, with the second of each pair of semibreves
receiving a downstem.
Text: on the New Jerusalem, perhaps for the anniversary of the
dedication of a church; see the discussion of this text in chapter 4.

Cuius de manibus
Quadri[ ]ivium

Source: Ob 7, fol. 266 (RISM no. 11).
Literature: Ed. in PMFC XVI, no. 103 and in Lefferts, "Motet," pp.
67–72. Facs. in EECM 26, pl. 54. Lefferts, "Motet," pp. 61–65.

Form: freely-composed five-section voice-exchange motet a4 (2+2) with coda:

$$95B = 2(12B) + 2(6B) + 2(7B) + 2(8B) + 2(11B) + 7B$$

The surviving voices are the second and fourth; from them almost all the counterpoint can be reconstructed through voice exchange. See the discussion of this motet in the section on the rear leaves of *Ob 7* in chapter 2.

Notation: tempus imperfectum, prolatio maior.

Text: nearly illegible; to the BVM?

Remarks: the page is so badly rubbed that it obviously was once either the outer leaf in its parent music book or else the outer flyleaf in the binding of some MS, perhaps the present one. The name of the fourth voice reads as given above, i.e., apparently longer than the word "quadrivium" by at least a few minim strokes.

Omnis terra
Habenti dabitur
Tenor

    Source: Ob 7, fol. 266v–267 (RISM no. 12).

    Literature: Ed. in PMFC XV, no. 22. Facs. in EECM 26, pl. 55–56. Apfel, *Studien* I, p. 31; Harrison, MMB, pp. 148–49; Hughes, "Reappraisal," p. 125.

    C.f.: unidentified; Hughes suggests the tenor is "In omnem" (presumably "In omnem terram," a phrase from Ps. 18:5 and Rom. 10:18), but no chant setting that text has yet been found to match.

    Form: bipartite isorhythmic motet a3 with diminution by one-half; two *colores* and nine *taleae*:

$$162B = 108B + 54B$$

I	$= (29 + 48 + 24 + 11)B + 3(12B) + 14B$
II	$= (28 + 3(24) + 13)B + 3(2 + 10)B + (2 + 11)B$
III	$= 4\frac{1}{2}(24B) + \frac{1}{2}(4\frac{1}{2}(24B))$

Text: triplum and duplum stand in strong contrast. The former praises God in language that recalls Genesis and may be a paraphrase of Psalm 103(104), which tells a creation story; the latter apparently launches an attack upon the flourishing of evil men in this world to the detriment of the righteous. Lines 1 through 4 of the duplum are Matt. 13:12.

Deus creator omnium
Rex genitor ingenite
T. Doucement me reconforte

    Source: Ob 7, fol. 267v–268 (RISM no. 14).

    Literature: Ed. in PMFC XV, no. 23; partial ed. in EBM II, pp. 32–36.

Facs. in EECM 26, pl. 57–58 and in EBM I, pl. XII–XIII. Apfel, *Studien* I, p. 31; Brewer, "A Fourteenth-Century Polyphonic Manuscript," p. 10; Lefferts, "Motet," p. 61.

C.f.: probably taken from a polyphonic setting of a *fatras* distich. See the discussion in Chapter 2 and see also Brewer, op. cit. Sung three times.

Form: strophic repeat with variation and exchange in motet a3; hocketing, in part melismatic, over the third tenor statement.

I 102B $= 6(9B) + 8B + 12B + 28B$
II $= 4B + 2(10B) + 2(7B) + 8B + 10B + 9B + 13B + 24B$
III $= 3(34B) = 3(16 + 18)B$

Notation: tempus perfectum maior.

Text: on Jesus and the Holy Trinity. Texts begin with the incipits of two well-known Latin-texted Kyries.

Remarks: notable rhythmic integration of tenor and upper voices; marked repetition of counterpoint over first two tenor statements, including exchange between upper voices; passages where the tenor moves in *s* and *m* produce counterpoint in parallel thirds, sixths, and 6-3 harmonies.

Pura placens
Parfundement
Tenor

Source: Ob 7, fol. 268v–269 (RISM no. 15); *F-Pn 23190 (Trém),* index, xliv; also known to have been the first motet in a manuscript of French motets now lost (see the reference in Besseler, cited below).

Literature: Ed. in PMFC XV, no. 24; partial ed. in EBM II, pp. 36–40. Facs. in EECM 26, pl. 59–60 and EBM I, pl. XIV–XV. Apfel, *Studien* I, p. 31; Besseler, "Studien I," pp. 184 and 222, n. 1; idem, "Studien II," p. 239.

C.f.: unidentified.

Form: bipartite isorhythmic motet a3 with diminution by one-half; four *colores* and six *taleae:*

135B $= 90B + 45B$
I $= (6+6+3+13+3)+(5+6+3+13+3)+(5+6+3+13)+(10+2(15)+7)B$
III $= (16+16)B + 2(14+16)B + 2(15B) + 13B$

Text: to the BVM; triplum in Latin and duplum in French.

Domine quis habitabit
De veri cordis adipe
T. Concupisco

Source: Ob 7, fol. 268v–269 (RISM no. 16), Latin texts; *F-CA 1328,* fol. 17v–18 (RISM no. 40), French texts; *F-Pn 23190 (Trém),* index, xvi, French texts; *I-IVC 115,* fol. 25v–26 (RISM no. 40), French texts.

Literature: Ed. in PMFC V, 16 (French) and 16a (Latin); partial ed. in EBM II, pp. 40–43. Facs. in EECM 26, pl. 59–60; EBM I, pl. XIV–XV.

Form: bipartite isorhythmic motet a3 with diminution by one-half; four *colores* and eight *taleae:*

$$108B = 72B + 36B$$

I	$= 16B + 3(4+3+11)B + 8B + 2(9B) + 12B$
II	$= 4B + 3(18B) + 16B + 3(9B) + 7B$
III	$= 4(18B) + 4(9B) = 4(1+5+12)B + \frac{1}{2}(4(1+5+12))B$

Text: Ob 7 version has Latin texts addressed to God and Jesus, paraphrasing Psalms and assonant slightly to one another; Continental sources preserve courtly French love poetry with the incipits "Se paour d'umble" and "Diex tan desir." The French texts are original, for the tenor ("Concupisco," meaning "I lust") was evidently selected with their sentiments in mind.

Parce piscatoribus
T. Relictis retibus

Source: Ob 7, fol. 269v (RISM no. 17).
Literature: Facs. in EECM 26, pl. 61.
C.f.: unidentified; the textual incipit, found in Matt. 4:20 and 4:22, suggests a source in the liturgy for Saint James or Saint Andrew.
Form: triplum and tenor of a bipartite isorhythmic motet a4 with diminution by one-half; two *colores* and eight *taleae:*

$$144B = 96B + 48B$$

I	$= (21+8)B + 2(16+8)B + (16+5)B + 3(8+4)B + 10B$
II	$= 4(24B) + 4(12B) = 4(12+12)B + \frac{1}{2}(4(12+12))B$

Text: on Saint James. See chapter 4, figure 50.

Ob 81

A solis ortus cardine
Tenor

Source: Ob 81, fol. 1 (RISM no. 1).
Literature: Ed. in PMFC XVI, 94. Facs. in EECM 26, pl. 62. Bent, "Rota versatilis," pp. 74–76; Harrison, NOHM III, pp. 89–91.
C.f.: no c.f. per se; melodic paraphrase of hymn in opening bars of upper voice. See chapter 2, figure 8.
Form: large-scale sectional voice-exchange motet a4 (2+2); a second upper part is reconstructible through exchange, and it is possible to recompose a "quartus cantus" modeled on those of other motets of this type.

This motet may be the first part of a larger composition with *Ob 81*, 2. See the discussion in chapter 2.

Text: the Christmas story following Luke 2, beginning as a paraphrase of the hymn "A solis ortus."

Ovet mundus
Ovet mundus
Tenor
Quadruplex

Source: Ob 81, fol. iv and 44 (RISM no. 2).

Literature: Ed. in PMFC XVI, no. 95; Wibberley, "English Polyphonic Music," pp. 239–44; Wulstan, *Three Medieval Conductus.* Facs. in EECM 26, pl. 63–64; dipl. facs. in Apfel, *Studien* II, pp. 52–56. Apfel, *Studien* I, p. 29; Bent, "Rota versatilis," pp. 74–76; Harrison, MMB, pp. 146–47; idem, NOHM III, pp. 89–90; idem, "Ars Nova," p. 75; Dom A. Hughes, NOHM II, pp. 395–96; Sanders, "English Polyphony," pp. 102–3.

Form: large-scale sectional voice-exchange motet a4 (2+2); may form the second half of a longer motet with *Ob 81,* 1. See the discussion in chapter 2.

Text: for Christmas, on the miracle of the virgin birth.

Hostis Herodes impie
Hic principes
Tenor etc.
Quartus cantus etc.

Source: Ob 81, fol. 44v–45 (RISM no. 3).

Literature: Ed. in PMFC XVI, no. 96; Wibberley, "English Polyphonic Music," pp. 245–57; Wulstan, *Three Medieval Conductus.* Facs. in EECM 26, pl. 65–66; dipl. facs. in Apfel, *Studien* II, pp. 57–60. Apfel, *Studien* I, p. 29; Bent, "Rota versatilis," pp. 68–70, 76; Harrison, NOHM III, pp. 90–91; idem, "Ars Nova," p. 74; Dom A. Hughes, NOHM II, pp. 396–97; Sanders, "English Polyphony," pp. 102–3.

C.f.: no c.f. per se; melodic paraphrase of hymn in opening bars of voice I. See chapter 2, figure 8.

Form: large-scale sectional voice-exchange motet a4 (2+2), notated in condensed format (as is the version of *Rota versatilis* in *Lbl 24198*). See the extended discussion in chapter 2.

Text: on Epiphany, paraphrasing and expanding on the hymn "Hostis Herodes" following Matt. 2 : 1–12.

Remarks: The irregular pattern of declamation of the very first phrase ("Hostis Herodes") by comparison with the third ("quid Christum times hodie") is a result of the use of chant paraphrase in the former.

Salve cleri speculum
Salve iubar presulum
T. [Sospitati dedit egros]
T.ii.

Source: Ob 81, fol. 45v and 2 (RISM no. 4).

Literature: Ed. in PMFC XV, no. 11 and Wulstan, *Three Medieval Conductus.* Facs. in EECM 26, pl. 67–68; dipl. facs. in Apfel, *Studien* II, pp. 61–64. Apfel, *Studien* I, p. 29; Harrison, NOHM III, pp. 91–93; idem, "Ars Nova," p. 74; idem, "Rota and Rondellus," p. 103; Sanders, "English Polyphony," pp. 197–98; idem, "Motet," p. 543; idem, "England: From the Beginnings," pp. 283–84.

C.f.: the prose for Saint Nicholas, *Sospitati dedit egros* (*AS,* pl. 360), set as a whole chant.

Form: five-section voice-exchange motet a4 (2+2) on c.f., with no coda, exploiting the double-versicle structure of the chant melody for four periods of exchange. The first section is freely composed.

Text: to Saint Nicholas, elaborating the c.f. text. To follow the familiar sequence of the Nicholas prose, though, text stanzas 7 and 8 must be reversed.

Remarks: Sanders likens the texture of this motet to the "stile brisé" ("English Polyphony," p. 197).

Ob 143

... nec Herodis ferocitas
Primus tenor

Source: Ob 143, fol. 1 (RISM no. 1).

Literature: Facs. in EECM 26, pl. 70 and EBM I, pl. XVI. Harrison, NOHM III, p. 99.

C.f.: unidentified; note insular designation as "Primus."

Form: duplum and tenor of a bipartite panisorhythmic motet a4 (2+1+1) and diminution by one-half with melismatic hocketing; two *colores* and eight *taleae:*

$$120B = 80B + 40B$$
$$I = (6+11)B + 3(9+11)B + 3B + 40B$$
$$II = 4(20B) + \tfrac{1}{2}(4(20B))$$

Text: to Saint James.

Remarks: Harrison credits this fragment with being an instance of the English adoption of isorhythm. Just possibly the c.f. is missing and the "primus tenor" is in fact a mislabeled contratenor.

Regne de pité
Regne de pité
Tenor de Regne de pité
Ct.

    Source: Ob 143, fol. 1v–2 (RISM no. 3).
    Literature: Ed. in PMFC XVII, no. 57; partial ed. in EBM II, pp. 47–48. Facs. in EECM 26, pl. 71–72; EBM I, pl. XVII–XVIII; Mustanoja, "Les neuf joies," following p. 8.
    C.f.: motet apparently freely composed. Tenor is sung twice, the second time in retrograde with change of mensuration.
    Form: bipartite motet with change in mensuration from *tempus imperfectum* to *tempus perfectum.*
    Notation: use of *cauda hirundinis; signum rotundum* marks change of mensuration; trochaic reading of binary c.o.p. ligatures.
    Text: See the section on vernacular texts in chapter 4 and see also Mustanoja, "Les neuf joies," a 90–page monograph on this poem with an edition and commentary. Listed in Långfors, *Les incipit,* pp. 346–47, and edited in Faral and Bastin, *Oeuvres complètes de Rutebeuf* 2, no. XLIX, pp. 247–52.

Ob 652

On this source see Bent, "Rota versatilis," pp. 70–71, 81–82.

Rex sanctorum angelorum

    Source: Ob 652, fol. i, iiv (RISM no. 2).
    Literature: Facs. in EECM 26, pl. 209.
    Form: isoperiodic phrasing: $72L = 6(12L)$.
    Text: incipit identical to that of a metrical litany from the Easter liturgy (see *GS,* pl. 114–15).

Regina celestium
Tenor de regina

    Source: Ob 652, fol. iv–2 (RISM no. 3).
    C.f.: first 21 notes of the BVM antiphon *Regina celi letare;* sung three times.
    Form: two lower voices of a motet a3 with *medius cantus;* irregular long-breve declamation, and no periodic phrase structure.

Salve sancta virgula
T. Salve sancta parens

> *Source: Ob 652,* fol. iv–2 (RISM no. 4).
> *C.f.:* whole-chant setting of the BVM introit.
> *Form:* triplum and tenor of a motet a4(?) with isoperiodicity in texted
> voice only:
> $$56L = 3(4+8)L + (4+7+9)L.$$

... rogativam potuit

> *Source: Ob 652,* fol. 69v–70 (RISM no. 5).
> *Form:* fragment of a refrain motet with melodic repetition in verse
> section. See chapter 2, table 9 and figure 16. Part of a decorative initial is still
> visible in the margin of the upper left-hand corner of the page, which has been
> trimmed along the top and right-hand borders. Based on the visible spacing of
> surviving music and text, one can estimate that three staves of music and two
> lines of text are lost, translating into four musical phrases and three stanzas of
> text. If this is correct, then either the refrain was stated only twice (V R V R) or
> the first verse section was shorter than that of the second, perhaps even
> allowing for an initial statement of the refrain (R V R V R).
> *Text:* apparently on Christmas.

Omc 266/268

Trowell's remark ("A Fourteenth-Century Ceremonial Motet," p. 74) that
Omc 268 preserves fragments of two isorhythmic motets has been repeated by
Sanders ("Medieval English Polyphony," p. 262). In *Omc 266* and *268,* which
belong together, there are in fact bits of three motets, and it is likely that none
is isorhythmic, strictly speaking.

... baptizas parentes
... sacer presul

> *Source: Omc 266,* fol. 26v (RISM no. 1).
> *Form:* fragmentary remains of two voices; RISM indicates they are
> perhaps from different pieces, but the texts and clefs suggest they are likely an
> upper and lower part from the same motet, though it has not been possible to
> join them.
> *Notation:* ternary breve-semibreve notation, with a perfect long and
> underlying patterns of first mode.

Text: on Saint Martin of Tours. See the discussion of provenance in chapter 4. I would like to thank Professors Peter Dembowski, Nancy Helmbold, Braxton Ross, and Howard Brown (all of the University of Chicago) for help and encouragement as I struggled to read the text and make this identification.

Remarks: overall range may have been as great as a sixteenth (Bb–cc).

Inter usitata
Inter tot et tales
T.

Source: Omc 266/268, fols. 26v, 26 respectively (RISM no. 2).

Literature: Ed. in PMFC XVII, no. 56.

C.f.: unidentified; rubric instructs performance: "Hic ter cantetur medio retro gradietur." See figure 23.

Form: motet a3 with some periodicity of phrase structure; motet begins and ends with rests in all voices, due to requirements of notation of tenor for retrograde performance. See chapter 2, figure 23 and the section on the later fourteenth century.

$$I \quad 110B = 2B + 5(16B) + 19B + 7B + 2B$$
$$II \qquad = 2B + 2(15+14)B + 16B + 15B + 17B + 2B$$
$$III \qquad = 3(36B) + 2B$$

Text: to the BVM, with reference to her Immaculate Conception, and also mention of Saint Paul.

Flos anglorum inclitus
. . . nobilis festum colentes

Source: Omc 266/268, fols. 26v, 26, respectively (RISM no. 3).

Form: two upper voices of a motet a3(?a4) that may have had a periodic phrase structure in perfect longs:

$$I \quad 12B + 30B + \ldots$$
$$II \quad 6B + 9B + 9B + 15B + \ldots$$

Notation: tempus imperfectum maior, with a perfect long subdivided according to second mode.

Text: to Saint Edmund.

Remarks: later addition to the MS, in a smaller hand.

Onc 57

O pater excellentissime

Source: Onc 57, fol. 1 (no. 1).

Literature: Partial transc. in Wibberley, "English Polyphonic Music," pp. 185–89. Facs. in EECM 26, pl. 78. Lefferts and Bent, "New Sources," pp. 352–53; Wibberley, op. cit., pp. 182–84.

Form: torso of a freely-composed five-section voice-exchange motet a4 (2+2), with texted coda that possibly also uses voice exchange. Most of the counterpoint can be reconstructed from the two surviving parts, which are the duplum and second tenor. Formally, this motet occupies an intermediate position between those motets with phrase-by-phrase exchange and those with larger sectional exchanges. See the discussion of voice exchange in chapter 2 and figure 4.

Text: on Saint Bartholomew; only the second half of each stanza survives, but recognition of the events of his legend was facilitated by a reference to the figure Polimius.

Remarks: Very similar to *Quid rimari (CAc 128/2,* 2) both in melodic idiom and handling of the two lower voices.

O crux vale
T.

Source: Onc 57, fol. 1v (no. 2).

Literature: Facs. in EECM 26, pl. 79. Lefferts and Bent, "New Sources," pp. 352–53; Wibberley, "English Polyphonic Music," pp. 182–84.

Form: probably triplum and "tenor primus" of a motet a4 (2+2) in three large sections of contrasting length, mensuration, and text versification, followed by a brief texted coda. See chapter 2, in the section on other insular motet types.

Section	Length	Mensuration	Phrases
1	34L	2nd mode	9L 8L 8L 9L
2	34L	1st mode	12L 12L 10L
3	41L(82B)	binary	15,18,17,12,20B
coda	5L	1st mode	

Note that the first and second sections are identical in length. The first two phrases of the second section, each of 12L, are articulated into three 4L subphrases. There is motion in *l* and *b* in the odd-numbered bars and in *s* in the even-numbered bars. Further, there are isomelic correspondences between these 12L phrases, especially between the middle 4L of each. The necessity of cutting short the final phrase (10L instead of 12L) to reach exactly 34L probably caused this phrase to stand outside of the relationship set up between the 12L phrases.

The third section, given its binary long, extensive declamation on chains of paired semibreves, and irregular phrasing, pozes a puzzle. Its numerical structure stands in no apparent relation to the 34L (102B) of the first two sections, and there also seems to be no larger grouping of binary longs, or of breves, disguised within the prevailing motion of either surviving voice.

Notation: there is the use of the *signum rotundum* at the end of each section (except between the third section and the coda) in both voices.

Text: to the Holy Cross, quoting in the final line the last line of a sequence to the Holy Cross, *Salve crux sancta.*

Remarks: the motet appears to be freely composed, with tonal closure on C, a heavy emphasis on supertonic D, and a final cadence to an 12-8-5 harmony. Identical melismatic tags link sections 1-2 and 2-3, and a variation of this refrain tag links section 3 to the coda. Declamation and phrase structure are not entirely regular (with real consistency only in the first section), but the musical phrases are carefully shaped melodically and suggest a composition composed "from the top down." Judging by the fact that the surviving upper part is texted throughout, it seems likely that the motet was polytextual. There is no sign of sectional voice exchange, though in rhythmic, harmonic, melodic, and formal style *O crux* is most closely related to large-scale sectional voice-exchange motets such as *Rota versatilis,* and to other free compositions a4.

Onc 362

Apello cesarem
T. Omnes

> *Source: Onc 362,* fol. 84 (RISM no. 1).
> *Literature:* Facs. in EECM 26, pl. 80. Harrison, NOHM III, p. 84.
>
> *C.f.:* neuma from the respond of the Christmas gradual *Viderunt omnes;* fourteen statements of the *color,* ten in second mode and four in first mode (81L + 32L).
>
> *Form:* duplum and tenor of a motet a4 with varied rhythmic patterning of the tenor *color.* No regular periodicity of musical phrases and no strong cadential articulation at the change of mode.
>
> *Text:* on the persecution of a good man.

Ianuam quam clauserat
Iacintus in saltibus
T. Iacet granum
Quartus cantus
Tenor per se de Iacet granum

Source: Onc 362, fol. 84v–85 (RISM no. 2).

Literature: Ed. in PMFC XV, no. 1; Stevens, *Music in Honour of St. Thomas,* no. 8. Facs. in EECM 26, pl. 81–82; dipl. facs. in Apfel, *Studien* II, pp. 39–41. Apfel, *Studien* I, p. 28; Harrison, NOHM III, pp. 84–87; idem, "Ars Nova," pp. 70–71; Sanders, "English Polyphony," pp. 218–19; idem, "Motet," p. 543; Stevens, "St. Thomas," pp. 329–31.

C.f.: whole-chant setting of respond used at matins and in procession at first vespers on feast of Saint Thomas.

Form: motet a4 (2+1+1) with isoperiodic phrases in upper voices over unpatterned tenor and quartus cantus:

$$\text{I} \quad 112L = 14(8L)$$
$$\text{II} \quad\quad = 3L + 9L + 11(8L) + 7L + 5L$$

Text: on Saint Thomas of Canterbury (marginal note: "de sancte Thoma cantuarie").

Remarks: one of two earliest known examples of a *solus tenor* combining functions of tenor and quartus cantus, thus reducing texture from a4 to a3 (see also the "Tenor pro iii" of *D-W499(W3),* item 1).

Balaam de quo
Balaam de quo
T. Balaam

Source: Onc 362, fol. 86 (RISM no. 4), voice II only; *F-MO,* fol. 392v–393v, written as two motets (RISM nos. 323, 324; Rokseth nos. 340, 341).

Literature: Ed. in PMFC XV, no. 2; Rokseth, *Polyphonies* III, pp. 258–62; Stevens, TECM I, 5; Tischler, *Montpellier* III/6–7, pp. 224–27. Facs. in EECM 26, pl. 84 (*Onc*); Rokseth, ibid. I, fol. 392v–393v (*F-MO*); dipl. facs. of the second half in Apel, NPM, facs. 63 (*F-MO*). Apel, NPM, p. 315; Bukofzer, SMRM, pp. 24–25; Dalglish, "Hocket," pp. 353–59 with very full references to other analyses on p. 353, n. 24–28; Harrison, MMB, pp. 133–34; idem, NOHM III, p. 93; idem, "Ars Nova," p. 71; Handschin, "Sumer Canon II," pp. 73–74; Sanders, "English Polyphony," pp. 193–95; idem, "Motet," p. 542; idem, "England: From the Beginnings," p. 283. Recorded on disc Nonesuch H-71308.

C.f.: verses four and five of the Epiphany sequence *Epiphaniam Domino.* Denis Stevens assumes that a performance of this motet would embed the motet within the sequence at mass. He observes in the liner notes for the Nonesuch disc that

a noted missal of the Sarum Use [*Paris, Bibliothèque de l'Arsenal (F-Pa 135)*] gives a clear clue to the performance of this work by starting the sequence in plainsong notation, changing to measured notation for the verses cited above, and then changing back again when they come to an end. The two troped verses enshrine the customary repeat of the melody on the vowel "a." [See *F-Pa 135,* fol. 240v, col. 1.]

Harrison points out, however, that in the Use of Salisbury the melody of the *Balaam* verses was used for the *Benedicamus Domino Alleluia* at Offices of Epiphany, citing the *Missale Sarum* (ed. Dickinson, 1861–63), col. 85, note: "Et cantus huius versus Balaam dicatur super Benedicamus cum Alleluia ad utrasque vesperas et ad matutinas secundum usum Sarum Ecclesie." Hence the choice of c.f. arguably makes this motet suitable for use in the office as a *Benedicamus* substitute rather than as a motet for use at mass. (Harrison, "Ars Nova," p. 71 and n. 8; idem, NOHM III, p. 93 and n. 1.)

Form: bipartite voice-exchange motet a3 with single text that is repeated on exchange; the two sections are written as separate motets in *F-MO.* See the beginning of the section of chapter 2 on isomelic motets.

dcf	hgf'	jif"	ijf"	x	y	z	w
cge	ghe'	ije"	jie"	y	x	w	z
AAB	AAB	AAB	AAB	C	C	C	C

Text: for Epiphany; tropic paraphrase of the language of the sequence verses used as the c.f.

Remarks: Dalglish calls the motet a "hocket variation," demonstrating in "Hocket" that the melismatic hocket sections in each half are variations on their respective texted sections. He wrongly describes voice I as "omitted" from *Onc 362* ("Hocket," pp. 358–59).

Civitas nusquam
T. Cibus esurientum
Cives celestis

Source: Onc 362, fol. 86v–87 (RISM no. 5).

Literature: Ed. in PMFC XV, no. 3 and in Stevens, TECM I, no. 17. Facs. in EECM 26, pl. 85–86; dipl. facs. in Apfel, *Studien* II, pp. 42–43. Apfel, *Studien* I, p. 28; Harrison, "Ars Nova," pp. 71–72; Sanders, "English Polyphony," pp. 250–51. Recorded on discs Expériences Anonymes EA-0024 and Harmonia Mundi France HM 1106.

C.f.: unidentified; texted with lines "Cibus esurientum, salus languentum, solamen dolentum."

Form: bipartite duet motet a3 with *medius cantus* and some varied repeat of counterpoint over return of tenor bars 1–10 as the final ten bars of the piece; the section break is defined by a cadence in all voices. No periodic phrase structure, but tenor is patterned:

$$50L = 24L + 26L = (4+6+4+6+4)L + (6+4+6+4+6)L.$$

Notation: counterpoint of two *s* against three *s* suggests the trochaic (2+1) reading of *s* duplets.

Text: to Saint Edward (marginal note: "de sancto Edwardo"). Voice I paraphrases Matt. 5:14–15 and 25:14–30.

Remarks: parallel counterpoint of outer voices mostly in sixths, with some stretches of noncadential parallel fifths.

Excelsus in numine
Benedictus Dominus
Tenor de Excelsus

Source: Onc 362, fol. 86v–87 (RISM no. 6).

Literature: Ed. in PMFC XVI, no. 99; Marrocco and Sandon, *Oxford Anthology,* no. 48; Stevens, *Music in Honour of St. Thomas,* no. 7. Facs. in EECM 26, pl. 86; dipl. facs. in Apfel, *Studien* II, pp. 44–45. Apfel, *Studien* I, p. 28; Hohler, "Reflections," p. 31; Sanders, "English Polyphony," p. 102; Stevens, "St. Thomas," pp. 342–43. Recorded on disc Peters PLE 115.

C.f.: a *pes*-like free voice in melodic double versicles.

Form: bipartite voice-exchange motet a3 with melismatic prelude and texted coda; double text sung alternately. See the beginning of the section in chapter 2 on isomelic motets.

Text: on Saint Thomas of Canterbury (marginal note: "de sancto Thoma cantuarie"). Hohler suggested in "Reflections" that the motet was originally conceived not for Becket but for the occasion of the canonization of Thomas of Hereford (1320). However, in private correspondence with me he has withdrawn that suggestion. I thank Mr. Hohler for kindly drawing my attention to significant textual allusions to Ps. 4:4, 7 and the language of the *Benedictus* at lauds (Luke 1:68–79).

Remarks: unusual tonality for the English repertoire in general and for free pieces in particular (G final with signature B♭). Fairly "open" counterpoint with extensive use of rests to lighten the texture.

Ade finit perpete
Ade finit misere
T. A definement d'este lerray

Source: Onc 362, fol. 87v (RISM no. 7); *F-TO 925,* fol. 166 (Anderson no. 8), with voice I beginning at 42,2.

Literature: Ed. in PMFC XV, no. 4 (*Onc*), with additional commentary in PMFC XVII; Facs. in EECM 26, pl. 87 (*Onc*); dipl. facs. in Apfel, *Studien* II, pp. 45–46 (*Onc*). Anderson, "New Sources," esp. p. 16; Apfel, *Studien* I, p. 28; Caldwell, "Letter to the Editor," pp. 384–85; Harrison, "Ars Nova," p. 73;

idem, NOHM III, p. 86; Sanders, "English Polyphony," pp. 220–21; idem, "Motet," p. 532. Recorded on disc Expériences Anonymes EA-0024.

C.f.: three statements of a tuneful melody identified in *Onc* as above, and in *F-TO* by the shorter "A definement." Caldwell, op. cit., draws attention to the fact that "the vernacular poem associated with the tenor of [this motet] has been located in the Bodleian MS Douce 308 (fol. 209), as the fourteenth item in the fourth section, devoted to *pastourelles.*" He cites some relevant literature, to which one can add Robert White Linker, *A Bibliography of Old French Lyrics* (1979), which anticipates Caldwell in the identification of the poem with the motet tenor (see no. 265–68). The melodic shape of the c.f. is a simple ab b′c b′c′ (= abb′).

Form: strophic repeat with variation in a motet a3 incorporating a phrase structure of mixed periodicity:

$$\text{I} \quad 72L = (13 + 11)L + 2(11 + 13)L$$
$$\text{II} \qquad = 8(9L)$$
$$\text{III} \qquad = 3(24L) = 3(6(4L))$$

The two lower voices share the same range, with the duplum generally beneath the tenor when the tenor is in the upper fourth of its range. There is a remarkably high degree of motivic ecomony and repetition both within each strophe, matching the melodic repetitions in the tenor melody, and between strophes. For example, see I, 1–4 = 25–28 = 49–52, or II, 56–60 = 64–68.

Text: on the Resurrection (marginal note: "de resurrectione" in *Onc*).

Remarks: the *F-TO* version is generally preferable to *Onc*.

Alta canunt assistentes
Quadruplum

Source: Onc 362, fol. 88 (RISM no. 8).

Literature: Facs. in EECM 26, pl. 88.

C.f.: not extant; possibly the motet was a whole-chant setting of an Alleluia (see below under *Text*).

Form: voices II and IV of a bipartite motet a4 (2+1+1?) with strophic repetition and varied voice exchange; change of mensuration after central cadence from second mode to first mode. The design of the motet may be represented as follows:

$$126L = 53L + 73L.$$

$$53L = 3L + 2(8L) + 2(8L) + (8+9)L + 1L$$
$$ \text{x} \qquad \text{AA}' \qquad \text{BB}' \qquad \text{CC}'$$

$$73L = (8+10L) + 2(9L) + 2(12L) + 12L + 1L$$
$$ \text{DD}' \qquad \text{EE}' \qquad \text{FF}' \qquad \text{F}''$$

Text: tropic expansion on the *Alleluia Pascha nostrum;* this is apparent because of the textual references: *Alta . . . miseria | Pascha no . . . immolatus est.* The sectional break divides Alleluia from verse.

Caligo terre scinditur
Virgo mater et filia
Tenor

Source: Onc 362, fol. 88v (RISM no. 9).
Literature: Ed. in PMFC XV, no. 5; Marrocco and Sandon, *Oxford Anthology,* no. 49. Facs. in EECM 26, pl. 89; dipl. facs. in Apfel, *Studien* II, pp. 46-47. Apfel, *Studien* I, p. 28; Caldwell, "Review," pp. 469-70; Harrison, NOHM III, p. 86; idem, "Ars Nova," p. 73. Recorded on disc Peters PLE 115.
C.f.: voice labeled "Tenor" is actually free; the c.f. is disguised in voice II. It is the virelai *Mariounette douche,* also used as the tenor of *Solaris ardor* (*Onc 362,* 10), where the French textual incipit is given.
Form: stratified motet a3 without regular phrase structure in triplum:

$$\text{I} \quad 49L = 5+6+8+4+5+4+7+5+5L$$
$$\text{II} \qquad = (7+4)L + 2(4+4)L + 2(7+4)L$$
$$\text{III} \qquad = 3(4L) + 12(3L) + 1L$$

Text: to the BVM at Christmas; duplum follows the shape of the virelai. Caldwell, op. cit., observes that lines 1-2, 5-6 of the triplum quote the second stanza of the Prudentius hymn *Nox et tenebrae et nubila* (*AH 50,* pp. 23-24), transforming "a hymn for daybreak into one for Christmas." The only change is the substitution of "partu" for "vultu" in line 6 of the motet text.

Solaris ardor Romuli
Gregorius sol seculi
Petre tua navicula
T. Mariounette douche

Source: Onc 362, fol. 89 (RISM no. 10).
Literature: Ed. in PMFC XV, no. 6 and in *History of Music in Sound* II, pp. 61-64. Facs. in EECM 26, pl. 90. Apfel, *Studien* I, p. 28; Harrison, "Ars Nova," p. 73; Dom A. Hughes, NOHM II, p. 403; Sanders, "English Polyphony," p. 221; idem, "Motet," p. 544. Recorded on disc RCA LM-6015 (History of Music in Sound II).
C.f.: a French virelai identified only by the textual incipit *Mariounette douche;* also used as the c.f. of *Caligo terre* (*Onc 362,* 9), where it is used at a level of transposition a fifth higher.

Form: isoperiodic motet a4 (3+1) with a module of 9L; some strophic repeat of counterpoint following the melodic shape of the tenor (ABBAA):

$$
\begin{aligned}
\text{I} \quad 54L &= 10L + 4(9L) + 8L \\
\text{II} \quad &= 14L + 4(9L) + 4L \\
\text{III} \quad &= 8L + 3(9L) + 2(5L) + 9L \\
\text{IV} \quad &= 12L + 2(9L) + 2(12L)
\end{aligned}
$$

Text: on Saint Augustine of Canterbury.

Virgo sancta Katerina
De spineto
T. Agmina

Source: Onc 362, fol. 89v, 82 (RISM no. 11).

Literature: Ed. in PMFC XV, no. 7. Facs. in EECM 26, pl. 91–92; dipl. facs. in Apfel, *Studien* II, pp. 48–49. Apfel, *Studien* I, p. 28; Harrison, "Ars Nova," p. 70; idem, NOHM III, p. 84; Sanders, "English Polyphony," pp. 248–50.

C.f.: neuma from the Saint Katherine responsory *Virgo flagellatur*. This *color* is sung in five rhythmically varied statements (29L + 20L + 17L + 11L + 13L), the second of which mixes first and second mode (see table 14).

Form: motet a3 that begins as if isoperiodic on a module of 9L (90L = 10(9L)) but then becomes more irregular due to varied rhythmic *taleae* in tenor (see the discussion of isoperiodicity in chapter 2):

$$
\begin{aligned}
\text{I} \quad 90L &= 3(9L) + 2(8L)+5L + (8+5+7)L + (4+7)L + 11L \\
\text{II} \quad &= 2L + 3(9L) + 3(8L) + 10L+9L + 8L + 10L \\
\text{III} \quad &= 9(3L)+4L +9(2L)+5L +3(4L)+5L +2(4L) +2(3L)+5L
\end{aligned}
$$

Text: to Saint Katherine; marginal rubric no longer visible. Text language is very close to that of the rhymed office texts for Katherine (*AS*, pl. V–Z). Regularly versified, with shift in scheme in the middle.

Remarks: variants to PMFC XV ed.: III: 50–52 *lb bbb l* (CB AFG F)/ 57–58 *lb l* (FG F).

Regi regum enarrare
T. Regnum tuum

Source: Onc 362, fol. 82v (RISM no. 12).

Literature: Facs. in EECM 26, pl. 93.

C.f.: whole-chant setting of the Gloria prosula; double-versicle structure of the c.f. is ignored in the setting.

Form: triplum and tenor of an isoperiodic motet a4 (2+2) with module of

7L; in order to accommodate the whole chant, tenor *taleae* are isoperiodic but not isorhythmic:

$$I \quad 84L = 9L + 8(7L) + 13L + 6L$$
$$II \qquad\; = 12(7L)$$

Text: a prayer to God, tropic to the tenor text.

Iam nubes dissolvitur
Iam novum sidus oritur
[T. Iam lucis orto sidere]

Source: Onc 362, fol. 83 (RISM no. 15), lacking tenor.

Literature: Ed. in PMFC XV, no. 8. Facs. in EECM 26, pl. 94. Handschin, "Sumer Canon II," pp. 75–76.

C.f.: the tenor does not survive in *Onc;* it was identified by Dr. Paul Hawkshaw who (like Handschin) reconstructed a contrapuntally acceptable voice under the upper parts, which was then recognized as the familiar tune of the hymn *Iam lucis,* stated two and one-half times.

Form: motet a3 isoperiodic in a module of 4L over the middle three of five tenor periods of 9L, with a textless *cauda* over the first tenor period and a more irregular scheme over the last:

$$I \quad 45L = (4+3)L + 7(4L) + (3+3+4)L$$
$$II \qquad\; = (2+3+4)L + 6(4L) + (3+4+5)L$$
$$III \qquad = 5(9L)$$

Text: to the BVM on her Nativity; listed in Chev. 38325 and ed. in *AH* 45b, p. 45.

Remarks: another thirteenth-century motet shares the same pair of texts set to different music; it appears, among other places, as *F-MO,* no. 258 (Rokseth no. 275). RISM B/IV/1 incorrectly reports that the *Onc* motet is merely a variant of the *F-MO* piece. This error is transmitted in two recent editions of the other setting: Tischler, *Montpellier* 2, p. lxv, wrongly indicates the *Onc* motet as a direct concordance, and further wrongly suggests that the *Onc* piece was not considered by Rokseth; Anderson, *Las Huelgas* 2, p. xxxv (in the notes to no. 34) also wrongly claims that the *Onc* motet is a direct concordance.

The two motets are, however, remarkably similar in formal design and stylization of declamation on the repeated word "iam." One may well have been modeled on the other. The *F-MO* piece has a tenor consisting of two statements of *Solem iusticie.* Roughly the middle half of the motet is isoperiodic, with a textless *cauda* over the first quarter and a more irregular scheme over the last quarter:

$$I \quad 40L = 2L + 7(4L) + 3L + 2(2L) + 3L$$
$$II \qquad\; = 8(4L) + 4(2L)$$
$$III \qquad = 20(2L)$$

(In both motets, modules of 4L have been counted such that the hocket falls over the last 2L of each unit.)

Whatever the direction of influence, it seems probable that the *Onc* motet is English in origin, on the basis of its appearance in an English source, the assonance of tenor text to the upper voices, some strophic repeat of counterpoint with varied voice exchange upon repeat of the tenor (as for instance in bars 13–14 compared with 31–32), and tonal closure.

O homo de pulvere
O homo considera
Quartus cantus de O homo
Filie ierusalem, tenor de O homo

Source: Onc *362,* fol. 83v, 90 (RISM no. 17).

Literature: Ed. in PMFC XV, 9; Marrocco and Sandon, *Oxford Anthology,* no. 50. Facs. in EECM 26, pl. 95–96; dipl. facs. in Apfel, *Studien* II, pp. 37–38. Apfel, *Studien* I, p. 27; Harrison, "Ars Nova," p. 70; Sanders, "English Polyphony," pp. 192–93; idem, "England: From the Beginnings," p. 283; idem, "Motet," pp. 541–42. Recorded on disc Peters PLE 115.

C.f.: beginning of a respond for the feast of a martyr or confessor (*AS,* pl. L); sung three times.

Form: motet a4 (2+1+1) with varied voice exchange (*Oxford Anthology* misleadingly labels as "isorhythmic"). Within each of the three sections there is a near-literal restatement of melody in the tenor for which there is corresponding voice exchange:

b	a′	b″		b		...c...d...
a	b′	a″	with	a	=	...d...c...
x	x′	x″		x		...v...v′...
y	y	y		y		...w...w′...

(See bars 8–12/16–20; 35–39/43–47/62–66/70–74.)

Text: homiletic; concordance for the pair in an earlier English motet, *Lbm 5958,* no. 2 (PMFC XIV, no. 79). Listed in Chev. 41870–71 and in GennB, nos. 212a/212b.

Remarks: narrow range (a thirteenth), narrow width of counterpoint (rarely exceeding an octave), lack of regular phrase structure, irregular declamation on long, or long and breve, and triadic final harmony all point to a date of composition in the later thirteenth century. (Both published editions amend the final note in the quartus cantus from an F to an A. Several thirteenth-century English motets a4 have a third in the final harmony, however. See chapter 1, table 4).

Rosa delectabilis
Regalis exoritur
T. Regali ex progenie

Source: Onc 362, fol. 90v–91 (RISM no. 18).

Literature: Ed. in PMFC XV, no. 10. Facs. in EECM 26, pl. 97–98; dipl. facs. in Apfel, *Studien* II, pp. 50–52. Apfel, *Studien* I, p. 28; Harrison, NOHM III, pp. 87–88; idem, "Ars Nova," p. 73; Sanders, "English Polyphony," pp. 239–40; idem, "Motet," p. 546.

C.f.: whole-chant setting of an antiphon for the Nativity of the BVM.

Form: duet motet a3 with *medius cantus* remarkably similar in design to *Jhesu redemptor omnium* (*Cfm,* 3); see chapter 2, figure 22.

Notation: first mode with elaborate subdivision of the breve using English circle-stem notation; see chapter 3, figure 35. Edition in PMFC lacks rhythmic consistency and accuracy.

Text: to the BVM.

Remarks: later entry in the MS as palimpsest over erased music that is now unreadable even under ultraviolet illumination.

TAcro 3182

... geret et regem gencium

Source: TAcro 3182, fol. B (no. 2).

Literature: Facs. in EECM 26, pl. 210; MEMG 4, pl. 203 (page labeled fol. 1). Lefferts and Bent, "New Sources," pp. 354–56.

Form: very fragmentary voice of a motet, probably the duplum; regularly versified text but irregular declamation and no regular phrase structure.

Notation: ternary breve-semibreve notation with a few melismatic minims.

Text: to the BVM.

Remarks: most similar to *Ancilla Domini* (*Lli 146,* 6).

... rex piaculum homo

Source: TAcro 3182, fol. Bv (no. 4).

Literature: Facs. in EECM 26, pl. 202. Lefferts and Bent, "New Sources," pp. 354–56.

Form: very fragmentary voice of a polyphonic composition using voice exchange. Not clearly a motet; possibly a whole-chant setting of an Alleluia (judging from what is legible of the text), of which there remains most of the verse. The setting alternates *cum* and *sine littera* sections and has a very wide range (a thirteenth, a–ff), which together suggest that this voice might be made to combine with itself in counterpoint through voice exchange. Professor Paul

Doe (University of Exeter) generously shared this observation and his discovery that parts of the voice can indeed be made to combine in this manner.

Notation: tempus imperfectum maior.

WF (Ob 20)

Lingua peregrina
T. Laqueus

    Source: Ob 20, fol. 25 (RISM no. 44 = *WF,* 44).

    Literature: Ed. in Dittmer, MSD 2, no. 44. Facs. in Dittmer, *Oxford, Latin Liturgical D 20,* p. 38. Dom A. Hughes, WMH, p. 67.

    C.f.: neuma from the beginning of the verse of the gradual for martyrs, *Anima nostra,* on the word "Laqueus." The tune is interesting, with an embedded melodic double versicle; apparently stated five times.

    Form: triplum (duplum?) and tenor of a motet a3 (a4?) with varied rhythmic patterning of the tenor in repeated *taleae* of 4L. See the section of chapter 2 concerning motets with varied tenor patterning. The upper voice has phrases of 4L and 8L, cadencing in the third bar of a 4L unit if there is antipenultimate stress on the last word; if the stress is penultimate, then there is a feminine cadence with longs in the third and fourth bars. Occasionally there is a rest of 1L that falls outside the 4L structuring (as in bars 5, 18, 35, 68, 101, 138, 150); hence there cannot have been complete synchronization of this upper part with the tenor throughout.

    Notation: larga-longa notation, on which see chapter 3 in the section concerning binary mensuration.

    Text: to the BVM.

    Remarks: palimpsest added over erased music; in the same hand that added *Peregrina moror* (*WF,* 47) and *Rex omnipotencie* (*WF,* 48).

WF (WOc 68)

Peregrina moror
T.

    Source: WOc 68, frag. xxxv, fol. 1v (RISM no. 47 = *WF,* 47).

    Literature: Ed. in Dittmer, MSD 2, no. 47. Facs. in Dittmer, *Worcester Add. 68,* p. 70. Dittmer, MSD 2, pp. 42–43; Dom A. Hughes, WMH, pp. 67, 98.

C.f.: unidentified; two statements of a lengthy *color* with embedded melodic double versicles (form **ABBCCD**) that is probably the neuma from a responsorial chant.

Form: triplum (duplum?) and tenor of a motet a3 (a4?) with varied rhythmic patterning of the tenor in repeated *taleae* of 4L. In these 4L units the third and fourth longs are often replaced by a double long. In the upper voice there is further articulation of the 4L units in synchronization with the tenor, especially by introducing a double long, two perfect longs, or a perfect long followed by a long-rest for the third and fourth longs of each unit. This defines a strict binary mensural organization on two successive levels above the long. It may be that the missing upper voice was set out of phase with the surviving two in much the same way that one finds phase shift in *Lingua peregrina* (*WF*, 44).

Notation: as in motet above.

Text: to the BVM.

Remarks: palimpsest over erased music; in same hand as the motet above.

Rex omnipotencie

Source: WOc 68, frag. xxxv, fol. iv (RISM no. 48 = *WF,* 48).

Literature: Ed. in Dittmer, MSD 2, no. 48. Facs. in Dittmer, *Worcester Add. 68,* p. 70. Dittmer, MSD 2, p. 43; Dom A. Hughes, WMH, p. 101.

Form: isolated voice, perhaps the triplum of a motet exhibiting strophic repetition with only slight variation; regular periodicity of phrase structure:
$$48L = 2(24L) = 2(4+3+3+4+3+3+4)L.$$

Text: to Mary and Jesus.

Remarks: use of C1 clef with signature B-natural above throughout. Palimpsest over erased music; in the same hand that added *WF,* 44 and 47.

Ut recreentur celitus
Secundus tenor

Source: WOc 68, frag. xii, fol. 1 (RISM no. 78 = *WF,* 78).

Literature: Ed. in Dittmer, MSD 2, no. 78. Facs. in Floyer and Hamilton, *Catalogue,* frontispiece. Dittmer, MSD 2, p. 58; Dom A. Hughes, WMH, p. 105.

Form: duplum and second tenor of a freely composed bipartite motet a4 (2+2) with isoperiodic phrase structure and a change of mensuration and modular number for the second half; each half ends with a textless coda.

$$178L = (80+4)L + (90+4)L$$

I	$= 8(10L) + 4L + 6(12L) + 22L$
II	$= (5+6)+(4+6)+8+3(6+4)+2(10)+5L+6+6(12)+5+6+5L$

Melodic resemblances, especially between alternate phrases, suggest some sort of varied strophic repeat. In each half, unsupported fourths calling for a second lower part occur in exactly the same place in each phrase (fourth and fifth bars in the first half; first and second bars in the second half).

Text: extant texted voice quotes stanzas 1–2, 5–6 of the hymn *Veni creator spiritus* as third and fourth lines of each of eight stanzas; the missing upper voice may have sung the same hymn verses (as the first two lines of each stanza), or may have set the skipped-over verses of the hymn so that the hymn text was sung in its entirety.

Remarks: palimpsest over erased music.

Inter choros paradisicolarum
Invictis pueris inter flammas

    Source: WOc 68, frag. xxi, fol. 1v (RISM no. 79 = *WF,* 79).

    Literature: Ed. in PMFC XIV, App. no. 26; Dittmer, MSD 2, no. 79. Facs. in Dittmer, *Worcester Add. 68,* p. 27. Dittmer, MSD 2, p. 58; Hohler, "Reflections," pp. 29–30; Dom A. Hughes, WMH, p. 94; Sanders, "English Polyphony," pp. 225–30 with transc.

    C.f.: none survives; reconstructed in PMFC XIV as a whole chant with no melodic recurrences.

    Form: two upper voices of an isoperiodic motet a4 (3+1) with a module of 12L; phrase scheme as follows, with I and IV hypothetical:

$$\text{I} \quad 64\text{L} = 4(12\text{L}) + 16\text{L}$$
$$\text{II} \qquad = 8\text{L} + 4(12\text{L}) + 8\text{L}$$
$$\text{III} \qquad = 4\text{L} + 5(12\text{L})$$
$$\text{IV} \qquad = 2\text{L} + 15(4\text{L}) + 2\text{L}$$

In the 10*pp* lines of text, the extension of the pickup to a full-bar anacrusis has been displaced to the third syllable, as a rule, for patterning of declamation.

    Text: to Saint Winifred (presumably the one whose relics are at Shrewbury and whose feast is November 3, but note the doubts raised by Hohler, "Reflections," pp. 29–30).

    Remarks: palimpsest over erased music.

Regnum sine termino
T. Regnum tuum solidum

    Source: WOc 68, frag. xii, fol. iv (RISM no. 80 = *WF,* 80).

    Literature: Ed. in Dittmer, MSD 2, no. 80. Facs. in Dittmer, *Worcester Add. 68,* p. 27. Dittmer, MSD 2, p. 59; Dom A. Hughes, WMH, p. 41; Sanders, "English Polyphony," p. 225 and n. 72.

    C.f.: whole-chant setting of the Gloria prosula; text is only partially underlaid and perhaps not intended to be sung.

Form: duplum and tenor of a motet a4 (2+2); sectional structure defined by the melodic shape of the c.f. (ABBCCD), with rhythmic repetition in tenor accompanied by voice exchange in the upper parts (over BB and CC):

$$88L = 16L + 2(22L) + 2(9L) + 10L.$$

Text: prayer to God, tropic to the prosula text.

Remarks: palimpsest over erased music; rhythm and handling of declamation suggest units of 2L are a mensural feature, with inconsistency only in the two 9L units of the third section.

Yc

On this source see not only Lefferts and Bent, "New Sources," pp. 358–61 but also Bowers, "Performing Ensemble," pp. 188–92.

Inter amenitatis tripudia
O livor anxie
T. Revertenti

Source: Yc, fol. 19v (no. 2), voice I only; *F-Pn 146,* fol. 21v (RISM no. 21), voices I and III only (in this source, the *Roman de Fauvel,* the index lists this motet under "Notez a tenures sanz trebles"); *F-Pn 23190 (Trém),* index, xxxi; *I-TR 87,* fol. 231v–232 (no. 177).

Literature: Ed. in PMFC I, no. 22 (*F-Pn 146*); von Ficker, *Sieben Trienter Codices: geistliche und weltliche Motetten,* p. 1 (*I-TR 87*). Facs. in EECM 26, pl. 213 (*Yc*) and in facsimile editions of *Fauvel* and the Trent codices. Lefferts and Bent, "New Sources," pp. 358–61.

C.f.: from the matins responsory *Revertenti Abraham* (*AS,* pl. 142), disposed in three *colores* and eight *ordines.*

Form: motet a3 with stratification of rhythmic activity and no regular phrase structure; phrase endings inconsistent with either first or second mode.

Text: see Dahnk, *L'Hérésie,* p. 104ff.

GB-YOX

This is a source of motets and other polyphony newly uncovered in Yoxford by Adrian Bassett, who is preparing a substantial report on it. I thank him for sharing information about the motets with me, from which the following brief account is drawn. The motets are on a single isolated bifolium, not the center of a gathering, now used as binding material in a Suffolk manorial extent of the fifteenth century.

Sub Arturo plebs vallata
Fons citharizancium
T. In omnem terram exivit sonus
  eorum et in fines orbis

    Source: GB-YOX, fol. 1 (no. 1), II and III; *F-CH 564,* fol. 70v–71 (RISM no. 111); *I-Bc Q15,* fol. 225v–226 and 342v (no. 218).
    Literature: Ed. in PMFC V, no. 31; CMM 39, no. 12; Bent, *Two Fourteenth-Century Motets in Praise of Music,* pp. 1–7; von Ficker, *Sieben Trienter Codices,* pp. 9–11; Günther, "Das Wort-Ton Problem," pp. 169–74. Facs. in Wolf, *Musikalische Schrifttafeln,* pl. 30–31 (*F-CH*); Gennrich, *Abriss der Mensuralnotation,* pl. xviii a–b (*F-CH*). Bent, "Transmission," pp. 70–72; Günther, "The Fourteenth-Century Motet," pp. 38–45; idem, "Das Wort-Ton Problem," pp. 163–78; Leech-Wilkinson, "Compositional Procedure," pp. 170–71; Trowell, "A Fourteenth-Century Ceremonial Motet;" Carapetyan, "A Fourteenth-Century Florentine Treatise," pp. 89, 91.
    Form: tripartite isorhythmic motet a3 with sectional diminution in the ratio 9:6:4 and broad phrase structures in the same length as the *taleae;* three *colores* and nine *taleae:*
    $152B = 72B + 48B + 32B = 3(24B) + 3(16B) + 3(64M)$.
    Notation: use of *cauda hirundinis* in *GB-Yoxford.*
    Text: a musicians motet. See discussion of musicians motets in chapter 4.
    Remarks: the tenor is cited in an Italian vernacular music treatise of the late fourteenth century. See Carapetyan, op. cit. and his edition of the treatise, *Notitia del valore delle note del canto misurato* (AIM: CSM 5, 1957).

Texted voice-part and tenor

    Source: GB-YOX, fol. 1v (no. 2).
    Text: on John the Baptist.

Texted voice-part and *Solus tenor*

    Source: GB-YOX, fol. 2 (no. 3).
    Text: employs musical imagery.

Degentis vita
Cum vix
T. Vera pudicicie
Ct.

Source: GB-YOX, fol. 2v (no. 4), I and III; *B-Ba 758,* fol. 53v (RISM no. 2); *D-Nst 9,* fol. 1 (RISM no. 1); *E-Bcen 971,* fol. 8v–9 (RISM no. 6); *F-CH 564,* fol. 62v–63 (RISM no. 103); *F-Pn 23190 (Trém),* index, lvii; *F-Sm 222,* fol. 81v (RISM no. 140).

Literature: Ed. in PMFC V, no. 23/23a; CMM 39, no. 2.

Form: unipartite isorhythmic motet a4; two *colores* and four *taleae:*

$$144B = 4(36B) \text{ (ideal)}$$

I	141B	$= 8B + 3(5+11+3+17)B + (5+11+3+6)B$
II		$= 9B + 3(9+8+19)B + (9+8+7)B$
III		$= 3(36B) + 33B$
IV		$= 10B + 3(7+16+13)B + (7+16)B$

Notation: tempus imperfectum minor with perfect *modus.*

Text: addressed to Jesus and Mary on the moral corruption of the world.

D-W 499 (W3)

This source consists of flyleaves from a Wolfenbüttel codex (Helmstadt 499) of Scottish provenance. They were seen by Wolf and referred to in HNK I, p. 286; Ludwig mentions them in "Die Quellen," p. 192, note, at which time they were missing. There is an entry for them in RISM B/IV/I, pp. 205–6. The contents are early fourteenth-century English troped chant settings a4 (2+2) of Alleluias for the BVM. Very similar to the settings in *Cjc 23* in style and technique.

... solis vel syderis
Tenor pro iii
Quartus
Tenor pro iiii

Source: D-W 499 (W3), fol. 1 (RISM no. 1).

Remarks: Two of the three surviving parts, aside from a brief bit of text for an upper voice, are the tenor and quartus cantus of a setting a4; where the tenor is regularly phrased it shows periodicity first in 9L and then in 11L. The "Tenor pro iii" condenses the first two into a single part; this is one of the two earliest examples of a *solus tenor,* along with the "Tenor per se de Iacet granum" of *Onc 362,* 1.

Alleluya concrepando pange musica
Alleluya consonet presens familia

Source: D-W 499 (W3), fol. 1v (RISM no. 2).

Form: bipartite, with a strong central cadence before the start of the verse. In the second section the triplum is periodic in 7L.

Quartus
Tenor pro iiii

>*Source: D-W 499 (W3),* fol. 2 (RISM no. 3).
>*Form:* two fragmentary lower voices of a bipartite setting. Tenor shows some periodicity in 4L in the second section.

Alleluya confessoris almi presentia

>*Source: D-W 499 (W3),* fol. 2v (RISM no. 5).
>*Remarks:* single voice-part, probably with division into bipartite form at the end of second staff. Notated with groups of two to four syllabic *s,* with a downstemmed semibreve used in groups of three. High-cleffed, usually C1 with B-natural above, but also using G2 with B-natural on staff 3 and the very unusual F5 clef, with total range e–gg.

F-Pn 23190 (Trém)

O dira nacio
Mens in nequicia
Tenor

>*Source: F-Pn 23190 (Trém),* fol. 2v (RISM no. 4); listed in the *Trém* index, ix.
>*Literature:* Ed. in PMFC XVII, no. 55. Facs. in Droz and Thibaut, "Un Chansonnier de Philippe le Bon." Besseler, "Studien II," pp. 188, 190–91; Wright, *Music and Musicians,* p. 150.
>*C.f.:* unidentified whole chant with embedded double versicle.
>*Form:* motet a3 with sectional structure defined by declamation patterns in the triplum. See chapter 2 at the end of the section on English isorhythm.
>*Notation: tempus imperfectum maior* in imperfect modus with very few minims.
>*Text:* on Thomas (presumably Thomas of Canterbury); text is fairly corrupt.
>*Remarks:* As Besseler observes, this is by all appearances one of the most old-fashioned pieces in *F-Pn 23190,* and it suggests to him the style of the Fauvel era. The fact that it sets a whole chant, has imperfect long and breve, and extensively exploits imperfect consonances, suggests its kinship with a Fauvel motet like *Quoniam novi–Heu fortuna–T. Heu me* (*F-Pn 146,* fol. 30; RISM no. 24), though *O dira nacio* does not have the latter's Petronian semibreves. The same musical features, along with the subject matter, use of duet passages and patterned declamation, and general avoidance of three or more semibreves per breve (even melismatically), suggest the possibility of English authorship.

F-TO 925

This source was brought to public attention in a 1982 article by Gordon Anderson, "New Sources." The editions of music that accompanied this article were clearly prepared from rough copy; it would seem that at the time of his death Anderson had only been able to provide the publisher with finished editions and translations of the Latin texts. The four complete motets have been reedited for PMFX XVII (in a Supplement to PMFC XV) by Frank Ll. Harrison, who also supplies some important revisions to details reported by Anderson. Since two pages are still pasted down, the original relationship between the leaves cannot fully be determined; the contents list as presented below will certainly have to be revised at some future point. Note that except for the tenor of *Ade finit*, none of the lyrics identified by textual incipit in these tenors has been traced elsewhere.

Pastedown material. *F-TO 925*, fol. I.

Exulta Syon filia
Exulta Syon filia
Exulta Syon filia
T. En ai ie bien trouve

    Source: F-TO 925, fol. Iv (Anderson no. 1).
    Literature: Ed. PMFC XVII, Suppl. no. 1; Anderson, "New Sources," pp. 4–6, 17–18.
    C.f.: double versicle with *ouvert* and *clos;* sung six times.
    Form: motet a4 texted 3+1 but with pairing of voices I and II (often echoing one another in imitation), and voice II functioning in range and rhythmic activity as a counterpart to the tenor, hence (2+2). Mixed periodicity, with extensive strophic repetition of counterpoint.

$$\begin{aligned}
\text{I} \quad & 54\text{L} = 4(8\text{L}) + 6\text{L} + 2(8\text{L}) \\
\text{II} \quad & \phantom{54\text{L}} = 4(10\text{L}) + 4\text{L} + 10\text{L} \\
\text{III} \quad & \phantom{54\text{L}} = 3(11\text{L}) + 4\text{L} + 17\text{L} \\
\text{IV} \quad & \phantom{54\text{L}} = 6(9\text{L}) = 6(4+4+1)\text{L}
\end{aligned}$$

    Notation: use of repeated breves instead of single imperfect long in III from bar 38 to the end, perhaps to highlight a carefully shaped melody in two tuneful double versicles with *ouvert* and *clos* paralleling the tenor tune. Note predominance of *ssbb* rhythms in I and II.
    Text: for the BVM at Christmas.

Erased three-voice motet.
    Source: F-TO 925, fol. 165 (Anderson no. 6).

S...
Syderea celi cacumina
T. Se iavoie a plaingant.
Tii. Tenor cont. Si javoie etc.

Source: F-TO 925, fol. Iv–165 (Anderson no. 7).
Literature: Text ed. in Anderson, p. 10.
C.f.: melodic double versicle with *ouvert* and *clos;* sung three times in changing rhythms.
Form: motet a4 (2+2) isoperiodic in upper voices over two supporting voices locked in hocketing rhythmic exchange:

$$\text{I} \quad 38\text{L} = ??$$
$$\text{II} \qquad = 4(7\text{L}) + 10\text{L}$$
$$\text{III/IV} \quad = 19(2\text{L})$$

Notation: binary long.
Text: to the BVM at Christmas.

...ma insuper et tymiamata
T. Or sus alouete

Source: F-TO 925, fol. II (Anderson no. 2).
Literature: Text ed. in Anderson, pp. 6–7.
C.f.: two melodic couplets followed by twofold statement of melodic double versicle with *ouvert* and *clos;* overall melodic shape AA BB CC'CC'.
Form: duplum and tenor of motet a3 with stratification of rhythmic activity and rhythmic patterning of semibreve declamation, looking something like *Laus honor* (*Cpc 228,* 3).
Text: to the Holy Cross.

Valde mane diluculo
Valde mane diluculo
T. Va dorenlot

Source: F-TO 925, fol. II (Anderson no. 3).
Literature: Ed. in PMFC XVII, Suppl. no. 2; Anderson, pp. 7–8, 18–19.
C.f.: brief tune (shape AAB); sung seven times.
Form: motet a3 with stratified rhythmic activity and some mixed periodicity:

$$\text{I} \quad 56\text{L} = 3(9\text{L}) + 11\text{L} + 8\text{L} + 10\text{L}$$
$$\text{II} \qquad = 3(8\text{L}) + 16\text{L} + 2(8\text{L})$$
$$\text{III} \qquad = 7(8\text{L})$$

Note hocket section over fifth tenor statement and predominance of *ssbb* rhythms in voice I.

Text: Easter texts telling the story of Mary Magdalene at the tomb.

Isolated tenor fragment, "In virtu. Sai[ant]?"
    Source: F-TO 925, col. II.

Corona virginum
Columba prudencie
T. Cui proclamant

    Source: F-TO 925, fol. IIv (Anderson no. 4).
    Literature: Ed. in PMFC XVII, Suppl. no. 3; Anderson, pp. 8–9, 19–20.
    C.f.: melodic double versicle with *ouvert* and *clos;* stated five times.
    Form: motet a3 with mixed periodicity:

$$\text{I} \quad 60\text{L} = 2(10\text{L}) + 5(8\text{L})$$
$$\text{II} \qquad = 6(10\text{L})$$
$$\text{III} \qquad = 5(12\text{L}) = 5(6{+}6)\text{L}$$

    Text: to the BVM.

Mons olivarum ecce rumpitur
Mors amari moritur

    Source: F-TO 925, fol. IIv (Anderson no. 5).
    Literature: Texts ed. in Anderson, pp. 9–10.
    Form: two upper voices of a bipartite motet a3:

$$80\text{L} = 48\text{L} + 32\text{L}$$
$$\text{I} \qquad = (2{+}6{+}2{+}10{+}2{+}6{+}2{+}6{+}2{+}10) + (10{+}10{+}2{+}10)\text{L}$$
$$\text{II} \qquad = 8{+}8{+}8{+}\ldots = ?6(8\text{L}) + 4(8\text{L})$$

    Text: Christ's Passion and death.
    Remarks: in the context of the rhythmic language of the other motets in this source, motion here in a double-long foot under second mode is decidedly old-fashioned.

Ade finit. See above under *Onc 362,* no. 7.

Vide miser et iudica
Vide miser et cogita
T. Wynter

    Source: F-TO 925, fol. 166 (Anderson no. 9).
    Literature: Ed. in PMFC XVII, Suppl. no. 5; Anderson, pp. 10–11, 20–21.

C.f.: three statements of a tune comprising two melodic double versicles. The one Middle English lyric with the same incipit (Brown, *Register,* no. 2655; Brown and Robbins, *Index,* no. 4177) does not appear to fit the melody.

Form: motet a3 with extensive strophic repeat and variation over each melodic double versicle of the tenor; also, periodic phrase structure:

$$\text{I} \quad 72\text{L} = 4(15\text{L}) + 12\text{L}$$
$$\text{II} \quad\quad = (11+14)\text{L} + (11+12)\text{L} + (11+13)\text{L}$$
$$\text{III} \quad\quad = 3(24\text{L}) = 3(2(6\text{L}) + 2(6\text{L}))$$

Text: homiletic; c.f. incipit clearly apt in tone.

Pastedown material. *F-TO 925,* fol. 166v.

US-PRu 119A

Si lingua lota
Mors amar...

Source: *US-PRu 119A,* fol. 5v and 2 (RISM no. A5).
Literature: Partial facs. in EECM 26, pl. 212. Levy, "New Material," p. 225.
Form: fragments of the triplum and duplum of a motet a3; no evident regularity of phrase structure but some clear melodic repetition in the triplum, as in bars 10–15 = 38–43 = (24)-29 and bars 5–9 = 49–52 = 20–22.
Text: apparently to the BVM, though the "mors" incipit implies Easter. One motet fragment in *F-TO 925, Mons olivarum– Mors amara (F-TO 925,* 5) begins similarly in the duplum and may have been a textual concordance, but there is no musical correspondence.
Remarks: the piece has rhythmic subdivision of the breve in idiomatic figures typical of early fourteenth-century English music; combined with the fact that it is on the same leaf as *Thomas gemma,* it would seem reasonable to presume it to be of the same general age. Possibly, though, some errors in rhythmic notation (square breves instead of a long and a breve) may point to an origin in English mensural notation, with a conversion to longs and breves from paired rhombs (or paired square breves) not entirely successfully carried out.

US-SM 19914

In ore te laudancium

Source: *US-SM 19914,* fol. 1 (RISM no. 1).
Form: isolated voice of a motet, judging by its range and text, a duplum; no evident periodic phrase structure.

Notation: tempus imperfectum maior.
Text: prayer to Jesus.

Textless

Source: US-SM 19914, fol. 1 (RISM no. 2).
Remarks: Not a motet. RISM incorrectly states that there is a single voice here. In fact there are two parts, making a crude but complete composition in two 15B sections notated in *tempus perfectum maior;* perhaps a discant setting of a c.f.

... Maria diceris mater
Soli fines ex gracia
T.

Source: US-SM 19914, fol. 1v–2 (RISM no. 3).
Literature: Dom A. Hughes, NOHM II, pp. 391–92.
C.f.: unidentified; a whole chant, probably a melisma, having embedded double versicle and overall shape AAB.
Form: three voices of a motet that was probably a4 (2+2), akin to an unipartite isorhythmic motet with four *taleae* (see chapter 2 in the section on English isorhythm):

$$96B = 4(24B) = 4(12+12)B.$$

Notation: tempus perfectum maior. Red coloration in the tenor changes the *modus* from imperfect to perfect.
Text: to the BVM; triplum text, *Maria diceris,* has reference to Carmelites. See chapter 3 in the section on external references in the motet texts.
Remarks: final cadence to 12–8–5 harmony; counterpoint similar to that in the *tempus perfectum* section of *Regne de pité* (see figure 28).

US-Wc 14

This source consists of two flyleaves of music taken from a fourteenth-century manuscript by John Britton on the laws of England. This book has an original English binding of the later fourteenth century (a point made in RISM and verified for me by the Library of Congress), and as Reaney observes in RISM B/IV/2, p. 371: "It is clear that the music was with the principal manuscript from the beginning." Günther flatly states in *The New Grove* ("Sources, MS, VII, 3") that *US-Wc 14* is French, but this is contradicted by the nonmotet items discussed below. The music clearly circulated in England and in all likelihood was copied by English scribes.

The two nonmotet items of *US-Wc 14* are of interest here. One (*US-Wc 14*, 1) is according to RISM a "single voice part sporadically underlaid with a Latin text, which is not easily legible." The text is in fact that of the *Alleluya Virga Iesse floruit*, and the voice is a melodic paraphrase of the chant, sounding a c.f. pitch every two breves. The paraphrase is the lowest voice of a setting that was probably a2 and similar in style to settings like the *Alleluia Salve virgo* a2 found in *Omc 267*, fol. 89v and *Lbl Egerton 3307*, fol. 46, which however has the c.f. in the top voice. The other item (*US-Wc 14*, 2) consists of two contrapuntally self-sufficient voices (an upper part, and the wrongly labeled "Tenor de et in terra") of a Patrem setting with drastically truncated text. Given the width of counterpoint and text omissions, it is likely this setting was a4, with a second upper voice telescoping the text and a contratenor in the tenor range. Both pieces can only be English and are in the same text and music hands as the motets.

Deus compaignouns de Cleremunde

> *Source: US-Wc 14*, fol. 2 (RISM no. 3).
> *Form:* uppermost six staves of music (five of text) of an isolated duplum (judging by C3 clef, phrase structure, and form of text) of an unipartite isorhythmic motet:
> $$20B + 5(16B) + \ldots$$
> *Notation: tempus imperfectum maior.*
> *Text:* alternately in French and Latin. Reaney says in RISM: "the bilingual motet . . . suggests North-Eastern French origin." Cleremunde could be the town of Clermont northwest of Paris near Beauvais, with its strategic Bourbon fortress (the dukes of Bourbon were counts of Clermont in the fourteenth century), or the important cathedral town in central France (now Clermont-Ferrand). Very possibly this voice-part, with its mention of good companions and good singing and reference to at least two individuals by name (one of whom is a Gwillelmus nicknamed Malcharte), is from a musicians motet (see the discussion of this text genre in chapter 4).

Rex Karole Iohannis genite
Leticie pacis concordie
T. Virgo prius ac posterius
Contratenor
Solus tenor

> *Source: US-Wc 14*, fol. 2v (RISM no. 4), fragment of II; *F-CH 564*, fol. 65v–66 (RISM no. 106), I, II, III, V; *F-Sm 222*, fol. 7v (RISM no. 10), I, IV, V with ascription to Royllart.

Literature: Ed. in PMFC V, no. 26; CMM 39, no. 5. Günther, "The Fourteenth-Century Motet," pp. 39, 44.

C.f.: last section of the Marian antiphon *Alma redemptoris mater;* sung twice.

Form: unipartite isorhythmic motet a4 with *introitus;* two *colores* and five *taleae:*

$$\text{I} \quad 160\text{B} = 10\text{B} + 18\text{B} + 4(28\text{B}) + 20\text{B}$$
$$\text{II} \qquad\quad = 5\text{B} + 19\text{B} + 4(28\text{B}) + 24\text{B}$$
$$\text{III} \qquad\quad = 18\text{B} + 5\text{B} + 4(28\text{B}) + 25\text{B} \qquad (28 = 6+5+17)$$
$$\text{IV} \qquad\quad = 18\text{B} + 4(28\text{B}) + 30\text{B} \qquad\qquad (28 = 4+10+14)$$

Very stylized formally, with hocket over the last 10B of every 28B *talea* and a double long in all parts at the beginning of each section.

Notation: basically *tempus perfectum minor,* with a shift to *tempus imperfectum minor* in the hocket that ends each period.

Text: motet dedicated to Charles V, king of France (1364–80) and to the BVM. See the section on "External References" in chapter 4.

Appendix 3

Thirteenth-Century English Motet Repertoire

Brackets are used to enclose information not in the sources.

A single asterisk in the left margin indicates a motet of Continental origin that survives in an insular source. Double asterisks mark motets of probable English origin that survive only in a Continental source. Some of the candidates for English origin that have been brought forward by Handschin, Tischler, Dittmer, and Apfel from among motets in Continental repertoires have been omitted. None of the motets of probable thirteenth-century origin that remain in the repertoire of the early fourteenth century are listed here.

This list attempts to exclude all troped chant settings (see chapter 1, table 1) and the voice-exchange motets in troped chant settings of Alleluias (see chapter 2, table 6), except for *Alle psallite,* which survives independently in *F-MO.*

The motets known only from the *Lbl 978 (Lo Ha)* index are excluded (see chapter 4, table 26). References to the index are made in this list where concordances survive.

Other *exclusa* include at least the following additional fragments found in English sources:

Ccc 8, items in binding strips
Cjec 5, 4, 5, 6, 8
Cjc 138, 1
Ctc, 1, 2, 3, 5, 7
Lbl 3132, 2, 3, 4, 5, 6
Lbl 5958, 4, 5, 6, 7
Ob 25, 2a, 4
Omec 1, 2
D-Gu, 3
US-PRu 119, C items.

Motet	Sources
...a quo fecundata ...archangelorum quam	Cjec 5, 3
A superna paranimphus	D-Gu, 4
**Ade costa dormientis T.	Lbl 978, 7.19 F-Pn 146, 20
Alle psallite Alle psallite Alleluya	F-MO, 322 (Rok 8.339) WF, 19 (Ave magnifica) WF, 56 (Ave magnifica) Ob 400, H (Ave magnifica)
Alleluia celica rite Alleluia celica rite T. [Pes]	US-PRu 119A, 3
*Amor veint tout fors Au tens d'este ke cil T. Et gaudebit	Lbl XVIII, 1 F-MO, 243 (Rok 7.260)
*Au queer ay un maus Ja ne mi repentiray T. Jolietement my teent	Ob 139, 3 F-MO, 15 (Rok 2.23)
*Ave gloriosa mater Ave gloriosa mater T. Ave gloriosa [Domino]	Lbl 978, 4 F-MO, 44 (Rok 4.53) and other Continental concordances
Ave miles de cuius Ave miles O Edwarde Quartus cantus Tenor. Ablue	Lwa 33327, 7
**Ave parens Ad gracie T. Ave Maria	Lbl 978, 7.40 F-MO, 60 (Rok 4.69)
Barbara simplex animo Barbara simplex animo Tenor [Hodierne lux diei]	US-Cu, 9

Benedicta domina	WF, 3
**Benigna celi regina Beata es Maria T. Veritatem	F-MO, 62 (Rok 4.71)
Campanis cum cymbalis Honoremus dominam T. Campanis [Primus pes] T. Honoremus [Secundus pes]	Ob 60, 13
Conditio nature defuit [O natio nephandi] T. [Pes]	WF, 64
Creatoris/ O maria T. [Agmina]	US-CU, 1/2
[Domine celestis rex] Dona celi factor Quartus cantus Tenor. Doce	Lwa 33327, 5
Dona celi factor T.	US-Cu, 3
Dulciflua tua memoria Precipue michi dat Tenor de Dulciflua [pes]	WF, 41 Lbl 978, 5.3
Dulcis Jesu memoria Pes de Dulcis Jesu memoria	WF, 75
En averil al tens O Christi clemencie T.	Cjc 138, 2
Eterne virgo memorie Eterna virgo mater T. [Pes]	WF, 15
...ex te verbum nunc	WF, 8

Fons ortorum riga morum   WF, 30
Pes

[Fulgens stella]   WF, 74
Pes de Fulgens stella

In odore [In odorem]   Ob 497, 5
Gracia viam [In odoris]   F-MO, 61 (Rok 4.70)
[Quartus cantus]
T. In odorem

**Jhesu dator venie   F-Pn 146, 32
Zelus familie
Tenor

Loquelis archangeli   WF, 18/66
Quartus cantus

*Mellis stilla   Ob 18, 1
T. Mellis stilla [Domino]   F-MO, 32 (Rok 4.40)

Miles Christi gloriose   Cjc 138, 4
Plorate cives anglie
[Pes]

Mirabilis Deus invisibilis   Ob 19, 1
T. Ave Maria
T. Ave Maria

*Nobili precinitur   Lbl 5958, 1
Flos de virga nascitur   F-MO, 58 (Rok 4.67)
T. Proles Marie virginis

O debilis o flebilis   WF, 73
Pes super O debilis
Primus Pes super O debilis

O decus predicancium   WF, 37
T. [Agmina]

O homo considera   Lbl 5958, 2
O homo de pulvere
T. [In seculum]

O Maria singularis T.	Ctc, 6
O Maria stella maris Jhesu fili summi patris T. [Pes]	Ob 497, 9
[O mores perditos] ...calbatio o gravis T. Opem [nobis]	D-Gu, 1/5 Cjec 5, 1
O mors moreris O vita vera Quartus cantus Tenor. Mors	Lwa 33327, 3
O nobilis nativitas O mira Dei misericordia O decus virginem Tenor. Apparuit	Lwa 33327, 2
O quam glorifica O quam beata domina O quam felix femina T. [Pes]	WF, 10
O regina celestis O regina celestis	WF, 22
O regina glorie T. [Pes]	WF, 36
O sancte Bartholomee O sancte Bartholomee T. O Barthomomee (pes)	Cjc 138, 3
O spes et salus ...de virgo semper T.	Ob 60, 15
O venie vena T. Illumina	WF, 13

Orbis pium Orbis pium T. O bipartitum partum	US-Cu, 8
... omnipotencie	WF, 24
Opem nobis o Thoma Salve Thoma virga Quartus cantus Tenor. Pastor cesus	Lwa 33327, 6
Patris superni Patris superni T. Pia pacis inclita	US-Cu, 7
Pro beati Pauli O pastor patris O preclara patrie Pes [T. Pro patribus]	Lwa 33327, 4 WF, 70
Pro beati Pauli O pastor patris O preclara patrie T. [Pes]	WF, 40
... profero in te rex	WF, 38
Prolis eterne genitor Psallat mater gracie Pes super Prolis et Psallat	WF, 6
Psallat choros in novo Eximie pater egregie T. Aptatur	Lwa 33327, 8 F-MO, 51 (Rok 4.60)
Puellare gremium Purissima mater Pes super Puellare et Purissima	WF, 76
Quam admirabilis Quam admirabilis Pes	WF, 16
Quatuor ex partibus	Ob 60, 14

Quem non capit	WF, 7
[Quem non capit]	Lbl 978, 5.1
Pes super Quem non capit	
...salvatoris	Ob 25, 3
T.	
Salve gemma confessorum	WF, 39
	Lbl 978, 7.29
**Salve mater misericordie	F-MO, 63 (Rok 4.72)
Salve regina misericordie	
T. Flos filius	
[Salve Simonis quia hic]	Cjec 5, 7
Salve Symon Montisfortis	
Tenor de Salve simonis quia hic [pes]	
Sanctorum omnium	WF, 23
T. [Pes]	
Senator regis curie	WF, 11
Primus Pes	D-Gu, 2
Secundus Pes	
Sol in nube tegitur	WF, 17
Pes	
Sospitati dedit egros	Cjec 5, 8a
...ferno cum timore	Lwa 33327, 1
...per te fides	
Spirans odor	
T. Kyrie	
Sub...scit	US-PRu 119B, 2
O...libate	
T. [Pes]	
Super te ierusalem	WF, 95
Sed fulsit virginitas	Lbl 978, 5.2
Primus tenor	F-MO, 59 (Rok 4.68)
T. Dominus	

Te Domine laudat	WF, 71
Te Dominum clamat	
Pes super de Te Domine	
et de Te dominum	
Tota pulchra es	US-PRu 119A, 2
Anima mea liquefacta	Lbl 978, 5.8
T. [Pes]	
Trahis suspirium	F-Pn 25408, 1
Mordax detractio	
T. [Epiphaniam]	
Tu capud ecclesie	DRu, 2
Tu es Petrus a petra	
T. [Veritatem]	
Veni mater gracie	Lbl 29, 1
T. Dou way Robin [pes]	US-PRu 119B, 1
Virginis Marie	WF, 72
Salve gemma virginum	Lbl 978, 5.12
Pes [T. Veritatem]	
*Virgo decus castitatis	Ob 72, 5
T.	F-MO, 49 (4.58)
[Virgo flagellatur]	Cjec 5, 2
Virgo regalis	WF, 12
[Virgo regalis]	
Pes	
... virtutum spolia	Ctc, 4
... virtutum spolia	
[Quartus cantus]	
T. [Et confitebor]	
Worldes blisce	Ccc 8, 2
T. [Benedicamus Domino]	

Notes

Chapter 1

1. This neglect continues to the present day in such broad surveys as Richard Hoppin's recent textbook, *Medieval Music* (published in 1978). See his chapter 20, pp. 502–8. and chapter 14, pp. 346–47.

2. See especially Handschin, "Sumer Canon"; Dittmer, *Worcester Fragments* (hereafter cited as MSD 2 to avoid confusion between the book and the source(s) of the same name); Apfel, *Studien* and its later offshoots, most importantly *Grundlagen*; Harrison, *Music in Medieval Britain*, "Ars Nova," and PMFC XV.

3. Bent, "Preliminary Assessment," p. 65; see also her elaboration of this point in "Transmission," pp. 65–67.

4. Sanders, "England: From the Beginnings," p. 289.

5. Here are some similarly approximate figures for comparison: from thirteenth-century England, more than 80 motets (see appendix 3); from thirteenth-century Continental Europe, about 500; from the fourteenth-century French tradition, more than 200; from the fourteenth-century Italian tradition, just over a dozen.

6. The motets are relatively easy to bring under exhaustive bibliographic control thanks to the existence of the *Répertoire international des sources musicales* (hereafter RISM), and to the cooperation between scholars in sharing the news of new discoveries that came to light since. Lefferts and Bent, "New Sources," provides a review of all relevant items that came to light between the publication of the RISM volumes (B/IV/1 in 1966 and B/IV/2 in 1969) and late 1981. To the time of this writing (late 1985), additional relevant sources have come to my attention: *D-W 499(W3)*, *GB-BERc 55*, *GB-LIc 52*, *GB-YOX*, and *F-TO 925*. On these, see the critical reports in appendix 2.

7. We speak of these motets as being freely composed, in the sense that they are free of a Gregorian tenor. The "popularity" of the style of the *pes* tenors is of course hypothetical, but plausible on account of their tonal closure, phrase regularity, and repetitiveness. For examples of dance-like tenors see Sanders, "Die Rolle," pp. 43–44. Some *pes* tenors bear a text or text incipit. In later motets, the use of the term *pes* to identify the tenor may hide a cantus firmus identified in another source. For instance, the "Pes de pro beati" in *WF*, 70 is in fact the Gregorian tenor "Pro patribus," and the "Tenor de Regina" in *Ob 652*, 3 is the plainsong "Regina celi letare." In general, however, terms such as "Pes de" or "Tenor de" indicate that the tenor is non-Gregorian. See, for example, the "Tenor de Excelsus" of *Onc*

362, 6 or the "Tenor de Dulciflua" of *WF*, 41. The term *pes* is mainly found in thirteenth century sources; the reference to the "Pes de Alma mater" in *BERc 55*, 1, referring to what seems to be an untexted rondeau, is an interesting exception.

8. For more on this markedly un-Continental approach to the motet, see the discussion of voice-exchange motets in chapter 2.

9. Table 1 augments the lists of Sanders in "Medieval Polyphony," chapter IIB, especially pp. 124–25. The division by century is made to correspond with a similar division of motets, and is in some respects artificial—for one, the same liturgical categories figure in both parts of table 1, and further, some of the items in the fourteenth-century list are among those motets that for stylistic reasons can be considered the very earliest in the later repertoire. There is a marked similarity between the categories of liturgical item cultivated in troped chant settings and those used for the mostly later repertoire of English discant: Mass Ordinary items, some Mass Propers, office responsories. See the contents of PMFC XVI.

10. One might also add that most thirteenth-century English troped chant settings appear to have been copied in gatherings of such pieces, rather than simply mixed with motets. See, for example, *WF*, *Lbl 979 (LoHa)*, *Ob 60*, and *Ob 400*. Fourteenth-century collections such as *Cjc 23*, *D-W 499(W3)*, and *Llc 52*, and polyphonic tropers preserving the repertoire a3 in score notation, such as *Ob 14* or *Ob 384*, also appear to have lacked motets.

11. My one qualification: I will in general not treat as motets the settings in *Cjc 23*, *D-W 499(W3)*, and *Llc 52*.

12. See, for instance, the remarks by Rokseth, *Polyphonies* IV, pp. 240–45, those by Harrison in the introduction to PMFC V, or those by Besseler in "Studien II," pp. 184–87.

13. See especially the review of provenances by Bent, "Transmission," pp. 72–75, and more recently by Harrison in the introduction to EECM 26, pp.xi–xvi. The quotation is from Bent, p. 72.

14. Bent, "Transmission," pp. 73–74; Ker, *Medieval Libraries*. The new data in Lefferts and Bent, "New Sources," only reinforce this picture. Note that in general music books seem to have suffered the fate of liturgical books, a fate different than that of the holdings of the monastic libraries as a rule because liturgical books were normally housed separately.

15. See Harrison, *Music in Medieval Britain*, pp. 17–38; 156–77. Bowers's work reached preliminary form in his 1975 East Anglia thesis, "Choral Institutions," and an expanded treatment has been announced for publication by Cambridge University Press. A similar treatment of monastic choirs would be a highly desirable complement. The main deficiency in the approach of Harrison and Bowers is their failure to develop the evidence regarding the decline in monastic choirs. New institutions are easy to trace; continuing institutions like monastic choirs, anonymous and not liable to leave many records behind, are not necessarily for that reason moribund. Bent ("Transmission," p. 72) points out the contradiction in the emphasis of Harrison and Bowers on this swing from monastic to secular while the manuscript provenance of sources remains resolutely monastic.

16. Bowers, "Performing Ensemble," p. 175.

17. See Bowers, "Performing Ensemble," p. 184.

18. Harrison, in the Introduction to EECM 26 (pp. xvi–xvii), distinguishes between ritual and nonritual genres of chant and polyphony. The ritual class of plainsongs includes those that are "essential and integral to the service concerned."

19. See Gordon Anderson, "Responsory Chants," for a statistical overview of tenor sources for Continental motets. He excludes English pieces with the remark (p. 119) that their tenors would form part of the substance of a later article, which did not come out before his untimely death. A further problem is that it may not be possible to identify a tenor with a single context, as there may be no way to decide which of its multiple functions in the liturgy is primary. See *Balaam* and *Ianuam quam* for two motets with tenors that have multiple uses in the liturgy.

20. Harrison, introduction to EECM 26, p. xvi.

21. See Wulf Arlt, *Ein Festofficium aus Beauvais,* and Ruth Steiner, "Mass I, 5: Two Medieval Masses; Later Developments."

22. See Harrison, introduction to PMFC XVI. This thesis grew out of Harrison's theory of clausula function, as expressed in *Music in Medieval Britain,* pp. 123–28, and elaborated elsewhere, including in his contribution to a roundtable at the IMS Congress in 1974 (KB Salzburg II, pp. 69–70); "Benedicamus, Conductus, Carol," pp. 35–40; and the introduction to EECM 26, pp. xvi–xviii.

23. Students of the clausula such as Norman Smith ("The Clausula of the Notre Dame School," pp. 84–92), Jürg Stenzl (*Die vierzig Clausulae,* pp. 166–69), and Rudolph Flotzinger (*Der Discantussatz im Magnus Liber,* pp. 63–66) have taken pains to indicate the conjectural nature of Harrison's theories. In their studies, Stenzl and Flotzinger propose a number of alternate theories. Sarah Fuller, in her work on St. Martial polyphony ("Aquitanian Polyphony," pp. 27–34), demands recognition of the separate ritual functions of versus and Benedicamus verse-trope, rejecting the interchangeability of conductus and Benedicamus versus. While acknowledging the conversion of some conductus to a Benedicamus function, she does not accept that there was a replacement of the latter by the former in the thirteenth century. The conductus, indeed, has other, more frequently encountered and readily identifiable functions, especially in processions and as a preface or benediction before a reading (while at the same time reading terminations, like Benedicamus terminations, are rare).

24. This objection rests on the assumption that if the motet were liturgical there would be systematic coverage of major feasts by a specific corpus of motets. One might expect the possibility that in some corpus all the motet tenors would be from, say graduals, or, at the very least, that they would all be used in the same place in the liturgy.

25. Bent, "Old Hall MS," p. 526.

26. See also the comments on liturgical placement in Lefferts, "Simon de Montfort," pp. 210–13, especially the remarks on the possible use of a motet in a memorial. A memorial is a short service performed at the close of lauds or vespers; it consists of an antiphon, versicle, and collect dedicated to some saint or the BVM. It is a perfect example of a frequently performed service that is outside of the normal round of mass and office, and that might well be a performance context for a motet. (*Parata paradisi porta* sets a BVM antiphon for memorials of Our Lady during Eastertide.) Motets might also have been used to augment a repertoire of rhymed proses for matins, rhymed offertories for Mass, or nonpsalmodic rhymed antiphons for offices, processions, and other devotional services.

27. The problem of motet function is not limited to the fourteenth-century English motet, but rather is a subject of continuing debate and research for Continental repertoires, especially of the fifteenth and sixteenth centuries. The recent article by Cummings, "Toward an Interpretation of the Sixteenth-Century Motet," is an excellent treatment of the issue for a

much later time period. He has collected evidence which tends to support the conclusion that the motet was used mostly at mass (as what he prefers to call a "paraliturgical" insertion) to accompany ritual action, especially at the offertory.

28. Casting the net a little wider would involve broadening the period to encompass the repertoire dating from around 1250 to 1450 or so, from the very first emergence of the *pes* motet and an idiomatic English harmonic style to the final abandonment of the isorhythmic tenor motet.

29. See chapter 3, table 17, for a list of sources of thirteenth-century English polyphony. Appendix 3 provides a list of thirteenth-century English motets.

30. See Bent, "A Lost English Choirbook" and "The Progeny of Old Hall: More Leaves From a Royal English Choirbook." For the subject matter of the *H6* motets, see the discussion of "Other Repertoires" in chapter 4.

31. Sandon, "Fragments of Medieval Polyphony," pp. 41–44. The fragment *Cant 3* had a motet by Dunstaple on John the Baptist (*Preco preheminencie*) and an anonymous work (*Ave miles triumphalis*) that is possibly on Saint Bartholomew.

32. Hohler, "Reflections," p. 30.

33. Hughes, "Re-Appraisal," pp. 105–6, discussing *En Katerine solennia*. Dates for this motet vary according to the occasion for which it is presumed to have been written. Hughes takes the position: "I do not think an event other than the Saint's Feast Day necessary for the motet."

34. Bent, "Transmission," pp. 70–72. Trowell has proposed that the motet was written in 1358, but it has features in common with the motets of the second layer of Old Hall, written ca. 1415.

35. Sanders makes this point in "Sources."

36. Note Mark Everist's assessment of the date of *Cjc 23* in Lefferts and Bent, "New Sources," p. 312. Page size, text hand, and the appearance of music and decoration suggest a date in the second half of the century, but the notation "need be no later than c. 1300."

37. Alejandro Planchart, "The Ars Nova and Renaissance," p. 157.

38. Bowers, "Performing Ensemble" and "Performing Pitch." The quotation is from "Performing Pitch," p. 22. His data from the latter article are separately included in chapter 1, table 2. Bowers observes that the double octave is regularly exceeded, in English polyphony at any rate, only beginning ca. 1460.

39. For Bowers's comments on the organic growth of range to this limit, see "Performing Ensemble," pp. 179–80.

40. See Lefferts, "Simon de Montfort," p. 220.

41. It can be argued just from considerations of range that one motet in the fourteenth-century repertoire, *Trinitatem veneremur* (*Lbl 24198*, 5), is of earlier origin. Its overall range is only a tenth, with part ranges of a ninth, eighth, tenth, and seventh, and every voice at some time assumes the role of the lowest sounding part; there is considerable voice-crossing. Bowers notes its anomolous disposition of voices in "Performing Ensemble," p. 172.

42. The emergence of writing in four real parts, with special emphasis on the English contribution, has been discussed by Ernst Apfel in "Über den vierstimmigen Satz," and "Zur Entstehung des realen vierstimmigen Satzes in England."

43. Rubrics in *Lwa 33327* refer to the motets a3 and a4 as "triplices" and "quadruplices," respectively. This one source has eight of the fourteen thirteenth-century motets a4 listed in chapter 1, table 3.

44. At least three thirteenth-century English compositions a3 survive in a scoring that could similarly be designated 1+2. These are *Mirabilis* (*Ob 19*, 1), whose supporting voices are both simply labeled "Ave Maria"; *O debilis* (*WF*, 73), whose supporting parts are labeled "Pes" and "Primus Pes"; and *Senator regis curie* (*WF*, 11; *D-Gu 220*, 2), whose supporting parts are labeled "Primus Pes" and "Secundus Pes" in *WF*, and "Pes" and "ii" in *D-Gu 220*.

45. The latter motet is found in *Onc 362* with a fifth voice, labeled "Tenor per se de Iacet granum," that is one of the two earliest known examples of a *solus tenor*. It combines the lines of tenor and quartus cantus, reducing their counterpoint to a single part of equivalent function that can be used in their place to allow a rehearsal or performance of the motet a3 instead of a4. (The other early example is the "Tenor pro iii" that combines the functions of quartus cantus and "Tenor pro iiii" in *D-W 499 (W3)*, 1.)

46. Parallel counterpoint in imperfect consonances permits fluent partwriting with rapid harmonic motion a3, but not a4. Partwriting in compositions a3 may be fairly continuous, or may itself be broken up in hocket fragmentation, as for instance in *Triumphat hodie* or *Salve cleri*. (Sanders, "English Polyphony," p. 197, has singled out the style of the second of these two motets as comparable to the *stile brisé* of the seventeenth-century French clavecinists.) This transparent style of writing, already remarked upon by Levy, "New Material," p. 231, is also a mark of late conductus-rondellus writing ca. 1300, as in *Fulget celestis* (*WF*, 31; *Onc 362*, 16).

47. We can be more certain that the terms "Pes" or "Pes de" and "Tenor" or "Tenor de" usually mean the same thing, i.e., a non-Gregorian tenor, and that the distinction between them is basically chronological, "Pes" being the earlier term. But there are exceptions to both of these generalizations, as observed above in note 7.

48. The editions of *O homo* in PMFC XV and Marrocco and Sandon, *Medieval Music*, both modify the "Quartus de O homo" to cadence to an 8–5 without the third. I do not approve of this editorial decision, but it is true that *O homo*, the only one of these pieces built on a cantus firmus, is also the only one to cadence to an 8–5–3 whose third (D–F) is minor, which may have caused the editors to edit it out. Note also that the concordance of *Pro beati Pauli* in *Lwa 33327* ends differently and, presumably, not on a full triad. See the critical report in PMFC XIV.

49. The four-voice motets *Virgo Maria* and *Tu civium* from *Cgc 512*, and *A solis–Ovet* and *Hostis Herodes* from *Ob 81*, do not indicate exactly how their final cadence is to be voiced, but the cadences probably move to 8–5, either a4 with doubling or simply a3.

50. *Barrabas dimittitur* and *Deus creator* are the only English motets a3 to cadence to 12–8; *Orto sole* (in its version a4), *Cuius de manibus*, *Soli fines*, *Regne de pité*, and *Humane lingue*, are the only English examples of motets a4 cadencing to 12–8–5. Comparable numbers drawn from PMFC V are 6 motets a3 (nos. 3, 7, 11, 12, 29, 30) and 10 motets a4 (nos. 2, 4, 6, 9a, 20, 24, 25, 26, 27, 28) out of a total of 34.

51. Harrison, introduction and "Notes on Transcription and Performance" in PMFC XV, and "Ars Nova," p. 72.

52. See especially Sanders, "Cantilena and Discant," pp. 10–23.

53. Table 4 includes all known sources except: (1) references to motets mentioned by English theorists or by theorists copied and known in England, but not found in an insular music source (mainly, if not exclusively, citations of Continental pieces); and (2) the Bridport, Guild Archives fragment, which is a "ghost reference" cited by H. Davey in *History of English Music*, p. 31 and picked up by Ludwig in *Repertorium* I, ii, pp. 677–78 but no longer locatable. See Ian Bent, "Polyphonic Verbum Bonum," p. 229. There is reported to have been some music for two voices plus a part labeled "Tenor de A toute hure."

54. Harrison discusses in "Ars Nova," pp. 68–70 the evidence that *Cgc 512* may have been copied some time during the years 1325 to 1336 and may have stayed in use at least until about 1355. Such evidence is practically unique among the sources in question here.

Chapter 2

1. Manfred Bukofzer, *Music in the Baroque Era*, pp. 365–69.

2. Sanders, "Motet," pp. 550–54, classifies Continental motets of the late Ars Antiqua into three types: the Petronian motet, the Latin double motet, and the French accompanied-song-style motet. The later isorhythmic motet in the French tradition exhibits unipartite, bipartite, and multipartite designs (see Günther, "Fourteenth-Century Motet," pp. 29, 41–42, following Besseler, "Studien II," p. 219). These are consistent and closely related types in concept and execution. The Italian motet of the fourteenth and early fifteenth centuries is basically of a single distinct type with its own tradition. (See Bent and Hallmark, *The Works of Johannes Ciconia*, p. XII; Bent also has an article forthcoming that is devoted to the Italian motet.) Neither the French nor the Italian tradition has the number of distinctly defined and recurrent structural plans that characterize the English output.

3. Consideration of text structure (i.e., versification) is secondary in this initial approach to typology, although it can be of critical interest to observe whether the text structure is independent of the musical phrase structure or whether they, to some degree, have isomorphic features, and whether in either case the resulting versification is regular or irregular. Some motet types normally accommodate regular texts, and it is probable that this consideration influenced the choice of motet type to be composed in individual instances. See the section on versification in chapter 4.

4. This typology is based on one by Sanders, who divides the English fourteenth-century motets into those exhibiting voice exchange, variation, or isoperiodicity, and comments on a number of interesting hybrids. (See Sanders, "English Polyphony," chapter III, pp. 192–263 and the later discussions derived from it in "Motet," pp. 538–50 and "England: From the Beginnings," pp. 283–89.) The divisions made here are roughly the same, though no single category of the present classification corresponds to the variation type of Sanders, "the successor to the *ostinato* pes-motet of the thirteenth century." (Sanders, "England: From the Beginnings," p. 287.) Rather, the motets on "*ostinati* and varied *ostinati* which are freely invented (or perhaps borrowed from popular sources)" are grouped with cantus firmus motets of similar isomelic structure, such as varied voice exchange, strophic repeat, or refrain types.

5. See, among other places, Harrison, NOHM III, pp. 88–94, where in addition *Balaam* is called a rondellus-motet, *Salve cleri* is called a conductus-motet with rondellus technique, and *Ovet mundus* is called a rondellus-conductus.

6. See Sanders, "English Polyphony," pp. 103–4, n. 74 and "Tonal Aspects," p. 24, n. 38.

7. Sanders, "English Polyphony," p. 122, summarizing chapter IIA (pp. 78–122), which is devoted to an investigation of this relationship.

8. Harrison (in "Rota and Rondellus," p. 101) insists on a further distinction beyond one of performance practice in discriminating rota from rondellus, arguing that "[in] a rota...some or all of the phrases of its melody extend over at least two units of interchange, while in the rondellus each phrase is the same length as the unit." This distinction is not observed here, and I take the only two true rotas in the repertoire to be the Sumer Canon (*Lbl 978*, 5; edited, among other places, in PMFC XIV, 4a) and *Munda Maria* (*WF*, 21; edited in PMFC XIV, 35). The Sumer Canon imposes a rota on an ostinato *pes* and for that reason can be regarded as a kind of voice-exchange motet. Barry Cooper plausibly argues that a similar situation obtained in *Salve Symon* (*Cjc 5*, 7). For this reason both have been listed as motets in table 5. (See Cooper, "A Thirteenth-Century Canon," and Lefferts, "Simon de Montfort.")

9. The only medieval authority who applies the term rondellus to compositions a3 such as diagrammed above is Walter Odington, who provides an example, *Ave mater Domini*, included in table 5. See Dittmer, "Beiträge," pp. 29–33, and see also Eggebrecht, "Rondellus," Falck, "Rondellus, Canon, and Related Types," and Sanders, "Communication." Bent, in "Rota versatilis," observes the kinship of rota and rondellus implied by the text and form of *Rota versatilis*, inspired by the legend of Katherine and the wheel. Despite this testimony I would still insist on the distinction between rondellus and voice exchange, and not use the term "rondellus" or "rondellus-motet" to describe *Rota*.

10. The following deals with pieces a3. There exists one conductus a2 with a rondellus section, namely *Karitatis* (*Omec 248*, 2). See Dom A. Hughes in NOHM II, p. 377. Examples fitting our definition of an independent rondellus a2 include *Salve mater salvatoris* (*Ob 343*, 1; ed. PMFC XIV, 6) and two better-known pieces cited by Harrison in "Rota and Rondellus," pp. 98–100, the "voice-exchange hymn" *Nunc sancte nobis* and the *Benedicamus* trope *Ad cantus leticie*, for both of which Harrison suggests a possible British origin. (On these two compositions, see also RISM B/IV/1, p. 15.)

11. As Table 5 shows, it is not possible to distinguish conductus from rondellus on the basis that the former is always notated in score, the latter in parts. When such compositions are written in parts, all the parts are texted. One isolated example shows what is best described as a polytextual conductus written in parts, namely *Salve fenestra vitrea* (*WF*, 34).

12. The sectional structures and isoperiodicity of phrase design in the motets may owe much to the phrase structures of the more elaborate rondelli.

13. They are edited in Dittmer (MSD 2, nos. 16 and 41) and by Sanders (PMFC XIV, nos. 53 and 55). Two other thirteenth-century motets, *Virgo regalis* (*WF*, 12) and *Loquelis archangeli* (*WF*, 18-66), also have four sections of exchange followed by a coda.

14. Its notation and rhythmic language is similar to that of *Triumphat hodie*, a voice-exchange motet a4 in the same manuscript.

15. An earlier French motet on the same tenor, spoofing English drinkers of good ale, has voice-exchange features. See *Hare hare hie Godalier–Goudalier on bien–T. Balaam* (*D-W 1099 (W2)*, fol. 197v–198v).

16. In *Onc 362* the motets *Civitas nusquam* and *Alta canunt* are also bipartite.

17. The phrases of *Balaam* are elided; the numbers shown here represent musical units rather than, strictly speaking, phrase lengths.

18. See Dalglish, "Variation" and "Hocket." Dalglish has a full analysis of *Balaam* in "Hocket," pp. 353–59. I do not agree that his analysis shows it necessary to regard the second half of *Balaam* ("Huic ut placuit") as an independent composition.

19. Justification for the assertion that these texted sections are "codas" is not hard to find. In *O pater* and *Viri Galilei* they are formally and textually anomalous. In the case of *Triumphat hodie*, the coda is defined by the handling of the tenor, which exhausts its French text and proceeds through a final double period (AA) in hocket between the two lower parts.

20. I say apparently because one upper part has not survived. However, the voice that remains is through-texted, and it interacted with the lost voice by singing the syllables of several words in hocket alternation.

21. Other motets do exist with a fivefold structure. These include *Suspiria merentis*, whose refrain is sung five times; *Candens crescit*, which has an overall five-section form defined by the rondo-like recurrence of a refrain (ABABA); and *Thomas gemma*, which can be analyzed as an irregularly proportioned five-section form framed by a short introduction and a coda and subdivided by a hocketing refrain. (See figure 10.) In none of the motets in which "5" plays a role is there an obvious symbolic meaning.

22. The idea of associating *A solis* and *Ovet* was proposed by Margaret Bent in "Rota versatilis," p. 76. My discussion is indebted to the observations and arguments she makes there.

23. For isolated instances, see *O spes et salus* (*Ob 60*, fol. 104–104v), or troped chant settings of Kyries such as *Virgo mater salvatoris* (*Cfm*, fol. 1–1v). Bent makes this point in "Rota versatilis," p. 76.

24. Harrison considers them to be conductus-related free settings, which is why they are edited in PMFC XVI rather than in PMFC XV. Sanders, "English Polyphony," p. 92, speaks of them as elaborate rondelli, a designation about which Apfel complains in *Grundlagen*, pp. 93–94. Like rondelli they are texted in all parts, but unlike rondelli, all voices do not sing all music or all text. Rather, all parts apparently are meant to sound their differing texts simultaneously. Texting, in fact, highlights the individuality (and interaction) of all the parts here, a motet-like trait quite opposite in conception from the highlighting of a single melodic line that is the function of text in the rondellus. Historically speaking, one could see them as furthering the tendency of *Fulget celestis curie* or of the two "conductus motets" in *US-Cu* to introduce polytextuality into a context that had traditionally lacked it. (The motets in *US-Cu* with sections in voice exchange (no. 7) and rondellus (no. 8) are "conductus-motets" because their upper parts have the same text, while their tenors bear a different text.)

25. This is an instance where modal terminology seems an apt way to characterize tonal features of, and distinctions between, medieval polyphonic compositions. *Virgo Maria* may be associated with the eighth mode, and *Tu civium* with the seventh mode.

26. Wibberley, "English Polyphonic Music," pp. 145–49.

27. Harrison, in PMFC XVI, bars the double long in these pieces. Edited that way, identical figures often recur in different halves of the bar. My numbers in figure 8 count single longs.

28. Four bars represent either four longs or four double longs, depending on which of the two versions of the notation of *Thomas gemma* is referred to. See chapter 3, figure 39.

29. Dalglish's analysis, in "Variation," pp. 46–47, distinguishes only two, not three, forms of the tenor. Levy first called attention to the ostinato and variation techniques in *Thomas gemma* in "New Material," p. 230.

30. Hohler, "Reflections," p. 31.

31. This layout is indebted to one arrived at by Alexander Blachly and W.T.H. Jackson for the notes to the record Nonesuch H-71292.

32. I am using "primary" and "subordinate" here to characterize the role of the musical phrase bearing this text, not to suggest that there is an original text and insertions. The full text of each voice must be regarded as having its own continuity.

33. Sanders, "English Polyphony," pp. 104–5. The *US-Cu* motet fragments 1–2 and 3, built on cantus firmi, are good further examples. Varied, rather than exact, voice exchange is seen in several thirteenth-century English motets including *O quam glorifica* and *Tota pulchra*.

34. The restriction to two or three tenor statements represents a marked decrease from the number of repetitions common in *pes* motets. Some of the motets from the early fourteenth-century source *F-TO 925* have more than three tenor periods (*Exulta Syon*, for instance, has six statements of a melodic double versicle), which speaks on stylistic grounds for their late thirteenth-century origin. Among later motets with declamation falling to breve and semibreve, *Orto sole* sets four statements of its tenor. Two pertinent fragments lacking tenors, *Duodeno sidere* and *Princeps apostolice*, can be shown to have had tenors stated three and two times, respectively.

35. Handschin, "Sumer Canon II," p. 90. For the other references, see the critical reports on all these pieces, appendix 2.

36. See also *Viri Galilei* and *Templum eya*. The recurring tag phrase "O Maria" in the thirteenth-century voice-exchange motet *Dulciflua* is an earlier example.

37. These English refrain motets are not related to the French motet with embedded refrain lines, the so-called *motet enté*. (See Hoppin, *Medieval Music*, pp. 338–40 and van den Boogaard, *Rondeaux et refrains*, esp. pp. 299–312.)

38. For the clearest available discussion of the meaning of isoperiodicity, with reference to many of the motets to be discussed below, see Sanders, "Motet," pp. 543–46. Isoperiodicity is not unknown among thirteenth-century motets, but is not nearly so often encountered as in the later repertoire, and is more frequent by far in England than on the Continent in the earlier period. There is a noticeable lack of such phrase structuring in the more modern Latin double motets of the *Roman de Fauvel*.

39. All three texted parts articulate eleven as eight longs followed by three long-rests (usually setting fifteen syllables per phrase) over a tenor moving in longs.

40. That is, a fourteen-syllable long line with rhyme and caesura regularly falling after eight syllables and a proparoxytonic (i.e., antepenultimate) final stress accent.

41. On the English propensity to manipulate a cantus firmus to provide tonal unity in a composition, see Sanders, "Tonal Aspects," pp. 31–34. From the fourteenth-century English motet repertoire at least *Veni creator*, *Barabbas dimittitur*, and *Nos orphanos*, in addition to *Petrum cephas*, show some manipulation of tenor pitch or design to create tonal closure. In this light, one of the curious features of *Parata paradisi porta* is that it states its tenor almost twice, but leaves off precisely the final phrase that would have provided tonal closure.

42. The break between the first six and final four phrases corresponds to a shift in narrative in the text, moving to direct discourse (the Lord addressing Paul).

43. The expression "medius cantus" makes just a single appearance in a motet source: the tenor of *Fusa cum silentio* in *D Rc 20* is identified as "Medius cantus. Manere." This term simply means middle voice. (Manuscript layout normally puts a *medius cantus*, like any other tenor, at the bottom of the page.) *Medius cantus*, as used in *D Rc 20*, has an equivalent in the vernacular English term *mean*, which was used to designate the middle voice in a composition a3 (as the second term in the constellation *treble/mean/burden*) in many late-medieval vernacular English texts. (See the references collected by Trowell, "Faburden," pp. 32–36, on the basis of which he argues that the terminology is applicable to a popular repertoire of improvised singing a3 in parallel harmonies that was the probable origin for fourteenth-century English cantilena and cantilena-style writing.) *Treble*, by comparison, is the English equivalent of *triplex* or *triplex cantus*, the term used, for instance, to identify the top part in a discant setting a3 of *Angelus ad virginem* in *Cu 710*.

44. Harrison, "Ars Nova," p. 72, and his introduction and "Notes on Transcription and Performance" for PMFC XV.

45. A number of other motets, mostly from the very earliest fourteenth-century sources, share tenor range with a lower texted part without exploiting this feature in the fashion of the duet motets. These include *Ade finit, Caligo terre, Corona virginum, Doleo super te, Orto sole, Patrie pacis, Regina celestium, Solaris ardor, Surgere iam est,* and *Trinitatem veneremur*.

46. The lower texted voice of *Fusa* is in long-breve declamation while the upper part has breve-semibreve declamation, so the two texts are not of the same length and are sung at different rates. Melismatic breves and semibreves in the lower part do, however, often move in sixths and tenths with the upper voice.

47. *Civitas nusquam* has a total span of only a twelfth with outer voices a fifth apart in range. It lacks any isoperiodic phrase structure, and occasionally engages in parallel counterpoint at the fifth, though counterpoint at the sixth is more common. All of this suggests that it may be an older motet than the others under consideration here.

48. In *Regne de pité* there is also simultaneous declamation of a single text throughout; one of the voices occasionally drops out for a few bars. Systematic parlando in duo beyond that seen in the duet motets is rare but not unknown; it can be heard in the second half of the *D Rc 20* version of *Orto sole* (the one a4), in the *Cgc 512* motets *Virgo Maria* and *Tu civium*, on the final phrase of *Doleo super te*, in the refrain motet *Suspiria merentis*, and in the upper two parts of *Trinitatem veneremur*. Probably there were also duet passages in *Parata paradisi porta*. It is interesting to see that in *Mulier magni meriti*, by contrast, increasingly lengthy bursts of semibreve declamation are not exploited for any prominent homorhythmic passagework between texted parts.

49. Bukofzer, SMRM, p. 97, cites examples of fifteenth-century English music manuscripts in which alteration is indicated by the numeral 2 below the affected pitch.

50. The tenor of *Inter usitata* also must be sung in retrograde (though this is conveniently explained in a verbal canon) and similarly provides rests at the beginning.

51. Harrison, in NOHM III, p. 86, remarks that "this practice [of placing a tenor in the middle voice] is of some interest in view of its regular adoption in English descant after *ca.* 1350 for ritual plainsong settings." See also Sanders, "Die Rolle," p. 45; idem, "Motet," p. 544; and Apfel, *Grundlagen*, Chapter IIh, pp. 133–35.

52. See the discussion of the mensuration of these cantilenas in the introduction to chapter 3, concerning table 16.

53. In *Cgc 512* this cantilena was mostly written out on two staves in score, but in one system it was written out on three, with the middle staff left blank. In *Cpc 228* it was written out entirely in two-stave systems, but it is followed on the same page by a separate voice-part that in fact is a middle voice for the first half of the piece. This third voice does not provide continuous enrichment of the texture, but rather supplements the harmony only at cadences in the outer voices and rests while the texted parts engage in their most extended spurts of homorhythmic patter. A similar empty staff has been left throughout the *Ob D.6* copy of the cantilena *Missus Gabriel* (PMFC XVII, no. 23), and the cantus firmus has been written out separately from the two outer parts of two discant items in score found in *US-NYpm 978*, 6 and 13 (PMFC XVI, no. 67 and XVII, no. 67, respectively).

54. *Alma mater* is of the same generation as the duet motets and cantilenas named above. It is of interest to note that in it the words "notulis modulis dulcissimis" are set to parallel motion in semibreves, albeit parallel fourths over a stationary tenor.

55. See Lefferts and Bent, "New Sources," pp. 334–37.

56. See Sanders, "Early Motets," especially pp. 36–37.

57. On this basis, for instance, the introduction of the minim in England is usually taken to be ca. 1350. See Harrison, "Ars Nova," p. 69. The *Quatuor principalia* cites the de Vitry motets *Cum statua* and *Vos quid* (CS IV, pp. 201–98), which are dated by Sanders to the 1330s ("Early Motets," p. 37). *Vos quid* appears in the English source *DRc 20*.

58. Levy, "New Material," pp. 230–31. See also Wibberley, "English Polyphonic Music," chapter III, "The Assimilation of Continental Trends."

59. Sanders, "English Polyphony," p. 234.

60. Sanders, "Motet," pp. 559–62 and "Vitry, Philippe de," pp. 26–27. Sanders suggests an influence on de Vitry of the sectional or strophic English motets in addition to the general influence of isoperiodicity on isorhythmic design. (Strophic is the term that is appropriate if there is a close correspondence between large textual subdivisions and the musical sections.)

61. Stratification of rhythmic activity does not necessarily imply stratification of range between triplum and duplum. In a number of Petronian motets triplum and duplum ranges overlap almost entirely, and the duplum frequently sounds over the triplum. *Caligo terre* and *Triumphat hodie* are clear examples.

62. I am limiting the association with Petrus de Cruce to those motets with sharp stratification. Declamation in chains of semibreves has also made its influence felt in well-defined motet types such as the refrain motets, motets with strophic repeat, the duet motets with *medius cantus*, and some of the motets with unusual periodicity, such as the three from *Cgc 512*: *Mulier, Orto sole,* and *Princeps.*

63. *Triumphus patet* is a fourth "Petronian" motet with carefully crafted duplum melody.

64. *Viri Galilei* or *Ut recreentur*, in some sense analogous free compositions a4, lie closer to recognizable norms for voice-exchange or isoperiodic compositions, respectively. See also *Candens crescit*, whose sectional structure has affinities to these large-scale free pieces.

65. Bent, "Transmission," pp. 66–67, raises the possibility that the motets of *Onc 362, Lbl 24198,* and *DRc 20* that have French-texted tenors are French in origin. I think there are good musical reasons (as I hope to show with the analyses in this chapter) as well as circumstantial ones, for taking these pieces to be English in origin. This position is

strengthened by the musical characteristics of the (mainly late thirteenth-century) motets with French tenors found by Anderson in *F-TO 925*, which all look distinctly English rather than Continental in form, counterpoint, and harmonic language.

66. See Craig Wright, *Music at the Court of Burgundy*, pp. 11–18 for documentation of the musical activity associated with this involuntary sojourn. Wright makes the intriguing suggestion that the keyboad intabulations of two de Vitry motets in the Robertsbridge codex (*Lbl 28550*, 4 and 5) may be linked with John's captivity in England and his interest in organ music (ibid., p. 16, n. 29). Wright also cites (p. 28) a later occasion when, in Tournai, four Englishmen sang a motet for young king Charles VI. The reference in the text of the triplum of *DRc 20*, 10 to a "J. Anglici" who sings in a "curia gallicorum" with six Frenchmen and Flemings indicates another way in which an Englishman might come into contact with French polyphony around midcentury (see the section on "External References" in chapter 4).

67. For more discussion of *Ob 7*, see Lefferts, "Motet," and for more on *DRc 20*, see Harrison, "Ars Nova." While it is beyond doubt that the *Ob 7* motets were compiled for (and perhaps at) Bury St. Edmunds, Nicholas Sandon has recently reminded us (in "Mary, Meditation, Monks and Music," p. 55, n. 21) that there is no hard evidence for the origin of the *DRc 20* motets at Durham. Nor, for that matter, is it necessary that they were used there, given that the host manuscript was donated to the cathedral priory by Prior Wessyngton in the midfifteenth century (clearly, we need to know more about the age and provenance of the binding, which if a local product might have used locally produced musical waste).

68. The assessment of the text hands is that of Margaret Bent (private communication); on rest-writing, see the pertinent section of chapter 3. I cannot agree with Roger Bowers ("Performing Ensemble," p. 168, n. 12), who holds that the rear leaves of *DRc 20* "seem to display no English features at all but, rather, to present an aspect consistent with a view that they are from a source of French origin."

69. Harrison, PMFC V, p. ix.

70. See the discussion of vernacular texts, and also of figure 50, in chapter 4.

71. Harrison, "Ars Nova," p. 69.

72. See RISM B/IV/2, pp. 282–83; Günther, "Problems of Dating," pp. 291–93; and Günther, "Sources."

73. See RISM B/IV/2, pp. 205–6 and Craig Wright, *Music at the Court of Burgundy*, pp. 148–58.

74. Besseler reports that no. 15 was the first motet in a Continental source of French Ars Nova polyphony now lost ("Studien I," p. 184.) There is no compelling reason to assume English authorship for any of the motets that have Continental concordances.

75. See the motets from *Ivrea* edited as PMFC V, nos. 7, 8, 11, 13, 32 and Machaut motets 2, 3, 4, 7, 10, 18.

76. The two Durham *unica* both have a prefatory *introitus*, though.

77. Harrison (NOHM III, p. 99) suggests an English origin for the *unicum Nec Herodis ferocitas*, but I know of no reason to think this.

78. The tenor and contratenor of *Virginalis concio* apparently had different mensural organizations on the modus level. This feature, together with the presence of an *introitus* and a four-voice texture, relate this motet particularly to Machaut motets 5, 21, and 23. In

addition to the motets by de Vitry named above in the text, *Impudenter circuivi* (*I–IVc 115*, 6) is of similar construction. See also *Nostris lumen* (*B-Br 19606*, 9) and PMFC V, nos. 2, 24, 27. Ernest Sanders has remarked on the evident skill of composition in *O vos omnes* and *Ad lacrimas flentis* and suggests because of their proximity to motets in *DRc 20* and *CH-Fc 260* known to be by de Vitry that they may be of his authorship. (Private communication.)

79. On the motet a4 in general, see Leech-Wilkinson, "Compositional Procedures."

80. See Sanders, "English Polyphony," pp. 92–93.

81. The nearest equivalents to the contrapuntal style of *Cuius de manibus* are in *Soli fines* and *Regne de pité*, which are discussed below; from the wider English repertoire one could cite the marvelous four-voice *Deo gratias* (*US-NYpm 978*, 9) and the *Alleluia Nativitas* (*Ccc 65*, 1) which are PMFC XVI, nos. 73 and 76, respectively.

82. A *fatras* is a short strophe of eleven lines with rhyme scheme AAB AAB BABAB that begins with the first line of a given couplet and ends with its second line. See Lambert C. Porter, *La Fatrasie et le Fatras*, pp. 69–105.

83. On Watriquet see Porter, *La Fatrasie*, pp. 149–59, and for a full list of all such French couplets, see van den Boogaard, *Rondeaux et refrains*. *Doucement* is published in Porter as no. 2, p. 149, and is no. 618 (Fatr. 14) in van den Boogaard.

84. This couplet is no. 26 in Porter, p. 157. The reference was first noticed by Ludwig, according to Dahnk, *L'Hérésie*, pp. 11–12. The motet is *F-Pn 146*, 4 (written prior to 1316). For the use of the *fatras* and *fatrasie* in fifteenth-century musical settings, see Rika Maniates, "Combinative Techniques," pp. 49–52.

85. I wish to thank Dr. Brewer for sharing with me a transcription of *Amis loial* and a copy of his article "A Fourteenth-Century Polyphonic Manuscript Rediscovered" about *PL-WRu I.Q.411*. The couplet is published in Porter as no. 11, p. 152 and is no. 121 (Fatr. 131) in van den Boogaard, *Rondeaux et refrains*.

86. There are strong reasons, primarily the repetitions of the tenor and the lack of sharp internal divisions reflecting the two lines of the distich, for disqualifying the motet in its entirety as a candidate for the original setting of the couplet.

87. The motet has a number of unusual, if not necessarily English, features. One can mention the wide range (a fifteenth), the paired ranges of the upper parts (c–dd), the relatively infrequently encountered mensuration (*tempus perfectum maior*), and the wide final cadential sonority (12–8 rather than 8–5, approached by a 10–6).

88. For remarks on this problem, see Harrison in NOHM III, pp. 99–100 and Hughes, "Re-Appraisal," pp. 125–26. We are equally in the dark as to the origins of the the canonic technique that appears so skillfully in Old Hall, especially in the compositions of Pycard. Two recent finds have begun to remedy this ignorance. Nicholas Sandon has found a chace-like canonic *Salve regina* in a Durham manuscript, now *Lbl Royal 7.A.vi* (fol. 35v–36), and Ernest Sanders has found a caccia-like canonic *Gloria* in *US-NYpm 978* (no. 14). See Sandon, "Mary, Meditations, Monks and Music," and PMFC XVII, no. 65.

89. The first of these has been published in a modern edition (Marrocco and Sandon, *Medieval Music*, no. 65) but the second, an incomplete piece, has not (the duplum has been erased and written over, so that it is impossible to read, even with the aid of ultraviolet light). For similar pieces in Old Hall, see the Credo by Pennard (*Lbl 57950*, no. 89) and the Gloria by Tye (*Lbl 57950*, no. 19; compare also the Gloria no. 23 by Leonel). Marrocco and Sandon suggest that the anonymous *Lbl 40011B* Gloria might also be by Pennard, forming a pair with the Old Hall Credo just cited.

90. The use of the ligature shapes of Robertus de Brunham in the tenor and contratenor parts of the *Ob 384* Gloria is discussed below in chapter 3 in the section "Breve-Semibreve Notation."

91. Günther dates *Rex Karole* to 1375. It ought to be noted here that the Strassbourg source attributes *Rex Karole* to Phillipus Royllart, who may be tenuously associated with the otherwise unknown Rowlard who contributed a Gloria to Old Hall (*Lbl 57950*, 29) that also survives as *Lbl 40011B*, 2. See Günther, CMM 39, p. xxxi.

92. See Trowell, "A Fourteenth-Century Ceremonial Motet"; Günther, CMM 39, p. lii; Bent, "Transmission," pp. 70–72; and Bent, *Two Fourteenth-Century Motets in Praise of Music*. Bowers's arguments, not yet in print, rely on additional archival evidence of the lives and careers of the musicians mentioned, along with careful attention to the (present or past) tense of the verbs used to describe them.

93. See Günther, "The 14th-Century Motet and its Development," and CMM 39, pp. vii, li–lii. The motet *En Katerine solennia* (*Lbl 57950*, 147) is representative of the more advanced style seen in Old Hall. It is tripartite, with successive diminution of the tenor in the ratio 3:2:1, and has a rhythmic character marked by a great deal of syncopation, as well as the simultaneous use of conflicting mensurations (with minim equivalency). See also Bent, *Dunstaple*, pp. 52–54 for a discussion of the basic scheme of Dunstaple's isorhythmic motets.

94. Its choice of tenor and use of the *cauda hirundinis* tend to confirm its English origin. (See the critical report in appendix 2.)

95. On the text of this motet, see the section "External References" in chapter 4.

96. This mensural shift recalls the sectional changes of mensuration in the late fourteenth-century cantilena, and the shifts in the sectional, nonisorhythmic English motets of the fifteenth century.

97. Besseler, "Studien II," pp. 190–91.

Chapter 3

1. There is near total neglect of the subject in Apel, *The Notation of Polyphonic Music* (hereafter NPM), except for the brief remarks on p. 243. Parrish, *Notation*, has a number of relevant plates (XXXII–XXXIII, XLIII, XLIV), but does not discuss with any insight their peculiarly insular features. There are useful plates and discussion in Besseler and Gülke, *Schriftbild*, pl. 12, 13, 15, 28, 31. In this light, the work of Wolf in GMN and HNK, relying on a familiarity with some relevant music sources and the texts edited by Coussemaker, is worthy of respect. However, Wolf's article "Early English Music Theorists" is trivial.

2. This presentation is deeply indebted to the work of Sanders and Bent. I would like to acknowledge the benefit of hearing a 1977 presentation by Professor Bent entitled "A View of Early Ars Nova Notations and their Relationship to the English Tradition." In addition, see her brief survey in section vi of "Notation III, 3" in *The New Grove*.

3. Odington's treatise is edited by Coussemaker in CS I, pp. 182–250 and edited by Hammond in CSM 14; translation by Huff of part VI in *Walter Odington*. Odington is thought to be the Benedictine monk-scholar of Evesham active at Gloucester College (the Benedictine house at Oxford) who flourished ca. 1300–1316 (see CSM 14, p. 21).

4. Handlo's treatise is edited by Coussemaker in CS I, pp. 383–403; translation by Dittmer (not without its problems) in *Robert of Handlo*. Handlo's treatise is basically a version of the widespread form into which the teachings of Franco of Cologne were condensed (normally beginning "Gaudent brevitate moderni"), here enriched with extremely important, unique testimony on the development of notation after Franco. The explicit of the treatise dates the work to 1326.

5. Hanboys's treatise is edited by Coussemaker in CS I, pp. 403–48. Hanboys is usually taken to be a fifteenth-century compiler (see most recently Hughes, "Hanboys" and Wibberley, "Notation," p. xx) on the basis of identifications by early antiquarians, but on internal evidence the treatise must be a work of the later fourteenth century, and Bent dates it to ca. 1375? in "Notation," p. 368. The treatise of Hanboys incorporates most of Handlo but is reorganized, updated, and substantially amplified in content. Hanboys quotes Franco not just through Handlo but also directly from the *Ars cantus mensurabilis*. Reaney points out the possibility that Handlo and Hanboys are one and the same individual, with the name Hanboys merely a scribal corruption of Handlo or vice versa ("The Question of Authorship," p. 12). The later treatise would have to be the work of a very old man.

6. The *Quatuor principalia* is edited by Coussemaker in CS IV, pp. 200–98; fourth *Principale* also in CS III, pp. 334–64 (Anon. I). A colophon dates the compilation to 1351 but Reaney has his doubts, suspecting on the basis of internal evidence that it may be later ("The Question of Authorship," p. 11). According to Sweeney (CSM 13, p. 9, n. 5), "It is conceivable that the date 1351 given in 3 manuscripts of the *Quatuor principalia* is basically correct, though the discussion of slightly later notational features towards the end of the treatise suggests a date c. 1380."

7. The unitalicized letters s and m will be used here not to stand for semibreve and minim, but to indicate syllabic or melismatic groups of semibreves. The terms duplets and triplets will be used as shorthand for groups of two or three semibreves per breve (s2, m2; s3, m3) with no implication that the subdivision of the breve is into smaller values equal to each other.

8. Here are the six notational groupings following Harrison in PMFC XV, translating his descriptions into the terminology of this study:

Group	Characteristics	Motets (PMFC nos.)
i	only s2,m2	1,4,9,14,16,27,36
ii	C-dot, O-dot	22,23,24,29,34,35
iii	s2,m2 with rare s3,m3	11,18,20,30,32
iv	s2,(s3) with m2–5 and use of dot	2,6,7,8,15,17
v	parlando, with dot	3,5,13,19,26,28,31
vi	use of stems	10,12,21,25,33

Harrison's total sample was small; this has led him on the one hand to put together disparate items in the same group (as group i, where PMFC XV, nos. 14 and 16 use dots of division and also have an imperfect long while no. 36 is in typical French Ars Nova *tempus perfectum minor*) and on the other to make a distinction (the separation of groups i and iii) that is perhaps too fine. (It is a distinction necessary for Harrison on account of his rhythmic interpretation of semibreve groups, which will be discussed below.) To quibble over another small point, no. 30 (put by Harrison in group iii) is not really m2,(m3); in fact m2 are rare in this piece and m3 common.

9. Stems were added to the motets in the front leaves of *Ob 7* by a later hand or hands. None appears to be the work of the original scribe(s). This activity may have been confined to a single gathering of the original book. (See Lefferts, "Motet," pp. 58–59.)

10. Though stems are added in *Ob 7*, they are apparently original in *Cgc 512* and are both original and more extensive in *DRc 20*. Harrison, in the "Notes on Transcription and Performance" for PMFC XV, sees no chronological development among the sources of motets with stems (his group vi), but he is led astray in this regard by failing to take into consideration that *Rosa delectabilis* (with stems) is a palimpsest much younger than the rest of the contents of *Onc 362*.

11. *Ave celi regina* (*Cgc 512*, 11 = *Cpc 228*, 5) is edited in PMFC XVII, no. 38. *Salamonis inclita* (*Cgc 512*, 10 = *US-NYpm 978*, 9) is edited in PMFC XVII, no. 37.

12. The statements of Anon. IV on the peculiarities of English practice are quoted, among other places, in Wibberley's contribution on notation in the introduction to EECM 26.

13. See especially Bukofzer, "Sumer Canon: a Revision," Handschin, "Sumer Canon," Levy, "New Material," and Dittmer, "The Dating and the Notation of the Worcester Fragments."

14. See also the discussion of the monophonic dance in *Ob 139* by Arlt in "The 'Reconstruction' of Instrumental Music," pp. 87–98.

15. Wibberley, "English Polyphonic Music," p. 63.

16. For a facsimile and partial transcription of *O spes et salus* see Lefferts and Bent, "New Sources," pp. 338–42. *Fulgens stella* arguably has a first-mode ligature pattern, but features of declamation (in particular, the location of *fractio*), and the slant of the note-heads (interpreted following Wibberley's hypothesis as described below) point to second mode.

17. See Wibberley, "English Polyphonic Music," pp. 61–134 (esp. 61–106), and "Notation," p. xxv. Presumably the singer, having established the mensuration by inspection of the most heavily ligated voice (usually the tenor), could apply it to his own part by the principle of *convenientia modorum* (see Sanders, "Duple Rhythm," p. 266 and Wibberley, "English Polyphonic Music," p. 66; both borrow the term from Anonymous VII in CS I, p. 379). Wibberley's hypothesis confirms Sanders's conclusions (against Dittmer's) in most instances. (Wibberley does not consider *WF*, 14.) No compositions in EMN use regular third mode, for instance. Candidates for duple rhythm according to Sanders include *WF*, 14, 15, 16, 17 (in EMN); *WF*, 32 (square breve); *US-Cu*, 3, 5, 8, 9 (in EMN); and *US-Cu*, 1, 6, 7, 10 (square breve). Wibberley argues that the following additional pieces have binary subdivision of the long: *WF*, 18=66, 24, 25, 95. Using his test, Wibberley further concurs with Sanders's transcription of the *Ob 139* monophonic dance in ternary longs (see "Duple Rhythm," pp. 289–91) but argues that the original notation of the Sumer canon indicated binary longs, and he supports Bukofzer's interpretation of *Veni mater gracie* (*Lbl 29*, 1) in duple meter (Wibberley, "English Polyphonic Music," p. 72; Bukofzer, NOHM III, p. 112).

18. Thirteenth-century compositions surviving in two notational versions include the following:

Opem nobis	*Cjec 5*, 1 = *D-Gu*, 1/5
Amor veint	*Lbl XVIII*, 1 = *F-MO*, 243 (Rok 7.260)
Ave gloriosa mater	*Lbl 978*, 4 = *F-MO*, 44 (Rok 4.53)
Nobili precinitur	*Lbl 5958*, 1 = *F-MO*, 58 (Rok 4.67)

Au queer	*Ob 139*, 3 = *F-MO*, 15 (Rok 2.23)
In odore	*Ob 497*, 5 = *F-MO*, 61 (Rok 4.70)
Salve sancta parens	*WF*, 9 = *Ob 60*, 1
Senator regis curie	*WF*, 11 = *D-Gu*, 2
Ave magnifica	*WF*, 19 = *F-MO*, 322 (Rok 8.339)
Pro beati Pauli	*WF*, 70 = *Lwa 33327*, 4
Gloria	*WF*, 88 = *Ob 60*, 10
Super te Ierusalem	*WF*, 95 = *F-MO*, 59 (Rok 4.68)
Regis aula	*US-PRu 119A*, 1 = *Lbl 24198*, 3

19. In *Campanis cum cymbalis* (*Ob 60*, 13) the ternary c.o.p. *sine perfectione* is likewise best interpreted *bbb*, as Sanders has done in the edition for PMFC XIV (no. 59). Though this piece has no surviving version in EMN, the rhythmic interpretation of the ligature must be predicated on EMN practice.

20. See Reaney and Gilles, *Ars Cantus Mensurabilis Franconis de Colonia* (CSM 18) and the earlier edition in CS I, pp. 117–36. There is a translation of the latter by Oliver Strunk in *Source Readings*, pp. 139–59. The dating of Franco's treatise is controversial. Wolf Frobenius recently proposed the date 1280 ("Zur Datierung von Francos *Ars cantus mensurabilis*"). This date has been accepted, at least in principle, by most scholars but not by all; some still argue for the traditional date about twenty years earlier. See for instance Anderson, Review, pp. 454–55 and Levy, "Organum Duplum," p. 184.

21. Strunk, *Source Readings*, p. 151; CSM 18, pp. 58–59.

22. To my knowledge only Handlo and one of the authorities he cites, Petrus le Viser, make an explicit distinction between melismatic and syllabic values ("coniuncta" and "divisa"). See CS I, pp. 388, 396–98. However, the distinction is important; syllabic, rather than melismatic, subdivision of the breve is the critical parameter. Further, all examples showing the manner of Franco, as well as those showing the slightly later manner of Petrus de Cruce, use syllabic semibreves.

23. Nonetheless, according to Apel (NPM, p. 318), "the greatest shortcoming of Franco's system was the lack of rhythmic variety in the realm of small values." Note that Handlo, in speaking of Franco, says chains of semibreves in the Franconian system are to be interpreted 2+2+2+...+2+3 (unless clarified by the use of the *divisio*, presumably). See CS I, pp. 387–88. In Franco's treatise and in the discussion by Hanboys (CS I, p. 424), it would seem that the opposite procedure ought to hold, i.e., that because semibreves stand in much the same relation to breves as breves to longs, one ought to group chains of semibreves by threes. This of course leads to a problem if one is left over, for that is impermissible. Hence Handlo probably reports Franco's intention.

24. The rhythmic modes of Lambertus are printed in CS I, pp. 279–81, and they are discussed by Gordon Anderson in "Magister Lambertus and Nine Rhythmic Modes" (on mode six, the *ssbb* pattern, see especially p. 67 and n. 41). Anticipating the problem of rhythmic interpretation of these semibreves, it should be noted that Anderson raises the possibility that the semibreves are equal, but in my opinion Lambertus offers no justification for this interpretation. In fact, the notation best corresponds to Petrus le Viser's *mos lascivus*, in which the interpretation of semibreves is explicitly Franconian, i.e., unequal.

25. In the *Onc* version of *Ade finit* the *ssb* figure is used twice (bars 14 and 63), while otherwise all such figures are represented by ternary descending c.o.p. ligatures. The figure *ssb* appears even more frequently in the newly discovered concordance to *Ade finit* in *F-TO 925*, where it again is clearly interchangeable with the c.o.p. Further, in *Lux refulget* the

descending ternary c.o.p. and the *bss* figure are both used, so they presumably do not both represent *ssb* rhythms. The straightforward interpretation of the *bss* figure may seem obvious, but in fact there is a controversy in the musicological literature over the interpretation of this symbol, which may at certain times and places have been intended to be read as *ssb* (i.e., as a substitute for a descending ternary c.o.p., or looked at another way, moving from shorter to longer values, as one would evaluate a coniunctura in Notre Dame modal notation). The *ssb* reading may be correct for most appearances of this figure in the old corpus of *F-MO*, fascicles 2–6. See Johannes Wolf, *Geschichte der Mensural-Notation* I, p. 52 and the review of that work by Ludwig in *Sammelbände der International Musik Gesellschaft* 6, p. 627. Wolf interprets the figure as *bss*, while Ludwig interprets it as *ssb*. See also Apel, "NPM," pp. 297 and 304, and Parrish, *Notation*, p. 136.

26. The kind of notation of free semibreves described here is especially characteristic of the notation of the more modern items in the *Roman de Fauvel* and the chansons of Jehannot de Lescurel found in *F-Pn 146*.

27. See Bent, "Notation III, 3" and Apel, "NPM," p. 296. The reference to Amerus, an Englishman writing in Italy in 1271, is in Ruini, CSM 25, pp. 99–100; Dietricus is mentioned in Apel, "NPM," p. 296, n. 1. Odington's retrospective statement that "Alii...dividunt...brevem in duas semibreves et raro in tres" might be stretched to imply that some divide the breve into two equal semibreves, but this moves securely into the realm of conjecture. See CSM 14, pp. 139 and Huff, *Walter Odington*, p. 9. In addition to theoretical testimony, the name itself can be taken to mean "half a breve" (however see Apel, ibid.). It is important to observe that, in the sources of the early to middle thirteenth century, groups of two semibreves are more common than groups of three semibreves and syllabic semibreves are rare (see Apel, ibid.).

28. The evidence has been reviewed by Sanders in "Duple Rhythm," pp. 250–62. On Odington see Hammond, CSM 14, pp. 138–39; on Anonymous IV see CS I, pp. 361–62. It should be added that Amerus also describes a notational system with a binary long and binary breve. See the discussion in Gallo, *La teoria della notazione in Italia*, pp. 13–17.

29. Apel, "NPM," p. 296.

30. The positions of both are to be found in articles in *The New Grove*. For Sanders, see "Petrus de Cruce," pp. 598–99, and for Bent, see "Notation III, 3," p. 364. For Jacques de Liège on Petrus de Cruce, see CSM 3/7, pp. 37–38, 84–86, 89–90 (CS II, pp. 401–2, 428–29). These passages have been read to mean that for Petrus just as three are equal, so are four, five, six, or seven. In fact, however, "equales" only directly modifies "tres." Harrison, in the introduction to PMFC XV, incorrectly reports that in the practice of Petrus de Cruce both duplets and triplets subdivide the breve equally.

31. See Sanders, "Duple Rhythm," pp. 250–56 and the modification to his explication of Petrus in "Petrus le Viser"; see also Bent, "Rota versatilis," pp. 83–84 and scattered remarks in her critical commentaries at the end of the article.

32. See CSM 14, p. 129; Huff, *Walter Odington*, p. 10.

33. See CSM 8, p. 29.

34. Sweeney, CSM 13, p. 42; CS III, p. 185.

35. CS III, p. 378.

36. That context is what I call breve-semibreve notation. See the section of chapter 3 devoted to this notation.

37. The distinctive non-Franconian doctrine of Lambert concerning propriety in ligatures was still being transmitted alongside the Franconian teaching in the fourth *Principale* nearly a century after it was formulated. (I am indebted to Reese, *Fourscore Classics*, p. 29 for this observation.) The *Quatuor principalia* relies on Magister Lambert as one of its chief authorities. See also Reaney, "The Question of Authorship," p. 12, and Reckow, "Proprietas und perfectio," pp. 137–39. This should should further alert us to the longevity and diversity of Ars Antiqua practices.

38. Sanders, "Duple Rhythm," p. 275, n. 134 and p. 276.

39. Bent, "Preliminary Assessment," p. 67.

40. Wibberley, contribution on "Notations" in the introduction to EECM 26, p. xxvi.

41. My concern in stressing this point is to make clear that any large-scale generalization about English rhythmic preferences ought to be made on the basis of data collected separately for each clearly distinguishable kind of notation. In fact, to anticipate the conclusions that will emerge below, I do agree that there seems to be a large-scale avoidance (or disregard) of a rhythmic category common across the Channel, i.e., iambs, in English music of the thirteenth and fourteenth centuries. This must be a conclusion, though, not a presumption.

42. In his argument Wibberley cites as evidence the Worcester version of *Thomas gemma*, which is actually in the paired semibreve type of breve-semibreve notation, not a version of Franconian. He also cites the cantilena *Salamonis inclita*, a piece not relevant to his argument because the trochaic rhythms designated by a later source for it apply on a different level (subdivision of the perfect semibreve rather than subdivision of the perfect breve) than the one at issue either in his discussion or the present one. See EECM 26, p. xxvi.

43. Harrison, "Notes on Transcription and Performance" in the introduction to PMFC XV.

44. I am not totally unsympathetic to this view as an editor. But to justify such flexibility one has to examine pieces one at a time, asking of each if it reflects stylistic conventions simpler than, earlier than, or at least different than those of the motets for which we normally judge Franconian precepts to be applicable.

45. These are grounds for the most telling criticism of the methods of transcription used by Rokseth (and more recently, Tischler) for *F-MO*, as well as by Harrison in PMFC XV. When editing, I believe it best to amend inconsistency when spotted. Harrison's policy, by contrast, is to assume inconsistency is intentional, and so he leaves unmodified certain inconsistent rhythmic details in *Mulier magni meriti, De flore martirum,* and *Rosa delectabilis,* for example.

46. As Bent notes ("Preliminary Assessment," p. 70), where there are hocketing semibreves the possibility exists for clarifying the subdivision of the breve through an examination of the rests. This can be seen, for instance, in the careful rest-writing in the "In seculum" hockets of a Continental source, the Bamberg codex (*D-BAs 115*). However, in the English motets, results of an examination of rest-writing are ambiguous. Where there are hocketing semibreves in *Triumphat hodie* and *Balaam de quo,* the scribe of *Onc 362* shows a preference for the form sitting on the line whether in pre- or postsemibreve position. The scribe of *Lbl 24198* seems to prefer the form hanging from the line before the semibreve and the form sitting on the line after the semibreve.

47. The problem is one we have already encountered. Are these rhythms a modernization of the original? Were groups of s4 under a binary breve never equal for the young de Vitry and his generation, as they could be for Petrus le Viser? There are some grounds for the possible interpretation of groups of s4 as equal in English sources, if the instances just cited are taken as representative of the simplest forms of circle-stem notation. (See group D(i) in figure 35.)

48. Bent, "Notation III, 3," p. 368.

49. Handlo, CS I, pp. 388–90, 396, 398; Hanboys, CS I, pp. 424–25. This Johannes de Garlandia is a different individual from the Johannes de Garlandia who was an important midthirteenth-century Continental theorist. (Neither musician is to be confused with the well-known thirteenth-century Parisian scholastic author.) The later musician, this shadowy Garlandia "the younger," must have been an important figure around 1300, working after Franco and Petrus de Cruce (and probably after Petrus le Viser) but before Admetus de Aureliano (CS I, pp. 397–98) and probably before de Vitry's *Ars Nova* (in any case, before the 1326 date of Handlo). See Bent, "Preliminary Assessment," p. 75, n. 6, and Sanders, "Duple Rhythm," p. 253ff.

50. CS I, p. 427. The notation is mentioned by J. Wolf in *Handbuch der Notationskunde* I, p. 271. Dittmer's transcription of this motet, accompanying a facsimile of it in his edition of Handlo, is not entirely reliable in its readings of rhythms and of text. See Dittmer, *Robert de Handlo*, p. 21 (facsimile) and pp. 22–24 (transcription).

51. There is a marked similarity in shape between the *minorata* and the shape described by Handlo for the major semibreve (CS I, p. 396).

52. Bent, "Preliminary Assessment," p. 69. Similar superfluous use of the circle can be cited from the *Kyrie Cuthberte* in group D(ii).

53. See Bent, "Preliminary Assessment," p. 69. The Latin is as follows (from CS I, p. 428, discussing subdivision of the imperfect breve): "Si sit de semibrevi imperfecta, distinguendum est an sit de curta mensura: quatuor equales pro brevi, vel de longa mensura: vidilicet octo equales pro brevi."

54. See the comparative editions published by Apel in CEKM I.

55. The dotted barlines in figure 34 are meant to draw attention to the fact that the subdivisions seem to group more naturally into 2B than into 3B units. For full editions of these versions of the *Kyria christifera*, see PMFC XVI, nos. 6 and 7.

56. For instance, *Veni mi dilecte* and *Virgo salvavit* are cantilenas that move basically in long-breve notation, *O lux beata* is an ornamented form of an English discant setting of a hymn and moves in ternary breve-semibreve notation, and the *Lbl 1210* Gloria, lacking a consistent modus level of organization, basically has an ornamented form of binary breve-semibreve notation.

57. See the remarks by Ernest Sanders in the preface to PMFC XVII.

58. The *Kyrie Cuthberte* is edited in PMFC XVI, no. 8, and *Stella maris* (*Cgc 334*, 7) is edited in PMFC XVII, no. 33.

59. Wright, *Music at the Court of Burgundy*, p. 16, n. 29.

60. For some of these statements, see Trowell, "Faburden—New Sources, New Evidence," pp. 39–40 and his notes.

61. The binary-breve version is seen in some free cantilena-style settings of the Gloria, such as *Lbl XXIV*, 1 and *Lbl 40725*, 1. It is used in the Gloria *Lbl 1210*, 5 with rhythmic diminution as in group D(ii) of the notational complex just discussed. Further, it occurs as a contrast to ternary breve-semibreve notation in a number of pieces such as the Gloria *Lbl 38651*, 6 and the troped Gloria *DRc, Communar's Cartulary*, 1.

62. The total of eight sources includes a very fragmentary concordance for *Mutato modo* in *Lbl 38651*. Note that there are very few free pairs of semibreves in *Spiritus et alme*, and that in two of the pieces the major semibreve is occasionally given a downstem, i.e., in *O lux beata* and *Rosa delectabilis*, which are examples of breve-semibreve notation ornamented according to group B practice in the circle-stem notational complex.

63. Sanders, "Duple Rhythm," pp. 275–76 and Bent, "Preliminary Assessment," pp. 66–69. Their arguments and evidence include the following. (1) It is reasonable to assume that the different notational states in which the cantilena *Includimur nube caliginosa* and the motet *Thomas gemma* have been preserved, represent the same rhythms, thus equating paired semibreves with square breve and semibreve in *Includimur* and paired semibreves with long and breve in *Thomas*. (2) When there are ornamental figures in one or more sources of a piece, these may indicate through spacing or the use of stems the underlying binary or ternary character of the breve and its prevailing mode of subdivision. For instance, concordances of the cantilena *Mutato modo geniture* indicate in a number of small details that the breve is ternary and its customary subdivision is 2+1. (3) Pieces may yield other empirical evidence such as the use of the binary c.o.p. ligature in contexts requiring it to be read 2+1. (4) There is some small amount of theoretical testimony indicating the possibility of a trochaic interpretation of paired semibreves, primarily the statement in the *Quatuor principalia* (cited above with a number of other relevant quotations). (5) There is a thirteenth-century predilection for trochaic rendition of paired rhomboid breves, and this may devolve upon these paired rhomboid semibreves (though it must be clarified that the context here is not Franconian). To these I would add a sixth, namely (6) that there are strong stylistic similarities between breve-semibreve pieces (with or without paired semibreves) and compositions in similar styles and genres written one level of notation higher, in longs and breves. I will elaborate on this point shortly below.

64. CS IV, p. 257; CS III, p. 337.

65. John Stevens describes the notation of *Angelus ad virginem* in the polyphonic settings of the Dublin Troper as simply "full black mensural...perhaps late fourteenth to early fifteenth century," but this is not sufficient, nor entirely accurate, in my view. See Stevens's description in *Cambridge Music Manuscripts*, ed. Fenlon, p. 81. For more on the *Angelus* settings, see below.

66. To anticipate a point, if the evolutionary hypothesis concerning the halving of values that I propose below holds, then perhaps the semibreves are ternary because their larger equivalent, the Franconian breve, is ternary. Incidentally, *tempus perfectum* is very much less common than *tempus imperfectum* on the Continent in the fourteenth century, as can be seen, for example, by a perusal of the works of Machaut or the motets of PMFC V. The reverse is true of breve-semibreve notations in England; perhaps this is so because, on the larger level, the binary long is less common than the ternary long in Ars Antiqua sources.

67. *Mutato modo* is edited in PMFC XVII, no. 36. Just as one would not expect to see a maximodus level of organization in a long-breve cantilena, so one does not expect to see a modus level of organization in a breve-semibreve piece. In both cases construction is essentially additive, perfection by perfection.

68. Bukofzer, NOHM III, pp. 115–17; Sanders, "Duple Rhythm," p. 276; and Bent, "Preliminary Assessment," p. 68.

69. NOHM III, p. 116. It should be added that the top voice at "concipies" supports his decision as well.

70. "Preliminary Assessment," p. 68. Bent's argument is somewhat obscured there by the misprint "trochaic" for "iambic" five lines up from the bottom of the page.

71. There are many stylistically similar pieces in long-breve notation with few or no semibreves, flowing conjunct melodies in stepwise sequential melodic descent, counterpoint in parallel 6-3s tempered by occasional 8-5s and cadences to 8-5s. See, for example, *Beata viscera* (*WF*, 91), *Spiritus procedens* (*Onc 362*, 13, and *Ob 14*, 6), and the *DRc 8* Latin-texted Kyries. These are representative of the late thirteenth- and early fourteenth-century generation of conductus, rondellus, and cantilena-style compositions.

72. Though long goes to breve, *ssb* goes to *ssb* in this example. Discant pieces move from cantus-firmus motion in longs to motion in breves early in the fourteenth century, and from breves to semibreves late in the century. For an example of this later, further shift to shorter values, see the setting of *Alma redemptoris mater* in *Occ 144* (PMFC XVII, no. 12), and other examples in Old Hall.

73. Sanders and Bent both argue (Sanders, critical report to *Thomas gemma* in PMFC XIV, 61; Bent, "Preliminary Assessment," p. 69 and also p. 75, n. 8) that the long-breve version might be a later notational clarification of the paired semibreves of *Thomas*, and further, it might be later because of the desire to introduce ornamental rhythmic subdivision on the semibreve level found in the long-breve versions, which would be impossible to accommodate in the breve-semibreve notation. In addition, Sanders has remarked that the necessity of reading paired semibreves unequally in the breve-semibreve version corresponds to the tradition of thirteenth-century EMN in its handling of paired rhomboid breves (PMFC XIV, 61, critical report). Of course one might also say that long-breve notation is vulnerable to rhythmic elaboration, and the long-breve original may have been simpler in rhythmic character. One can also point out an analogous relationship, both stylistic and notational, between cantilenas in long-breve and breve-semibreve notation, observing their basic equivalency except in regard to ornamental subdivision (and to some extent, in declamation on the longest perfect value—more frequent on perfect breve than on perfect long). I will argue shortly that the mensuration of *Thomas gemma* is fundamentally a binary one, and that the long-breve notation is best regarded as a "duplex long-long" version used to write rhythms unavailable on a purely long-breve level without a binary long, which in effect is the version we have in breves and semibreves.

74. It is probably identical to a composition listed early in the *Lbl 978 (LoHa)* index. For an edition of both versions, see PMFC XVII, no. 15a/15b.

75. If Hanboys's ascription is correct, Brother Robert is clearly a major figure in the development of middle fourteenth-century English music. Brunham is one of these shadowy figures whose activities need to be dated and localized. He is identified as "frater" by Hanboys (CS I, p. 477) and by a Trinity College copy of the musical treatise *Declaratio*, there attributed to Frater Robertus de Brunham but elsewhere usually associated with the name of Torkesey (*Cambridge, Trinity College, MS O.9.29.*, fols. 53v and 94). See CSM 12, p. 36 and n. 8. On Brunham, see also Bent, "Preliminary Assessment," pp. 68, 70. Brunham's devices are introduced in Hanboys's section devoted to the semibreve practices of the moderns, as opposed to those of the ancients. Brunham probably was active in the

years 1330 to 1350 or so. One other innovation credited to Brunham, some special forms for perfect long, breve, and semibreve rests, appears in many fourteenth-century English sources (see below in the section devoted to rest-writing).

76. Hanboys writes "Ergo vitiose assignatur alteratio, quando assignatur per duos tractulos, et potest assignari per punctus." See CS I, p. 432; for the *Quatuor principalia*, see CS IV, p. 271 (CS III, p. 349).

77. *Cu 710*, 1 (*Angelus ad virginem*); *Ob 384*, 2 (*Gloria*); *TAcro 3184*, 2 (*Magnificat*); and *Occ 144*, 3 (*Fulgens stella*). Two other appearances are worthy only of a footnote: in *US-PRu 103*, 3 (*Salve regina*), the descending form is used in I:107 against the normal oblique descending form in a parallel part; and in *LEcl 6120*, 1/2 (*Frangens evanuit*), a Brunham shape appears at the final cadence in voice I, probably representing some attempt at a rhythmic readjustment to a problematic spot in the piece.

78. CS I, p. 432.

79. I have in mind a discant setting of Sarum Agnus 9 that survives in both Old Hall (*Lbl 57950*, 134) and the Fountains fragments (*Lbl 40011B*, 14). Figures written in the ternary-breve section of this piece as breve-plus-semibreve (2+1) in Fountains appear in c.o.p. ligatures in Old Hall. These are read 1+2 in Bent and Hughes's edition. Their decision is based on the prevailing rhythmic language and conventions of the manuscript, but it does seem to be the case that an anti-Franconian reading of the ligatures, following the rhythms designated in Fountains, would improve the counterpoint in at least two spots.

80. Margaret Bent also stresses the importance of the violation, or hesitancy to violate the *similis ante similem rule* (Private communication). Sectional changes of mensuration do not always prove the intent to use Ars Nova prolations exclusively, as is seen by the pieces cited above in n. 61 that alternate ternary and binary breve-semibreve notation. The cantilena *Frangens evanuit* (*LEcl VR 6120*, 1/2) moves between an apparent *tempus imperfectum maior* (perhaps a version of circle-stem notation Group C) and *longa mensura* (Group D(ii)).

81. See PMFC XVI, 22, a Kyrie with concordances in *Ob 14*, *Ob 55*, and *NWcro 299*.

82. A good number of the newer motets in the *Roman de Fauvel* have a binary long. Late thirteenth-century English examples include compositions in English mensural notation from *US-Cu* and *WF* (see figure 30) and examples in square-breve notation from *Ob 60* (the *Gloria: Spiritus et alme*) and *F-TO 925* (the motet *Syderea celi*).

83. See CS I, pp. 404–5. By contrast, for Franco three simple figures sufficed: *longa, brevis,* and *semibrevis*.

84. The concept that not all rhythmic values can be found together in one voice is not new in Hanboys's formulation. Handlo, for instance, qualified the use of the long by making it clear that longs cannot be associated with the very smallest values, *minimae* and *minoratae*, and he closed his discussion relative to this point with the following remark: "Patet igitur que note cum quibus haberi possunt." (CS I, p. 391).

85. The largest note value found in the repertoire is the triple long used in the tenor of *Quare fremuerunt*, the smallest the one-eighteenth of a breve found in the lowest voice of *Beatus vir*.

86. Dittmer, MSD 2, p. 42 (in the critical notes to *WF*, 47) and in "The Dating and the Notation of the Worcester Fragments," p. 6. In this article he wrongly includes *WF*, 48 (written in the same hand as *WF*, 44 and 47) with the others in larga-longa notation.

87. Dittmer, "The Dating and the Notation," p. 6.

88. See CSM 12, p. 25.

89. The *Quatuor principalia* also only refers to the *duplex longa*. (Handlo acknowledges an "immeasurably long" long for the tenors of organa.)

90. CS I, p. 405.

91. The larger values are conveniently well-determined and customarily available as units of declamation. One avoids the binary long and breve on the next level down, or the use of the minim as a unit of declamation two levels down. Further, the rhythms of the longs and breves in the Worcester pieces follow second-mode patterns; on the minim level the equivalent to these iambic rhythms was rarely seen until after midcentury (it is one of the progressive traits in the later works of Machaut).

92. This section of *Rota versatilis* has one ornamental c.o.p., and there are ornamental semibreve duplets and triplets in *Thomas gemma*. These intrusions of semibreves may be considered accidental rather than essential to the basic character of the mensuration of these motets.

93. The final phrase probably cadenced to a double long in the last two bars of the section, omitting any bars of rest. If this is so, the section was probably 56L (2x28L), and the phrase structure might have been something like 16L+12L+14L+14L (with truncation of the last phrase to 12L).

94. CS I, p. 391; *Lbl 4909*, p. 8 (fol. 4v).

95. Bent, "Rota versatilis," pp. 76–78. I am indebted to her article for drawing my attention to Handlo's quotation of the incipit.

96. For Bent's version of the incipit, see "Rota versatilis," pp. 77, 92.

97. CS I, p. 415; *Lbl 8866*, fol. 70v.

98. This is so despite the phrase structures in *O crux*, which are in some sense ternary in their groupings of breves. See the critical report in appendix 2.

99. In PMFC XVI, Harrison transcribes the last section of *Ovet mundus* in three-half time (three two-four bars), and transcribes the two sections of *Hostis Herodes* in three-quarter time.

100. Together these phrase lengths comprise the four consecutive whole numbers 12 through 15. This permutation of consecutive integers has the same kind of deliberate circularity that Bent has noted in the lengths of verse in each new stanza (i.e., 12, 13, 11, 15, 14). See "Rota versatilis," pp. 84–85.

101. The ternary long on the last syllable of the fourth phrase and the subsequent ternary long-rest argue for an interpretation in ternary longs. One might also add that the ternary interpretation creates a most elegant proportional number scheme in longs (see the critical report in appendix 2).

102. Bent, "Rota versatilis," p. 66; see also pp. 83–84.

103. PMFC XV, p. xiv. *Triumphus patet* also provides an example of the use of the *brevis erecta*, whose appearances in practical sources always correspond to innovative insular stemming practices.

104. Bent discusses uses 1, 3, 5, and 6 in "Rota versatilis," pp. 79–80. See also Wolf, *Handbuch der Notationskunde,* p. 268.

105. In *O pater* the circle is used as a kind of *signum congruencie* at the ends of sections. In one source of *Rota versatilis, Lbl 40011B*,* a small dot placed over the first note of the section is used instead of the circle. In two instances, *Hostis Herodes* and the Robertsbridge codex intabulation *Flos vernalis,* three or four circles arranged vertically in the place of a staff division mark a sectional and mensural change. Though I would emphasize the role of the circle in mensural, not merely sectional demarcation, Bent, for example, interpets the latter as the primary meaning.

106. Hammond, CSM 14, pp. 128–29, 145; Huff, *Walter Odington,* p. 10. Odington's practice is not seen in *Lbl 1210* (contrary to Sanders, "Duple Rhythm," p. 253, n. 13 or Hammond, CSM 14, p. 129, n. 5); rather, the use of the circle in this source is as in (6) in the discussion below, to mark off each third of a ternary breve or each half of a binary breve.

107. See the discussion of this note form in Bent, "Preliminary Assessment," pp. 73–74, with reference to the definitions of Handlo (CS I, p. 383) and the nearly identical ones in Hanboys (CS I, pp. 413, 417). Bent notes that the only other references to *longe* and *breves erecte* are in the London version of de Vitry's *Ars Nova* (CSM 18, pp. 77–78), where "it may have been introduced into the text by an English compiler" (Bent, p. 73).

108. In regard to the long, Handlo writes: "longe... vocantur erecte quia ubicunque inveniuntur per semitonum eriguntur" (CS I, p. 383).

109. Sources in which the *brevis erecta* is found include *Lpro 23, Lbl 1210, Ob 384,* and *Ob 60.* Bent reports finding other examples in nonmotet items of *Ob 14* and *B-Br 266* (Bent, "Preliminary Assessment," p. 76, n. 32).

110. See CS IV, p. 446 and Reaney and Gilles, *Ars Cantus Mensurabilis,* p. 55.

111. See the discussion of this rest-shape in the edition by Sweeney of the Anon. dictus Theodoricus (CSM 13, p. 21), and see also the comparative chart of rest-shapes in the studies by Johannes Wolf (*Geschichte der Mensural-Notation* I, pp. 88–89; *Handbuch der Notationskunde* I, p. 336). The theorist known to Wolf as CS III, Anon. VI and thought perhaps to be English, has been identified as Petrus de Sancto Dionisio, whose treatise, a compilation relying mainly on the *Notitia artis musicae* of Muris, has been edited recently by Michels (*Johannis de Muris,* pp. 147–66; for the perfect semibreve-rest, see p. 163).

112. The discussion of Brunham's rest forms in CS IV, p. 447 omits (inadvertently, I believe) the eleventh, minima-rest.

113. In addition to the following discussion, see Bent, "Preliminary Assessment," pp. 70–71.

114. The addition of the mensuration sign reverse-c-dot at the beginning of both voices of this motet may be, like the scribe's use of Brunham's rests, an attempt to update it in appearance.

115. *Thomas gemma* does not use any of the distinctive rest forms.

116. See Bukofzer, *Studies in Medieval and Renaissance Music,* pp. 97–98 where he remarks on the distinctly English rest-writing in *Lbl 40011B,* and also Bent, "Preliminary Assessment," pp. 70–71. Note that the form of perfect semibreve-rest that projects above and below the staff line also occurs in Italian sources—in the music of Jacopo da Bologna and in the Rossi codex—as Sweeney has pointed out (CSM 13, p. 21).

Chapter 4

1. Vernacular texts (Middle English or Anglo-Norman) are exceptional in the English repertoire. See below in the section "Vernacular Texts."

2. See Clarkson, "On the Nature of Medieval Song," chapter III: "The Lyric Structure of the Fourteenth-Century Motet."

3. Van der Werf, Review, pp. 201–2.

4. Hohler, in "Reflections," has recently made a stimulating foray in this direction. Rigg, "Medieval Latin," in *Editing Medieval Texts*, pp. 113–16, makes some telling comments on the amount of unstudied Latin poetry in late medieval British anthologies, and two recent surveys of the broader European scene only reinforce his concern (see Diehl, *The Medieval European Religious Lyric*, pp. 237–42, and Nichols, "Latin Literature," in *The Present State of Scholarship in Fourteenth-Century Literature*, esp. pp. 195–200). Until this material is better controlled, and until we have a better picture of the genres of liturgical Latin poetry actively being written in the fourteenth century (sequences, rhymed offices, and the like), the motet texts will necessarily have to be viewed quite narrowly.

5. The contents of the texts of a polytextual English motet almost never address their subject matter in exactly the same way, but at the same time almost never show the sharp differences in subject matter occasionally encountered in Continental motets. *Petrum cephas* is typical, with a triplum citing New Testament stories of Peter's calling, his naming, and his designation as keeper of the keys, while the duplum refers to later events and legends, most specifically Peter's encounter with the magician Simon Magus. *Trinitatem veneremur* is an untypical instance where the various texts sound different themes (all appropriate in an address to God, however).

6. "Ego" is heard, for instance, in the two texts of *Zorobabel abigo* and the duplum text of *Zelo tui* (beginning "Reor nescia quit sit sapiencia").

7. The level of detail in a typical motet text is comparable to that of a sequence, in other words, more explicit and extended than any other liturgical item except for the vastly larger-scaled lessons at matins.

8. See Bent, "Rota versatilis," p. 67. Harrison's assertion ("Ars Nova," p. 80, n. 1.) that two items in the rear leaves of *DRc 20* are numbered is incorrect. However, the front and rear leaves of *Ob 7* and *DRc 20* indicate by their contrasts in repertoire that the collections from which they came were probably grouped stylistically; further, the front leaves of *Ob 7* may have grouped insular motets by features of form and structure. See Lefferts, "Motet," pp. 58–60. The earliest Continental motet collections were arranged either in liturgical order by cantus firmus, or alphabetically. Fascicles 2 through 6 of *F-MO* (a large anthology) group motets systematically according to the number of voices, method of texting, and text language. Within each fascicle, however, the rationale for ordering is not clear.

9. For *Ob 652*, see Bent, "Rota versatilis," pp. 81–82; for *Lpro 2/261*, see the report by Lefferts and Bowers in Lefferts and Bent, "New Sources," p. 334; and for the Berkeley castle rotulus *BERc 55* see the forthcoming report by Wathey.

10. In table 26 all abbreviations and contractions have been silently expanded, and an indication of date or subject has been added on the right-hand side. The contents of this index have been printed in Ludwig, *Repertorium* I, 1, pp. 270–76, and Wibberley, "English Polyphonic Music," pp. 179–81. Holschneider, *Die Organa von Winchester*, pp. 48–53,

tabulates the Alleluias only. See also Schofield, "The Provenance and Date of 'Sumer is Icumen in,'" pp. 82–84; Ian Bent, "A New Polyphonic 'Verbum bonum et soave,'" p. 229; and Sanders, "Sources, English." Table 26 does not indicate those pieces in the index for which there survive possible concordances, of which there are only a few.

11. In his discussion of *LoHa*, Hohler ("Reflections," pp. 13–14) observes that the Alleluias ought to define very precisely the provenance of the index, but tracing though surviving liturgical books has not yet yielded a concordant series. Other evidence suggests the institution may have been Reading abbey (though Hohler raises some cogent objections to this), and the Alleluia cycle identical to that one known to have been composed by one W. de Wycombe. See Sanders, "Wycombe, W de." Incidentally, Hohler ("Reflections," p. 16) asserts that the heading in *LoHa* that reads "postea Rx W.de Wic" may not refer to the Alleluias, as is usually assumed.

12. As Sanders has noted in regard to a more limited sample of thirteenth-century pieces, when only the free compositions of the Worcester fragments are considered the percentage of Marian pieces becomes still higher, reaching two-thirds. See Sanders, "English Polyphony," p. 104, n. 76; for the percentage he calculates on cantus firmus items, see ibid., pp. 125–26.

13. The elimination of the motets of probable thirteenth-century origin surviving in fourteenth-century sources, along with such items as the troped-chant settings of the "Regnum tuum solidum" Gloria prosula, would cause the motets on saints to stand out even more.

14. See Anne Walters Robertson, "The Reconstruction of the Abbey Church of St-Denis," esp. pp. 193–99.

15. This argument presupposes that the collections being discarded were of a medium size (60 to 100 items) rather than small, selective samplings of the available repertoire in circulation.

16. Hohler, in "Reflections," p. 32, singles out these three saints as not particularly monastic, thus cautioning against the view that the motets are of monastic provenance. But his argument is countered by the fact that these three are among the very most popular saints in all of Western Christendom, as can be seen, for instance, by a casual perusal of the *Register* of the *Analecta Hymnica*. They are as highly ranked in the monastic Benedictine calendars of medieval England as in the calendars of the secular rites of Salisbury, Hereford, or York. (See Wormald, *English Benedictine Calendars after 1100*, and the calendar of the Worcester antiphonal in Mocquereau, *L'Antiphonaire Monastique de Worcester*, for instance.)

17. Again, this piece of evidence, if that is what it is, may be telling us something about the role of the motet in the liturgy. Concerning the liturgy of the papal chapel at Avignon in the fourteenth century, Andrew Tomasello has recently written "that polyphony may have been more easily introduced into the service on those feasts that were less rigidly controlled by ancient and solemn liturgical tradition" (*Music and Ritual*, p. 116 and the author's note).

18. There is an interesting correspondence in the provision of many additional pieces for the BVM in some sequence collections. In terms of numbers, the Hereford Missal contains 79 sequences, of which 14 (18 percent) are Marian. Similarly, the Dublin Troper contains 75 sequences in its first series, of which 10 (13 percent) are Marian, but in addition, 42 more Marian sequences appear in a second series. The supplementary series of Marian Alleluias in the *LoHa* index provides another parallel.

19. See for example the *Stella maris* of John of Garland, *Les Miracles de Nostre Dame* of Gautier de Coinci, or the *Cantigas de Santa Maria* compiled for Alphonso X of Spain.

20. The motet might have served as an elaborate *Benedicamus Domino* substitute for Trinity Sunday. However, given the obvious striving for assonance in the texts of all parts in most English motets, and since the blessing formula is so frequently encountered in the liturgy of this feast, I would argue that its use as a *Benedicamus* substitute is not inevitable.

21. Rokseth notes the difficulty with this topic in her discussion of the texts of the *F-MO* motets (*Polyphonies* IV, p. 231).

22. "Non vox sed votum, non musica cordula sed cor, Non clamor sed amor sonat in aure Dei" or "Deus non verborum sed cordis est auditor" are examples of the pithy way the sentiment might be stated. See Siegfried Wenzel, *"Fasciculus Morum,"* p. 232. It may be that in the homiletic motet texts we see the influence of the friars; perhaps it is significant in this regard that there are so few of this type.

23. The lamenting tone of *Herodis in pretorio* for Holy Innocents Day (December 28) and the threatening picture of Herod in *Hostis Herodes* (for Epiphany) also may be cited in this regard. One might even stretch the point to include the observation that the tenor of *O homo*, "Filie Ierusalem," is from a respond for feasts of a martyr.

24. These are the Sundays when the matins lessons are read from the book of Kings, the so-called *Hist.Reg.* period. See *Brev.Sar.* I, p. mclxxii.

25. Sanders, "Motet," p. 548. It may be that the Biblical figures in these motet texts are meant to stand for contemporary persons; if so, the composer's intended referential or allegorical meaning is obscure. Perhaps, like some sequences, the motet could be sung "in dominicis diebus per estatem." This is the rubric in the Dublin Troper, *Cu 710*, for the sequences *Quicumque vult salvus* and *Voce iubilantes*. The topical specificity of *Doleo* does seem, I grant, insufficiently neutral to be suited for most Sundays.

26. See von Simson, *Gothic Cathedral*, pp. 8, 11, 134, and elsewhere for a discussion of this tradition.

27. See AH 55, p. 35 (no. 31).

28. See Karl Strecker, *Die Lieder Walters von Chatillon* I, no. 9, pp. 13–14. Strecker's critical notes examine the relationship of *Templum veri* to *Rex Salomon fecit*.

29. This motet (*WF*, 12) has been edited by Dittmer in MSD 2, no. 12 and by Sanders in PMFC XIV, no. 51. Hohler, in "Reflections," pp. 24–25, points out the unsuitability of the text for the nonmartyred Eadburga.

30. See Bowers on *Cfm* in Lefferts and Bent, "New Sources," pp. 289–91.

31. See under the Latin equivalents of this subject heading in the *Analecta Hymnica: Register*. Two such texts appear in *Lbl 978* (fols. 10v–11) between the motet *Ave gloriosa mater* and the Sumer Canon. They are *Felix sanctorum* and *Petrus Romanis reseravit*.

32. Dickinson, *Missale Sarum*, pp. 661*–63*; Henderson, *Missale Herefordense*, pp. 370–71; Chevalier, *Repertorium*, no. 815.

33. Hohler (writing in "Reflections,") has an enviable control over medieval English liturgical books, and discusses problems in the determination of provenance with information on subject matter drawn from sequence collections. But though some English sequence repertoires are widely available for study (such as those in the Salisbury, Hereford, and

York missals), there is little published analysis of them (though see Messenger, "Hymns and Sequences of the Sarum Use"). Recently, the leading expert on the hymns and hymnaries of medieval England, Helmut Gneuss, has made a call for sequence work comparable to the work he has done on the cycle of hymns (see Gneuss, "Hymns," pp. 416–17).

34. The texts of *Baptizas*, which are hard to read, run more or less as follows:

> *Triplum*
>
> . . . . . den . . . .
> . . . . ine
> . . o . . catholicorum
> . . . . . . dor ruine
> . . . . obvans . . . . .
> . . . . . os in fine
>
> baptizas parentes
> Dei cum virtute
> obviantem larvam
> [. . .]dis cum salute
> tuis provi votis
> requiescunt tute
>
> trium mortuorum
> eras [. . .]itator
> neophitus primus
> celle speculator
> flentis alternatus
> trinus colli lator
>
> [. . .]certant cives
> turonum pictorum
> sacrum petunt corpus
> tutele suorum
> sed hoc per fe[. . .]ram
> traxit gens priorum.
>
> O Martine fulgens in gloria
> nobis tua assint subsidia.
>
> *Duplum*

. . . . sacer presul . . . . . abrahe . . . . sinus nullus . . . . s gestibus suppremus nucus hic brachus . . . . contem . . obiureli commer . . . . fecit globus ignem . . . . respuit cesaris miliciam ut fortis defendat (ecc)lesiam nostram p . . . arunt chorus monachorum superstes ut . . . . etor sis . . . . .

35. Hohler points out, for instance ("Reflections," p. 15), that "until the mid-fourteenth century S. Edmund was apparently patron of the English 'nation' in the University of Paris."

36. On Coxford and *Cfm*, see the report by Roger Bowers in Lefferts and Bent, "New Sources," pp. 282–86.

37. On *Llc 52* see the report by Susan Rankin in Bowers and Wathey, "New Sources," pp. 149–53.

38. Hohler, "Reflections," p. 31.

39. Hohler incorrectly identifies *Excelsus in numine* as pertaining to Thomas of Hereford and misidentifies *Solaris ardor* with Saint Gregory ("Reflections," p. 31).

40. On *Ob D.6* see Hughes, "New Italian and English Sources," pp. 174–75 and see also the critical report on *Augustine par angelis* in appendix 2.

41. Hohler, "Reflections," pp. 24–30.

42. See Lefferts, "Simon de Montfort," p. 203.

43. See Levy, "New Material," p. 224.

44. See Lefferts, "Simon de Montfort," pp. 206–9. I do not see *Trinitatem* as a product of the 1260s, however, but perhaps of the 1290s.

45. The others are *Musicalis sciencia-Sciencie laudabili* (*F-Pn 67*, 5), *Apollonis-Zodiacum* (*I-IVc 115*, 20 and several other Continental sources), *Alma polis-Axe poli* (*F-CH 564*, 108), and *Sub Arturo plebs*; other possibilities include *Deus compaignouns de Cleremunde* (*US-Wc 14*, 3) and perhaps one or two in Bent's reconstructed manuscript (see "The Progeny of Old Hall," p. 22). See also Bent, *Two Fourteenth-Century Motets In Praise of Music*. Besseler ("Ars Antiqua," col. 687) mentions six motets of the late thirteenth century that name musicians, and texts of Italian Trecento polyphony also occasionally name musicians.

46. I would like to thank Craig Wright, Reinhard Strohm, and Andrew Tomasello for kindly checking their archival data for these names; see also Wright, *Music at the Court of Burgundy* and Tomasello, *Music and Ritual at Papal Avignon*. The royal court would probably have been identified as the "curia francorum" rather than "curia gallicorum."

47. My thanks to Andrew Tomasello for alerting me to the desiderius/Didier relationship and the Avignon church. Anglés mentions a certain "Johannes Pipudi, canonicus Sancti Desiderii Avinionensis" who is named as the author of two medieval music treatises in *Seville, Biblioteca Colombina, MS 5-2-25* ("De cantu organico," p. 1325).

48. Harrison, *Music in Medieval Britain*, pp. 77–81.

49. Stäblein-Harder, *Mass Music in France* (MSD 7), pp. 17–18.

50. On the musicians named, see Trowell, "A Fourteenth-Century Ceremonial Motet," and Bent, "Transmission," pp. 70–72.

51. Günther has suggested (CMM 39, p. lii) that *Sub arturo* was written in direct response to, and emulation of, the musicians motet *Apollonis eclipsatur*.

52. See Günther's discussion in CMM 39, pp. xxix–xxxi.

53. The surviving text of *Alme pater* reads as follows:

> Alme pater pastor vere
> Christicolarum omnium
> per te diu dolvere
> mentes nostrorum omnium

[...]isera turcibus
sustulisti tam perversa
heu captivarum manibus
Neepolitani nobiles

quos diligebas tantum
heu non fuerunt nobiles

ulcissi tuum munere
egena illorum atria
repleveras innumere
ingrata tua patria

dudum Christi[...]lacrimis
nostre sunt uncte facies
quod te dum malos comprimis
atrox obcedit acies

intra suos vidit muros
omni cantanda feria
casus diu pati duros
te flebiles Luceria.

54. For two standard narratives of these events, see Ludwig Pastor, *The History of the Popes* I, pp. 134–38, and Mandell Creighton, *A History of the Papacy* I, pp. 85–97.

55. Contrafacture cannot be wholly ruled out, especially since the text may be defective, or may not have been set in full (one stanza appears to be incomplete and the fit of text to isorhythmic structure is clumsy).

56. The first two stanzas of the triplum of *Inter usitata* read as follows:

Inter usitata
novum quid cantemus
quia nova grata
frequenter habemus
cons(tanter) psallamus

se ad opus cuius
Domine tam pure
sancti Pauli huius
novelle structu(re)
simulque dicamus.

57. See Smet, "Carmelites," and Staring, "Simon Stock" in the *New Catholic Encyclopedia*. Wibberley, "English Polyphonic Music," pp. 151–57, suggests an association of Simon Stock and the Carmelites with the texts of the motet *Virgo Maria* (*Cgc 512*, 3).

58. The manuscript in which this motet appears as a flyleaf, *US-SM 19914*, has associations with the Augustinian house of St. Osyth, but no evident Carmelite connections.

59. English cantilenas are almost exclusively devoted to the BVM. Exceptions include settings for Saint Margaret, (*Virgo vernans velud rosa, Cgc 230*, no. 2); for Jesus (*Hic quomodo seduxerat, LEcl 6120*, 9 and *Jhesu christe rex, GLcro 678*, 2); for Christmas and Easter (*Christi messis, LEcL 6120*, 11 and *Frangens evanuit, LEcl 6120*, 1/2, respectively); and for king Edward III (*Singularis laudis digna US-NYpm 978*, 1 = *Occ 144*, 1 and *Regem regum, US-NYpm 978*, 3). The second Edward setting could also be read as pertaining to Edward the Confessor.

60. For the text fragments see Bent, "A Lost English Choirbook," p. 262 and "The Progeny of Old Hall," pp. 21–22.

61. See Bukofzer, *John Dunstable Complete Works*, and Bent, *Dunstaple*. Dunstaple's works also include two nonisorhythmic motets, on Saint Katherine and the Holy Cross. The surviving motets of Leonel Power are by contrast all nonisorhythmic and Marian, setting the texts of votive antiphons. This emphasis on Mary is in fact the direction taken by the English motet in the fifteenth century, culminating in such collections as the Eton choirbook.

62. On the motets in *I-MOe 1.11 (ModB)* see Hamm and Scott, "A Study and Inventory of the Manuscript Modena," in the inventory under fols. 125v, 126v, and 135v; for *CAc 128/3* see chapter 1, n. 30. As one further example dedicated to a saint there is the bipartite motet a4 *Cantemus Domino–T. Gaudent in celis* (*Lbl Egerton 3307*, fol. 75v–77) in honor of the feast of Saint Dunstan. See McPeek, *The British Museum Manuscript Egerton 3307*, no. 51, pp. 96–101 and Bowers, "The Performing Ensemble," pp. 191–92.

63. Sanders, "Motet," p. 532.

64. Sanders, "Peripheral Polyphony," p. 277.

65. Rokseth, *Polyphonies* IV, pp. 227–31.

66. All of those identified with feasts of the Christian calendar have been identified by Sanders as English (70, 340–41) or peripheral (60), or have been identified by Tischler as belonging outside the central stylistic group. See Sanders, "Peripheral Polyphony," and Tischler, preface to *The Montpellier Codex*. See also Sanders, "Motet," p. 533 on the "peripheral" Latin double motets.

67. See Hans Tischler, "Classicism and Romanticism in 13th-Century Music," "Intellectual Trends in 13th-Century Paris as Reflected in the Texts of Motets," and "Latin Texts in the Early Motet Collections: Relationships and Perspectives."

68. Tischler, "Intellectual Trends," p. 6.

69. Tischler, "Latin Texts in the Early Motet Collections."

70. See especially Sanders, "Motet," pp. 556–57 and "The Early Motets of Philippe de Vitry," with references in the latter to the extensive earlier literature on motet subject matter.

71. The carol usually consists of a burden alternating with uniform stanzas (commonly rhymed aaab). Note that the texts of the refrain motets are not in carol form.

72. R.L. Greene, *The Early English Carols*, 2nd ed.

73. J. Stevens, *Mediaeval Carols* and *Early Tudor Songs and Carols*.

74. Stevens, "Round-Table: The English Carol," p. 298.

75. See Harrison's contribution to Stevens, "Round-Table: The English Carol," pp. 302–3.

76. These hymns have been edited three times recently by different scholars: R.L. Greene, *The Lyrics of the Red Book of Ossory* (Oxford, 1974); E. Colledge, *The Latin Poems of Richard Ledrede, O.F.M.* (Toronto, 1974); and Th. Stemmler, *The Latin Hymns of Richard Ledrede* (Mannheim, 1975). Stemmler could, to a certain extent, take into account the editions of Greene and Colledge. An important critical review of all three editions, by A.G. Rigg, appears in *Medium Aevum* 46 (1977), pp. 269–78. None of the editions is wholly satisfactory, though each has particular strengths.

77. Greene, *The Lyrics*, p. v.

78. Colledge, *Latin Poems*, p. xli.

79. Greene, *The Lyrics*, p. 6.

80. Performance context is one of the sources of greatest controversy among students of the carol. See Stevens, "Round-Table," esp. pp. 285–86.

81. It has often been printed, most recently in Colledge, *Latin Poems* and Greene, *The Lyrics*. Greene (p. xxvii) remarks on the similarity to a note given with the musical settings of the *Libre Vermell*, (*E-MO*, 1). On this source, see RISM B/IV/2, pp. 99–102.

82. D.L. Jeffrey, *The Early English Lyric and Franciscan Spirituality*, p. 17. On Jeffrey's work, however, see the scathing comments by Edward Wilson (Review) and Siegfried Wenzel (*Verses in Sermons*, pp. 102–3). Wenzel specifically complains that Jeffrey completely misunderstands the Latin contexts of the English lyrics (p. 102).

83. See R.H. Robbins, "The Authors of the Middle English Religious Lyrics," and Jeffrey, *The Early English Lyric*. See also Christopher Page, "Angelus ad virginem." Jeffrey's theory that all the secular lyrics were written by Franciscan friars "has not met with much critical approval" (Fisher, "English Literature," p. 25), but their predominant influence—"from 65 to 90 percent of work up to 1350" (Diehl, *Religious Lyric*, p. 243)—is unquestionable.

84. Jeffrey, *The Early English Lyric*, pp. 184 and 214, respectively. However, in Wenzel's opinion (*Verses in Sermons*, p. 103), "Jeffrey's view that these English verses in *Fasciculus morum* (a Franciscan handbook for preachers) were sung from the pulpit need not be taken seriously. There is no evidence that the verses in this handbook are composed in song or carol form or were intended for singing."

85. On the important relation of the two vernacular motet texts, *Worldes blisce* and *Regne de pité*, to Franciscans and the devotional literature, see below in the section "Vernacular Texts." However, as I have already pointed out in Lefferts, "Simon de Montfort," p. 213, the scarcity of insular motets setting Middle English in the late thirteenth and early fourteenth centuries can be given a direct explanation: Middle English lyrics and motet composition do not overlap because they represent the creative activity of two distinct spheres, the parish church and the cloister, and were destined by their authors, friars and monks, for very different audiences and occasions.

86. On the popularity and significance of *Dulcis Jhesu Memoria*, see Raby, *Christian-Latin Poetry*, pp. 329–31.

87. See the critical reports on the motets of *CAc 128/2* in appendix 2.

88. See the critical report on *Laus honor vendito* (*Cpc 228, 3*) in appendix 2.

89. The use of hymns as a source of texts is another area of common ground. (The Franciscans showed a keen interest in translating favorite hymns into English.) However, motet texts are in general not as heavily dependent on hymns as are, for example, the carols, many of which incorporate Latin lines or phrases drawn from hymns. On the carol and the hymn, see especially Greene, *The Early English Carols*, 2nd ed., pp. lxxxi, lxxxv–xciv. Concerning the hymn and the motet, see tables 28 and 30 below.

90. The only language other than French or Latin used in the upper parts of thirteenth-century Continental motets is Provençal; see Gennrich, *Bibliographie*, nos. 102, 319, 537; one motet in *Darmstadt 3317* has German in the tenor ("Brumas e mors . . . o weh der not"). For one fourteenth-century isorhythmic motet with Provençal text, . . . *bon milgrana–Mon*

gauch-T. Idem est (*E-GER*, 7), see PMFC V, no. 33 and the discussion in Zaslaw, "Music in Provence," esp. pp. 103–14. For one fourteenth-century motet with Flemish text among the Cambrai fragments, *Saghen dat min corser ic*, see Fallows, "L'origine de MS.1328," p. 280.

91. These lines occur at the end of the text of the duplum of a motet in Old Hall (*Lbl57950*, 146) that was intended as a *Deo gratias* substitute. The French composer referred to may be Mayshuet. See Hughes and Bent, *The Old Hall Manuscript* I, 2, pp. 419–23; Bent, "Transmission," pp. 66–67; Hughes, "Re-Appraisal," pp. 104–5; and Bent, "The Progeny of Old Hall," pp. 6–7.

92. See Rokseth, *Polyphonies* IV, p. 158 and Gennrich, *Bibliographie*, p. 112. See also chapter 1, table 1.

93. See the critical report in appendix 2 of this study and also the edition in PMFC XV of *Herodis in atrio* (*DRc 20*, 1), whose tenor, ("Hey hure lure") is an interesting if controversial example.

94. Musically the tenor of *Veni mater* is employed in a way quite similar to that of the Latin-texted *pes* in an English motet of similar age, *O sancte Bartholomee-O sancte Bartholomee-T. O Bartholomee miseris*, a melodic double versicle whose origin is likewise clearly not Gregorian. These are the sorts of tenor that lead us to believe that the *pes* tenors of the thirteenth-century motet repertoire and some of the *pes*-like tuneful, untexted tenors of the fourteenth-century repertoire are unidentified melodies drawn from popular sources. On *Veni mater* (*Lbl 29*, 1 = *US-PRu 119B*, 1) see Levy, "New Material," p. 225 and Bukofzer, NOHM III, pp. 111–12. It has been edited twice in recent years, in Dobson and Harrison, *Medieval English Songs*, no. 18 and PMFC XVII, no. 52. *O sancte Bartholomee* (*Cjc 138*, 3) is edited in PMFC XIV, no. 45.

95. *Herodis in atrio*, though from a later source (*DRc 20*) and written with minim stems, is similar to *Caligo terre* in many features of style (as noted in chapter 2) and probably was composed at about the same time.

96. See the critical report for *Ade finit* (*Onc 362*, 7) in appendix 2.

97. On *Ccc 8* see RISM B/IV/1, pp. 451–53. On *Worldes blisce*, see Bukofzer, "The First Motet With English Words," and NOHM III, p. 111. The motet has been edited recently by Dobson and Harrison for *Medieval English Songs*, no. 17, and by the present author for PMFC XVII, no. 53.

98. This book is *National Library of Scotland, Advocates' Library, MS 18.7.21*. The excerpt is found on fol. 124. See Wilson, *A Descriptive Index*, no. 200, and the notes to the edition of *Worldes blisce* in PMFC XVII. Grimestone's book is also an early source for vernacular carol texts. See Greene, *Early English Carols*, 2nd ed., p. cliv.

99. See the thirteenth-century motets listed in appendix 3, including *Ave gloriosa mater (Duce creature)*, *Au queer*, and *En averil*, as well as the juxtaposition of English and Anglo-Norman in monophonic collections such as *Lbl Arundel 248*.

100. See the critical report on *Deus compaignouns* (*US-Wc 14*, 4) in appendix 2.

101. See the literature on Rutebeuf and *Regne* cited in the critial report on *Ob 143*, 3 in appendix 2.

102. On Bohun, see Colledge, *Latin Poems*, p. xxxv.

103. Most distinctive in *Ob 143*, besides *Regne de pité*, are two settings in English discant of unusual chants, *Alleluia. Hic est vere martir* and *O benigne redemptor* (PMFC XVI, no. 79 and XVII, no. 3, respectively).

104. The quotation is from Colledge's description (*Latin Poems*, p. 1) of the Latin lyrics of the *Red Book of Ossory*, which are richly annotated for such references in his edition. (See his discussion of them on pp. xliv–lix.) Incidentally, as is discussed by both R.L. Greene and Colledge, eight of the Red Book poems (nos. 48 through 55) are derived from a single longer Latin poem, "De Maria Virgine," known from fourteenth-century English sources. See, for instance, Greene, *The Lyrics*, pp. vi–viii.

105. This term was suggested to me by Prof. Peter Dembowski, University of Chicago, in a discussion of his work on saints' lives.

106. See the critical reports on *Onc 362*, 15 and 17 in appendix 2.

107. See also the multiple settings of "Dona celi factor" in *Lwa 33327*, 5 and *US-Cu*, 3; the settings of "Pro beati Pauli" in *WF*, 40 and *WF*, 70 (= *Lwa 33327*, 4); and the settings of "Conditio nature defuit" in *WF*, 65 and in a continental motet that survives in the Montpellier codex and elsewhere (*F-MO*, 42 = Rok 4.51).

108. The Sarum Breviary is a convenient source for *legenda*, in the matins lessons, but it is uncertain how stable these were, and hence to what degree they reflect a fourteenth-century reading. One has recourse to other versions of these lives in the *Acta sanctorum*, the *Legenda Aurea* of Jacob de Voragine, or the *Nova legenda angliae* edited by Horstmann, for instance, for basic comparative work.

109. Richard Rolle (d. 1349) was a hermit and holy man associated at the end of his life with the Cistercian nunnery of St. Mary at Hampole near Doncastre in Yorkshire. His main literary contribution was to the mystical tradition of devotional prose in the vernacular. The *Canticum amoris*, a 38–stanza poem to the BVM in Latin, is probably a very early work; its incipit ("Zelo tui langueo virgo speciosa") is nearly identical to its explicit ("Zelo tui langueo virgo regia"), which is shared with the motet. See Hope Emily Allen, *Writings Ascribed to Richard Rolle*, pp. 89-93 and Raby, *The Oxford Book of Medieval Latin Verse*, no. 290, pp. 442–48.

110. Assonance has a more technical meaning (i.e., the partial rhyme of stressed vowels only, or the simple repetition of vowel sounds) that is narrower than the sense in which I will be using the term.

111. One could argue for an English origin of (or influence on) the *DRc 20* motet *Virgo sancta-Virginalis concio* on account of the deliberate assonance apparent in the texts. The later thirteenth-century motets of *Lwa 33327* demonstrate the last vestiges of a text relationship not seen in the later repertoire, the incorporation of the tenor text into the last line of duplum and triplum. For instance, the tenor of *Lwa 33327*, 5 (Dona celi) is *Docebit*, and the duplum ends "qui nos prudencie et iusticie vias docebit." The tenor of *Lwa 33327*, 7 (Ave miles) is *Ablue*, and the duplum ends "dona nobis prospera et scelera ablue."

112. In one motet, *Trinitatem-Trinitas-Trinitatis-T. Benedicite*, there is emphatic reiteration of the word Trinity over an appropriate but nonassonant chant for Trinity Sunday.

113. In *Mulier* or *Orto sole* the *pes*-like tenors, if taken from some popular stock of melodies instead of being newly composed, might (like *Floret* or *Babilonis flumina*) actually have some appropriate textual incipit that was intended to be recognized, but which simply was not recorded in any surviving source.

114.   Assonance helped identify the tenors of *Surgere–T.Surge et illuminare* and *Iam–Iam–T.Iam)*, and may help in future with *Suffragiose–Summopere–T.* and *Inter choros–Invictis–T.* Reliance on assonance can help to correct text readings, as in the case of the duplum of *Civitas–Cives–T.Cibus*, which reads "Tu es" in *Onc 362*, or in the duplum of *Orto sole–Origo viri–O virga*, which simply reads "virga" in both sources (see the critical report in appendix 2).

115.   Some fourteenth-century pieces, in particular the later French "realistic" virelais, explore illustrative, especially onomotapoetic effects.

116.   For a list of such schemes, see Dag Norberg, *Introduction*, pp. 216–17. One can speak of a motet of varied versification, as in the refrain motets or *Rota versatilis*, where successive stanzas or pairs of stanzas differ in verse design.

117.   Anderson, "The Motets of La Clayette," p. 6; see pp. 6–7 of his article for a statistical survey. See also Sanders, "Motet," p. 514.

118.   The versification of the fourteenth-century isorhythmic motet has been explored in detail by Clarkson in "On the Nature of Medieval Song," and the relationship of word to music has been examined by a number of writers, most notably by Günther in "Das Wort-Ton-Problem" and by Reichardt in "Das Verhältnis zwischen musikalischer und textlicher Struktur."

119.   The differentiation of the triplum from the duplum by the amount of text and rapidity of declamation was characteristic of the motet from its earliest days and reaffirmed in the stratified motet of the early fourteenth century, though not always expressed with such rigidly worked out logic as in the isorhythmic motet. It is interesting to note, by contrast, that the English isoperiodic motets tend to have equivalent texts. In cases where only a single texted voice of an isorhythmic motet survives, the distinction between text structures makes the identification of a voice as a triplum or duplum staightforward (so, for instance, one can say immediately that *Nec Herodis ferocitas* and *O vos omnes* are duplum parts, or that *Parce piscatoribus* is a triplum).

120.   With a *pp* stress there may be a secondary stress on the final syllable, but the masculine accent is not a critical feature of this sort of Latin verse.

121.   This tendency to break up long verses has not been taken to its limit; for instance, *8p* is frequently made up of *2x4p*, but these smallest constituents have not been noted.

122.   To cite just two, Crocker, "Sequence, (i), 1–9," and Stäblein, "Hymnus B."

123.   Knapp, "Musical Declamation," is mainly concerned with this verse form.

124.   It should be mentioned here that the *7pp7pp6p* "Vagantenzeile" is not particularly common. To the best of my understanding I see no classical meters. Virtuoso exercises in versification (such as in the thirteenth-century English motet *Lwa 33327*, 1) do not make an appearance.

Bibliography

Allen, Hope Emily. *Writings Ascribed to Richard Rolle*. New York: Modern Language Association, 1927.

Analecta Hymnica Medii Aevi. 55 vols. Ed. Guido M. Dreves, Clemens Blume, and Henry M. Bannister. Leipzig, 1886–1922; R 1961.

Analecta Hymnica: Register. 3 vols. Ed. Max Lütolf. Berne and Munich, 1978.

Anderson, Gordon A., ed. *The Las Huelgas Manuscript*. 2 vols. American Institute of Musicology: Corpus Mensurabilis Musicae, 79. 1982.

————. "Magister Lambertus and Nine Rhythmic Modes." *Acta musicologica* 45 (1973), pp. 57–73.

————. "The Motets of the Thirteenth-Century Manuscript La Clayette: A Stylistic Study of the Repertory." *Musica disciplina* 28 (1974), pp. 5–37.

————. "New Sources of Mediaeval Music." *Musicology* vii. Melbourne: The Musicological Society of Australia, 1982, pp. 1–26.

————. "Notre Dame and Related Conductus: A Catalogue Raisonné." *Miscellanea Musicologica (Aus)—Aidelaide Studies in Musicology* 6 (1972), pp. 153–229 and 7 (1975), pp. 1–81.

————. "Responsory Chants in the Tenors of Some Fourteenth-Century Continental Motets." *Journal of the American Musicological Society* 29 (1976), pp. 119–27.

————. Review of *Die Copula*, by Fritz Reckow. *Music and Letters* 54 (1973), pp. 453–57.

Anglés, Higinio. "De cantu organico: tratado de un autor catalán del siglo xiv." *Anuario musical* 13 (Barcelona, 1958), pp.3 –24. Reprinted in *Hygini Anglés. Scripta Musicologica*, 3 vols. Ed. José Lopez-Calo. Rome: Edizioni di Storia e Letteratura, 1975–1976. Vol. III, no. 62, pp. 1321–56.

Apel, Willi, ed. *Keyboard Music of the Fourteenth and Fifteenth Centuries*. American Institute of Musicology: Corpus of Early Keyboard Music, 1. 1963.

————. *The Notation of Polyphonic Music*. 5th ed., rev. Cambridge, Mass.: The Medieval Academy, 1953.

Apfel, Ernst. *Anlage und Struktur der Motetten im Codex Montpellier*. Annales Universitatis Saraviensis; Reihe: Philosophische Fakultät. Heidelberg: Carl Winter, 1970.

————. *Beiträge zu einer Geschichte der Satztechnik von der fruhen Motette bis Bach*. Munich: Eidos Verlag, 1964–1965. See esp. chapter two, "Die Motette im 13. und beginnenden 14. Jahrhundert in England."

————. *Grundlagen einer Geschichte der Satztechnik vom 13. bis zum 16. Jahrhundert*. Grundlagen einer Geschichte der Satztechnik, 1. Saarbrücken: author, 1974.

————. *Studien zur Satztechnik der mittelalterlichen englischen Musik*. 2 vols. Abhandlungen der Heidelberger Akademie der Wissenschaft, Philosophisch-Historische Klasse, Jahrgang 1959, 5. Abhandlung. Heidelberg: Carl Winter, 1959.

_____. "Uber den vierstimmigen Satz im 14. und 15. Jahrhundert." *Archiv für Musikwissenschaft* 18 (1961), pp. 34–51.

_____. "Zur Entstehung des realen vierstimmigen Satzes in England." *Archiv für Musikwissenschaft* 17 (1960), pp. 81–99.

Arlt, Wulf. *Ein Festofficium des Mittelalters aus Beauvais.* Cologne: Volk, 1970.

_____. "The 'Reconstruction' of Instrumental Music: The Interpretation of the Earliest Practical Sources." *Studies in the Performance of Late Mediaeval Music.* Ed. Stanley Boorman. Cambridge, 1983, pp. 75–100.

Bent, Ian. "A New Polyphonic 'Verbum bonum et soave'." *Music and Letters* 51 (1970), pp. 227–41.

Bent, Margaret. *Dunstaple.* London: Oxford University Press, 1980.

_____, ed. *The Fountains Fragments.* Clarabricken, Ireland: Boethius Press, forthcoming.

_____. "A Lost English Choirbook of the Fifteenth Century." *International Musicological Society. Report of the Eleventh Congress, Copenhagen, 1972*, pp. 257–62. Kassel: Barenreiter, 1976.

_____. "Notation, III, 3—Western, c. 1260–1500." *The New Grove Dictionary* (1980), vol. 13, pp. 362–70.

_____. "Old Hall MS." *The New Grove Dictionary* (1980), vol. 13, pp. 526–29.

_____. "A Preliminary Assessment of the Independence of English Trecento Notations." *L'Ars Nova italiana del Trecento IV (1975).* Ed. Agostino Ziino. Certaldo: Centro di studi sull'Ars nova italiana del Trecento, 1978, pp. 65–82.

_____. "The Progeny of Old Hall: More Leaves from a Royal English Choirbook." *Gordon Athol Anderson (1929–1981) In Memoriam.* Ed. Luther Dittmer. Henryville, Pa.: Institute of Medieval Music, 1984, pp. 1–54.

_____. "Rota versatilis: Towards a Reconstruction." *Source Materials and the Interpretation of Music: A Memorial Volume to Thurston Dart.* Ed. Ian Bent. London: Stainer and Bell, 1981, pp. 65–98.

_____. "The Transmission of English Music 1300–1500: Some Aspects of Repertory and Presentation." *Studien zur Tradition in der Musik.* Ed. Hans Eggebrecht and Max Lütolf. Munich: Katzbichler, 1973, pp. 65– 83.

_____, ed. *Two Fourteenth-Century Motets in Praise of Music.* Lustleigh, Devon: Antico Edition, 1977.

_____ and Anne Hallmark, eds. *The Works of Johannes Ciconia.* Polyphonic Music of the Fourteenth Century, 24. Paris and Monaco: Editions de L'Oiseau Lyre, 1985.

Besseler, Heinrich. "Ars Antiqua." *Die Musik in Geschichte und Gegenwart* (1949–1951), vol. 1, cols. 679–97.

_____. *Die Musik des Mittelalters und der Renaissance.* Handbuch der Musikwissenschaft, ii. Potsdam: Bücken, 1931.

_____. "Studien zur Musik des Mittelalters." Part I in *Archiv für Musikwissenschaft* 7 (1925), pp. 167–252 and Part II in 8 (1926), pp. 137–258.

_____ and Peter Gülke. *Schriftbild der mehrstimmigen Musik.* Musikgeschichte in Bildern, III/5. Leipzig: VEB Deutscher Verlag für Musik, 1973.

Bond, Francis. *Dedications and Patron Saints of English Churches.* London: H. Milford, Oxford University Press, 1914.

Boogaard, Nico H.J. van den, ed. *Rondeaux et refrains du iixe siècle au début du xive.* Paris: Klincksieck, 1969.

Bowers, Roger D. "Choral Institutions Within the English Church: Their Constitution and Development, 1340–1500." Diss. University of East Anglia, 1975.

_____. "The Performing Ensemble for English Church Polyphony, c. 1320–c. 1390." *Studies in the Performance of Late Mediaeval Music.* Ed. Stanley Boorman. Cambridge: Cambridge University Press, 1983, pp. 161–92.

_____. "The Performing Pitch of English 15th-Century Church Polyphony." *Early Music* 8 (1980), pp. 21–28.

_____ and Andrew Wathey. "New Sources of English Fourteenth- and Fifteenth-Century Polyphony." *Early Music History* 3 (1983), pp. 149–53.

Bragard, Roger. *Speculum Musicae Jacobi Leodensis.* 7 vols. American Institute of Musicology: Corpus Scriptorum Musicae, 3. 1961–1973.

Brewer, Charles. "A Fourteenth-Century Polyphonic Manuscript Rediscovered." *Studia Musicologica Academiae Scientiarum Hungaricae* 24 (1982), pp. 5–19.

Brown, Carleton. *A Register of Middle English Religious and Didactic Verse.* Oxford: Bibliographical Society, 1916.

_____ and R.H. Robbins. *The Index of Middle English Verse.* New York: Columbia University Press, 1943. *Supplement* by R.H. Robbins and J.L. Cutler. Lexington: University of Kentucky Press, 1965.

Bukofzer, Manfred. "The First Motet with English Words." *Music and Letters* 17 (1936), pp. 225–33.

_____, ed. *John Dunstable Complete Works.* 2nd rev. ed. prepared by Margaret Bent, Ian Bent, and Brian Trowell. Musica Britannica, 8. London: Stainer and Bell, 1970.

_____. *Music in the Baroque Era.* New York: Norton, 1947.

_____. "Popular and Secular Music in England." *New Oxford History of Music,* III. Ed. Dom Anselm Hughes and Gerald Abraham. London: Oxford University Press, 1960, pp. 107–33.

_____. *Studies in Medieval and Renaissance Music.* New York: Norton, 1950.

_____. "'Sumer is icumen in'; a revision." *University of California Publications in Music* II, 2. Berkeley, CA.: University of California Press, 1944, pp. 79–114.

Butler's Lives of the Saints. Rev. and ed. Herbert Thurston and Donald Attwater. 4 vols. New York: Kenedy, 1956.

Caldwell, John. "Letter to the Editor." *Music and Letters* 63 (1982), pp. 384–85.

_____. "Review of *Motets of English Provenance: Polyphonic Music of the Fourteenth Century, XV,*" ed. Frank Ll. Harrison. *Music and Letters* 62 (1981), pp. 466–70.

Carapetyan, Armen. "A Fourteenth-Century Florentine Treatise in the Vernacular." *Musica disciplina* 4 (1950), pp. 81–92.

_____, ed. *Notitia del valore delle note del canto misurato.* American Institute of Musicology: Corpus Scriptorum Musicae, 5. 1957.

Chevalier, Cyr Ulysse. *Repertorium Hymnologicum.* 6 vols. Louvain and Brussels: Lefever, et al., 1892–1921.

Clarkson, George Austin Elliott. "On the Nature of Medieval Song: The Declamation of Plainchant and the Lyric Structure of the Fourteenth-Century Motet." Diss. Columbia University, 1970.

Colledge, Edmund. *The Latin Poems of Richard Ledrede, O.F.M..* Toronto: Pontifical Institute, 1974.

Cooper, Barry. "A Thirteenth-Century Canon Reconstructed." *The Music Review* 42 (1980), pp. 85–90.

Coussemaker, Edmund de. *Scriptorum de Musica Medii Aevi.* 4 vols. Paris, 1864–1976; R 1963.

Creighton, Mandell. *A History of the Papacy from the Great Schism to the Sack of Rome.* 6 vols. London: Longmans, Green, and Co., 1887–94.

Crocker, Richard. "Sequence (i), 1–9." *The New Grove Dictionary* (1980), vol. 17, pp. 141–51.

Cummings, Anthony M. "Toward an Interpretation of the Sixteenth- Century Motet." *Journal of the American Musicological Society* 34 (1981), pp. 43–59.

Dahnk, Emilie. *L'Hérésie de Fauvel.* Leipziger Romanistische Studien. II. Literaturwissenschaftliche reihe. No. 4. Leipzig: Selbstverlag des Romanischen seminars, 1935.

358   Bibliography

Dalglish, William E. "The Hocket in Medieval Polypony." *Musical Quarterly* 55 (1969), pp. 344–63.

_____. "The Use of Variation in Early Polyphony." *Musica disciplina* 26 (1972), pp. 37–51.

Davey, Henry. *History of English Music.* London: J. Curwen and Sons, 1895.

Dickinson, Francis W., ed. *Missale Sarum.* Oxford and London: J. Parker and Soc., 1861–1883; R 1969.

Diehl, Patrick S. *The Medieval European Religious Lyric. An Ars Poetica.* Los Angeles: University of California Press, 1985.

Dittmer, Luther. "Beiträge zum Studium der Worcester-Fragmente." *Die Musikforschung* 10 (1957), pp. 29–39.

_____. "The Dating and the Notation of the Worcester Fragments." *Musica disciplina* 11 (1957), pp. 5–11.

_____, ed. *Oxford, Latin Liturgical D 20; London, Add. MS. 25031; Chicago, MS. 654 App.* Institute of Medieval Music: Publications of Medieval Musical Manuscripts, 6. Brooklyn, 1960.

_____, trans. and ed. *Robert de Handlo.* Institute of Medieval Music: Music Theorists in Translation, 2. Brooklyn, 1959.

_____, ed. *Worcester Add. 68; Westminster Abbey 33327; Madrid, Bibl. Nac. 192.* Institute of Medieval Music: Publications of Medieval Musical Manuscripts, 5. Brooklyn, 1959.

_____, ed. *The Worcester Fragments.* American Institute of Musicology: Musicological Studies and Documents, 2. 1957.

Dobson, Eric J. and Frank Ll. Harrison. *Medieval English Songs.* London: Faber, 1979.

Dronke, Peter. *Medieval Latin and the Rise of the European Love Lyric.* 2 vols. 2nd ed. Oxford: Clarendon Press, 1968.

Droz, E. and G. Thibaut. "Un Chansonnier de Philippe le Bon." *Revue de musicologie* 7 (1926), pp. 1–8.

Eggebrecht, Hans. "Rondellus/rondeau, rota." *Handwörterbuch der musikalischen Terminologie.* Wiesbaden: Steiner, 1972.

Expériences Anonymes EA 0024. "English Polyphony of the XIIIth and Early XIVth Centuries." *Music of the Middle Ages,* disc 4. 1957.

Falck, Robert. *The Notre Dame Conductus: a Study of the Repertory.* Henryville, Pa.: Institute of Medieval Music, 1981.

_____. "Rondellus, Canon, and Related Types before 1300." *Journal of the American Musicological Society* 25 (1972), pp. 38–57.

Fallows, David. "L'origine du MS.1328 de Cambrai." *Revue de musicologie* 62 (1976), pp. 275–80.

Faral, Edmond and Julia Bastin. *Oeuvres Complètes de Rutebeuf.* 2 vols. Paris: Picard, 1959–1960.

Fenlon, Iain, ed. *Cambridge Music Manuscripts, 900–1700.* Cambridge: Cambridge University Press, 1982.

Ficker, Rudolph von, ed. *Sieben Trienter Codices: geistliche und weltliche Motetten.* Denkmäler der Tonkunst in Österreich, Jahrgang XL, 76 (Trienter Codices, VI). Vienna: Universal-Edition, 1933; R 1960.

Fischer, Kurt von, and Max Lütolf, eds. *Handschriften mit mehrstimmiger Musik des 14., 15., und 16. Jahrhunderts.* 2 vols. RISM B/IV/3–4. Munich and Duisberg: Henle, 1972.

Fisher, John H. "English Literature." *The Present State of Scholarship in Fourteenth Century Literature.* Ed. Thomas D. Cooke. Columbia, Mo.: University of Missouri Press, 1982, pp. 1–54.

Flotzinger, Rudolph. *Der Discantussatz im Magnus Liber und seiner Nachfolge.* Wiener Musikwissenschaftliche Beiträge, 8. Vienna: Bohlaus, 1969.

Floyer, J.K. and S.G. Hamilton. *Catalogue of Manuscripts Preserved in the Chapter Library of Worcester Cathedral.* Oxford: J. Parker and Co., 1906.

Frere, Walter H., ed. *Antiphonale Sarisburiense.* London: Plainsong and Medieval Music Society, 1901–1924/25; R 1966.

———, ed. *Graduale Sarisburiense.* London: Plainsong and Medieval Music Society, 1891–1894; R 1966.

———, ed. *The Use of Sarum.* 2 vols. Cambridge: Cambridge University Press, 1898–1901; R 1969.

Frobenius, Wolf. "Zur Datierung von Francos *Ars cantus mensurabilis.*" *Archiv für Musikwissenschaft* 27 (1970), pp. 122–27.

Fuller, Sarah Ann. "Aquitanian Polyphony of the Eleventh and Twelfth Centuries." 3 vols. Diss. University of California at Berkeley, 1969.

Gallo, F. Alberto. *La teoria della notazione in Italia dalla fine del XIII all'inizio del XV secolo.* Bologna: Tamari Editori, 1966.

Gaselee, Stephen. *The Oxford Book of Medieval Latin Verse.* Oxford: Clarendon Press, 1928.

Gennrich, Friedrich. *Abriss der Mensuralnotation des XIV. und der ersten Hälfte des XV. Jahrhunderts.* 2nd ed. Langen-bei-Frankfurt, 1965.

———. *Bibliographie der ältesten französischen und lateinischen Motetten.* Summa Musicae Medii Aevi, 2. Darmstadt, 1957.

———. *Die Kontrafaktur im Liedschaffen des Mittelalters.* Summa Musicae Medii Aevi Band XII, Fundamenta II. Langen-bei-Frankfurt, 1965.

Gilles, André and Gilbert Reaney, ed. *Torkesey, Johannes: Declaratio Trianguli et Scuti.* American Institute of Musicology: Corpus Scriptorum Musicae, 12. 1966.

Gneuss, Helmut. "Latin Hymns in Medieval England: Future Research." *Chaucer and Middle English Studies.* Ed. Beryl Rowland. London: George Allen and Unwin, 1974, pp. 407–24.

Göllner, Theodor. *Die mehrstimmigen liturgischen Lesungen.* 2 vols. Tutzing: Schneider, 1969.

Greene, Richard L., ed. *The Early English Carols.* 2nd ed., rev. and enlarged. Oxford: Clarendon Press, 1977.

———, ed. *The Lyrics of the Red Book of Ossory.* Oxford: Blackwell, 1974.

Günther, Ursula. "The 14th-Century Motet and its Development." *Musica disciplina* 12 (1958), pp. 29–58.

———, ed. *The Motets of the Manuscripts Chantilly and Modena.* American Institute of Musicology: Corpus Mensurabilis Musicae, 39. 1965.

———. "Problems of Dating in Ars Nova and Ars Subtilior." *L'Ars Nova italiana del Trecento IV (1975).* Ed. Agostino Ziino. Certaldo: Centro di studi sull'Ars nova italiana del Trecento, 1978, pp. 289–301.

———. "Sources, MS, VII, 3: French Polyphony, 1300–1420, Principal Individual Sources." *The New Grove Dictionary* (1980), vol. 17, p. 661–65.

———. "Das Wort-Ton Problem bei Motetten des späten 14. Jahrhunderts." *Festschrift Heinrich Besseler.* Leipzig, 1961, pp. 163–78.

Hamm, Charles and Ann Besser Scott. "A Study and Inventory of the Manuscript Modena Biblioteca Estense, α.X.1.11 (ModB)." *Musica disciplina* 26 (1972), pp. 103–43.

Hammond, Frederick, ed. *Walter Odington. Summa de speculatione musicae.* American Institute of Musicology: Corpus Scriptorum Musicae, 14. 1970.

Handschin, Jacques. "The Sumer Canon and Its Background." Part I in *Musica disciplina* 3 (1949), pp. 55–94 and Part II in 5 (1951), pp. 65–113.

Handwörterbuch der musikalischen Terminologie. Ed. Hans Eggebrecht. Wiesbaden: Steiner, 1972–.

Harrison, Frank Ll. "Ars Nova in England: A New Source." *Musica disciplina* 21 (1967), pp. 67–85.

———. "Benedicamus, Conductus, Carol: A Newly-Discovered Source." *Acta musicologica* 37 (1965), pp. 35–48.

_____. Contribution to "Symposium: Das Organum vor und ausserhalb der Notre-Dame-Schule." *International Musicological Society. Report of the Ninth Congress, Salzburg, 1964.* Kassel: Barenreiter, 1964, pp. 68–80.

_____. "English Church Music in the Fourteenth Century." *New Oxford History of Music*, vol. III. Ed. Dom Anselm Hughes and Gerald Abraham. London: Oxford University Press, 1960, pp. 82–106.

_____. *Motets of English Provenance.* Polyphonic Music of the Fourteenth Century, 15. Paris and Monaco: Editions de L'Oiseau Lyre, 1980.

_____, ed. *Motets of French Provenance.* Polyphonic Music of the Fourteenth Century, 5. Paris and Monaco: Editions de L'Oiseau Lyre, 1968.

_____. *Music in Medieval Britain.* 2nd ed. London, 1963; R 1980.

_____. "Rota and Rondellus in English Medieval Music." *Proceedings of the Royal Musical Association* 86 (1959/60), pp. 98–107.

_____, Ernest H. Sanders, and Peter M. Lefferts, eds. *English Music for Mass and Offices.* Polyphonic Music of the Fourteenth Century, 16 and 17. Paris and Monaco: Editions de L'Oiseau Lyre, 1983–1985.

_____ and Roger Wibberley, eds. *Manuscripts of Fourteenth-Century English Polyphony: A Selection of Facsimiles.* Early English Church Music, 26. London: British Academy, 1981.

Henderson, W.G., ed. *Missale Herefordense.* Leeds: McCorquodale and Co., 1874; R 1969.

Hesbert, Dom René-Jean, ed. *Le Tropaire-Prosaire de Dublin: Cambridge University Library MS. Add. 710.* Monumenta Musicae Sacrae, 4. Rouen: Imprimerie Rouennaise, 1966 (1970).

Hohler, Christopher. "Reflections on Some Manuscripts Containing 13th-Century Polyphony." *Journal of the Plainsong and Medieval Music Society* 1 (1978), pp. 2–38.

Holschneider, Andreas. *Die Organa von Winchester.* Hildesheim: Olms, 1968.

Hoppin, Richard. *Medieval Music.* New York: Norton, 1978.

Horstmann, Carl. *Nova legenda Angliae.* Oxford: The Clarendon Press, 1901.

Huff, Jay A. *Walter Odington (born ca. 1278). A Translation of Part VI of De Speculatione Musicae.* American Institute of Musicology: Musicological Studies and Documents, 31.

Hughes, Andrew. "English Sacred Music (Excluding Carols) in Insular Sources, 1400–c. 1450." 3 vols. Diss. Oxford University, 1963.

_____. "Hanboys, John." *The New Grove Dictionary* (1980), vol. 8, p. 80.

_____. "The Old Hall Manuscript: A Re-Appraisal." *Musica disciplina* 21 (1967), pp. 97–129.

_____. "New Italian and English Sources of the Fourteenth to Sixteenth Centuries." *Acta musicologica* 39 (1967), pp. 171–82.

_____ and Margaret Bent. *The Old Hall Manuscript.* 3 vols in 4. American Institute of Musicology: Corpus Mensurabilis Musicae, 46. 1969–1973.

_____ and Margaret Bent. "The Old Hall Manuscript: An Inventory." *Musica disciplina* 21 (1967), pp. 130–147.

Hughes, Dom Anselm. *Early Medieval Music Up to 1300.* History of Music in Sound, 2 (booklet for record in series of same name). New York: Oxford University Press, 1953.

_____. "The Motet and Allied Forms." *New Oxford History of Music*, vol. II. Ed. idem. London: Oxford University Press, 1954, pp. 353–404.

_____, ed. *Worcester Medieval Harmony of the Thirteenth and Fourteenth Centuries.* Burnham: Plainsong and Medieval Music Society, 1928; R 1971.

James, Montague Rhodes. *A Descriptive Catalogue of the Manuscripts in the Library of St. John's College, Cambridge.* Cambridge: Cambridge University Press, 1913.

Jeffrey, David L. *The Early English Lyric and Franciscan Spirituality.* Lincoln, Nebr.: University of Nebraska Press, 1975.

Ker, Neil R. *Medieval Libraries of Great Britain: A List of Surviving Books.* Royal Historical Society Guides and Handbooks, 3. 2nd ed. London, 1964.

Knapp, Janet. "Musical Declamation and Poetic Rhythm in an Early Layer of Notre Dame Conductus. *Journal of the American Musicological Society* 32 (1979), pp. 383–407.

Knowles, David and R.N. Hadcock. *Medieval Religious Houses: England and Wales*. 2nd ed. New York: St. Martin's Press, 1972.

Korhammer, P.M. "The Origin of the Bosworth Psalter." *Anglo-Saxon England* 2 (1973), pp. 173–87.

Långfors, Artur I.E. *Les incipit des poèmes français antérieurs au xvi⁰ siècle*. Paris: E. Champion, 1917.

Leech-Wilkinson, Daniel. "Compositional Procedure in the Four-Part Isorhythmic Works of Philippe de Vitry and His Contemporaries." Diss. Cambridge University, 1982.

Lefferts, Peter M. "The Motet in England in the Fourteenth Century." *Current Musicology* 28 (1979), pp. 55–75.

————. "The Motet in England in the Fourteenth Century." Diss. Columbia University, 1983.

————. "Text and Context in the Fourteenth-Century English Motet." *L'Ars nova italiana del Trecento VI (1984)*. Ed. Giulio Cattin. Certaldo: Centro di studi sull'Ars nova italiana del Trecento. Forthcoming.

————. "Two English Motets on Simon de Montfort." *Early Music History* 1 (1981), pp. 203–25.

———— and Margaret Bent. "New Sources of English Thirteenth- and Fourteenth-Century Polyphony." *Early Music History* 2 (1982), pp. 273–362.

Levy, Kenneth Jay. "A Dominican Organum Duplum." *Journal of the American Musicological Society* 27 (1974), pp. 183–211.

————. "New Material on the Early Motet in England: A Report on Princeton Garrett 119." *Journal of the American Musicological Society* 4 (1951), pp. 220–39.

Liber Usualis. Paris: Desclée, 1952.

Linker, Robert White. *A Bibliography of Old French Lyrics*. Romance Monographs, 31. University, Miss.: Romance Monographs, 1979.

Ludwig, Friedrich. "Die Quellen der Motetten ältesten Stils." *Archiv für Musikwissenschaft* 5 (1923), pp. 185–222, 273–315.

————. *Repertorium organorum recentioris et motetorum vetutissimi stili*. Vol. I: Catalogue Raisonné der Quellen. Part I: Handschriften in Quadrat-Notation. 2nd ed. Institute of Medieval Music: Musicological Studies, 7. 1964. Part II: Handschriften in Mensural-Notation. Institute of Medieval Music: Musicological Studies, 26. 1978.

————. Review of *Geschichte der Mensural-Notation von 1250–1460*, by Johannes Wolf. *Sammelbände der International Musik Gesellschaft* 6 (1904–1905), pp. 597–641.

McPeek, Gwynn S. *The British Museum Manuscript Egerton 3307*. London: Oxford University Press, 1963.

Maniates, Maria Rika. "Combinative Techniques in Franco-Flemish Polyphony: A Study of Mannerism in Music from 1450 to 1530." Diss. Columbia University, 1975.

Marrocco, Thomas and Nicholas Sandon, eds. *Medieval Music*. The Oxford Anthology of Music, 1. London: Oxford University Press, 1977.

Messenger, Ruth Ellis. "Hymns and Sequences of the Sarum Use." *Transactions and Proceedings of the American Philological Society* 59 (1928), pp. 99–129.

Michels, Ulrich, ed. *Johannis de Muris: Notitia artis musicae et compendium musicae practicae. Petrus de sancto Dionysio: Tractatus de Musica*. American Institute of Musicology: Corpus Scriptorum de Musica, 17. 1972.

Mocquereau, Dom André, ed. *L'Antiphonaire Monastique de Worcester. Codex F.160 de la Bibliothèque de la Cathédrale de Worcester*. Paléographie Musicale, 12. Tournay: Desclée, 1922.

Mone, Franz Joseph, ed. *Lateinische Hymnen des Mittelalters*. 3 vols. Freiburg-im-Breisgau: Herder, 1853–1855; R 1964.

Mustanoja, Tauno F. "Les neuf joies Nostre dame, a Poem Attributed to Rutebeuf." *Suomalainen tiedakatemia. Toimituksia. Annales Academie Scientiarum Fennicae.* Ser. B, vol. 73, no. 4, pp. 1–90. Helsinki, 1952.

The New Grove Dictionary of Music and Musicians. 20 vols. Ed. Stanley Sadie. New York: MacMillan, 1980.

The New Oxford History of Music. 11 vols. Ed. Egon Wellesz, Anselm Hughes, et al. London: Oxford University Press, 1954–.

Nichols, Fred J. "Latin Literature." *The Present State of Scholarship in Fourteenth-Century Literature.* Ed. Thomas D. Cooke. Columbia, Mo.: University of Missouri Press, 1982, pp. 195–257.

Norberg, Dag L. *Introduction à l'étude de la versification latine médiévale.* Stockholm: Almquist and Wiksell, 1958.

Page, Christopher. "Angelus ad virginem: A New Work by Philippe the Chancellor?" *Early Music* 11 (1983), pp. 69–70.

Parrish, Carl. *The Notation of Medieval Music.* New York: Norton, 1957; R 1978.

Pastor, Ludwig. *The History of the Popes from the Close of the Middle Ages.* 40 vols. Trans. Frederick Antrobus et al. London: K. Paul, Trench, Trübner and Co., 1891–1953.

Planchart, Alejandro. "The Ars Nova and Renaissance." *The Schirmer History of Music.* Ed. Leonie Rosensteil. New York: Schirmer, 1982, pp. 19–295.

Polyphonic Music of the Fourteenth Century. Ed. Leo Schrade, Frank Ll. Harrison, and Kurt von Fischer. Paris and Monaco: Editions de L'Oiseau Lyre, 1956– .

Porter, Lambert C. *La Fatrasie et le Fatras: Essai sur la poésie irrationelle en France au Moyen Age.* Paris: Minard, 1960.

Procter, Francis and Charles Wordsworth, eds. *Breviarium ad usum Insignis Ecclesie Sarum.* 3 vols. Cambridge: Cambridge University Press, 1879–1886; R 1970.

Raby, F.J.E. *A History of Christian-Latin Poetry from the Beginnings to the Close of the Middle Ages.* 2nd ed. Oxford: Clarendon Press, 1953.

––––––. *The Oxford Book of Medieval Latin Verse.* Oxford: Clarendon Press, 1959.

Reaney, Gilbert, ed. *Manuscripts of Polyphonic Music: Eleventh–Early Fourteenth Century.* RISM B/IV/1. Munich and Duisberg: Henle, 1966.

––––––, ed. *Manuscripts of Polyphonic Music (c. 1320–1400).* RISM B/IV/2. Munich and Duisberg: Henle, 1969.

––––––. "The Question of Authorship in the Medieval Treatises on Music." *Musica disciplina* 18 (1964), pp. 7–17.

––––––and André Gilles, eds. *Ars Cantus Mensurabilis Franconis de Colonia.* American Institute of Musicology: Corpus Scriptorum Musicae, 18. 1974.

––––––, André Gilles, and Jean Maillard, eds. *Ars Nova Philippi de Vitriaco.* American Institute of Musicology: Corpus Scriptorum Musicae, 8. 1964.

Reckow, Fritz. *Der Musiktraktat des Anonymous IV.* 2 vols. Beihefte zum Archiv für Musikwissenschaft, 4–5. Wiesbaden: Steiner, 1967.

––––––. "Proprietas und perfectio." *Acta musicologica* 39 (1967), pp. 115–43.

Reese, Gustave. *Fourscore Classics of Music Literature.* New York: Liberal Arts Press, 1957; R 1970.

––––––. *Music in the Middle Ages.* New York: Norton, 1940.

Reichert, Georg. "Das Verhältnis zwischen musikalischer und textlicher Struktur in den Motetten Machauts." *Archiv für Musikwissenschaft* 13 (1956), pp. 197–216.

Répertoire international des sources musicales. Series B/IV: Manuscripts of Polyphonic Music. Ed. Gilbert Reaney et al. Munich and Duisberg, 1966–.

Rigg, A.G, ed. *Editing Medieval Texts: English, French, and Latin Written in England.* New York: Garland Press, 1977.

_____. Review of *The Lyrics of the Red Book of Ossory*, by Richard L. Greene; *The Latin Poems of Richard Ledrede*, by Edmund Colledge; and *The Latin Hymns of Richard Ledrede*, by Th. Stemmler. *Medium Aevum* 46 (1977), pp. 269–78.

Robbins, Rossell Hope. "The Authors of the Middle English Religious Lyrics." *Journal of English and Germanic Philology* 39 (1940), pp. 230–38.

Robertson, Anne Walters. "The Reconstruction of the Abbey Church of St.-Denis (1231–81): The Interplay of Music and Ceremony with Architecture and Politics." *Early Music History* 5 (1985), pp. 187–238.

Rokseth, Yvonne. *Polyphonies du xiiiᵉ siècle*. 4 vols. Paris: Editions de L'Oiseau Lyre, 1935–1939.

Ruini, C., ed. *Practica Artis Musice Ameri*. American Institute of Musicology: Corpus Scriptorum Musicae, 25. 1977.

Sanders, Ernest. "Cantilena and Discant in 14th-Century England." *Musica disciplina* 19 (1965), pp. 7–52.

_____. "Communication to the Editor." *Journal of the American Musicological Society* 31 (1978), pp. 168–73.

_____. "Duple Rhythm and Alternate Third Mode in the 13th Century." *Journal of the American Musicological Society* 15 (1962), pp. 249–91.

_____. "The Early Motets of Philippe de Vitry." *Journal of the American Musicological Society* 28 (1975), pp. 24–45.

_____. "England: From the Beginnings to c. 1540." *Music from the Middle Ages to the Renaissance*. Ed. F.W. Sternfeld. New York: Praeger, 1973, pp. 255–313.

_____, ed. *English Music of the Thirteenth and Early Fourteenth Centuries*. Polyphonic Music of the Fourteenth Century, 14. Paris and Monaco: Editions de L'Oiseau Lyre, 1979.

_____. "Medieval English Polyphony and its Significance for the Continent." Diss. Columbia University, 1963.

_____. "The Medieval Motet." *Gattungen der Musik: Gedenkschrift Leo Schrade*. Vol. I. Ed. Wulf Arlt et al. Berne and Munich, 1973, pp. 497–573.

_____. "Peripheral Polyphony of the 13th Century." *Journal of the American Musicological Society* 17 (1964), pp. 261–87.

_____. "Petrus de Cruce." *The New Grove Dictionary* (1980), vol. 14, pp. 598–99.

_____. "Petrus le Viser." *The New Grove Dictionary* (1980), vol. 14, pp. 600–601.

_____. "Die Rolle der englischen Mehrstimmigkeit des Mittelalters in der Entwicklung von Cantus-Firmus-Satz und Tonalitätsstruktur." *Archiv für Musikwissenschaft* 24 (1967), pp. 24–53.

_____. "Sources, MS, V: Early Motet" and "Sources, MS, VI: English Polyphony 1270–1400." *The New Grove Dictionary* (1980), vol. 17, pp. 655–61.

_____. "Tonal Aspects of Thirteenth-Century English Polyphony." *Acta musicologica* 37 (1965), pp. 19–34.

_____. "Vitry, Philippe de." *The New Grove Dictionary* (1980), vol. 20, pp. 22–28.

_____. "Wycombe, W. de." *The New Grove Dictionary* (1980), vol. 20, pp. 552–53.

Sandon, Nicholas. "Fragments of Medieval Polyphony at Canterbury Cathedal." *Musica disciplina* 30 (1976), pp. 37–54.

_____. "Mary, Meditations, Monks and Music: Poetry, Prose, Processions and Plagues in a Durham Cathedral Manuscript." *Early Music* 10 (1982), pp. 43–55.

Schofield, Bertram. "The Provenance and Date of 'Sumer is Icumen in.'" *The Music Review* 9 (1948), pp. 81–86.

Schrade, Leo, ed. *The Works of Philippe de Vitry, etc.* Polyphonic Music of the Fourteenth Century, 1. Paris and Monaco: Editions de L'Oiseau Lyre, 1956.

Simson, Otto von. *The Gothic Cathedral*. 2nd rev. ed. Bollingen Series, 48. Princeton: Princeton University Press, 1962.

Smet, J. "Carmelites." *New Catholic Encyclopedia* (1967), vol. 3, pp. 118–21.

Smith, Norman. "The Clausula of the Notre Dame School: A Repertorial Study." Diss. Yale University, 1964.

Sowa, Heinrich, ed. *Ein anonymer glossierter Mensuraltraktat 1279.* Königsberger Studien zur Musikwissenschaft, 9. Kassel, 1930.

Spanke, Hans G. *Raynauds Bibliographie des altfranzösische Lieds, neu bearbeitet und erganzt.* Leiden: E.J. Brill, 1955.

Spitzmüller, Henry. *Poésie latine chrétienne du moyen age, iiiᵉ–xvᵉ siècle.* Bruges: Desclée, 1971.

Stäblein, Bruno. "Hymnus, B. Der lateinische Hymnus." *Die Musik in Geschichte und Gegenwart* (1957), vol. 6, cols. 993–1018.

Stäblein-Harder, Hanna. *Fourteenth-Century Mass Music in France.* American Institute of Musicology: Corpus Mensurabilis Musicae, 29 and Musicological Studies and Documents, 7. 1962.

Stainer, J.F.R., C. Stainer, and John Stainer, eds. *Early Bodleian Music.* 2 vols. London: Novello, 1901; R 1967.

Staring, A. "Simon Stock." *New Catholic Encyclopedia* (1967), vol. 13, pp. 224–25.

Steiner, Ruth. "Mass I, 5: Two Medieval Masses; Later Developments." *The New Grove Dictionary* (1980), vol. 11, pp. 776–81.

Stemmler, Theo. *The Latin Hymns of Richard Ledrede.* Mannheim: University of Mannheim, Department of English, 1975.

Stenzl, Jürg. *Die vierzig Clausulae der Handschrift Paris, Bibliothèque nationale, Latin 15139 (St. Victor).* Bern: Paul Haupt, 1970.

Stevens, Denis. "Music in Honor of St. Thomas of Canterbury." *Musical Quarterly* 56 (1970), pp. 311–48.

――――, ed. *Music in Honour of St. Thomas of Canterbury.* London: Novello, 1970.

――――, dir. *Music in Honor of St. Thomas of Canterbury.* Nonesuch H-71292.

――――, ed. *The Treasury of English Church Music Vol. I: 1100– 1545.* London: Blandford Press, 1965.

――――, dir. *The Treasury of English Church Music Vol. I.* HMV CSD 3504.

――――, ed. *The Worcester Fragments.* London: Basil Ramsey, 1981.

――――. "The Worcester Fragments." *Musical Times* 116 (1975), pp. 784–85.

――――, dir. *The Worcester Fragments.* Nonesuch H-71308.

Stevens, John, chairman. *Early Tudor Songs and Carols.* Musica Britannica, 36. London: Stainer and Bell, 1975.

――――. " 'La Grande Chanson Courtoise:' The Chansons of Adam de la Halle." *Proceedings of the Royal Music Association* 101 (1974–1975), pp. 11–30.

――――. *Mediaeval Carols.* 2nd ed. Musica Britannica, 4. London: Stainer and Bell, 1958.

――――. "Round-Table: The English Carol." *International Musicological Society. Report of the Tenth Congress, Ljubljana 1967.* Kassel: Bärenreiter, 1970, pp. 284–309.

Strecker, Karl. *Die Lieder Walters von Chatillon in der Handschrift 351 von St. Omer.* Die Gedichte Walters von Chatillon, 1. Berlin: Weidmann, 1925.

Strunk, Oliver. *Source Readings in Music History.* New York: Norton, 1950.

Summers, William. *English Fourteenth-Century Polyphony: Facsimile Edition of Sources Notated in Score.* Münchner Editionen zur Musikgeschichte, 4. Tutzing: Schneider, 1983.

Szövérffy, Joseph. *Die Annalen der lateinischen Hymnendichtungen.* 2 vols. Berlin: E. Schmidt, 1964–1965.

Tischler, Hans. "Classicism and Romanticism in 13th-Century Music." *Revue Belge de musicologie* 16 (1962), pp. 3–12.

――――. "Intellectual Trends in 13th-Century Paris as Reflected in the Texts of Motets." *The Music Review* 29 (1968), pp. 1–11.

――――. "Latin Texts in the Early Motet Collections: Relationships and Perspectives." *Musica disciplina* 31 (1977), pp. 31–44.

_____, ed. *The Montpellier Codex*. Recent Researches in the Music of the Middle Ages and Early Renaissance. Vols 2–7. Madison, Wis.: A-R Editions, 1978.

Tomasello, Andrew. *Music and Ritual at Papal Avignon 1309–1403*. Studies in Musicology, no. 75. Ann Arbor, Mich: UMI Research Press, 1983.

Trowell, Brian. "Faburden—New Sources, New Evidence: A Preliminary Survey." *Modern Musical Scholarship*. Ed. Edward Olleson. London: Oriel Press, 1978 (1980), pp. 28–78.

_____. "A Fourteenth-Century Ceremonial Motet and its Composer." *Acta musicologica* 29 (1957), pp. 65–75.

Van der Werf, Hendrik. Review of *The Montpellier Codex*, ed. Hans Tischler. *Speculum* 56 (1981), pp. 200–205.

Walther, Hans. *Initia Carminum ac Versuum Medii Aevi Posterioris Latinorum*. 2nd ed. Göttingen: Vandenhoeck und Ruprecht, 1969.

Wenzel, Siegfried. "The English Verses in the *Fasciculus Morum*." *Chaucer and Middle English Studies*, ed. Beryl Rowland. London, 1974, pp. 230–48.

_____. *Verses in Sermons*. Cambridge, Mass.: The Medieval Academy of America, 1978.

Wibberley, Roger. "English Polyphonic Music of the Late Thirteenth and Early Fourteenth Centuries: A Reconstruction, Transcription, and Commentary." Diss. Oxford University, 1976.

_____. "Introduction: Notation in the Thirteenth and Fourteenth Centuries." *Early English Church Music*, 26, 1981, pp.xix–xxviii.

Wilson, Edward. *A Descriptive Index of the English Lyrics in John of Grimestone's Preaching Book*. Medium Aevum Monographs, New Series, II. Oxford: Blackwell, 1973.

_____. Review of *The Early English Lyric and Franciscan Spirituality*, by David L. Jeffrey. *The Review of English Studies*, N.s. 28 (1977), pp. 318–21.

Wolf, Johannes. "Early English Music Theorists from 1200 to the Death of Henry Purcell." *Musical Quarterly* 25 (1939), pp. 420–29.

_____. *Geschichte der Mensural-Notation von 1250–1460*. 3 vols. Leipzig, 1904; R 1965.

_____. *Handbuch der Notationskunde*. 2 vols. Leipzig, 1913–1919; R 1963.

_____. *Musikalische Schrifttafeln*. Leipzig, 1927.

Wooldridge, H.E. and H.V. Hughes, eds. *Early English Harmony from the 11th to the 15th Century*. 2 vols. London, 1897–1913; R 1976.

Wormald, Francis. *English Benedictine Kalendars after A.D. 1100*. 2 vols. Henry Bradshaw Society, 77 (1939) and 81 (1946).

Wright, Craig. *Music at the Court of Burgundy, 1364–1419: A Documentary History*. Henryville, Pa.: Institute of Medieval Music, 1979.

Wulstan, David, ed. *Three Medieval Conductus for Christmas*. Oxford: Oxenford Imprint, forthcoming.

Zaslaw, Neal. "Music in Provence in the 14th Century." *Current Musicology* 25 (1978), pp. 99–120.

Zwick, G. "Deux motets inédits de Philippe de Vitry et de Guillaume de Machaut." *Revue de musicologie* 27 (1948), pp. 28–57.

Index